Issues in Historiog

General editor
R. C. RICHARDS(
University of Winch

Debates on the Holocaust

MANCHESTER
1824

Manchester University Press

Issues in Historiography

Already published

The Debate on the Norman Conquest
Marjorie Chibnall

The Debate on the French Revolution
Peter Davies

The Debate on the English Revolution
R. C. Richardson

The Debate on the American Civil War Era
H. A. Tulloch

The Debate on Black Civil Rights in America
Kevern Verney

The Debate on the Rise of the British Empire
Anthony Webster

Issues in Historiography

Debates on the Holocaust

TOM LAWSON

MANCHESTER
UNIVERSITY PRESS
MANCHESTER AND NEW YORK

distributed exclusively in the USA by Palgrave Macmillan

Copyright © Tom Lawson 2010

The right of Tom Lawson to be identified as the author of this work has been asserted by him in accordance with the Copyright, Designs and Patents Act 1988.

Published by Manchester University Press
Oxford Road, Manchester M13 9NR, UK
and Room 400, 175 Fifth Avenue, New York, NY 10010, USA
www.manchesteruniversitypress.co.uk

Distributed in the United States exclusively by
Palgrave Macmillan, 175 Fifth Avenue, New York,
NY 10010, USA

Distributed in Canada exclusively by
UBC Press, University of British Columbia, 2029 West Mall,
Vancouver, BC, Canada V6T 1Z2

British Library Cataloguing-in-Publication Data
A catalogue record for this book is available from the British Library

Library of Congress Cataloging-in-Publication Data applied for

ISBN   978 0 7190 7448 6 hardback

ISBN   978 0 7190 7449 3 paperback

First published 2010

The publisher has no responsibility for the persistence or accuracy of URLs for any external or third-party internet websites referred to in this book, and does not guarantee that any content on such websites is, or will remain, accurate or appropriate.

Typeset
by Helen Skelton, Brighton, UK
Printed in Great Britain
by TJ International Ltd, Padstow

In memory of Michael Cousins 1971–2008

And for Elisa

CONTENTS

ACKNOWLEDGEMENTS

This book is primarily designed as an introductory text for students and teachers. As such it seems appropriate to begin these acknowledgements with some thanks to those teachers who shaped my education and especially those who encouraged my engagement with the past. Joan Harcourt, Roy Petter, Brian Higgins, Beverley Hough, and Ian Wilson were all genuinely inspiring, all demonstrating the joy of learning for learning's sake. They may never read this book, nor even know of its existence, but I thank them for helping make me able to write it. Perhaps the most important person of all in that regard is my father Peter Lawson. Throughout my life he has shown me that knowledge is precious. He read this book in manuscript form, and highlighted many errors (grammatical and conceptual) and I am very grateful for his labours. But his contribution is much more profound than some proof reading, so thanks for everything Dad.

Of course learning is not confined to when we are young, and it is not just adults that can teach. My children Arthur, Florence, and their friends Frank, Megan and Sam (all 4 and under) are constant reminders of the wonder of life and of learning. On an emotional level, I think that they have collectively taught me something about the scale of the loss incurred during the Holocaust and thus made me feel much more deeply the scar on humanity that it represents. I thank them for this, and I am utterly thankful for them. In some ways I wish that they didn't have to grow up to learn about events like those discussed here and discover what an ugly place the world can be.

I wrote this book mainly during a period of research leave and teaching relief in 2008 and 2009. I am grateful to the University of Winchester, and to my colleagues in History in particular, for providing the time to write. The book has benefited immeasurably from being read and commented on by Tony Kushner, Donald Bloxham, Colin Haydon and Andrew Schütte. I thank them all for their insights and their honesty. Thanks also to Roger Richardson, the editor of the series in which this appears, for his comments. The mistakes here are all mine however. Thanks also to all those students who have been subjected to a working through of this book's conclusions over the last few years. Thanks are also due to the friends who have sustained me with their company while writing this book, and to all the Cavaliers, who know more than most cricket teams that it is not the winning that counts.

This book is dedicated to two remarkable people. The first, Michael Cousins, was a friend at the University of York and then my companion in Durham when I studied for the MA which really focused my interest in Holocaust historiography. Mike was studying for his PhD in Physics at the time, but he held a probing interest in my work which was often very challenging. He was first and foremost a very dear friend, and remained so after I left Durham. Mike died tragically in May 2008. I miss him very much. I hope this book, as a history of ideas, is a fitting tribute to a man who was truly an intellectual. The second person is my wife Elisa. She has listened patiently to all of the conclusions that I have tried to draw here, nursed me through various moments of angst and been a constant source of support and encouragement; while at the same time being virtually a single parent and doing her own stressful and demanding job at the University of Southampton. I owe her everything and love her with all of my heart. It is my name on the cover, but this book would not have been written without her.

T.L.
November 2009

ACRONYMS AND ABBREVIATIONS

DAF	*Deutsche Arbeitsfront*, German Labour Front
GDR	German Democratic Republic
HSSPF	*Höhere Schutzstaffeln- und Polizeiführer*, Higher SS and Police Leader
IfZ	*Institut für Zeitgeschichte*, Institute of Contemporary History, Munich
IKL	*Inspektion der Konzentrationslager*, Inspectorate of Concentration Camps
IMT	International Military Tribunal, Nuremberg
IPN	*Instytut Pamięci Narodowej*, Institute of National Remembrance, Poland
IWM	Imperial War Museum, London
JHI	Jewish Historical Institute, Warsaw
NSDAP	*Nationalsozialistische Deutsche Arbeitpartei*, National Socialist German Workers (Nazi) Party
OS	*Oneg Shabbat* (Joy of the Sabbath), archives organised by Emanuel Ringelblum in the Warsaw ghetto
OSS	Office of Strategic Services (the forerunner to the CIA)
POW	Prisoner of War
RKFDV	*Reichskommissariat für die Festigung des Deutschen Volkstums*, Reich Commisariat for the Strengthening of Ethnic Germandom
RSHA	*Reichssicherheitshauptamt*, Reich Security Main Office
RuSHA	*Rasse und Siedlungshauptamt*, Race and Resettlement Office
SA	*Sturmabteilung*, paramilitary Nazi 'stormtroopers' or 'brownshirts'
SD	*Sicherheitsdienst*, Security Service of the SS
SS	*Schutzstaffeln*
SSPF	*Schutzstaffeln- und Polizeiführer*, SS and Police Leader
T4	Codename for the Euthanasia Programme, derived from the original headquarters at Tiergartenstrasse 4, Berlin.

USHMM   United States Holocaust Memorial Museum
Vatican II   The Second Vatican Council, 1962–65
WVHA   *Wirtschafts Verwaltungshauptamt*, Economic and
              Adminstrative Main Office of the SS
YIVO   Yiddish Scientific Institute, New York

GENERAL EDITOR'S FOREWORD

History without historiography is a contradiction in terms. The study of the past cannot be separated from a linked study of its practitioners and intermediaries. No historian writes in isolation from the work of his or her predecessors nor can the commentator – however clinically objective or professional – stand aloof from the insistent pressures, priorities and demands of the ever-changing present. In truth there are no self-contained academic 'ivory towers.' Historians' writings are an extension of who they are and where they are placed. Though historians address the past as their subject they always do so in ways that are shaped – consciously or unconsciously as the case may be – by the society, cultural ethos, politics, and systems of their own day and they communicate their findings in ways which are specifically intelligible and relevant to a reading public consisting initially of their own contemporaries. For these reasons the study of history is concerned most fundamentally not with dead facts and sterile, permanent verdicts but with highly charged dialogues, disagreements, controversies, and shifting centres of interest among its presenters, with the changing methodologies and discourse of the subject over time, and with audience reception. *Issues in Historiography* is a series designed to explore such matters by means of case studies of key moments in world history and the interpretations, reinterpretations, debates and disagreements they have engendered.

Tom Lawson's subject is one of the most recent topics in this series – still one, indeed, for some, within painful living memory – so its historiography is necessarily shorter in its time-span. But, as the book's title announces, it is emphatically plural in nature. This book rejects the possibility of packaging the Holocaust's complexities within a single over-arching framework. Lawson deals with depictions of perpetrators, victims and bystanders, Jew and non-Jew, German and non-German. He charts the opening up of archives; the reunification of Germany, understandably, made a vital difference in this respect. He has a clearly foregrounded agenda, and reflects helpfully on relationships between text and context and between past and present. Though broadly thematic in its treatment the book keeps chronology constantly in view and examines the shifting preoccupations of the debates, the development of different perspectives (gender, for instance), and the kinds of metanarratives – intentionalist and functionalist – which have emerged and been challenged. Key terms like 'Holocaust' and 'Final Solution' are carefully unpacked and shown to have changing resonances and meanings. The coverage is extremely broad and a very large number of historical writings and other texts come under scrutiny. Writers as different as Raphael Lemkin, Hannah Arendt, David Irving, and Saul Friedlander are discussed and situated in their times. Dialectical relationships between text and context come into prominence; crude determinism is avoided.

This is a subject which, unsurprisingly in view of its moral and emotional impact, has claimed the attention of the public at large and not simply that of the historians' professional community. Survivor testimonies discussed here, some of them unleashed by the trial of Adolf Eichman in 1961, helped fuel it. It is entirely fitting, therefore, that some attention is given in this book to contributions to debates on the Holocaust which originated outside academia. Hochhuth's discomforting play 'The Deputy' (1963) receives an extended treatment. So do the deliberately stage-managed text of *The Diary of Anne Frank* (1947) and Binjamin Wilkomirski's *Fragments* (1996), an influential forgery. Major films like *Schindler's List* (1993) and the nine-hour epic documentary *Shoah* (1985) which have had a huge impact are considered. More recent films like *The Pianist* (2002) and *The Boy in the Striped Pyjamas* (2008) are further indicators of an unflagging interest in this subject. Television programmes on the Holocaust, both drama and documentary, have abounded.

Lawson's forcefully argued book makes compelling, and sometimes deeply moving, reading. Students will find it a helpful and reliable guide to one of the most controversial subjects of modern times and will surely pause as a result of reading it before subscribing to glib verdicts and generalisations.

R.C. Richardson
December 2009

INTRODUCTION

In October 1943 Heinrich Himmler addressed a group of senior SS commanders in Posen. Speaking for more than three hours, he ended with a candid discussion of the 'extermination' of the Jewish people. Extolling the virtues that the SS had displayed in carrying out this murderous task, Himmler instructed that the 'Final Solution' was to remain secret. It was an unwritten and 'never to be written' page of glory in Germany's great history. Some three years previously, Emmanuel Ringelblum, a young Jewish historian imprisoned in the Warsaw ghetto, had presciently anticipated this desire to erase him, his people and their destruction from the historical record. He had established *Oneg Shabbat*, a clandestine archive dedicated to documenting all that Himmler and the Nazis sought to destroy, and to establishing a narrative of the destruction itself. Ringelblum accepted that the Jews might die, but hoped their memory and history would live on.

Ultimately, despite Himmler's hopes, the history of the Holocaust has been written and rewritten. Ringelblum's archive was discovered in the ruins of post-war Warsaw and has formed the basis of much historical writing about the Nazis' Jewish victims. Himmler's speech is itself a part of the voluminous historical record of the perpetration of the genocide, which was first haltingly pieced together in the post-war trials. The Holocaust has been reconstructed in increasing detail ever since. Indeed such is the sheer scale of contemporary Holocaust historiography that any attempt to interrogate its history can only be partial and incomplete. Nevertheless this book does attempt such a task – to survey the development of Holocaust historiography, from its birth during the Second World War while the death camps were still claiming their victims, to the present day. What follows is then a history of history-writing about the Holocaust, a history of the ongoing attempt to subvert Himmler's desire for obliteration. Before that survey can begin however, I think it is necessary to reflect on the methodological principles on which it rests.

This is not a book about the past itself, but about the ways in which the Holocaust has been rendered and represented as History.[1] Although not always understood in terms that we may recognise, the *Shoah* has been present in Western historical consciousness since before the guns of World War Two fell silent. From court-rooms to history books, efforts to grapple with and award meaning to the genocide of the Jews, in historical terms, have been a consistent feature of post-war intellectual culture and it is these representations that are the subject of this book. Those texts, it is argued here, need to be considered in contexts other than the past – such as their differing methodological approaches, or opposing moral, political and theological assumptions, or indeed the different national contexts in which they were produced. By analysing these wider contexts I hope to create a history or narrative of how History (as a discipline) has sought to deal with and understand what we call the Holocaust. In doing so I also hope to offer an analysis of where contemporary Holocaust historiography has, as it were, come from.

This is not simply an esoteric exercise – an example of the discipline of History turning in on itself. As James Young has argued, we cannot separate what we know about the Holocaust from the ways in which we have been told it.[2] Studying the contexts from which histories emerged may therefore lead to a greater and more nuanced understanding of the past itself. Nor is this a philosophical exercise designed to pour scorn on the (in)ability of historians to illuminate the past. After all I am an historian too. I am not suggesting that where interpretations have been grounded in extrinsic contexts, where we can understand an interpretation of the Holocaust with reference to the present as much as the past, they are not worthwhile. But they are complex. The relationship between present and past that they betray *is* worthy of study. As such this book intends to reveal the complexity of historians' efforts to uncover the Holocaust past, and the degree to which that past can be held to have a great variety of different meanings. In doing so, as well as showing the processes by which Holocaust History has been made, I hope also to demonstrate that historians and history-writing have an enduring social and political relevance. In fact I am trying to show that history-writing about the Holocaust has very often been engaged in and concerned with a moral, political discourse about 'now' as well as 'then'. *Debates on the Holocaust* are concerned with fundamental questions of moral and political identity, nothing less than existential questions about the human condition in general, about who 'we' are.

There is no doubt that this book is informed by the 'postmodern' critique of History, although I would not describe myself as a 'postmodernist'. I am however, like most historians today, sceptical of our ability to show the past 'as it really was'. Thus I begin here from the critical position that History is a representation of the past made in the present. Furthermore, I believe that the process by which 'History' represents 'the past' can be scrutinised – telling us something about (in this instance) the representation of the Holocaust, and about history-writing in general. In other words, an historiographical work of this type begins from the premise that history-writing *constructs* rather than records or reflects the past.

There is actually little that is contemporarily controversial about such thinking. We are, to a certain extent, all postmodernists now. Historians in the twenty-first century are nearly all writing under the influence of the 'linguistic turn' if only in the vast extension of the source material that they are interested in and comfortable dealing with. Indeed, contrary to the claims of some of the foremost theorists, postmodern historiography has proved liberating for the discipline of History which appears to be in rude health.[3] Keith Jenkins may well be predicting the 'end of History' in the light of the postmodern challenge – but his is almost a lone voice.[4] Most historians in the contemporary West accept that past and present collide in their markedly provisional narratives, and are indeed comfortable with that knowledge.[5]

However, Holocaust History seems to exist somewhere outside of this consensus. The Holocaust is routinely referred to in debates about the discipline of History, usually as the *sine qua non* of conservative rejectionists of the postmodern challenge. The existence of Holocaust deniers is typically held up as an example of the dangers of relativism. If all interpretations are valid, the argument goes, then we no longer have the critical faculty to distinguish between honest historical appraisals of the Holocaust and the dishonest fictions of deniers. The Holocaust is also used to critique the idea that the past does not exist outside representations like History. Although such a view is logically irrefutable (the past self-evidently does not exist), it is argued that the Holocaust reveals it to be somehow *morally* dubious. As Richard Evans states baldly: 'Auschwitz was not a discourse.'[6] As such the reality of past suffering is used to avoid the problematics of representing that suffering in the present.

In moral terms it may be that Auschwitz-Birkenau has a history which marks it as the 'epicentre of human suffering' but that does not mean its meaning is fixed. In that sense, Auschwitz *is* a discourse and what is more, its meanings are manifold, changing and contested. The history of the site is itself complex – it was at various times (and indeed the same time) a Prisoner of War (POW) camp, a political punishment facility, a slave-labour installation, and an extermination centre in both the Euthanasia programme and the 'Final Solution'. Visitors to the site today witness an ongoing struggle to represent all of those significances. Indeed the site itself has been and is the subject of an ongoing battle as to its meaning in the past, present and future – we might think of aggressive placing of crosses outside camp walls during the 1980s,[7] or the groups of Israeli students bedecked in national flags who claim the site as theirs today.[8] These actions are rather transparent attempts to create and cement a mythical status of Auschwitz as representative of either Christian martyrdom, or Jewish suffering and redemption; but the historiography of the site can be similarly deconstructed.

Take these two, perhaps extreme, cases as examples. Philip Friedman's *This Was Oswiecim* (a history first published in 1946) searched for the universal significance of a camp where Jews from around Europe, Poles and Soviet POWs had all been murdered. Friedman's research had been used in a post-war trials programme concerned to highlight the impact of the German murderers on the martyred Polish nation as a whole, not just its Jewish community. Thus it cast Auschwitz in a universal light.[9] Half a century later, Robert Jan van Pelt's architectural history of the site, *The Case for Auschwitz* from 2002, emerged from the David Irving libel trial.[10] As a result it was overwhelmingly concerned to document the history of Jewish suffering at the camp. Although a libel trial, the proceedings became in effect an investigation of the existence of lethal gas chambers at Auschwitz; hence the emphasis on the particularity of the Jewish experience. Both Friedman's and van Pelt's narratives are full of insights into the past and history, but we can only really understand them if we engage with the particular contexts in which they were produced.

Nor does understanding that the history of Auschwitz has changed and is changing, that therefore the history and historiography of the Holocaust has been constructed in the present, legitimate Holocaust denial. To say that *all* interpretations are valid, that all meanings grafted onto the past are of equal interpretative value and potential, is simply an act of intellectual nihilism. As critics of postmodernism have indicated the historian must be bound by her sources, this is as self evident a truth as the idea that the past does not exist. But, acknowledging that the construction of the past is complex is *not* the same as claiming that it is equivalent to fiction, even if the processes by which the past is reconstructed may well be very similar to the process of making fiction, or indeed of making a history whereby the Holocaust didn't happen.

Many deniers ape the tools of the historian – the Institute for Historical Review, the pseudo-scholarly publishers of much denial literature, produce essays replete with footnotes that look like work from scholarly journals.[11] But, however much it might look like it, their work is not History and they are not historians. What sets them apart from historians is not the mechanisms by which they present the past, but their attitude to sources, and their invention of a meaning for the past made *wholly* in the present.

Scholarly investigations of the Holocaust are conversations *between* past and present – the sources provide the fragments of the past that are missing in the work of deniers. Historical knowledge is thus the product of that process, that clash between 'then' and 'now'. How else can we explain the shifting sands of historiography, or that the past is written anew by successive generations, when the past by definition remains unmoved and does not change? This constant revisionism may be the result of newly discovered sources, as it were aspects of the past previously obscured from view. But, it is also the result of changes in the contexts in which those sources are considered, and in which their meanings are sought – changes, as it were, in the present rather than the past. As such I can say without fear of endorsing denial that the Holocaust has been constructed, and reconstructed, in the post-war world.

Of course this is not a novel idea – studies of Holocaust memory have become vogue and indeed there now exists an orthodox interpretation of the narrative of that memory from the 1940s to the present day. To use Alan Mintz's pithy phrase, the argument is commonly proposed that the Holocaust has gone 'from silence to salience'. That in the aftermath of war the Holocaust was little discussed, but that situation has changed to such a degree that since the 1990s the Holocaust has had an almost ubiquitous memorial presence in the Western world.[12] Indeed some have famously discerned a surfeit of memory, the presence of the '*Shoah* business' or an 'Holocaust Industry' in contemporary culture.[13] While such claims are disputable, the idea that each age and indeed each culture has an understanding of the *Shoah* tailored to its needs has become firmly established.

Although Historians are often said to have contributed to the culture of silence in the post-war period, intriguingly the genres of representation that have been studied to create this narrative do not usually include the work of historians. Studies of Holocaust memory tend to concentrate on films, novels, courtrooms, museums or other genres of representation. Why? The exclusion of History appears to result from the similar assumptions to those which underpin the use of the Holocaust as a stick with which to beat postmodernists. Holocaust *History* somehow resists deconstruction for moral and ethical reasons. History must be seen, not as a vector of memory, but as a window on the past.

In part this is the result of claims made by historians themselves. Especially during the 1970s and 1980s, the notion that the Holocaust was/is somehow unique – both historically and morally – was regularly proposed. It is a concept that seemed to cover a multitude of purposes. First and foremost it was an articulation of despair, an attempt to draw attention to the scale of the challenge that the murder of Europe's Jews posed. It also gave vent to anguish at the lack of attention that the Holocaust apparently received both in the historical profession and in Western culture more generally.[14] Uniqueness also articulated a fear of the potential consequences of antisemitism in a world where threats to the state of Israel were growing.[15] Yet, uniqueness was posed as an historical argument in and of itself – suggesting that the Holocaust could not be compared with other cases of mass violence or genocide, that it was *sui generis*.[16]

Regardless of the historical validity of such claims, and they are dubious to say the least, their impact was to mystify rather than explain. The idea of uniqueness removed the Holocaust from mainstream academic discourse. The use of the Holocaust as a way of cutting off debates about the nature of History as a discipline and an epistemology is evidence enough of this. And yet even those historians who were the most prominent proponents of the uniqueness argument, such as Lucy Dawidowicz, recognised that their histories of the Holocaust were not objective windows on to the past. Dawidowicz implied, even if she did not mean to, that the historian was more present in the construction of Holocaust History as a moral actor than elsewhere.[17] The natural corollary of such an argument is that Holocaust History is more openly constructed in the present than other subjects of historical writing. On the contrary however, uniqueness has been employed to suggest that the Holocaust past is more fixed and more stable than other histories. *Debates on the Holocaust* rejects the idea that Holocaust History is necessarily more stable – either than other types of History or than other representations of the past. The book aims to show not only that Holocaust History has been constructed but also that it *is* one of the carriers of the social memory of the Holocaust in the post-war world.

What is more, one of the consequences of studying Holocaust history-writing as a construction of the past is that we are forced to reconsider orthodox narratives of the development of Holocaust memory. The idea of post-war silence is unsustainable. In actual fact the study of historical writing about the Holocaust between 1945 and 1955 reveals that the genocide of the Jews *did* impinge on historical consciousness, although not in ways that we might always recognise. The persecution of Jews was most notably investigated inside the context of a more widespread Nazi destructiveness and violence – and as such the genocide of the Jews was not recognised on its own terms, indeed was not believed to be unique. We should not however make the mistake of thinking that this means that it evaded the attentions of scholars all together.

The observation that a much wider definition of the Nazis' genocidal violence was proposed in the aftermath of war, raises further fundamental questions and problems. If, during the war and indeed in the post-war years, the Nazi campaign against the Jews was not (or perhaps could not) be separated from the extraordinary general violence which provided its context – area bombing, the violence of the Eastern front and the murderous treatment of Soviet POWs, barbaric Nazi occupation policies throughout Europe – then: just what do we mean by the Holocaust anyway?

This is a difficult question to answer. Tracing the development of the term 'Holocaust' is almost impossible. We certainly cannot identify when it became adopted as the more or less universal signifier of the 'Judeocide'.[18] It is definitely a problematic term. Its heritage in religious language, indeed in a Christian discourse, is potentially disturbing – suggesting the sacrifice of the Jews and concomitantly a redemptive purpose for the genocide.[19] Carried to its logical conclusion, the term could be taken to imply that the Nazis were the agents of God. But, putting those problems aside, for good or ill, it is now the universal signifier of the Nazi campaign against the Jews. Thus it also has an exclusive definition, in that other victims of the Nazis are not designated victims of the Holocaust. Such exclusivity, such uniqueness, may be morally problematic – but it is a reality, a reality in some way imposed by the historiography surveyed here.

In many ways the story of Holocaust history-writing is at first the story of an attempt to build a distinct narrative for Nazi policies towards Jews, a development which was ultimately concluded, or speeded to a conclusion, by the application of the term Holocaust. The first two chapters of this book chart the emergence of the idea of the persecution of the Jews as a separate set of events. I am in this sense, ironically, a prisoner of my sources, which have overwhelmingly applied the label Holocaust to the destruction of the Jews, not to any wider suffering unleashed by the Third Reich. If, therefore, because in my moral and historical opinion the term Holocaust *should* include all victims of National Socialist extermination policies, I was to survey the development of the historiography of all these areas, I would, I fear, be imposing a narrative on the past from *my* present. Because of this I will confine my study to the historiography of the Nazi campaign against the Jews.

The irony here should not be lost on readers – is it possible for a book which proceeds from the observation that history-writing is constructed in the present not the past, to claim at the same time that we cannot impose the present on the past in this work of History? In many ways this is an irresolvable contradiction. If my observations about the discipline of History are to hold true then they must be applicable for my work too. As such this book might be nothing more than an autobiographical account of the development of my understanding of the Holocaust. It is up to the reader to decide how far this matters. But, remember that it is not my claim here that all History is forged *only* in the present, indeed I argue forcefully later in the book for the transformative impact of the discovery of new documents from the past on some areas of Holocaust historiography. As such it bears repeating that we are proceeding from the assumption that all History is a conversation between past and present. This does not mean that it is impossible to know the past, just that it is only possible to know the past through representations of it.[20] My study of those representations is in that sense a work of History that is ripe for deconstruction too.

This is not the only irony at work here or in any historiographical reader. The book that follows does construct a narrative and thus imposes some coherence on the chaos of Holocaust History. This is unavoidable. In that sense History may be constructed in the present and thus an utterly imperfect way of accessing the past – but as this study demonstrates, it is perhaps the only way we have. Where historians and other scholars have attempted to embrace more radical approaches than I do here, such as in the study of Holocaust victims and survivors which argue explicitly that we should jettison the desire for coherence, then the past, or at least the historicist past, seems to my mind to slide even further out of view.[21] This is then a work that is, as I have already stated, sceptical of some of the claims made on behalf of history-writing, but that is also a work of history-writing too.

The narrative constructed here follows a broadly chronological path through Holocaust historiography. It charts the various debates conducted: on the role of ideology and antisemitism in the origins of the 'Final Solution', on whether Nazi anti-Jewish policy followed a smooth plan or developed haphazardly, on the relationship between German society and the persecution of the Jews in their name, on the links between anti-Jewish action and other policies pursued by the Nazi regime through to more general questions of the comparative context for the Holocaust and its relationship to modernity and micro-histories concerned with the motivations of individual perpetrators. At the same time as reviewing such debates I also seek to demonstrate how the scholars concerned are usually attempting to articulate much wider philosophical reflections – concerned with issues as wide-ranging as the philosophy of History as a discipline or the very nature of human society and interaction.

Despite attempting a chronological survey, an entirely linear narrative is as impossible in a work of historiography as it should be in a work of History. The chronology thus breaks down in two important ways. First, themes which may dominate certain historiographical eras are seldom played out entirely within them. Chapter 1 suffices as an example. There was broad interest in the pre-history of German antisemitism in the immediate post-war era but such debates were not confined to that period and they continue now. The analysis in Chapter 1 reflects that. Second, for good or ill, Holocaust History has often been characterised using the trinity of the perpetrators, the bystanders and the victims. In part this division reflects national boundaries – the first histories of the bystanders and the victims emerging from British and Israeli historiographies respectively. Such is the dominance of this division in contemporary Holocaust studies, it is repeated here and the narrative which traces the development of perpetrator history is interrupted by a study of the bystanders and followed by an analysis of the historiographies of the Holocaust's victims. While this is just another example of the manner in which the present and the past overlap in this study too, the roots of this divided historiography are traced – and the possibility for integrated histories of the Holocaust is discussed in the conclusion.

Studies of historiography often proceed from E.H. Carr's instruction that you must study the historian before the history. And indeed there have often been suggestions in Holocaust historiography that its practitioners can be easily divided – if not in political than at least in national or even ethnic grounds. It is certainly the case that while the grand political narratives that have shaped other historiographies, most notably Marxism, are not present to the same degree in the historicisation of the *Shoah*; there are national tendencies within Holocaust history-writing. In the most general terms Jewish and Israeli historians have been more concerned with the victims of the Holocaust than a German historical profession that in the end sought to account for their own descent into the abyss. With the first histories of the Holocaust, it is possible to detect a certain autobiographical purpose even – survivor historians wanted to document the history of their own suffering or the heroism of those amongst them who resisted; while the first German historians to confront the Nazi past, themselves veterans from the generation of the Hitler Youth, inevitably focused more on the perpetrators and the society that supported them.

Yet it is not just because this is only generally true, that such an approach to Holocaust historiography is, I believe, unhelpful. It can also lessen our ability to understand the ways in which historians have produced innovative narratives of the Holocaust era that can be read as more than just a kind of ethnic or national appropriation of the past. Take this rather lengthy case study as an example. In 1987 leading German historian, about whom you will read much in this volume, Martin Broszat engaged in a dialogue with the Jewish historian Saul Friedländer about the possibilities of the normalisation and historicisation of the Nazi era and thus the Holocaust. In this exchange Friedländer was content to argue that historians could be divided between the survivors of the perpetrators and the victims – and any historian who had faith in their ability to escape such heritage was working under an 'epistemological illusion'. At the same time he suggested that Broszat's work on everyday life in National Socialist Germany, the scholarship that had in a way sparked this debate, could not be read simply as a contribution to historical understanding because Broszat's Germanness inevitably rendered his scholarship part of a political discourse concerned with the creation of positive German national identities. Meanwhile Broszat, in an earlier contribution, had suggested that German historians had to contend, in their efforts to dispassionately and perhaps scientifically analyse the Nazi past, with a 'mythical memory' of the Holocaust created by its surviving victims – of which Friedländer was one. In other words both scholars cast doubt on the other's ability to escape their personal connections to the past.[22]

Of course that Broszat had been in the Hitler Youth, and Friedländer had lived the war in hiding in France is important in understanding their work. And their history-writing was a contribution to discourses about German and Jewish identities in the present as well as the past. However, it is important that we get beyond the idea that national and ethnic origins are all important, because taken to its logical conclusion such a view suggests (as Friedländer and Broszat implied in their at times bitter exchange) that either all German historiography is apologia and all Jewish historiography concerned with the creation of a memorial culture of victimhood. Because Holocaust historiography has been dominated by, broadly speaking, liberal historians the dangers of suggesting a kind of ethnic determinism are heightened even further.

Bearing this in mind, the book that follows does not begin only with the historian then, although it does attempt to place historians in their contexts. We start here the with historians' texts – as opposed to just their contexts as it were. Each chapter uses a specific text as a gateway to debates about the Holocaust. Each text has been selected because it appears to capture typical approaches to the study of the Holocaust at that point in the chronological narrative and each chapter begins with a brief analysis of these texts themselves. Such analyses often reveal a great deal about the wider political, social and cultural contexts in which the Holocaust has been rendered as History.

It is undeniable that there is no text without reading, and as such the book is also concerned to trace (as much as is possible) the manner in which those texts have been read, and are read, in order that the inter-textual relationships evident in Holocaust historiography can be reconstructed. After all, despite their commitment to the ideal of the lone scholar, historians seldom work alone, but in communities. Most historical works are in some ways shaped by those which precede them, even if only as acts of revisionism, and this book will guide the reader through these relationships – in order to understand the contexts in which these texts must be situated, and indeed in which they have been understood.

Despite the apparent philosophical similarity of historical approaches to the Holocaust, the investigations that follow here reveal that the cleavages in Holocaust History mark fundamental moral, political and indeed philosophical divides – especially with regard to the discipline of History itself. In that sense Holocaust

History has always been, in part, concerned with History as an epistemology – a further irony. The first chapter reveals that attempts to wrestle with the destruction of the European Jews in the immediate aftermath of war, although not always performed by historians, were the beginnings of a discourse about how to understand the particular suffering (and the particularities of the suffering) of a specific victim group in the universal horror of war. They also represent a case study in the vexed relationship between war-crimes prosecution and historical understanding. Chapter 2 confronts the first attempts to form historical narratives of the murder of the European Jews *per se*, and finds a discourse that is as much concerned with the moral politics of judgement in the post-war world as it is with the *Shoah*.

At the same time, Chapter 2 also charts the beginning of an enduring conflict as to how the Holocaust is best situated in the context of long-term historical development. In the very first instance Holocaust historiography was concerned with the question of the relationship between the destruction of the European Jews and modernity. Such a discourse continues to this day, and is as much about the moral politics of the present as it is the past – put simply whether the Holocaust reveals the potential violence of modernity or the potential violence of its antitheses, unreason and irrationality, and as such whether the Holocaust reveals the brutality of 'us' or our enemies. In this the Holocaust is revealed as the site of a much wider morality play concerned with the very human condition itself.

Chapter 3 breaks the narrative of the development of the history of the perpetrators, and argues that once it had been created by historians, others began to ask how institutions and individuals external to Nazi-occupied Europe had responded to the Holocaust. Again a divided historiography is uncovered, and again the divisions are as much concerned with what does and does not constitute legitimate historical enquiry as with the issues of responses to the Holocaust themselves. Chapters 4, 5 and 6 re-focus on the history of the perpetrators – and, as well as charting the progress of debates on the perpetration of genocide, delve beneath that surface to uncover renewed debates on both the moral responsibilities of the historian and on the nature of morality itself. At the heart of this discourse is a fundamental, almost theological, debate about what constitutes morality and moral

behaviour, and whether morality is (as historians might traditionally have argued) contingent or both universal and eternal.

Despite primarily trying to demonstrate the degree to which
history-writing can disguise debates about the present, past and
future within scholarship concerned ostensibly only with the past,
this book also wishes to assert the role of primary documentary
evidence in making History. In other words it investigates and at
times recognises the primary importance of the past in historical
writing. The study of historiography too seldom concentrates on
what historians do with documents and indeed how they do it,
whereas most historians would assert this as the defining feature
of their practice. This does not mean that throughout Holocaust
historiography documents play a determining role. Chapter 3
argues that documents are somewhat irrelevant in the ritualised
scholarship around the issue of Catholic responses to the murder
of Europe's Jews. But, in the post-Cold War world it is the massive
expansion of the documentary evidence base for Holocaust studies
which has, I argue, transformed historical understanding.

The final two chapters are concerned with the victims and
survivors – who were often excluded from more general Holocaust
narratives. Again what is at issue is the purpose of history-writing
itself; Chapter 7 concentrates on History's function in the
formation of post-war Jewish identities. Chapter 8 then returns to
the fundamental question of the very ability of historians to represent the past. An analysis of work on the testimonies of
surviving victims finds that debates about how best to use this
material are in essence a discourse concerned with the moral
possibilities of history-writing and the degree to which it can,
despite the fundamental desire to generalise, produce narratives
that can deal meaningfully with individuals.

Overall then, this book reveals the provisionality of historical
narratives, and the conversation between the past and the present
that they disguise. At the same time this is not an exercise in
debunking history-writing, but one that asks that its full complexity be recognised. It is after all an unresolved irony that this is a
History book too, written now about the past. And ultimately, the
act of writing it would have been an empty exercise indeed if I did
not believe that this was a book that could tell its readers something both about the past and the way that the past has been and
is constructed in the present.

***

Finally, a note on how you might use this book. While ultimately that is a matter for the reader, some direction from me will at least help clarify my intentions. This book is an introduction to *Debates on the Holocaust*, the footnotes are full of references to be explored in order that topics covered briefly here can be understood in more detail. There is a brief guide to further reading at the end, but please consider this a bare minimum – in a way the whole book is a guide to further reading in and of itself.

Notes

1 Throughout the text History, the discipline, will be referred to using a capital 'H'. Where history is used to mean the past, or at least a means of ordering the past, a lower case 'h' will be used.

2 James Young, *Writing and Rewriting the Holocaust: Narrative and the Consequences of Interpretation* (Bloomington: IN, 1998), p. 1.

3 See Callum Brown, *Postmodernism for Historians* (London, 2005), pp. 180–1 which outlines the positive impacts of postmodernism on the history profession.

4 See for example Keith Jenkins, *Why History? Ethics and Postmodernity* (London, 1999) and the even more insistent *At the Limits of History: Essays on Theory and Practice* (London, 2009).

5 After all this is a point of view that is accepted by the most important rebuttal of postmodernism by an historian Richard Evans, *In Defence of History* (London, 1997), p. 195.

6 *Ibid.*, p. 124.

7 Isabel Wollaston, 'Sharing Sacred Space: The Carmelite Conspiracy and the Politics of Commemoration', *Patterns of Prejudice* (Vol. 28, Nos 3–4, 1994), pp. 19–27.

8 For a discussion of this see Jackie Feldman, *Above the Death Pits and Beneath the Flag: Youth Voyages to Poland and the Performance of Israeli National Identity* (New York, 2008).

9 Philip Friedman, *This Was Oswiecim* (London, 1946), p. ix.

10 Robert Jan van Pelt, *The Case for Auschwitz: Evidence from the Irving Trial* (Bloomington: IN, 2002).

11 See for example Jürgen Graf, *The Giant with the Feet of Clay: Raul Hilberg and his Standard Work on the Holocaust* (Capshaw: AL, 2001) – this is a pseudo-scholarly effort to attack the work of Raul Hilberg, which has all the trappings of history-writing but is in fact a work of denial.

12 Alan Mintz, *Popular Culture and the Shaping of Holocaust Memory in America* (Seattle: WA, 2001), p. 3.

13 Norman Finkelstein, *The Holocaust Industry: Reflections on the Exploitation of Jewish Suffering* (London, 2001).

14 See Lucy Dawidowicz, *The Holocaust and the Historians* (Cambridge: MA, 1981).

15 Gavriel D. Rosenfeld, 'The Politics of Uniqueness: Reflections on the Recent Polemical Turn in Holocaust and Genocide Scholarship', *Holocaust and Genocide Studies* (Vol. 13, No. 1, 1999), pp. 28–61.

16 Such an argument usually rested on the observation that the Nazis had required and intended the total annihilation of the Jewish race. This totality of intent was, it was suggested, not the case in the Turkish genocide of Armenians or indeed any other case of genocidal violence. See for example Steven T. Katz, *The Holocaust in Historical Context: Volume 2* (New York, 2003).

17 Lucy Dawidowicz, *The War Against the Jews 1933–45 – Tenth Anniversary Edition* (London, 1987), p. 21.

18 Some scholars use this term because it seems less problematic than Holocaust. See Arno Mayer, *Why did the Heavens not Darken* (New York, 1988) and more recently Deborah Dwork and Robert Jan van Pelt, *Holocaust: A History* (New York, 2003).

19 For a discussion of these issues see Tom Lawson, 'Shaping the Holocaust: Understanding the European Jewish Tragedy in Christian Discourse, 1945–2005', *Holocaust and Genocide Studies* (Vol. 21, No. 3, 2007), pp. 404–20.

20 Dan Stone, *Constructing the Holocaust* (London, 2003), p. xviii.

21 See Chapter 8 in this book.

22 Martin Broszat and Saul Friedländer, 'A Controversy about the Historicization of National Socialism', *New German Critique* (Spring/Summer, No. 44, 1988), pp. 85–126. This is reprinted in Simone Gigliotti and Berel Lang (eds), *The Holocaust: A Reader* (Oxford, 2005), pp. 264–300.

1

'The Theory and Practice of Hell': post-war interpretations of the genocide of the Jews

In 1946 Catholic Austrian Eugen Kogon published *Der SS Staat* – one of the first book-length 'Histories' of the Nazi concentration-camp system, which appeared a year later in English translation as *The Theory and Practice of Hell*.[1] Kogon, a sociologist and anti-Nazi who had been incarcerated since 1939, wrote the book at the behest of the American occupation forces. The work is typical of the manner in which the Holocaust was constructed in the immediate post-war era, chiefly because the persecution of the Jews was not its main focus and appears to have been lost amidst a general horror at Nazi persecution.[2]

Kogon's analysis was, to a great degree, autobiographical – based on his own experiences in Buchenwald. But he aimed also to say something about whole camp structure and its crimes. Buchenwald stood as representative of Nazi iniquity. Yet, as it was dedicated to mainly *political* punishment and latterly the distribution of slave labour, Buchenwald was entirely different to those 'death camps' in Eastern Europe, Belzec, Sobibor and Treblinka, where the racial enemies of the Reich had been put to death. It was also different to institutions like Auschwitz and Majdanek, which combined all the functions of the camp system. But, for Kogon, Buchenwald stood for all.

This popular account of the past – it had sold over 135,000 copies by 1947 in Germany alone[3] – also had a political purpose in the present and future. The text was part of a much broader programme of 're-education' which attempted to orient the German population away from Nazism, and then reorient them back to the West and away from communism too. The author hoped 'that this book may help to keep Germany from ever again surrendering to the powers of evil, that it may warn the rest of the world of the fate awaiting those who do surrender'.[4] Perhaps Kogon's academic background as a sociologist determined this universal focus as much as his involvement with the occupying powers in Western Germany. But because Kogon was both an anti-communist and an anti-Nazi – and as a Christian a recognisable German and Western victim of the Nazi state – he was used by the Allies.[5] As such Kogon helped to promote a narrative in which Nazism was primarily the enemy of Western values and politics.

At face value, Kogon's was primarily an effort to unravel the psychology of the SS Death's Heads Units (*SS-Totenkopf*) who administered the concentration camps, and thus to understand what had led Germany to the abyss. These SS men appeared as 'maladjusted and frustrated ... social failures' whose isolation from the norms of society had led them to find solace in the perverted ideology of Nazism. In other words, these were men who had departed from the moral and political norms of civilisation.[6] Such an analysis also supported an understanding of German society which found Nazism and its institutions separated from the community as a whole. As if to confirm the present political uses of this investigation of the past, the 1950 edition of *The Theory and Practice of Hell* contained additional chapters which explored the comparability of the Nazi concentration camp and the Soviet Gulag.[7]

It is a matter of received wisdom that the memory and history of the murder of Europe's Jews was shrouded in a cloak of silence in the period immediately after the Second World War – and Kogon's universalising approach is seen as typical.[8] Post-war reconstruction, followed by a Cold War which produced rather jaundiced versions of the past all served to orient interest away from what we call the Holocaust. It is commonly argued that nation-building in post-war Europe, be it liberal democratic or communist, required dominant narratives of the past which emphasised popular resistance to Nazism rather than the complex relationship between victimhood and collaboration exposed by the campaigns against Jews.[9] Peter Novick has shown that in the memory of post-war America too, the Nazis' 'Final Solution of the Jewish Question' just appeared to be the 'wrong atrocity' – in part because it allowed no comparison with the contemporary evil enemy in the Soviet Union. Even in Israel, a state in part created to give space for Holocaust survivors, the experience of the *Shoah* seemed often to remain obscured in the project of national construction.[10]

Unsurprisingly historiography has been found to have followed this general cultural trend, Dan Stone argues that 'undoubtedly the most striking fact about the immediate post-war historiography is its absence, or at least its silence'.[11] This silence is most notable amongst German historians and university History departments – where no professional study of the murder of Europe's Jews was produced before the 1960s. Disinterest was not confined to the scholarly sphere. Survivor narratives published from the 1960s onwards, often point to their inability to articulate or find anyone willing to listen to these stories immediately after the war.[12] Elie Cohen's study of behaviour in the concentration camps, first published in 1952, lamented that he was 'under no delusion that there was any great interest in the subject'.[13]

An analysis of Holocaust historiography in the post-war years might then be rather short, reflecting, as Michael Marrus did in his classic *The Holocaust in History* (first published in 1987), that 'it is well to remember how recent is the beginning of professional study of the Holocaust ... up to the time of the Eichmann trial in 1961, there was relatively little discussion of the massacre of European Jewry'.[14] But the idea of silence is misleading, first because it implies an absence, a void. It ignores the many voices that *were* discussing the murder of Europe's Jews in the immediate aftermath of the war – such as the courts and commissions responsible for post-war justice and retribution, other academic disciplines (most notably psychology), or surviving victims of the Nazis such as Eugen Kogon.

As *The Theory and Practice of Hell* actually shows, the murder of Europe's Jews was being discussed, but in a manner which does not conform to present-day conceptions of the Holocaust. The Nazis' genocidal campaigns were often rendered, for example, in a manner which utterly failed to acknowledge the specific role which Jews (and perhaps the Roma and Sinti 'Gypsy' populations) played in the Nazi imagination, and as such as victims of Nazi barbarism too. Yet these works, which include that by Kogon, did not ignore or fail to see the genocide of the Jews – even if the

apparent (to our eyes) specificity of Jewish suffering was somewhat lost amidst the desire to learn general and universal lessons
from Nazi cruelty. Indeed Nazi cruelty towards the Jews was seen
clearly. Yet, crucially, the meaning attached to that cruelty, and the
questions that were asked of it – were not geared to illuminating
and thus learning the lessons of the genocide of the Jews, but
rather non-specific Nazi 'hell': 'there', it is stated in the introduction to the English language edition of Kogon's book, 'but for the
grace of God go you and I'.[15]

This first chapter will explore these attempts to grapple with
the genocide of the Jews. Efforts to universalise the Jewish experience like Kogon's will be considered alongside the legal/
historical narratives that were developed in post-war courtrooms
– especially by survivor historians who went on to staff historical
institutes in Europe, the USA and Israel in the 1950s. And even
where survivors were talking only to themselves, I suggest that it
is important that we listen to what they were trying to say.[16] I will
also highlight the primary role played by social psychologists in
the academic study of what we would call the Holocaust during
the post-war era. Finally the chapter will analyse accounts of Jewish persecution subsumed within prominent renderings of the
Nazi state as totalitarian. Throughout I will argue that even where
the Nazi campaign against the Jews was rendered in a manner that
does not conform to the basic shape of our Holocaust narrative –
that Jews were murdered as Jews – it is crucial that, if we are
concerned to understand the development of Holocaust historiography, we engage with such discourses. By illuminating the
different meanings that were awarded to the genocide of the Jews
when it was discussed, for example, in studies of population movement in mid-century Europe, or when it was universalised in the
discourse of international law which surrounded efforts to try
Nazi war criminals, then we can begin to see that even with Holocaust History the past is passed through a set of ideological
assumptions which help give it shape. And as such the meanings
attached to it, and the many contexts in which historians now
demand that it is viewed, are not the permanent and unmoving
features of the landscapes of the past, but the binoculars of the
present through which the past is, currently, made visible.

The universalising of Jewish suffering

Kogon did not only submerge Jewish suffering, and it would be a simplification to claim that Jews were simply written out of *The Theory and Practice of Hell*. The specific tragedy that the Jews of Europe had faced was acknowledged. Some of the major perpetrators of the Holocaust appeared too – Odilo Globocnik, the Lublin SS and police leader (*Schutzstaffeln- und Polizeiführer,* or SSPF) who had co-ordinated the murder of the Jews of the General Government is cited, albeit mistakenly, as General Globocniy.[17] Furthermore, a narrative of Jewish suffering was established which acknowledged that Jewish policy had distinct phases, aims and outcomes between 1933 and 1944.[18] Kogon also began to ask some of the questions that underpin Holocaust historiography today – especially regarding the motivation of the perpetrators. He tried, very briefly, to associate the radicalism of the SS (in general terms) to its intra-organisational proliferation and competition – an idea at the centre of later characterisations of the development of Nazi anti-Jewish policy.[19] Despite this, a deliberate analysis of the Holocaust *was* passed over, too enormous for both author and reader alike to comprehend: 'it is impossible to present here anything like an exhaustive picture of the Jewish mass tragedy.'[20] Accordingly Kogon restricted himself to a few examples of Nazi anti-Judaism, in part 'to spare the sensibilities of those who need to suffer nothing worse than the reading'.[21]

Kogon's desire to shield the reader from the Jewish experience at Nazi hands was, of course, further acknowledgement of its specific barbarity and was a precursor to those claims that language itself is somehow 'balked at the Nazi divide' – that we lack the frameworks in which to communicate and understand it.[22] Yet Jews and Jewish suffering did appear elsewhere in Kogon's work – but as evidence of universal Nazi evil and universal reactions to it. Most notably Kogon celebrated Jewish resistance, in the shape of the Warsaw ghetto uprisings of January and then April 1943, as a moral and physical rejection of Nazism. His analysis of the 'psychology of the prisoners' of the Nazi camp system also relies, to a degree, on the experience of Jewish prisoners. Some of the imagery which would underpin much more explicit attempts to analyse the experience of Holocaust victims in later years appeared here too – for example citing the so-called 'Moslems' or 'Musselman' who feature in many, if not all, Holocaust testimonies and in the historiography of the Holocaust's victims to be discussed in later chapters. These 'men of unconditional fatalism' who went to their deaths 'without a sign of a fight' had been broken by the camp regime and by their persecutors and then murderers.[23] Despite this, Jews did not quite appear as Jews in Kogon's narrative. While the examples of 'Moslems' Kogon employed were Jews, they stood as representative of all victims of Nazism, examples of the universal psychology of the prisoners in Hell.

As such even the attempts to engage with the Jewish experience within *Der SS-Staat* returned the reader to the universal lessons that underpinned the book and thus removed focus on Jews suffering as Jews at Nazi hands. In doing so Kogon drew on a rich heritage of efforts to universalise Jewish suffering in, especially, the West – which may explain the endorsement of his narrative by the Allies. Allied propaganda during the war itself had been much more comfortable with non-Jewish victims of Nazism, such as the dissenting Protestant pastor Martin Niemöller, in part because of a desperate desire to avoid the idea that theirs was a war being fought on behalf of Europe's Jews.[24] Propaganda initiatives also involved historical interpretations of Nazi violence, or at least evaluations that placed that violence in context. The *Nazi Kultur in Poland* is an example of such work that preferred to concentrate on non-Jewish suffering at German hands – discussing the specifics of only Nazi anti-Christian politics and violence. But like Kogon's work, this publication from the British Ministry of Information was not silent on the persecution of the Jews, or at least their absence from the narrative was acknowledged. Again like Kogon, the contributors seemed to lack a vocabulary with which to discuss the persecution of the Jews, a 'subject too hugely horrible to be dealt with properly in a book'.[25] We are again faced with the paradox that it is a recognition of the very enormity of the crimes against the Jews which militated against specific efforts to engage with them.

So why did the persecution of the Jews evade focus in this way? An earlier History, first published in 1944, may shed some light here. Based on work done between 1940 and 1942, Polish-Jewish legal theorist Raphael Lemkin's *Axis Rule in Occupied Europe* was perhaps the most influential effort to historicise Nazi criminality prior to the end of the Second World War. Like Kogon,

Lemkin focused on the Nazi persecution of the Jews, but asked that it was seen mainly in its general context.

Historicising the Holocaust in a legal framework

Lemkin's purpose was legal – he developed the concept of genocide: the effort to destroy an entire people or community.[26] When one thinks of genocide in the context of the Second World War, one thinks, of course, of Nazi crimes against the Jews. However, it was not just Nazi anti-Judaism to which Lemkin wished to draw attention, or which he wished to identify as genocidal and therefore propose legal redress. Indeed, like Allied propagandists Lemkin defined the treatment of Jews not as an end in itself, but as a constituent part of a wider policy of barbarism – based on a sense of racial hierarchy.

That Lemkin's historical analysis of German anti-Jewish policy was part of an argument for international legal redress, explains the position it was awarded in his explanatory framework. Lemkin was concerned to demonstrate why Nazi rule in occupied Europe was a matter for the international community in *general*, in order that a specific and international legal response might be developed. As such the Nazi campaign against the Jews was understood as important because it was part of a generally genocidal policy. Consequently, although Lemkin acknowledged the specific status that Jews held in the Nazi imagination, and their specific legal status in all of the different occupation regimes that the Nazis unleashed on Europe,[27] he required that the genocide of the Jews be seen in the context of a policy of genocide that was to destroy Jews, Poles and independent Slavic nations too.

This desire to see the attack on the Jews in context meant that Lemkin's historical narrative focused on institutions such as the Reich Commissariat for the Strengthening of Ethnic Germandom (*Reichskommissariat für die Festigung des Deutschen Volkstums*, or RKFDV) and the Race and Resettlement Office (*Rasse und Siedlungshauptamt*, or RuSHA). These offices were responsible for the movement of populations which saw Poles and Jews moved out of areas to accommodate ethnic Germans, moving westwards from the Baltic states, to create a permanent racial reordering of Europe and destroy current ethnic and national groups. As such these were the agencies of genocide as much as the

SS Einsatzgruppen that were murdering Jews in the occupied Soviet Union.

Lemkin found the meaning of the genocide of the Jews as part of a general racial vision of the world. By implication this was also an analysis of the place of antisemitism within the Nazi imagination. Lemkin did not see this ideology as peculiarly significant, but simply a part of a more insidious desire to reconfigure racially the world: Jews 'extremely inhuman treatment' at Nazi hands, he wrote, was a 'propaganda device for the promotion of the anti-Christian idea of the inequality of human beings and of German racial superiority'.[28]

That Lemkin refused to award a specific priority to anti-semitism in his understanding of the Nazi state was typical of Western interpretations of the Third Reich in wartime.[29] The refusal of Allied governments to isolate the sufferings of Jews in their propaganda prompted groups and individuals to campaign first to draw attention to the specific plight of Jews and then for efforts to be made to rescue them.[30] The publications of these rescue campaigners also point toward the first real controversy within efforts to historicise the Holocaust. This discourse concerned the universality or specificity of the genocide of the Jews.

The publications of the Jewish Black Book Committee, a body consisting of Soviet and American campaigners on behalf of stricken Jewry active both during and after the war, represented a riposte to those who wished to see the persecution of Jews universally. If the efforts of this group during war had been directed towards persuading a recalcitrant watching world to rescue Jews, then in its aftermath they were directed towards ensuring that the judgement of both History and war crimes trials recorded Jews as specific victims of Nazi policy as a result of their specific place in the Nazi imagination. As *The Black Book* stated boldly in its indictment against Nazism, published in the America in 1946, the Third Reich had enacted a:

> plan to exterminate a whole people numbering millions, to do so not as an act of war, *but as part of an effort wholly unconnected with war*, to wipe out systematically a group of human beings.[31] (Emphasis added)

By declaring that the history of the 'Final Solution' could (and should) be understood separately from the progress of the Second

World War the writers of the Black Book Committee were asserting the specificity of Jewish suffering and that Nazi anti-Jewish
action was the result of a specific ideological conviction. This
directly contradicted Lemkin's account of the progress of Nazi
anti-Jewish policy as a deliberate policy of war.[32] The Nazi state's
total war effort against the nations and peoples of Eastern Europe
was, Lemkin argued, enacted to conform to a pre-existing plan of
genocidal destruction. One constituent part of this was the
destruction of the Jews.[33]

This early historiography and controversy amounted to a
historiography without documentation. It was based on an understood, and largely undisputed narrative of the events of Nazi
anti-Jewish action, established mainly through eyewitness
testimony. That narrative saw a legislative campaign against Jews
prior to 1939, followed by persecution which developed into mass
murder in the context of war.[34] Interpretations as to the impetus
for policy radicalisation or as to the meaning of events are not at
all explicable with reference to the documentary record. Nuances
of interpretation were thus the result only of the differences in aim
and outlook of those constructing these Holocaust narratives.
Lemkin's rationale was to demonstrate the general suffering
caused by Nazi occupation and to suggest that the world should
develop a legal response, the Black Book Committee were
campaigning that their co-religionists, so marginalised in Allied
propaganda and ignored in war aims and especially in terms
of rescue policy, be recognised as specific and special victims
of Nazism. Thus two different versions of the Holocaust were
provided.

Wartime Holocaust narratives did not lack complexity, even
when they could see only the general significance of Nazi violence.
Although Raphael Lemkin, for example, presented a Third Reich
planning for a genocidal war, his picture of the Nazi state did not
entirely suggest that its radicalism and as such its genocidal violence was the result only of the acting out of a planned and
ordered campaign. Indeed in his desire to demonstrate the legal
responsibility of individuals for actions contributing to genocide,
he constructed a picture of the SS and the German police operating in occupied Eastern Europe with considerable institutional and
individual autonomy. As such Lemkin's Nazi state was no totalitarian monolith – because in such a state all but the leaders may

have been able to plead a defence of deference to orders.[35] Instead Lemkin offered a picture of Nazi police organisations operating without orders and outside of legal frameworks, putting into practice the ideological desires of their leaders.

Prosecuting the Holocaust

Despite this complexity and nuance, simplistic narratives of Nazi anti-Jewish action came to dominate accounts of the Holocaust. Much more linear narratives of Jewish policy emerged from the International Military Tribunal at Nuremberg (IMT) and it was these that came to the fore. Contrarily, these narratives also had their roots in the works which I have just suggested constructed a more complex picture. But this contradiction is easily explained. Just as the legal motivation for Lemkin's work may have militated in favour of an interpretation which spread responsibility around the foot-soldiers of Nazi destruction, the desire to prove a conspiracy amongst the elites of German society worked in favour of a more monolithic presentation of power and responsibility in the Hitler state. As Donald Bloxham has argued the idea of the rational power relationships at work in the Nazi state, alongside the desire to find a widespread Nazi ideological conspiracy, inevitably impacted on the picture of the Holocaust presented in the Nuremberg courtroom. Some of the complexities of Holocaust narratives constructed in wartime were lost – as the murder of Europe's Jews was portrayed as the simple result of ideological planning on behalf of the Nazi elite.[36]

If the first histories were written without documents, the same cannot be said of the Holocaust narratives that emerged from courtrooms. Prosecutions at the IMT, and the subsequent proceedings at Nuremberg, provided the documentary basis for Holocaust studies for the next forty years – in the shape of material seized from the German ministries as well as the institutions of the Nazi movement itself. The documentation produced by the Nazi occupation regimes in the East was less plentiful however, as it remained under the control of the Soviet successor states in Eastern Europe. But the fact remains that a 'Nuremberg historiography' was in many ways novel, because it relied on the documentary evidence of the perpetrators. Indeed if the extant historiography prior to the trials had been mainly reliant on established narratives and eyewitness testimony, the trials offered a completely different method of reconstructing the past. Witnesses were rejected at the IMT because it was claimed that they offered less reliable evidence, for what was a court of law, than the seized documents of the Nazi state, and of course the indicted men themselves.[37]

This legal assumption has had a profound impact on all Holocaust historiography informed by the Nuremberg trials, most notoriously in the work of Raul Hilberg (whose work is the subject of a subsequent chapter of this book). As such it was not just the complexity of some wartime reconstructions of the Holocaust that was lost in the courtroom. The witnesses to the Holocaust, most often its surviving victims, have often been absent – written out of the narratives which sought to reconstruct the Nazi policy decisions and motivations that controlled their lives. And, it was not just the absence of the voices of the victims of the 'Final Solution' that obscured some of the Holocaust story. Legal imperatives moved Jewish suffering away from the centre of the picture constructed of Nazi depravity. The Nuremberg prosecutions needed to be anchored in extant international law, and as a consequence their main thrust had been to demonstrate a conspiracy to wage aggressive war, which it was argued was outlawed by Treaty obligations from the 1920s. All other forms of criminality it was suggested flowed from this fundamental criminal conspiracy, and as such crimes against the Jews were relegated to the background. Such a diminished focus on Nazi anti-Judaism was observed by some historians attempting to reconstruct the story of Nazi anti-Jewish action at the time.[38]

It was not just at the IMT that crimes against the Jews were subsumed within attempts to engage with Nazism in a wider context. Some of the US-led further proceedings also had this effect – which directly impacted on later historiography. As it had been in Lemkin's original analysis, the RuSHA appeared at the centre of attempts to implicate the Nazis' general racial vision of the world.[39] As a consequence the eighth of the twelve subsequent proceedings at Nuremberg became known as the 'RuSHA Trial'. This trial had perhaps a more direct impact on published academic work concerned with Nazi racism than any of the others, because it chimed with an extant interest amongst – particularly American – scholars on general population movement in Europe since the end of the Great War. This included those trials more focused on crimes against Jews, such as the prosecution of Oswald Pohl, the head of the Economic and Administrative Main Office of the SS (*Wirtschafts Verwaltungshauptamt*, or WVHA) in the so-called 'Concentration Camp Trial', and Otto Ohlendorf in the '*Einsatz-gruppen* Trial'.

A number of studies published in the wake of the RuSHA Trial reflected this. Russian American sociologist Eugene Kulischer's study proposed that the deportation and murder of Jews be seen only as a part of this racial re-ordering organised by the RuSHA and RKFDV as a part of his more general work on population displacement.[40] This search for a general context was not just the result of individual scholars' ethnic identity either. Joseph Schecht-mann's *European Population Transfers*, a project that had begun life under the auspices of the Institute for Jewish Affairs (which had been established precisely to document Jews' experiences in modern Europe) argued similarly that Jewish suffering could only be 'fully understood in the light of the wider National Socialist conception of the German mission in the European east'.[41]

That such work, and the RuSHA trial, shared a certain myopia was confirmed by Robert Koehl's study *RKFDV* which was based on the documentation produced for the trial.[42] His work placed little priority on the murder of Europe's Jews. Yet to indict all of this scholarship as evidence of silence would be a mistake. Jewish suffering is not absent at all, but it is placed in context. For example, the transition to the murder of Jews in the winter of 1941 was understood as part of a general radicalisation *not* of antisemitism, but of the population policies of the Third Reich. Such interpretations did attach meaning to the Nazi campaign against the Jews then, as indicative of the generally insidious Nazi racial imagination.

Away from Nuremberg, other prosecution attempts *were* more focused on crimes against the Jews. Charged with responsibility for investigating crimes committed in Poland by the Nazis, first the 'Soviet State Extraordinary Commission for the Investigation of Fascist and Nazi Crimes' and then the 'Polish Central Commission for the Investigation of German Crimes' led judicial and historical investigations into the 'Final Solution' on Polish soil. It was under the auspices of the latter body, and after district attorney Jan Sehn's investigation of Auschwitz-Birkenau that Rudolf Höss, the former commandant of the death-camp, was tried and executed. A Jewish Historical Commission also functioned in post-war Poland, and was largely based around the efforts of a group of survivor historians. This commission also had a role in judicial accounting; it was after a report by the Jewish Historical Commission that a prosecution was brought against the Polish men responsible for the massacre by fire of the Jewish inhabitants of the small town of Jedwabne in July 1941.[43]

It would still be possible to dismiss even these efforts at producing judicial accounts of Nazi anti-Judaism as contributing only to post-war silence. The Soviet State Commission ultimately abandoned all efforts to illuminate the sufferings of Jews as Jews, suppressing the publication of the report of the Jewish Black Book committee.[44] The Polish Historical Commission may well have overseen prosecutions of men guilty of crimes committed against Jews, but the historical narratives they produced clearly elided Jewish and Polish suffering too. While Jews were recognised as perhaps the primary victims of the camps (whose diversity of purpose was at times not recorded), their victimhood was also seen as a precursor to a universal Polish suffering and therefore not of peculiar significance. According to the authors of one investigation:

> The German Camps in Poland were one of the main instruments of the 'New Order' Policy. This order, based on the idea of the superiority of the 'Nordic' race and of the 'Master Race' in particular, gave typical expression to Nazi imperialism in the East. It aimed at the wholesale exploitation of the forces of the conquered nations for the benefit of Germany, and afterwards at their extirpation. The Jews were to be completely extirpated before the end of the war; while the Poles were intended to do slave work for the Germans before *sharing their fate*.[45] (Emphasis added)

Such universalisation is both entirely explicable and understandable. Crimes against Jews were part of the general panorama of German crimes against the Polish nation that the Historical Commission was charged with investigating.[46]

Yet by viewing Nazi crimes against Jews in an overall context the investigations of the historical commissions *did* provide insights into anti-Jewish action as well. And indeed they provided an *interpretation* of anti-Jewish violence – namely that it needed to be understood in the context of a system of government and occupation that pertained to, and relied on, the violent destruction of more than just Jews. Even today, the most ardent proponent of the uniqueness of Jewish suffering would accept that there was a functional link between the extermination of the mentally and physically handicapped in the so-called Euthanasia Programme and the 'Final Solution'. This was a link first established in the findings of the historical commissions. The technologies of killing developed in Euthanasia were applied to the mass murder of the Jews, and the technical expertise of Euthanasia personnel was also employed in later programmes of destruction. Christian Wirth was the most notorious example. He had been transferred directly from co-ordinating the activities of the Euthanasia facilities to the death camp at Belzec in December 1941, and would go on to perform a similar overseeing role in all of the death camps of Operation Reinhard in occupied Poland.[47] The Polish Historical Commission argued that the link between killing operations was not only practical but ideological:

> Extermination of psychiatric patients in Poland constitutes only one link, and a quite insignificant one at that, in the long chain of crimes committed by the Germans in this country in the years 1939–45. The Germans aimed at annihilation of elements considered either economically useless and consequently imposing an extra burden on the economy of the Third Reich or dangerous, for racial, national or political reasons to the German imperialistic and expansionist plans.[48]

Indeed some of the contextual associations made in the findings of the Polish Historical Commission have something to tell today's students of Holocaust history. Now, scant attention is given in most Holocaust histories to the relationship between the treatment of Soviet POWs and Jews, if only in terms of the escalation of levels of violence enacted by German troops. However the murderous treatment of those POWs was the subject of investigation by the Commission.[49]

While the investigations of the IMT and the Western trials provided a model of historical reconstruction that relied heavily on documentary evidence, the historical commissions in Poland much more successfully integrated the voices of the surviving victims. Thus Vassilli Grossman's reconstruction of Treblinka which ultimately was published in *The Black Book* relied solely on victim testimony. Grossman offered a picture which prefigured some of the iconography of much later Holocaust representation, although the eyewitness testimony did result in some misconceptions – such as the notion that people were put to death by steam. Yet the idea that in Treblinka 'everything was designed for death', and murder took place 'along the lines of a modern industrial enterprise' seem to offer profound insights into the nature of Nazi murder policy.[50] The investigation of Treblinka for the Polish Historical Commission, also based on testimony, drew a very sharp distinction, missing in Western Holocaust narratives at this time, between the camps of Operation Reinhard and Auschwitz-Birkenau, and the German camps liberated by the Western allies. While Belsen appeared to be the epitome of Nazi horror to the British for example,[51] eyewitness testimony for the Polish commissions identified that unlike either Auschwitz-Birkenau or Belsen, both of which had manifold purposes, 'Treblinka ... was in reality *just* a place of mass execution' (emphasis added).[52]

Survivor historians and the shaping of Holocaust research

The Polish Central Commission for the Investigation of German Crimes and the Central Jewish Historical Commission, which soon after became the Jewish Historical Institute (JHI) were the most important institutions for determining an historical understanding of the Holocaust in Poland. The heritage of the JHI lay in efforts, centred around the *Oneg Shabbat* archive of Emmanuel Ringelblum, to document the internal history of Jewish communities at the eye of the Nazi storm.[53] Indeed it was the members of the JHI who had previously contributed to *Oneg Shabbat*, such as Rachel Auerbach, who were primarily responsible for the recovery of the archive material in post-war Warsaw.

Philip Friedman headed the JHI, and was responsible for some of the most important publications that it produced. Friedman's later appointment at Colombia University demonstrates the extent of his journey into the echelons of professional, Western historiography. Importantly, while the JHI mainly produced work in Yiddish, Friedman's work was translated, primarily into English, almost immediately after publication. Friedman's *This was Oswiecim*, for example, appeared in a first English edition in 1946. Again this was a nuanced interpretation which drew distinctions between the different types of camps in Poland, and the different roles that they played in the 'Final Solution':

> Oswiecim devoured most of the Jewish victims ... the death camps in the eastern parts of Poland, Treblinka, Sobibor, Majdanek and Belzec, were primarily for the liquidation of Polish Jews ... but Oswiecim was an international slaughter camp.[54]

As well as understanding the variegated nature of the camp system (or systems), Friedman made some efforts to separate out the fate of Jews, as Jews, from the sufferings of other nationalities. Jews, he argued, were deported as Jews into Poland something which seemed to demonstrate their peculiar role in the Nazi imagination.

Commonly the survivor historians associated with the JHI left Poland in the post-war decade, most for either Israel or the USA. It was in these new contexts that they continued their work and that of Jewish research institutes destroyed by the Nazis. The Yiddish Scientific Institute in New York (YIVO), for example, which had relocated from Vilna in 1940 provided survivor historians with an outlet for their research. Although the majority of its publications were in Yiddish and thus inaccessible outside the Eastern European Jewish community, YIVO did also seek to make publications available in at least English, in order to broaden interest in the 'Jewish catastrophe'.[55] While not directly connected to the work of the Historical Commissions, the Wiener Library in London also offered an outlet for Holocaust research. The publications of the Library were concerned to prove Nazi 'guilt' for example through the publication of interviews with Holocaust survivors.[56]

More survivor historians ultimately came to work for and publish through *Yad Vashem*, the Israeli state institute for Holocaust research established in 1957, than any other institute. Rachel Auerbach, Joseph Kermish, who had headed the archives of the Central Polish Historical Commission, and Nachman Blumenthal, who had been head of the Warsaw Historical Commission, were all on the permanent staff at *Yad Vashem*.[57] Again survivor and witness testimony was at the forefront of research published through *Yad Vashem*, as it had been for the other post-war Holocaust research institutes. The most notable thing about the work of the institutes and the survivor historians that contributed to them was the recognition that there existed a specific Jewish experience at Nazi hands which required its own history and interpretation.[58]

It might be argued, however, that this recognition of the specificity of Jewish fate did little to puncture the dominant universal interpretation of Jewish suffering. Philip Friedman's analysis of Auschwitz-Birkenau was introduced by the Polish Ambassador to London who emphasised the privations of Poles, rather than exclusively Jews.[59] In many ways this reflects a fundamental and unresolved tension, particularly as Auschwitz I *was* an instrument in the punishment and domination of the Polish population as a whole after all.

Yet we should not make the mistake of assuming that what we have uncovered here is simply the beginnings of an ethnic historiography of the Holocaust – that non-Jews employed the process of universalisation as a means of understanding Nazi anti-Jewish action and rendering it meaningful, and that Jews employed the idea of specificity to draw attention to their own suffering. Clearly there is an element of appropriating Jewish victimhood in the suggestion that Auschwitz-Birkenau held only universal lessons and is only understandable as a site of universal suffering. But the attempt to find a general meaning for the persecution of Jews was also an honest interpretation of the 'very deep moral crisis' that war had exposed for the human race as a whole.[60] The context of Jewish suffering was recognised by Jewish historians too. Friedman's analysis of Auschwitz ended with testimony which suggested that all non-Germans would ultimately have been the victims of the 'Final Solution' at that point confined to Jews, and his overall analysis of the 'Extermination of the Polish Jews' also suggested that 'undoubtedly the Poles and the Russians were next on the list of candidates for mass extermination'.[61] In Britain too, the *Wiener Library Bulletin* stated that there 'could be no doubt that [the persecution of the Jews] would [have] soon developed into a general persecution of all religious forces'.[62] As such, the persecution of the Jews was the concern of all.

Locating the Holocaust in European history

The question of whether or not Jews suffered alone masked deeper questions over the roots of Nazi persecution politics. Had Nazi anti-Jewish urges come from inside or outside European history? Claims as to the universal meaning of Jewish suffering, that Jews had been the first victims of a general negation of European civilisation, were often accompanied by the suggestion that Nazism was a force alien to the progress of European history.

Such long-term views of history were commonly written from a liberal, even whiggish, perspective.[63] The 'Final Solution' was not allowed to disrupt narratives of progress and was argued to have been the result of an alien ideological mania which did not come from the traditions of European history. Even where a distinct antisemitism was detected it was deemed to have been a deviation from the dominant Christian culture of Europe.[64]

There were also efforts, inside and outside the discipline of History, to relate the 'Final Solution' to a more long-term narrative of *Jewish* history. There was distinct tendency, embodied in the publications of *Yad Vashem* from the mid-1950s, to cast the Holocaust inside a Zionist narrative of a catastrophe and redemption that ended with the formation of the State of Israel.[65] Indeed prior to the formation of Israel, historical interpretations of Jewish suffering in the Second World War often ended with hopeful predictions that the end of the story would be a Jewish national home:

> In the measureless martyrdom that they have had to endure, their chief solace is the hope that now, after these years of slaughter, when the day of settlement comes, they will experience the great act of historic reparation for which they have yearned and prayed throughout the centuries.[66]

During the years immediately following war, there were also significant efforts to understand the 'Final Solution' within the long-term history of Jewish/non-Jewish relations and particularly the history of antisemitism – in part motivated by this desire to understand whether the Holocaust was the product of European history or just an aberration. This was a discourse that had begun during the war itself, although not always within the discipline of History. James Parkes, a Church of England priest, historian, theologian and campaigner on Jewish/Christian relations,[67] argued often that there was a straight line from the medieval Christian pulpit to Auschwitz – in other words that there could be no distinction between the blood libels of the twelfth century and the Nazi drive to reshape the racial make-up of mankind.[68]

This question of the continuity or otherwise of racial anti-semitism also dominated post-war scholarship which attempted, self-consciously, to trace the roots of the Holocaust. Eva Reichmann stated quite explicitly that her analysis of the social bases of antisemitism was an effort 'to discover the causes of the catastrophe' she had herself fled in 1939.[69] Ultimately Reichmann found that modern political antisemitism was phenomenologically distinct from its religious counterpart because it bore no relation to any objective tensions between Jew and non-Jew. If religious antisemitism could be explained in part, according to Reichmann, by Jews refusal to submit to the light of Christ, then modern political antisemitism could be explained only with reference to the psychology of the antisemites themselves.[70]

Reichmann, and to a lesser extent Paul Massing (whose study of antisemitism was published around the same time) wished to see the ideology only in functional terms however,[71] and proposed an essentially Marxist analysis of its socio-economic causes. This new ideology was the preserve of a new class in Germany, the lower middle class, who were the product of an industrial revolution which showed them the economic potential of modernity but, because of the peculiarities of German history, denied them its benefits. Reichmann suggested this new class, the artisans and the traders, were cut off from the networks and the support of the workers but developed no new social bonds and responsibility of their own. Their 'inner disharmony [and] lack of unity',[72] what Hannah Arendt would describe as 'loneliness', drove them to a political antisemitism which articulated their despair with its powerful images of the capitalist Jew as the harbinger of the modern world which had cut them adrift and the socialist Jew from whose solidarity they were excluded. As such although Jews became the target of such an ideology, that ideology was actually only on the surface about Jews and indeed hatred of them. Such observations were 'especially illuminating' for those seeking to understand 'the character of the catastrophe' because it meant that to 'seek [its] causes ... in the Jewish Question ... would be to seek them where they cannot be found'.[73] Reichmann's analysis was thus the beginning of a discourse central to Holocaust historiography, regarding the connection between ideology and extermination.

Later scholarship on antisemitism (in the 1960s and beyond) rejected such determinism. Peter Pulzer and George Mosse suggested that we needed to investigate the content of ideologies themselves in order to understand them.[74] Mosse agreed with Reichmann's suggestion that the supporters of political antisemitism were often located in a specific socio-economic context – the lower middle class whom 'the industrial revolution had squeezed to the wall'.[75] But he insisted that Hitler's revolution *was* an anti-Jewish revolution.[76] Pulzer acknowledged that antisemitism required a specific social and economic despair to take hold – which is why it was only a latent tendency in German history prior to 1918. But whatever the social and economic demands of political antisemitism, its driving force, Pulzer argued, was antisemitism, not the other way around.[77]

Although not confronting directly the causes of the 'Final Solution', this scholarship on antisemitism established that ideological antisemitism did not descend on Europe from a clear blue sky. Political antisemitism was revealed as a constituent part of public conversation in Germany since the nineteenth century and, as Pulzer argued, without this there would have been no Holocaust. However such observations provoked further debate around long-term causation. Although Pulzer himself stated when his study was first published, and indeed subsequently, that he was precisely *not* arguing that German history progressed inexorably towards the 'Final Solution', there has been a tendency towards such an interpretation in studies of antisemitism in Germany. More recent scholars, such as Paul Weiss, Paul Lawrence Rose and Daniel Goldhagen, have all sought to demonstrate that a specific and lethal brand of antisemitic thought, or to use Rose's phrase 'revolutionary antisemitism', was axiomatic to German culture.[78] Such scholarship is methodologically problematic because it potentially leads scholars to read the undoubted antisemitism of, to take one example, Richard Wagner in the light of Auschwitz. Wagner's rhetorical exhortations for the 'destruction' of Judaism become in such a formula a call for the 'physical removal' of Jews.[79]

Scholars of antisemitism appeared to emphasise the uniqueness of German historical development. Indeed as much as the search for the antisemitic pre-history of the Holocaust was an attempt to contextualise it within the wider narrative of Jewish non-Jewish relations, it was also an effort to place the 'Final Solution' inside a long-term narrative of German history. Those attempts invariably paid homage to the *Sonderweg* thesis, which claimed a special path to modernity for Germany. This historiographical school (or schools) argued that Germany's route to modernity had been different from the rest of the West, which had produced a specific class constellation which, for example, left a middle class alienated in Germany, whereas elsewhere they were the stakeholders of modernity. The strange survival of an illiberal elite from Imperial Germany meant that at the end of the Weimar Republic there existed an authoritarian consensus in some parts of German society which Hitler and the Nazis could exploit.[80]

Tracing the roots of Nazi antisemitism back into the imperial German past was part of the *Sonderweg* project. Reichmann's analysis that Germans were susceptible to antisemitism because of their 'political immaturity', in turn a consequence of their 'delayed development', uses some of its key explanatory frameworks.[81] But as Peter Pulzer acknowledged, there is something inherently teleological about this. Marginal antisemites in imperial Germany, who were never electorally successful, only gain their importance through our knowledge of what came after.[82] From the very first instance then, awareness of the Holocaust challenged the limits of the discipline of History. Of course in many ways the *Sonderweg* thesis was very comforting, in that it suggested that the Holocaust emerged from historical traditions antithetical to the rest of Europe.

Social psychology and the Holocaust

Early historical debates about the Holocaust were not just confined to the attempt to locate the destruction of the European Jews within long-term continuities. As early as 1950 Philip Friedman defined at length what he believed to be the questions facing the historian of the Jewish experience to the First International Conference on World War II held in Amsterdam. Reading this list today is like reading a summary of the issues investigated by Holocaust historians.[83] This included the question of when the 'Final Solution' developed as policy and indeed the response of Jewish communities to Nazi persecution – around which there was a noisy public and scholarly conversation.[84]

But the issues that dominated research were universal ones. As was argued in the *Wiener Library Bulletin* in March 1947:

What is needed ... is this; to describe the internal life of a ghetto or concentration camp in such a way as to expand and enrich the field of social science. Again and again the question must be asked: what happens as a result of each order and prohibition. How do community and individual behave in the face of increased oppression? How much scope remains, within the steadily narrowing confines of existence, for any self-chosen activity? ... The procedure for normal society will have to be referred to for comparison with this highly abnormal society; the dwelling of an ordinary citizen, for example, as compared with the accommodation in a camp. Only by confrontations of this kind will it be possible to arrive at something like a psychology of the camps, in which terrible destinies were fulfilled under unfathomable circumstances – destinies from which have sprung impulses which will reverberate through the story of this age.[85]

The concentration camps therefore became the site of attempts to gain insight into the human condition, attempts that were articulated not within the discourse of History but social psychology. As Herbert Bloch wrote 'a remarkable opportunity for the study of social patterning and personality under a highly distinctive set of controlled circumstances was afforded by the horrible mass exploitation by the Third Reich of concentration camp inmates'.[86]

Psychological investigations of camp life were largely based on the testimonies and memories of survivors. In the case of Bruno Bettelheim, the analyst was himself a survivor.[87] Notwithstanding fears of the unconscious distortions of memory,[88] psychological investigations were thus another arena in which the memories of survivors contributed to academic discourse. The most prominent question asked was: what determined survival? As Hilde Bluhm wrote, 'death in a Nazi concentration camp requires no explanation, survival does'.[89] Psychologists often used the Freudian concept, the 'life instinct', in accounting for the tenacious survival of individuals.[90] The major point of disagreement between scholars concerned the types of human relationships that would best condition that survival. In other words, to use the language of the day and the discipline, was it the 'egocentric' or the 'altruistic' prisoner who was most likely to endure? Would those who cultivated human relationships in the camps have a greater chance of emerging than those who simply protected themselves?

Herbert Bloch's 1947 study of 547 women survivors from Buchenwald noted that 'even the most idealistic developed strong egocentric tendencies [and] lost their former sense of altruism' in the new moral world of the concentration camps.[91] Ernst Federn found that the 'totalitarian' concentration camp produced a 'war of all against all' in which only the strong and selfish survived.[92] Such arguments were not particularly novel, and they echoed those that had been heard during the war itself. Bruno Bettelheim had argued as early as 1943 that the essential characteristic of survival was the prisoner's adoption of Nazi attitudes to their fellow inmates and had thus implied that the categories of victim and perpetrator bled into one another in the Nazi scheme.[93] In studies that were prompted by a desire to learn something about the universal human condition, these were bleak conclusions indeed. But there were alternatives offered, both Bluhm and then (writing somewhat later, but drawing on the research of the 1940s) Cohen found examples of kindness and camaraderie to challenge this pervasive view of the decline and disappearance of moral life in the concentration camps, suggesting that altruism as well as selfishness could protect prisoners.[94]

Because of the Freudian foundations of their work, psychological theorists of the concentration camp were particularly interested in prisoner sexuality. Commonly it was found that sexual desires had been suppressed. For Paul Friedmann suppression of sexuality was indeed a necessary precondition for survival – because it was a symptom of regression to a more primitive state.[95] Hilde Bluhm agreed that sexual desire disappeared amongst male prisoners, but found that the 'counterpart in women' the 'cessation of menstruation', was less prevalent.[96] That Bluhm selected male desire and female reproductive capacity as points of comparison betrays much about Freudian assumptions regarding human sexuality. However it is noteworthy that scholars sought to variegate their analyses of the concentration camp prisoner using the category of gender.

However, while gender was, however questionably to today's eyes, used to bifurcate the 'universal' camp inmate, other forms of differentiation were (it appears) deliberately suppressed. This was, very much, a search for the universal. Perhaps Bettelheim established this breadth of focus by arguing that the fate of an individual was irrelevant in the Nazi universe, because the Nazis themselves believed the individual to be unimportant. He was therefore only interested in the 'trans-individual' results of camp life.[97] This universal vision however inevitably downplayed the differences between different types of prisoner in different types of Nazi camp. Elie Cohen's work on building a model of the camp experience is representative here. Cohen developed a picture of the life of the inmate that divided their incarceration into three distinct phases (reaction, adaptation, resignation) each of which could be applied across the board from the political detainee in Buchenwald in the 1930s to the Jewish inmate of Auschwitz in the summer of 1944.[98] As such Olga Lengyel's memories of being forcibly and internally examined by 'drunken soldiers' on arrival at Birkenau were understood not in relation to her experience as either a Jew or a women, but as representative of the 'fright' of arriving in a Nazi camp.[99]

While psychological investigations of the experience of the concentration camps were in many ways a response to the sufferings of Jews, they almost inevitably seemed to obscure that Jews had suffered as Jews, because their authors wished to find only lessons for 'modern man' as a whole.[100] Even where it was acknowledged that 'no prisoner has ever led such a life or suffered more wrongs than a Jewish prisoner had to bear in the Third Reich', the historical significance of that suffering was sought in the fact that the treatment of Jews was just a precursor to wider violence.[101] As such Jewish behaviour was rendered a case study in human reactions to 'totalitarian' cruelty.

It was not simply the victims of the Nazis who were the subject of psychological analysis. The perpetrators of destruction were also scrutinised. Typically such scholarship emanated from war crimes trials. Again it operated at the very broadest level; ignoring the different institutions and environments in which Nazi crimes were committed,[102] psychologists were concerned to discover what made 'men' descend into the depths of barbarism. Perhaps the most important contributors to this discourse were Leo Alexander and again Elie Cohen. Alexander had worked for the US prosecution team at the IMT and thus with the defendants; while Cohen, a survivor, relied heavily on the work of G.M. Gilbert, Alexander's British equivalent. Both sought to understand, through the study of individuals, why at a societal level, the 'religious-humane-cultural superego common to all civilised peoples' had given way under the Third Reich.[103] Despite the universal focus of such questions, their answers indicted a very specific German psychology – which Alexander suggested was more susceptible to 'tribal' rather than 'universal' loyalties and thus to the release of 'instinctual' or 'aboriginal' destructive urges. In other words, there was something innate in German culture which meant that the barbarian, which in the rest of the West had been overcome by enlightenment reason, lurked near to the surface – the psychological forerunner of the *Sonderweg* thesis.[104]

The emphasis on the universal also led inevitably to the interpretation of Nazi ideology in purely functional terms. Antisemitism became, for example, just a means of manipulation and control, or the means by which the destructive urges that 'lies within man himself' were released.[105] Perhaps the most extreme versions of this search for the psychology of the universal perpetrator can be found in the publications of the Institute for Social Research. The theorists Theodor Adorno and Max Horkheimer argued that there were certain personality types that were susceptible to Nazism, the 'authoritarian personality' found the essence of Nazism in a form of social and psychological dysfunction.[106] This is not to dismiss this scholarship as anything other than a genuine engagement with the perpetrators of National Socialist violence, but the scale of its separation from specific historical context limits its enduring historical relevance.[107]

However it is important to understand that one of the central questions of Holocaust historiography – simply put, why did the perpetrators of violence commit such atrocities – *was* being asked by academics in the immediate aftermath of war, and that these were questions that were at the very least prompted by horror at the sufferings of Jews. And more than that, psychologists asked these questions in the way that historians would a generation later, albeit when they were more interested in the genocide of the Jews *per se*. Leo Alexander's observations that the motivation for 'ideologically conditioned' war crimes might be as 'familiar as in ordinary crime'. 'Fear and cowardice, especially fear of ostracism by the group', presages directly explanations of the tendency to violence which would be rediscovered in analyses from the 1990s of the 'Ordinary Men' involved in the prosecution of the Holocaust.[108]

The Holocaust and the totalitarianism thesis

Universal explanations of Holocaust perpetrators that were proposed by psychologists and sociologists also fed into the discourse of totalitarianism which has been so often indicted as obscuring the specific genocide of the Jews. The tendency to attempt to explain a generalised 'terror as a system' inevitably downplayed emphasis on the ideological specificities of the Nazi system and thus the role of Jews in the Nazi imagination. That Nazism seemed to embody an anti-enlightenment irrationalism which had unleashed a 'primitive destructive drive coupled with magic thinking that is so prevalent in small children and primitive people' also encouraged comparison with that other anti-Western 'totalitarian' state – the Soviet Union.[109] Analyses of Nazi war crimes, especially those critical of war crimes trials, refused to consider Nazism in anything but a comparative context.[110]

I would suggest, however, that Holocaust scholars have been too quick to dismiss the totalitarianism thesis as failing to give priority to, or to understand, the murder of Europe's Jews. Clearly the crude identification of Soviet and Nazi brutality did little to engender specific knowledge of the Holocaust.[111] Indeed some of the more politicised accounts may even have been attempts to *deny* the specificity if not the reality of Jewish suffering.[112] But there is more to the idea of totalitarianism than crude anti-communism. This chapter will end with a brief discussion of Hannah Arendt's *Origins of Totalitarianism*, which is perhaps the most sophisticated and original statement of this concept and what is more should be understood as a specific response to the murder of Europe's Jews and an attempt to provide a conceptual framework within which it can be understood.[113] Arendt's work also referenced and contributed to many of the debates of post-war Holocaust scholarship and as such acts as a reminder of this intellectual vibrancy.

Crude images of totalitarianism had been vogue during the war. Western propaganda, both that directly produced by government and not, emphasised that the essence of totalitarianism could be found in the extent of government control over the lives of individuals – and as such interpreted all the crimes of Nazism, including antisemitic mass murder, as a part of this more profound horror. If Nazism was only significant because of its dictatorial grip on society – through the secret police institutions like the

Gestapo – it could be directly compared with the Soviet Union and the Cheka/NKVD. Inevitably perhaps, as Arendt wrote her thesis in the late 1940s, such tropes do occur: totalitarianism, she argued, 'with its more complete understanding of the meaning of absolute power, intruded upon the private individual and his inner life with equal brutality'.[114] But Arendt stated unambiguously that her project sought specifically to understand the triumph of anti-semitism in the 'establishment of death factories', and we cannot dismiss that simply because at times there is a comparative analysis grafted on to it. Indeed Arendt rejected those like Eugen Kogon who sought to look away from the 'outrageous' excesses of the Nazi regime, arguing that her task was to 'bear … consciously the burden which our century has placed on us'.[115]

Arendt investigated the origins, if not the specific causes, of the Holocaust, in a much wider context than just Germany.[116] Indeed in many ways her work can be best understood, in intellectual terms, as a discourse with the prototypes of the *Sonderweg* thesis.[117] Arendt's interpretation of the meaning of the Third Reich and its crimes represented the exact opposite of these, claiming that the 'reality is that the Nazis are men like ourselves'.[118] She did not entirely reject the ideas about class inherent in the *Sonderweg*, just the idea that Germany's development was somehow unique. The emergence of totalitarianism could, according to Arendt, be explained in the socio-economic arrangements of modernity – common to all of the West. If one of the key features of totalitarianism was the triumph of antisemitism this was the consequence of the emergence of the ideologically homeless 'masses' or the 'mob', whom modernity had emancipated but also terrified because it produced such a highly atomised society.[119] This suggests the determining role of Jewish suffering in the genesis of her thinking and therefore her recognition of the specificity of the German and indeed Jewish totalitarian experience – for it was antisemitism, according to Arendt, which drew atomised men together.[120]

Despite this, there is no denying that Arendt was, in many ways, the arch universaliser of Nazism. Her indicting of the colonial adventurers of Western imperialism as the forerunners of totalitarianism cannot really be read in any other way. The essence of the totalitarian system was to be found in the degree to which it transformed the moral worlds of both its adherents and victims alike. Colonialists such as Carl Peters, or even T.E. Lawrence, operated a moral framework, which according to Arendt was cut off from Western standards and as such could promote irrational racism and the maintaining of a racial hierarchy as a duty.[121] British imperialists in Africa predated Nazism when they declared that 'no ethical considerations such as the rights of man will be allowed to stand in the way of white rule' not because they espoused the doctrine of race, but because they subverted the traditional morality of the Judeo-Christian West.

But Arendt's location of the precursors of Nazism in European imperialism should not be taken as evidence of her failure to appreciate the profundity of the 'Final Solution', rather almost precisely the opposite. It was *because* Arendt realised the scale of the challenge represented by the death camps, that she sought its universal roots. Arendt recognised in Auschwitz a 'radical evil' which had attempted, and to some extent succeeded, in changing what it meant to be human itself, especially in terms of the obligations or otherwise that men had to one another. 'The whole of nearly three thousand years of Western Civilisation', she wrote in her concluding remarks 'as we have known it in a comparatively uninterrupted stream of tradition, has broken down, the whole structure of Western culture with all its implied beliefs, traditions, standards of judgment, has come toppling down over our heads'.[122] The Holocaust altered everything for Arendt, even the 'human structures of reality' itself,[123] because the 'Final Solution' had been an effort to reshape not just a society but the constitution of mankind itself.[124]

If that altering of the very human condition in the Nazi death camp and indeed the Soviet Gulag was the problem for Arendt, then the *Origins of Totalitarianism* was the beginning of her search for answers. Some of those answers lack clarity, and indeed are often contradictory – but in those contradictions Hannah Arendt contributed to a discourse which in many ways continues to provide some of the shape, vocabulary and metaphors of contemporary Holocaust studies. This alone seems evidence enough that the long silence narrative of the development of Holocaust consciousness and historiography is, to put it bluntly, wrong.

Arendt engaged with the question of whether, for example, the roots of Nazism and thus the Holocaust had been located inside or outside the Western tradition. Nazism appeared at times in her narrative as a fundamental break, a rejection and indeed the 'destruction [of] civilisation'.[125] However the very implication of the search for the origins of totalitarianism *inside* Western thought and history suggested that the death camps emerged from continuities rather than discontinuities. And indeed Arendt made this claim explicitly as well:

> Even the emergence of totalitarian governments is a phenomenon within, not outside, our civilisation. The danger is that a global, universally interrelated civilisation may produce barbarians from its own midst ...[126]

Ultimately the general drift of Arendt's argument appears to have been that totalitarianism was the product of continuities rather discontinuities, but that the inherent totalitarian potentiality of modernity had hitherto been obscured. It was the 'subterranean streams of Western history that had finally come to the surface' in the camps.[127] For our purpose however these conclusions are irrelevant, the debate which Arendt conducted with herself in many ways identified the fundamental question for Holocaust studies. Did the 'Final Solution' represent a reversion to barbarism or is it the intrinsic product of a modern state and society? Much of what follows in this book is concerned with scholars' attempts to answer these enduring questions.

Ultimately Holocaust scholarship in the immediate aftermath of war, genocide and liberation was noisy rather than muted or silent. Many of the central concerns and contentions of what today would be called Holocaust studies were established. It is correct to say that single research monographs concerned with the Nazi 'Final Solution' did not abound, but in other contexts both the wider meaning of the genocide of the Jews and its specific development as policy were debated. From the mid-1950s onwards single studies of the 'Final Solution' did begin to emerge, suggesting a narrowing of the universal focus that was engendered, in part, by the universal suffering of war – and those are the subject of the next chapter. The emphasis on the universal meaning of the genocide of the Jews was also a consequence of a desire to contextualise Jewish suffering, both on the part of Jewish (including survivors) and non-Jewish scholars. That search for context, whether it be in establishing the long-term continuities of genocide as a colonial crime, or the desire to see the movement of Jews as a part of general schemes of population transfer in the middle of the twentieth century, is a search that continues today.

Notes

1 Eugen Kogon, *Der SS-Staat: Das System der Deutschen Konzentrationslager* (Frankfurt am Main, 1946). The translation (and the version used here) is Eugen Kogon, *The Theory and Practice of Hell: The German Concentration Camps and the System Behind Them* (London, 1950).
2 Donald Bloxham, *Genocide on Trial: War Crimes Trials and the Formation of Holocaust History and Memory* (Oxford, 2003), p. 87.
3 Nikolaus Wachsmann, 'Looking into the Abyss: Historians and the Nazi Concentration Camps', *European History Quarterly* (Vol. 36, No. 2, 2006), p. 248.
4 Kogon, *Theory and Practice*, p. 12.
5 Robert Moeller, *War Stories: The Search for a Usable Past in the Federal Republic of Germany* (Berkeley: CA, 2001), p. 4.
6 Kogon, *The Theory and Practice*, p. 259.
7 Bloxham, *Genocide on Trial*, p. 88.
8 For example, Dan Stone, *Constructing the Holocaust* (London, 2003), p. 97.
9 See for example Tony Judt, *Postwar: A History of Europe Since 1945* (London, 2007), pp. 803–31.
10 Idith Zertal, *Israel's Holocaust and the Politics of Nationhood* (Cambridge, 2005), pp. 52–91.
11 Stone, *Constructing the Holocaust*, p. 87.
12 See Kitty Hart, *Return to Auschwitz* (London, 1983) for the harrowing account of her reception in England which she described as 'one of the unhappiest times of my life … probably the closest I ever came to total despair', in part because she was prevented from speaking about her experiences in Auschwitz.
13 Elie A. Cohen, *Human Behaviour in the Concentration Camp* (London, 1988), p. xxi.
14 Michael Marrus, *The Holocaust in History* (London, 1993), p. 4.
15 Kogon, *Theory and Practice*, p. 11.
16 Dan Stone for example acknowledges that survivor historians did discuss the Holocaust in the 1950s and 1960s but that they spoke 'to all intents and purposes only to each other'. Dan Stone, 'Ontology or Bureaucracy? Hannah Arendt's Early Interpretations of the Holocaust', *History, Memory and Mass Atrocity: Essays on the Holocaust and Genocide* (London, 2006), p. 54.
17 Kogon, *Theory and Practice*, p. 172.
18 *Ibid.*, p. 162.
19 *Ibid.*, p. 270.
20 *Ibid.*, p. 162.
21 *Ibid.*, p. 172.
22 The quotation is from Nora Levin, *The Holocaust: The Destruction of European Jewry* (New York, 1968), p. xii.

23 Kogon, *Theory and Practice*, pp. 284–5.
24 Tom Lawson, *The Church of England and the Holocaust: Christianity, Memory and Nazism* (Woodbridge, 2006), p. 49.
25 *The Nazi Kultur in Poland* (London, 1945), p. 219.
26 Raphael Lemkin, *Axis Rule in Occupied Europe: Laws of Occupation, Analysis of Government, Proposals for Redress* (Washington: DC, 1944), p. xi.
27 *Ibid.*, p. 75
28 *Ibid.*, p. xi.
29 Tony Kushner, *The Holocaust and the Liberal Imagination: A Social and Cultural History* (London, 1994), passim.
30 See Victor Gollancz, *Let My People Go!* (London, 1943) as an example.
31 *The Black Book: The Nazi Crime Against the Jewish People* (New York, 1946), p. 5.
32 Lemkin, *Axis Rule*, p. 80.
33 *Ibid.*, p. 81.
34 This is the narrative communicated by *The Black Book*, which offers chapters on 'The Law', the 'Strategy of Decimation' and 'Annihilation' which indicate the narrative drive of the publication.
35 Lemkin, *Axis Rule*, pp. 12–24 for an analysis of the German police.
36 Bloxham, *Genocide on Trial*, p. 185–6.
37 *Ibid.*, p. 61.
38 See for example Josef Gutman, 'The Fate of European Jewry in the Light of the Nuremberg Documents', YIVO Annual of Jewish Social Science (Vol. II–III, 1947–48), pp. 313–27.
39 Lemkin, *Axis Rule*, p. 222.
40 Eugene M. Kulischer, *Europe on the Move: War and Population Changes 1917–47* (New York, 1948), p. 1.
41 Joseph B. Schechtmann, *European Population Transfers* (New York, 1946), p. 266.
42 Robert Koehl, *RKFDV: German Resettlement and Population Policy 1939–45* (Cambridge: MA, 1957), p. 146.
43 Jan Thomas Gross, *Neighbors: The Destruction of the Jewish Community in Jedwabne, Poland* (Princeton: NJ, 2001), passim.
44 Zvi Gitelman, 'Politics and the Historiography of the Holocaust in the Soviet Union', in Gitelman, *Bitter Legacy: Confronting the Holocaust in the USSR* (Bloomington: IN, 1997), p. 19.
45 Sophie Czynska and Bogumil Kupse, 'Extermination, Concentration and Labour Camps in Poland in the Years 1939–45', Central Commission for Investigation of German Crimes in Poland, *German Crimes in Poland*, Vol. I (1945 – translation published New York, 1982), p. 14.
46 Czynska and Kupse, 'Extermination', p. 7.
47 Yitzhak Arad, *Belzec, Sobibor, Treblinka: The Operation Reinhard Death Camps* (Bloomington: IN, 1987), pp. 17–28.
48 Stanislaw Batawia, 'Extermination of Patients with Mental Disorders', *German Crimes in Poland*, Vol. II, p. 159.
49 Stanislaw Polski, 'German Crimes Against Soviet Prisoners of War', *German Crimes in Poland*, Vol. I, pp. 261–71.
50 Vassilli Grossman, 'Treblinka', *The Black Book*, p. 407.

51 Tony Kushner, 'From "This Belsen Business" to "Shoah Business": History, Memory and Heritage, 1945–2005', Suzanne Bardgett and David Cesarani, *Belsen 1945: New Historical Perspectives* (London, 2006), pp. 189–216.

52 Z. Lukaszkiewicz, 'Extermination Camp at Treblinka', *German Crimes in Poland*, Vol. I, p. 102.

53 Emmanuel Ringelblum, *Notes from the Warsaw Ghetto* (New York, 1985).

54 Philip Friedman, *This Was Oswiecim* (London, 1946), p. ix.

55 See 'Studies on the Epoch of the Jewish Catastrophe', *YIVO Annual of Jewish Social Science* (Vol. VIII, 1954).

56 See for example Mordechai Lichtenstein, 'Eighteen Months in the Oswiecim Concentration Camp', *Jewish Survivors Report: Documents of Nazi Guilt* (No.1, 1945). For a general overview of Wiener Library's activities, see Ben Barkow, *Alfred Wiener and the Making of a Holocaust Library* (London, 1997).

57 Boaz Cohen, 'The Birth Pangs of Holocaust Research in Israel', *Yad Vashem Studies* (Vol. 33, 2005), p. 203.

58 The title of the publication of Yad Vashem made this point explicitly: *Yad Vashem Studies on the European Jewish Catastrophe and Resistance*.

59 Henry Strasburger, 'Introduction', Friedman, *This Was Oswiecim*.

60 Strasburger, 'Introduction'.

61 Friedman, *This Was Oswiecim*, p. 58; Friedman, 'Extermination of the Polish Jews', *German Crimes in Poland*, Vol. I, pp. 166–7.

62 Leonard Montefiore, 'Achievements and Aspirations', *Wiener Library Bulletin* (Vol. 1, No. 1, 1946), p. 1.

63 The most obvious example being the postwar version of H.A.L. Fisher, *A History of Europe* (London, 1960).

64 See for example Stephen H. Roberts, *A History of Modern Europe* (London, 1948), p. 545; Sydney H. Lebel, *A History of Europe Since 1870* (Chicago: IL, 1948), p. 839; Walter Phelps Hall and William Sterns Davis, *The Course of Europe Since Waterloo* (New York, 1947), p. 725.

65 Stone, *Constructing the Holocaust*, p. 142.

66 Board of Deputies of British Jews, *The Jews in Europe: Their Martyrdom and Their Future* (London, 1945), p. 40.

67 See Colin Richmond, *Campaigner Against Antisemitism: The Reverend James Parkes, 1896–1981* (London, 2004).

68 Robert Everett, 'James Parkes: A Model for Christians in the Time after the Holocaust', Yehuda Bauer et al. (eds), *Remembering for the Future* (Oxford, 1989), p. 330.

69 Eva Reichmann, *Hostages of Civilisation: The Social Sources of Anti-Semitism* (London, 1950), p. 5.

70 *Ibid.*, p. 59.

71 Massing was also a German émigré to the USA, and former member of the German Communist Party. Paul Massing, *Rehearsal for Destruction: A Study of Political Anti-Semitism in Imperial Germany* (New York, 1949), pp. 147–8.

72 *Ibid.*, p. 164.

73 *Ibid.*, p. 101.

74 See for example George L. Mosse, *The Crisis of German Ideology: Intellectual Origins of the Third Reich* (London, 1966).

75 *Ibid.*, p. 7.

76 *Ibid.*, p. 294.

77 Peter Pulzer, *The Rise of Political Anti-Semitism in Germany and Austria* (London, 1988), *passim.*

78 Paul Lawrence Rose, *German Question/Jewish Question: Revolutionary Antisemitism from Kant to Wagner* (Princeton: NJ, 1992); John Weiss, *Ideology of Death: Why the Holocaust Happened in Germany* (Chicago: IL, 1996); Daniel Jonah Goldhagen, *Hitler's Willing Executioners: Ordinary Germans and the Holocaust* (New York, 1996).

79 Rose, *Revolutionary Antisemitism in Germany*, p. 366.

80 For a brief but very useful discussion of the *Sonderweg* see Jurgen Kocka, 'German History Before Hitler: The Debate about the German Sonderweg', *Journal of Contemporary History* (Vol. 23, No. 1, 1988), pp. 3–16. For a critique see David Blackbourn and Geoff Eley, *The Peculiarities of German History* (Oxford, 1984).

81 Reichmann, *Hostages of Civilisation*, pp. 126–41.

82 Pulzer, *Political Anti-Semitism*, p. xiv.

83 The research questions are printed in Philip Friedman, *Roads to Extinction: Essays on the Holocaust* (New York, 1980), pp. 571–6.

84 This issue is considered in Chapter 6 below and is as such not investigated here.

85 *Wiener Library Bulletin* (Vol. 1, Nos 3–4, 1947), p. 15.

86 Herbert Bloch, 'The Personality of Inmates of Concentration Camps', *The American Journal of Sociology* (Vol. 52, No. 4, 1947), p. 335.

87 As well as Bettelheim, scholars referenced in this study who had survived Nazi camps include Elie Cohen and Ernst Federn.

88 Cohen, *Human Behaviour*, p. 121.

89 Hilde Bluhm, 'How did they Survive? Mechanisms of Defence in Nazi Concentration Camps', *American Journal of Psychotherapy* (Vol. 2, No. 1, 1948), p. 3.

90 Cohen, *Human Behaviour*, p. 164.

91 Bloch, 'The Personality of Inmates of Concentration Camps', p. 337.

92 Ernst Federn, 'Terror as System: The Concentration Camp', *Psychiactric Quarterly* (Vol. 22, No. 1, 1948), p. 78.

93 Bruno Bettelheim, 'Individual and Mass Behaviour in Extreme Situations', *Journal of Abnormal and Social Psychology* (Vol. 38, 1943), p. 449.

94 Cohen, *Human Behaviour*, *passim*; Bluhm, 'How did they Survive?', p. 31.

95 Paul Freidmann, 'Some Aspects of Concentration Camp Psychology', *American Journal of Psychiatry* (Vol. 105, No. 8, 1949), pp. 604–5.

96 Bluhm, 'How did they Survive?', pp. 11–12.

97 Bettelheim, 'Individual and Mass Behaviour', p. 418.

98 Cohen, *Human Behaviour*, p. 115

99 *Ibid.*, pp. 120–1.

100 Bloch, 'The Personality of Inmates', p. 335.

101 Federn, 'Terror as System', p. 69.

102 For example 'The SS' appeared as a vast monolith for example, which ignored the different situational contexts in which the men of the *Einsatzgruppen*, the *SS-Totenkopf* divisions which guarded the camps, or indeed the research officers of the SD, operated. See Federn, 'Terror as a system', *passim.*

103 Leo Alexander, 'War Crimes: Their Social-Psychological Aspects', *American Journal of Psychiatry* (Vol. 105, No. 3, 1948), p. 174; Cohen, *Human Behavi*our, p. 260.

104 Leo Alexander, 'The Moulding of Personality Under Dictatorship: the importance of destructive drives in the socio-psychological structure of Nazism', *Journal of Criminal Law and Criminology* (Vol. 40, No. 1, 1949), pp. 3–27.

105 Ernst Simmel, *Anti-Semitism: A Social Disease* (New York, 1946), p. xxiii.

106 Theodor Adorno and Max Horkheimer (eds), *The Authoritarian Personality* (New York, 1950). For a discussion of their work and critiques of it see Christopher Browning, *Ordinary Men: Reserve Police Battalion 101 and the Final Solution in Poland* (London, 2002), pp. 165–6.

107 David Cesarani argues that accounts of Adolf Eichmann written under the influence of Adorno tell us nothing about Eichmann or his motivations. David Cesarani, *Eichmann: His Life and Crimes* (London, 2004), pp. 18–19.

108 Leo Alexander, 'War Crimes: Their Social-Psychological Aspects', *American Journal of Psychiatry* (Vol. 105, No. 3, 1948), p. 171.

109 The quotation is from Leo Alexander, 'Destructive and Self-Destructive Trends in Criminalised Society: A Study of Totalitarianism', *Journal of Criminal Law and Criminology* (Vol. 39, No. 5, 1949), p. 558. For an intellectual history of the idea of totalitarianism see Abbott Gleason, *Totalitarianism: The Inner History of the Cold War* (New York, 1995).

110 See for example , F.J.P. Veale, *Advance to Barbarism: How the Reversion to Barbarism in Warfare and War Trials Menaces our Future* (Appleton: WI, 1953).

111 The classic model of totalitarianism is Carl J. Friedrich and Zbiniew Brzezinski, *Totalitarian Dictatorship and Autocracy* (New York, 1956).

112 This is certainly the case with scholarship surrounding war crimes trials. Arguments against trials frequently sought to compare Nazi Germany and the Soviet Union, some of this anti-trial rhetoric has since been warmly commended by deniers see for example Richard Harwood, *Nuremberg and Other War Crimes Trials: A New Look* (Chapel Ascote, 1978).

113 As Samantha Power wrote, Arendt's *Origins* is nothing if not a response to 'Hitler's death camps'. Samantha Power, 'Introduction', Hannah Arendt, *Origins of Totalitarianism* (New York, 2004), p. x.

114 *Ibid.*, p. 315.

115 *Ibid.*, p. xxvi.

116 Indeed she rather regretted the title because it implied a more definite causality than she was prepared to put her name to. *Ibid.*, pp. 617–18.

117 See for example A.J.P. Taylor, *The Course of German History: A Survey of the Development of Germany Since 1815* (London, 1951)

118 This is a quotation from a 1945 essay used by Power, 'Introduction', p. xi.

119 Arendt, *Origins of Totalitarianism*, p. 19.

120 *Ibid.*, p. 468.

121 *Ibid.*, pp. 242–86.

122 *Ibid.*, p. 625.

123 Shiraz Dossa, 'Human Status and Politics: Hannah Arendt on the Holocaust', *Canadian Journal of Political Science* (Vol. 13, No. 2, 1980), p. 313.

124 Arendt, *Origins of Totalitarianism*, p. 565 (these arguments are repeated on p. 620 – which is the conclusion from the original 1951 edition).

125 *Ibid.*, p. 267.
126 *Ibid.*, p. 384.
127 *Ibid.*, p. xxvii.

2

'Eichmann in Jerusalem': war crimes prosecutions and the emergence of Holocaust metanarratives

On April 11 1961 Adolf Eichmann stood for the first time before a court in Jerusalem charged with being the Third Reich's 'executive arm for the extermination of the Jewish people'.[1] The case against him was outlined over the next four months, and constituted, in effect, a history of the Holocaust performed in front of the world's media, indeed it was televised live in several different countries.[2] Over 700 journalists reported the beginning of the trial, which is invariably hailed as a watershed moment in the development of Holocaust narratives. Because much of the prosecution case rested on surviving witnesses to Nazi persecution it transformed the role of survivors and persuaded many to tell their own stories for the first time. A plethora of publications followed – both from survivors and those examining the rapidly iconic Eichmann.[3] The most important was Hannah Arendt's *Eichmann in Jerusalem: A Report on the Banality of Evil*, a collection of her court reports previously published in the *New Yorker* magazine. According to Peter Novick the trial and the cultural noise which surrounded it broke the 'silence' shrouding the Holocaust, and for some it even represents the 'birth of Holocaust studies itself'.[4]

But historical change can rarely be convincingly simplified to a series of turning points, and the intellectual history of Holocaust historiography is no different. Both the narratives of the 'Final Solution' presented by Eichmann's prosecution, and the alternative versions constructed in the media and elsewhere, drew on the significant analytical perspectives on the Holocaust reviewed in the first chapter. Indeed Arendt's *Eichmann* relied on an extant historiography to which she gave a voice and developed into a universalist explanation of the perpetration of the 'Final Solution', which chimed with the post-war perception that the persecution of the Jews had revealed a general crisis in human behaviour. However, approaches to the study and understanding of the Holocaust *did* change around the time of the Eichmann trial. The genocide of the Jews began to be embedded as a singular event in the minds of scholars and even the popular imagination.[5] Such a singular event also demanded singular explanations, and Holocaust narratives in this era are defined by the desire to offer an overarching thesis on, especially, the causes and perpetration of the 'Final Solution'.

Ultimately these explanations, these metanarratives, can be grouped together around two poles – the first symbolised by the account given by the prosecution of Eichmann and the second related, albeit somewhat awkwardly, to Hannah Arendt's rejoinder in *Eichmann in Jerusalem*.[6] The former emphasised Nazi ideology in its explanation of both the emergence and then prosecution of genocide; the latter was more concerned by the cultural and structural preconditions and determinants of mass violence. This chapter compares and contrasts these opposing interpretations as a means of introducing the landscape upon which Holocaust studies has been constructed. It also considers the differing conceptions of not only the Nazi past but the entire philosophical exercise of accessing the past, of writing history, upon which those opposing interpretations stood. These interpretations would ultimately become known as 'intentionalism' and 'functionalism', reflecting a more widespread interpretative controversy in the study of the Third Reich. While that controversy was at first a function of the German historical profession, when concentrating on the Holocaust as a distinct subject it became a much wider conflict involving scholars from Europe, the USA and Israel.[7]

The chapter begins with an analysis of Eichmann himself, in order to explain why he could stand as symbolic of the entire 'Final Solution' both in the court and in historiography. While it is the differences between interpretations which are the focus, the chapter concludes with a short analysis of their central similarity – itself very important for shaping future scholarship: the sense that the genocide of the Jews was a subject, event or even epoch, which needed to be understood in its own right and on its own terms.

Why Eichmann?

Eichmann was abducted outside of his home in Buenos Aries by Israeli agents in May 1960. The furore surrounding his trial is only in part explained by these extraordinary events.[8] The world was captivated because Eichmann had emerged as symbolic of the Nazis' campaign against Jews since the end of the war. Although unknown to the Allies in May 1945 when he was in American custody as a Prisoner of War, Eichmann's name became indelibly associated with the 'Final Solution' because of the testimony of fellow Nazis. Dieter Wisliceny, who was Eichmann's deputy in the Jewish Affairs 'desk' of the Gestapo, waxed particularly lyrical about his role in genocide when offering testimony for the defence of Ernst Kaltenbrunner at Nuremberg. Kaltenbrunner had been Eichmann's overall superior after he assumed the leadership of the Reich Main Security Office of the SS (*Reichssicherheitshauptamt*, or RSHA) at the beginning of 1943.[9] Rudolf Höss, the former Kommandant of Auschwitz-Birkenau, reserved a special place for Eichmann in his 'autobiography', composed while awaiting execution in a Polish prison cell. While Höss confessed to feeling anxiety about the extraordinary crime in which he and Eichmann were partners, he reported that Eichmann 'was completely obsessed with the idea of destroying every single Jew he could lay his hands on. Without pity and in cold blood [he believed] we must complete this extermination as rapidly as possible'.[10] Eichmann was then indicted as the key executor of the 'Final Solution' within the early social-psychological histories of the Holocaust too.[11]

Eichmann's career certainly placed him at the centre of anti-Jewish policy in the Third Reich. He was the Security Service (*Sicherheitsdienst*, or SD) of the SS's expert in Zionism during the mid-1930s,[12] and worked more generally on SS emigration projects. Consequently Eichmann established, at the behest of Reinhard Heydrich, the Central Office for Emigration in Vienna after the *Anschluss* of March 1938.[13] The efficiency of the Eichmann operation ensured that the SD became the primary agency for Jewish emigration in the Reich, and the 'Vienna Model' was later applied to the rest of Greater Germany.[14] First Eichmann was sent to Prague, where a similar office was established to supervise the emigration of Czech Jewry,[15] and then in October 1939 he was transferred to Berlin to run the Central Office for Jewish Emigration that had been established there in March.[16] In October

1939 Eichmann was responsible for the first wartime deportations of Jews in German-controlled territory from Ostrava (in the modern-day Czech Republic) and then Vienna to Nisko, south of Lublin in Eastern Poland.[17] These deportations were supposed to be the precursor to the formation of a vast Jewish 'reservation', part of Himmler's more general population strategy as head of RKFDV. Plans for a reservation came to nought.

This was just the first failed innovation in anti-Jewish policy with which Eichmann and his office were concerned; he was also a key figure in the plan to deport four million Jews to Madagascar pursued from the middle of 1940, but which was aborted during 1941.[18] After the invasion of the USSR Eichmann's expertise in emigration and deportation was translated into an expertise in deportation and genocide. Eichmann's office, which had become part of the Gestapo, worked with Reinhard Heydrich after he had been detailed to prepare a 'Final Solution' of the Jewish Question in July of 1941. The precise details of Eichmann's activities during the second half of 1941 remain oblique.[19] What we know without doubt is that Eichmann was sent around occupied Poland to observe and consult on the many and invariably murderous anti-Jewish actions that had, for whatever reason, recently begun.

Whenever a fundamental decision to pursue genocide through-out German-controlled Europe was made, Eichmann was a key figure in its implementation. He took the minutes at the Wannsee Conference in January of 1942 when Heydrich attempted to cajole and coerce the hardly unwilling apparatus of the German state into the machinery of genocide. From that point on Eichmann's office became responsible for the transportation of Jews from around Europe often, but not exclusively, to the death camp at Auschwitz-Birkenau. Eichmann was then present on the ground when the Third Reich reached its destructive apogee in Hungary in the late spring and early summer of 1944. His entire office was moved to Budapest, and performed a crucial role in deporting Hungary's Jews to Auschwitz-Birkenau, approximately 400,000 of whom would die between the middle of May and July of that year.

A prosecutorial metanarrative: antisemitism equals genocide

At his trial, the prosecution sought to develop a picture of Eich-mann as the fanatical executor of Nazi ideology, driven to carry out murder by his devotion to Hitler's *Weltanschauung*, which in turn could be reduced to hatred of Jews. Unlike the efforts to contextualise antisemitism within a wider world view which had defined many of the accounts of Nazism reviewed in Chapter 1, this prosecutorial narrative identified antisemitism as both the means and the ends of the Nazis' ideological ambitions. Thus, Chief Prosecutor and Attorney General Gideon Hausner told the Jerusalem court that the explanation for Eichmann's actions was simple – 'his burning devotion to the utter destruction of Jewry' which he believed 'was the right and proper thing to do'.[20] From this starting point the prosecution then proceeded to offer an account not only of Eichmann's activities but of the destruction of Jewry as a whole. The antisemitism to which Eichmann subscribed was shown to be its fundamental cause. It is often acknowledged that the trial was in part a show trial, an effort to educate Israel and the world as to the dangers of antisemitism and to assert the 'sovereignty of Israel' to defend herself against such an ideology.[21] As such Eichmann sat in the glass booth generally representative of the Holocaust and its perpetrators and therefore the explanation of his behaviour proposed by the prosecution was an attempt to account for all perpetrator action. The trial thus produced an Holocaust metanarrative which had antisemitism at its very centre.

The prosecutorial narrative which indicted Eichmann's ideological intentions was typical of some emerging Holocaust historiography and as such had a much wider resonance than the Jerusalem court. More formally historical accounts of the 'Final Solution' proposed similar causal explanations, and maintained a close association with efforts to prosecute the perpetrators of atrocity. Jacob Robinson and Nora Levin's analyses of the Holocaust emerged, if in different ways, from the Eichmann trial itself and repeated the prosecutorial narrative. Robinson had been an advisor to the prosecution; Levin's popular *The Holocaust* was largely based on a repetition of the prosecution's case. That case had largely been built in association with the survivor historians at *Yad Vashem*.[22]

Other trials processes had a relationship with academic historiography too. The Institute of Contemporary History (*Institut für Zeitgeschichte*, or IfZ) in Munich produced narratives of various aspects of the Nazi regime to support the German war crimes trials programme which began in 1958. The director of the IfZ from 1959, Helmut Krausnick, produced the expert witness submission for the Frankfurt Auschwitz trial between 1963 and 1965. This was later published as 'The Persecution of the Jews',[23] and was the first attempt by a German scholar to explain the 'Final Solution' as a singular process.[24] Although the same cannot be said for all of the narratives emanating from the IfZ, which as an institution was most responsible for structuralist or functionalist accounts of the Third Reich, Krausnick offered a very similar thesis to that proposed by Eichmann's prosecutors in his statement for the Frankfurt court.

These prosecutorial narratives focused on two major themes – the role of ideological antisemitism and (somewhat perversely given their purpose) the centrality of Hitler in the initiation and legitimation of the politics and policy of annihilation. These foci also ensured that singular narratives of the 'Final Solution' could be designed because its specific root – Hitlerian antisemitism – could be easily identified. Ultimately it would be Lucy Dawidowicz, another survivor historian from Vilna, who would produce the most comprehensive account of the Holocaust from this direction – *The War Against the Jews*, published in the mid-1970s. Dawidowicz summarised what would become known as the 'intentionalist' reading of the 'Final Solution' when she wrote 'people are moved to action not by structures, but by their ambitions, intentions and goals. *They are motivated by ideas, values, beliefs and the force of passion*' (emphasis added).[25] In other words, like a criminal case which determined to prove an individual's *personal* responsibility, prosecutorial narratives of the Holocaust sought explanations which focused on individuals, their intentions and the choices they made.[26]

Although brought to the fore in courtrooms, similar causal narratives had been proposed before. Leon Poliakov published his *Harvest of Hate* in the mid-1950s. Poliakov, a French scholar of antisemitism, argued that this ideological hatred should be at the very centre of any attempt to historicise the Holocaust.[27] Jacob Robinson demonstrated that the prosecution of Eichmann had been predicated on a similar assumption when he wrote 'the attitude of the Nazi regime toward Jews was for the most part that felt towards a species that simply has to be physically destroyed. This attitude was the moving force behind Eichmann's deeds'.[28]

Helmut Krausnick similarly advised the Frankfurt court trying the former functionaries of Auschwitz that they could only understand the Nazi persecution of the Jews if they understood the 'philosophy' behind it,[29] a philosophy he explained with reference to the special path of German antisemitism.[30] Nora Levin, whose *The Holocaust* essentially represented a summary of extant research towards the end of the 1960s agreed, suggesting both that the Holocaust was explicable through Nazi ideology, and that there was 'no Nazi ideology aside from anti-Jewish ideology'.[31]

The development of anti-Jewish policy in these narratives was then explained as the progressive implementation of the Nazis' destructive urges. Helmut Krausnick argued that the Nuremberg Laws had been 'released' by Hitler after an intensive propaganda campaign had prepared the ground for them. Such narratives also suggested that each new policy deliberately contained the seeds of future developments. Again Krausnick said of the Reich Citizenship Laws, 'the party leadership ... regarded the Nuremberg Laws as merely a stage in the fulfilment of their Jewish policy'.[32] As such he implicitly suggested both the existence of a Nazi plan (or overall vision at least) for anti-Jewish legislation and extensive central control over that policy.

Prosecutorial narratives had to combine an account of the smooth progress of Nazi anti-Jewish policy with the obvious contradiction that that policy underwent a series of changes throughout the history of the Third Reich. This stumbling block was overcome through the depiction of ever-more powerful central authorities in the Nazi movement, who unleashed progressively more radical policies as they themselves could exert more control. As such the limited anti-Jewish policy in the aftermath of the seizure of power, confined to boycotts and attempts to 'aryanise' the civil service, could thus be explained because Nazi control over the state was circumscribed by a dominant conservatism. Hitler moved policy on to its next, logical, point in the plan whenever the expanding Nazi power base allowed. Hitler, Dawidowicz wrote, 'had the craft to plan and the patience to wait to carry out that plan'.[33] Of course war provided one such opportunity, and Hitler's Reichstag speech of January 1939 in which he prophesied the annihilation of the Jewish race in Europe in the event of another world war was consistently interpreted as a statement of genocidal intent. As Helmut Krausnick wrote, the 'day of reckoning had come'.[34]

Because prosecutorial narratives suggested that central power in the Nazi state was able to move policy in line with a pre-existing plan, they became acutely concerned with the moment of particular decisions, not least the transition between a policy of persecution and a policy of genocide. After all, only the latter was seen as the genuine expression of an ideological desire to rid the world of Jews. Of course a preoccupation with this particular decision, this particular moment in time, was somewhat perverse owing to the paucity of documentation surrounding it. There simply does not exist a single written authority for the 'Final Solution'. As Leon Poliakov wrote, it is a 'decision … shrouded in darkness'. Although Poliakov was prepared to speculate that this missing documentation may never have existed he was certain that the decision itself had been actively taken: 'undoubtedly it was the master himself, Adolf Hitler, who signed the Jews' death warrant.'[35] Krausnick suggested that the plan to exterminate all Jews was inherent in Nazi war aims and was implemented when the intensification of war provided the opportunity.[36] Dawidowicz agreed: war unleashed the 'relentless course' of anti-Jewish policy towards annihilation.[37]

The idea that war unleashed a newly destructive dynamic within the Nazi regime clearly suggested that the 'Final Solution' had diverse causal roots. However, prosecutorial narratives sought to depict the Holocaust as emanating from a single ideational cause. Lucy Dawidowicz was typical of the route out of this apparent interpretative impasse, arguing that the 'Final Solution' was inherent in ideology anyway. She argued that *Mein Kampf* was the Nazi blueprint for destruction. Its obfuscatory language was a deliberate ploy to disguise its murderous intentions. Those intentions may have been set free by war, but true 'believers … always knew' of their existence.[38]

Other scholars made similar arguments. Krausnick highlighted disagreements within the Nazi state over the role and utility of Jewish labour. Ultimately he explained away the apparent tension between labour and annihilation by suggesting that the will to murder Jewish slaves would always triumph in the end, because this reflected the purer, ideological commitment. The murder of Jewish slaves in the Lublin region in November of 1943 (known as

Operation Erntefest in Nazi semantics) was presented by Kraus-nick as simply in keeping with a murderous ideology. Events like this might actually point to the multifaceted 'Final Solution' or even the multivalent application of ideology within the Nazi system, but they were reduced instead to being, somewhat illogically, evidence of the driving force of Nazi ideology. *Operation Erntefest* appears more likely to have been a response to security concerns after the uprising in the Sobibor death camp and the mere existence of SS-controlled Jewish slaves suggest the enduring co-existence of labour exploitation and annihilation as policy goals.[39]

Similarly Nora Levin's *The Holocaust* dismissed initiatives such as the Madagascar Plan as a fiction, an 'official pretense' *because* it did not fit with the preconceived definition of a murderous, genocidal Nazi ideology.[40] Levin's argument reflected the desire to remove Nazi anti-Jewish policy from the general context in which it had previously been understood. After all the Madagascar Plan was part of a much wider project of demographic engineering and population movement. By labelling it a fiction, Levin asserted that Jewish policy should only be understood as a consequence of a murderous antisemitism.

This is not to say that these scholars never suggested that the 'Final Solution' was complex. Leon Poliakov's *Harvest of Hate* explicitly acknowledged that Nazi anti-Jewish policy shifted several times during the war years, and that those shifts were at times due to locally determined 'changes and adjustments'.[41] He prefigured the work of contemporary historians by some forty years by arguing that Jewish policy had to be understood as a series of interlocking and overlapping phases.[42] Lucy Dawidowicz equally pre-empted the work of more modern scholars when she argued that the SS developed a much more radical anti-Jewish policy during the early years of the Third Reich, aimed consistently at removing Jews, but that they were unable to impose this more generally.[43] However such complexity never dented the superstructure of narratives which ultimately always returned to monolithic interpretations of the 'Final Solution' as the result of, as Dawidowicz wrote, a National Socialist movement which understood the destruction of Jews as their 'basic programmatic task'.[44]

In summary then, prosecutorial explanations for the 'Final

Solution' tended to combine a picture of the Third Reich as operating around a fixed ideological programme of destruction, a shared comprehension of antisemitic goals; with an image of the state as a rather centralised dictatorship which was governed by a unified cabal of true believers. The latter conception was necessary to protect the integrity of the former, in that an understanding of the 'Final Solution' as the result of ideological intention *required* that it had been progressively put into effect as and when the opportunity arose. In order to demonstrate individuals' personal responsibility, in both a legal and moral sense, it had to be demonstrated, when prosecutions literally employed such narratives, that individuals shared and identified with these overarching ideological ambitions. Hence Adolf Eichmann was presented as both a willing and a knowing executioner.

A structural metanarrative I:
the moral imperative for genocide

The prosecution's account of Eichmann as an ideological warrior, and thus the idea that the 'Final Solution' could be explained purely with reference to ideological conviction, was not the only explanation to emerge from the Jerusalem court nor was it the most publicly resonant. Hannah Arendt's reporting of the trial combined Eichmann's own account of his behaviour (which also constituted the case for his defence), with extant perspectives on the Nazi genocide in order to produce an alternative thesis. For Arendt, Eichmann just did not match the picture of an ideological monster painted by the prosecution. This is not to say she questioned his involvement at the centre of the Nazis apparatus of destruction. She did not. However this willing *genocidaire* did not appear fiendish, instead he was 'terrifyingly normal'. As such she produced an account of the Holocaust which sought explanation not in the ideological specificities of the Nazi dictatorship but in the structures of totalitarianism and indeed the modern bureaucratic state in general.[45]

Versions of Eichmann, and the perpetrators of the Holocaust in general, that looked more like Arendt's everyman than Gideon Hausner's zealous tormentor of Jews, already abounded. As early as 1952, British historian Gerald Reitlinger had attempted to construct a chronological narrative of Nazi anti-Jewish policy, in which Eichmann featured only as a normal 'German civil servant'.[46] According to Reitlinger's *The Final Solution* the structure in which Eichmann operated needed to be included in the causal matrix along with the ideology which he served, because it was that structure which had shaped, sustained and carried out policy. So Reitlinger identified Reinhard Heydrich as the engineer of genocide, and while Eichmann may have been its executor it was actually a process that proceeded under 'its own momentum'.[47] That momentum had been triggered by the ideological authors of the project, but it was not a dynamism that could simply be explained with reference only to that ideology. As such Reitlinger explains the continued gassing of Jews in Auschwitz in late 1944, despite the apparent ending of the 'Final Solution', as a result of the system of mass murder – 'in the German bureaucratic grooves there was no other way of disposing of unproductive bodies'.[48] Most importantly the division of labour within the German civil service inured Eichmann and men like him from the consequences of their actions: 'like the aerial bomber, the bureaucrat does not see his kill. It is possible that Eichmann never saw a single one of the millions of Jewish corpses of which he boasted.'[49]

Arendt developed both Reitlinger's indictment of the German civil service, and his suggestion that Eichmann was both a conduit for his radical, ideological superiors, protected from the reality of his deeds by the structure in which he operated.[50] She also investigated Eichmann's own narrative further, in that he claimed before and during the trial that he had simply been law abiding and as such shouldered no legal responsibility for the crimes in which he freely admitted his involvement. Ultimately Arendt did not dissent from this suggestion that he had obeyed the law, but argued that the concept of obedience needed to be understood in the context to which Reitlinger had originally alluded. Within the German civil service Arendt suggested, to be 'law abiding means not merely to obey the laws but to act as though one were the legislator of the laws that one obeys. Hence the conviction that nothing less than going beyond the call of duty will do.'[51] Arendt thus complicated Eichmann's weasely defence of 'obedience', claiming that it was not possible to disentangle this obedience from ideological commitment and identification with his task. In stressing the importance of context Arendt related the Holocaust to a sociological interest in the power of organisational networks that spread far beyond studies of the 'Final Solution' at this time and was vogue in US social science in general.[52]

These observations of organisational context were crucial for an understanding of the Third Reich. In terms of the power structure of the Nazi state, Arendt's picture of Eichmann implied almost precisely the opposite of the totalitarian caricature of the centralised and monolithic state with which she is sometimes associated. It was a system in which the relationship between the obeyed and the obedient was two-way, and as such doing one's duty required an understanding of, and engagement with, the meaning and consequence of action, because it often required one to go beyond formal orders. This conception of duty was best explained through the role of the *Führer*. The *Führer* principle was a novel legal mechanism, because the historic will of the *Führer* now had a legal personality. But the *Führer*'s will was often oblique and ill-defined. In terms of Jewish policy the ambitions of rendering Nazi-occupied Europe *Judenrein*, of the *Vernichtung* of the Jews,[53] were public but were vague and certainly did not add up to policy. Eichmann's role in the SS allowed him to make policy in line with these vague goals, but in the absence of formal direction. Hence his innovations in deportation in the latter part of 1939 and the early part of 1940, which went far beyond any centralised directive. Indeed Eichmann understood this new structural and legal determinant to such an extent that it even allowed him to *disobey* orders given by his unquestionable superiors when they did not seem in keeping with the will of the *Führer*. Heinrich Himmler's order that Eichmann protect Hungary's Jews for use in ransom negotiations with the Allies was instructive for Arendt. Eichmann ignored him. According to Arendt he could disobey the *Reichsführer* SS because his instructions 'ran directly counter to the *Führer*'s order' on the 'Final Solution'.[54]

Of course the latter example looks like simple obedience to a command from the head of state. But Arendt suggested that it was significant in understanding the systemic radicalism of the Third Reich. Eichmann (and for him Arendt believed we could read all officials) understood that the *Führer*'s will had the force of law, and that will was usually pronounced in the vaguest terms but undoubtedly as an expression of the most radical, most National Socialist action. In terms of Jewish policy that became mass murder. As a consequence the system then made it very difficult to countermand, to draw back from, radical policy because that would have been to contravene and contradict the will of the *Führer*. Radicalism in the Nazi state thus, according to Arendt, came from the fact that policy was often established *de facto* rather than *de jure*. Such observations now represent something of an orthodoxy in studies of the Third Reich, represented by the concept of 'working towards the Führer', which Ian Kershaw popularised in his biographies of Hitler published at the turn of the century.[55]

Like Reitlinger then, Arendt insisted that *structural* determinants were added to the historical explanation of the 'Final Solution' which indicted only an ideological antisemitism. That said, like the *Origins of Totalitarianism* before it, Arendt's narrative of Eichmann and thus the Holocaust was not without contradictions. That Eichmann identified so completely with the *Führer* meant that he was a radical,[56] that he was an active supporter of the policy he administered.[57] But in her desire to demonstrate that Eichmann was not the 'perverted sadist' that the court believed him to be,[58] Arendt sometimes allowed ideological commitment and antisemitism almost entirely to disappear from her analysis of motivation and ergo from her causal explanation of the 'Final Solution' itself, just as her critics allege. For example Arendt's Eichmann did not even join the National Socialist German Workers (Nazi) Party (*Nationalsozialistische Deutsche Arbeitpartei*, or NSDAP) out of conviction but simply because of his alienation, a line of argument that betrayed the influence of psychological accounts from the 1950s which explained Nazism as a home for the socially dysfunctional;[59] an argument which actually contradicted Arendt's earlier observation that the most 'disturbing factor in the success of totalitarianism is … the true selflessness of its adherents' which was itself a consequence of the degree of their identification with the movement's *Weltanschauung*.[60]

At times Arendt's Eichmann could not, it appears, think *at all*. He could not engage with the ideological content and meaning of his actions, an argument she developed from *Origins of Totalitarianism* when she had proposed that the content of totalitarian ideologies was of little consequence, and far from taking these ideas seriously we need only regard them as 'clichés … mere devices to organise the masses'.[61] When it came to Eichmann in particular, Arendt concluded that 'he had no motives ... he merely, to put the matter colloquially never realised what he was doing'.[62]

Perhaps Arendt should not have put this colloquially. Critics have, especially in recent historiography, attacked her for suggesting Eichmann's thoughtlessness precisely because she appeared to imply that he lacked ideological commitment. Michael Thad Allen's study of the mid-level managers of the WVHA and their involvement in the 'business of genocide' sought to reassert the importance of ideological commitment to our understanding of the desk-bound perpetrators of atrocity. Allen describes Kurt Wisselinck, a low-ranking bureaucrat who was the SS representative to the German Labour Front, complaining that the prisoners of Gross-Rosen, slave labourers in other words, were being over-fed. This complaint had nothing to do with the efficiency of the slave labour operation and everything to do with an ideological commitment to the maltreatment of these men.[63] According to Allen the bureaucrats of the SS knew very well what they were doing.

But, Arendt's suggestion that Eichmann did not *know* what he was doing was intended to imply rather more than a lack of ideological commitment. It was an attempt to convey his emptiness, the distance he appeared to demonstrate from the global historical meaning of his activities. In other words his lack of conscience, with reference to the traditional precepts of Western morality. As such the idea of 'thoughtlessness' was a legal and a moral treatise on responsibility, as well as an historical argument about the culture of destruction in the Third Reich and the importance of the division of labour to the destruction process. The idea of responsibility in Western legal tradition revolves around the notion that the criminal is aware that his actions represent a transgression. But Arendt argued that inside the Third Reich Eichmann's efficient carrying out of the deportation of Jews, far from being a legal transgression, was actually the embodiment of the ideal. He overcame significant administrative challenges, such as the non-availability of rolling stock and the intransigence of the Reich railway authorities, in order to deliver Jews to slavery and/or death. As such *legally* Eichmann could hardly be suggested to have known he was doing the wrong thing, as he was self evidently within the context of the Third Reich doing the *right* thing. Retrospective war crimes prosecutions however operated around the idea that this strict legal ideal did not apply because involvement in the crime of genocide was so obviously a *moral* transgression that it could be pursued as criminal. Arendt disagreed with this suggestion, and as such questioned not only the prosecution of Eichmann, which rested on that idea, but also the very jurisdiction of the court to try him.

This argument for Eichmann's moral, and ergo legal, responsibility was built on the assumption that the moral framework of right and wrong is underpinned by certain eternal norms – in essence that there *are* essential moral truths (such as 'Thou Shalt not Kill'). But on the contrary Arendt believed that the Third Reich, and the totalitarian state in general, represented an entirely *new* moral world. Crucially this was a world in which the murder of Jews was promoted as the very opposite of a transgression and in which no public figure or organisation suggested that it was anything other than a moral duty. As Eichmann himself argued, after the Wannsee conference at which he had witnessed the 'Popes of the Third Reich' discuss the necessity and duty of genocide, on what basis could he question it? When Arendt argued then that he did not know what he was doing, what she was essentially saying was that Eichmann had no access to a moral framework or discourse which would allow him to 'know' that he was doing wrong. Eichmann's participation in the 'Final Solution' was thus not a failure of his conscience, it would only have been unconscionable for him to refuse.[64]

It is not that the man in the glass booth who personified the 'banality of evil' did not identify ideologically with the 'Final Solution' then or with the new morality that it represented. Those scholars who have subsequently caricatured Arendt as simply arguing that Eichmann mindlessly followed orders – as Yaacov Lozowick put it the 'drab bureaucrat carrying out orders' – have thus done her a disservice.[65] The relationship between ideology and destruction in Arendt's analysis is more complex. Locating Eichmann in a cultural and societal context, Arendt fundamentally proposes that ideological conviction in the Third Reich, and in any modern society, cannot be understood in terms of personal agency alone. As she wrote in her alternative judgement which she imagined delivering to Eichmann himself, a judgement that could have been applied to any middle-ranking supporter of the Nazi regime: 'you have carried out, and *therefore actively supported*, a policy of mass murder. For politics is not like the nursery; in politics obedience and support are the same.'[66] What she of course failed to understand, and what later scholars have highlighted, is the degree to which Eichmann and his *männer* were responsible for *shaping* the ideological atmosphere in which they operated. The degree to which policy was the result of innovations made by officials such as Eichmann and the staff of the Jewish affairs desk at the Gestapo, one of the only agencies in the Third Reich concerned solely with Jewish policy *throughout* German-controlled territory.[67]

Yet it is wrong to say that Arendt's Eichmann did not believe that he was doing the right thing. In effect the implication of her long discussion about the nature of morality in a totalitarian state is an investigation of the ways in which Eichmann could and did identify with his task, although she insisted that he did not have to filter these beliefs through any moral norms recognisable to us. But he was, as Hans Safrian, Yaacov Lozowick and David Cesarani have all demonstrated, more personally responsible for shaping the moral world in which he operated than Arendt allows for. Yet Arendt's arguments are not primarily empirical but philosophical. She proposed that moral values are transient and culturally constructed, in other words that there are no essential moral truths. Arendt saw Eichmann, and yes, everyman, as a product of their society.

Arendt's thesis was then primarily an account of both the structural and moral preconditions for and causes of the 'Final Solution'. She argued that one must go beyond simply antisemitism. Although universal in focus, this account was also specific to the German bureaucracy of which Eichmann was a part. In her analysis of Eichmann as a cog in a machinery of government and administration which drove the 'Final Solution' forward, she relied almost entirely on Raul Hilberg's *The Destruction of the European Jews*. It is to an analysis of this, perhaps the most important metanarrative of all, that we now turn.

A structural metanarrative II:
the state and the process of genocide

Raul Hilberg had been immersed in the documents of the Third Reich since cataloguing them for the US army prior to the Nuremberg prosecutions. As such it was natural that the subject of his doctoral dissertation be related to such work. Hilberg reported that from the outset his project was regarded as of marginal interest, although his dissertation did win a prize when it was completed.[68] From the outset he was determined to understand the perpetrators, with whom he had become intimately acquainted through his work with the documents. Hilberg felt that these men had not adequately been covered in the extant literature. Poliakov's *Harvest of Hate* was typical: 'his thesis, expressed in the title, that the root of the process was hatred, seemed in my eyes to be an antiquated supposition. The bureaucrats, I already knew, were not haters.'[69]

For Hilberg the 'Final Solution' was, above all, a systematic *process*. Of course he acknowledged that there were various pressures within the Nazi regime which tended towards pogrommatic violence against Jews. During the 1930s the *Sturmabteilung* (SA, the paramilitary Nazi 'stormtroopers' or 'brownshirts') and the NSDAP had both attempted to drive Jewish policy in that direction, and after 1939 Nazi forces commonly attempted to foment local violence against Jewish populations, most famously in Lithuania. But for Hilberg what marked the 'Final Solution' out was that it was a controlled, bureaucratic *process* of 'definition, expropriation, concentration and annihilation' which could be mapped in all of the areas under Nazi occupation during the Second World War.[70] It was the systematisation and bureaucratisation of this process which made the 'Final Solution' so lethal, because it was this which gave it its ceaseless dynamism.

In Hilberg's thesis there existed no overarching plan for Nazi anti-Jewish action. Each stage in the process dictated that its successor would be yet more radical, revealing both further possibilities and necessities in anti-Jewish action. The first stage was to find a working definition of a minority group (the Jews) – for example in the Nuremberg Laws, which then informed the desire to separate that minority and dissolve the personal and economic relations between them and the majority population – in the aryanisation of Jewish property and businesses. The necessity of the third stage – removal – was only revealed by the first two however, when, in the *Altreich*, the Germans were faced with a destitute victim population which appeared as a burden. Anything other than removal would have been to re-establish a relationship between Germans and Jews.[71]

While Hilberg accepted that the 'Final Solution' was a variegated process, in that it was applied (and indeed succeeded)
differently in different areas of Nazi occupied Europe, he insisted
that it was possible to build a model of its implementation.[72]
Indeed it was even possible to design a model of its variations too.
He argued that the destruction process in axis countries was determined by the 'extent of war enthusiasm in that state. The
implementation of the destructive program and the prosecution of
the war show close parallels.'[73]

Hilberg's desire to model the 'Final Solution' was directly influenced by Ernst Fraenkel and Franz Neumann who had made the
first efforts to map the National Socialist system during the
1940s.[74] Fraenkel had discerned a dual state, essentially split
between the 'normative' and 'prerogative', in the co-existence of
the rational, legal authorities of the traditional structures of
German governance, and the often duplicating and frequently
irrational structures of revolutionary Nazism which emanated
from the Nazi movement itself. Neumann, who was Hilberg's doctoral supervisor, had further nuanced this Manichean dichotomy
in his *Behemoth* which understood the Nazi state not as a state at
all but as a series of overlapping, competing and sometimes mutually reinforcing power-blocs, including a charismatic and
theoretically unrestrained *Führer*. Those power blocs included
industry, the armed forces and the Nazi movement itself. Hilberg
described *Behemoth* as giving him an 'indispensable tool of analysis'.[75] In the mid-1970s Peter Hüttenberger would further influence
Holocaust historiography with his development of Neumann's
thesis, an analysis of the National Socialist 'polycracy' in which
the competition (and conversely mutual reliance) between those
power blocs was further stressed in a system only 'held together by
the authority of Hitler'.[76]

Hilberg was the first scholar to apply these perspectives on the
National Socialist political community purely to the 'Final Solution'. It is notable how far this vision of the Third Reich differed
from the essentially top-down monolithic structure implied by
scholars such as Krausnick and later Dawidowicz. That an analysis
of the progress of Nazi anti-Jewish policy required a working theory of the functioning of the state in the Third Reich appeared
obvious to Hilberg. As there was no single agency in charge of
Judenpolitik, and because the driving force of that policy shifted

as the history of the Third Reich progressed, and especially because all anti-Jewish action – from aryanisation and emigration to deportation and annihilation – required multiple agency implementation; a study of the development of destruction policy required an understanding of the entire organised community.[77] Consider only the agencies involved in deporting Jews from Western Europe to the death camps. This frequently required the functional co-operation of Eichmann's Gestapo office, the Reichsbahn (German railway authorities), the Foreign Office, the civil and / or military occupation authorities from the deportation areas, the local police forces and even the local Jewish Councils and then the camp authorities at the destination and potentially the industrial concerns for which some Jews were used as slave labour, in addition to organisations such as *Einsatzstab Rosenberg*, geared to the expropriation of the assets that deported Jews had left behind.[78] This co-operation spread far beyond just the agencies of the state – the construction of the death camp at Auschwitz-Birkenau called upon the resources of the armed forces and private industry as well as the construction office of the WVHA.[79]

For Hilberg co-operation defined the total process of the 'Final Solution' which he declared was 'comparable in its diversity to a modern war, a mobilisation, or a national reconstruction'. Indeed he was struck by the unity of that process, in that despite the decentred power structure of the Third Reich and thus the lack of totalitarian central direction, 'the destruction of the Jews was not disrupted, continuity was one of its crucial characteristics'.[80] In fact, Hilberg argued that the unity, direction and thus destructiveness of the process was a result of, rather then despite, the peculiar nature of the Nazi system. Because the bureaucracy, from its lowest levels to the highest, lacked a 'master-plan' and indeed until comparatively late in the process a definable end goal, innovation and radicalism in Jewish policy filled that vacuum. The very 'Final Solution' itself was oblique, defined only in the vaguest terms. When Hitler prophesied 'annihilation' in January 1939 each stage of the process seemed to open up new possibilities – especially for lower-level bureaucrats not privy to the oral orders that were handed down from Hitler and Himmler. These possibilities could present themselves at the centre of Nazi power or on the periphery. It was, for example, only because of the appalling conditions which the ghettoisation of the Jews had created that Rolf Heinz Höppner could suggest to Adolf Eichmann in July of 1941 that it might be better to kill the Jews of Łódź than keep them alive. Höppner knew that such a suggestion did not represent any agreed *policy* but he also knew that it was in line with the vague and rhetorical goals that placed great priority on making German territory *Judenrein*.[81]

Hilberg's emphasis on the structure of Nazi rule appears at times to depersonalise the Holocaust. References to the fact that the destruction process was determined and that 'it is ... inevitable that a bureaucracy ... should push its victims through' the progressive stages in the process, seem to be faceless – indicting the bureaucracy or the machine rather than the individuals within it.[82] However Hilberg was in fact unambiguous about what drove the machinery onwards to ever more apocalyptic ends:

> The Germans killed five million Jews. The onslaught did not come from the void; it was brought into being because it had meaning to its perpetrators. It was not a narrow strategy for the attainment of some ulterior goal, but an undertaking for its own sake, an event experienced as *Erlebnis*, lived and lived through by its participants ... The German bureaucrats who contributed their skills to the destruction of the Jews all shared this experience, some in the technical work of drafting a decree or dispatching a train, others starkly at the door of a gas chamber. They could sense the enormity of the operation from its smallest fragments. At every stage they displayed a striking path finding ability in the absence of directives, a congruity of activities without jurisdictional guidelines, a fundamental comprehension of the task when there were no explicit guidelines.[83]

But despite his acknowledging the importance of the perpetrator's ideological conviction, there is little doubt that it was the structure of Nazi rule which created genocidal momentum in Hilberg's narrative.

After Hilberg and Arendt, the idea that Jewish policy had developed in the absence of an overall vision quickly became received wisdom especially amongst German scholars such as Uwe Dietrich Adam, Karl Schleunes and those grouped at the IfZ – also first publicly played out in the expert submissions that the IfZ provided to German courts.[84] Karl Schleunes, for example, began his investigation of pre-war antisemitic policy from the assumption that the 'Final Solution as it emerged in 1941 and 1942 was not the product of a grand design ... they had no specific plans for a solution of any sort', only a shared sense of a Jewish problem.[85] It was the Nazi system, according to Schleunes, which then forged the 'twisted road to Auschwitz'. This idea of the progressive development of policy filtered through the peculiar power structure of the Third Reich would become known as 'functionalism' or 'structuralism'.

Functionalist scholars were quick to acknowledge the influence of both Hilberg and Arendt in the development of their theses. Writing in the mid-1980s Hans Mommsen, perhaps the foremost functionalist historian of the Third Reich,[86] praised Hannah Arendt for having brought to public attention the 'simple but horrific truth [which she adopted from Hilberg] that the Holocaust had not been the result of a systematically executed political plan' and that the radicalism of the 'Final Solution' was the consequence of this vacuum and the peculiar state described by Hilberg.[87]

That structure that gave rise to genocide, according to both Hilberg and Arendt, included the *Judenräte* (Jewish Councils), which they controversially placed inside the machinery of destruction. In a double-pronged analysis, Hilberg argued first that the Jewish Councils were a mere cipher for the instructions of the Nazis and that they therefore aided the bureaucracy of destruction. Second he suggested that Jewish passivity in the face of the Nazi onslaught, the idea that the Jews went like 'lambs to the slaughter', was the result of an ingrained anticipatory compliance developed as the Jewish reaction to persecution over the last two millennia.[88] Hilberg was not actually the first historian to interpret the Jewish Councils in this way. Both Leon Poliakov and Gerald Reitlinger had identified the councils' role in expediting deportations. However, both historians were only openly critical of Chaim Rumkowski (who had been the leader of the Łódź ghetto) and as such implied no general culpability on the part of Jewish leaders.[89] Hilberg, and subsequently Hannah Arendt, did not differentiate in this manner. Indeed Arendt offered a universal *moral* evaluation of the *Judenräte*:

to a Jew this role of the Jewish leaders in the destruction of their own people is undoubtedly the darkest chapter of the whole dark story. It had been known about before, but it has now been exposed for the first time in all its pathetic and sordid detail by Raul Hilberg ... But the whole truth was that there existed Jewish community organisations and Jewish party and welfare organisations on both the local and international level. Wherever Jews lived, there were recognized Jewish leaders and this leadership, almost without exception, co-operated in one way or another, for one reason or another, with the Nazis. The whole truth was that if the Jewish people had really been unorganised and leaderless, there would have been chaos and plenty of misery but the total number of victims would hardly have been between four and a half and six million people.[90]

Unsurprisingly such an analysis engulfed Arendt, and by association Hilberg, in a wave of controversy. Nathan Eck, representative of the survivor historians grouped at *Yad Vashem*, dismissed Hilberg's historical research as 'slander' (indeed despite the recommendation of Philip Friedman *Yad Vashem* had refused the opportunity to publish Hilberg's work).[91] By interpreting Jewish Councils just in relation to the destruction process Eck argued that the cultural life of the ghetto had been ignored.[92] In fact Hilberg *had* acknowledged the complexity of the *Judenräte*, arguing that they both 'saved and destroyed their people' because of their roles in feeding the ghetto, ensuring productivity and in co-operating with and at times administrating deportation.[93] But he, and especially Hannah Arendt, also implied that the Jewish Council leaders had made choices in their dealings with the Nazis. For Eck and other critics like Jacob Robinson the implication of choice also suggested moral *responsibility*. The reality, according to Jacob Robinson, was that the victims were the only actors in this historical drama who could not be regarded as culpable: 'the murder of six million Jews was the direct responsibility of Nazi Germany which carried it out ... the destruction of six million Jews ... is the darkest chapter of Jewish history during the Nazi period, and indeed during all time.'[94]

The gulf between Hilberg, Arendt and their critics revealed by their opposing analyses of the *Judenräte* also highlights a disagreement about both the causes of the 'Final Solution' and indeed the entire purpose and method of historical explanation. Eck *et al.* indicted a peculiarly murderous antisemitic ideological conviction in their causal analysis. The Jewish Councils could not therefore be awarded any real significance in the progress of a 'Final Solution' that had been determined and driven by a fanatical anti-Judaism – for that would have been a contradiction in terms. For Hilberg *et al.* structural prerogatives needed to be added to the causal matrix in order to understand how ideology was translated into radical action. Jewish Councils had a *function* within the process, which embedded and accelerated destruction. The Jewish Councils' self-evident separation from ideology only further highlighted that the process was self-propelling and in part *structurally* determined.

Intentionalism, functionalism and the philosophy of History

In essence then two Holocaust metanarratives had emerged. An 'intentionalist' explanation rooted in the history of ideas and a 'functionalist' interpretation rooted in the more abstract social science of government and organisation. Yet from the outset this dichotomy was about much more than just an explanation of the 'Final Solution'. It was concerned with how one situated an account of the Holocaust within a more wide-ranging understanding of the modern world. It was also a debate over morality, ethics and the responsibility of the historian, and even the purpose of historical explanation itself.

From the outset Hannah Arendt had been concerned to understand the relationship between the Holocaust, modernity and modern social and political organisation. She wanted to understand the Holocaust in a context beyond the boundaries of the Third Reich and Nazi occupied Europe.[95] Hence her representation, intended or otherwise, of Adolf Eichmann as 'everyman' – in that he appeared as the universal functionary of modern bureaucracy. Whilst Raul Hilberg balked from his association with Arendt, that his analysis relied so heavily on the idea of the state and the bureaucracy as a machine which drove (almost by itself) the 'Final Solution' forward means that he too implied an association between modern bureaucratic forms and genocide. As he wrote in a later publication:

> That is the crux of the question when we ponder the meaning of Western civilisation after Auschwitz. Our evolution has outpaced our

understanding; we can no longer assume that we have a full grasp of the workings of our social institutions, bureaucratic structures, or technology.[96]

And, of course, Arendt's Eichmann was largely conceived in the light of Hilberg's analysis. If Hilberg's Third Reich was an ideological world it was also one, as we have seen, that was decentred and in which different agencies operated – in terms of Nazi anti-Jewish policy – in the absence of specific policy directives and in line with only vague ideological and rhetorical goals. That they could function at all in such a system was because they were able to rely on 'existing procedures ... [where] the usual practices [were] applied in unusual situations'. In other words the 'Final Solution' was a genocide that required and relied upon a specific form of bureaucratic organisation that was peculiar to the modern state.[97] As German functionalist Hans Bucheim phrased it:

> it must be remembered ... that concentration upon sheer achievement without regard for truth or ethics, the desire to do the maximum whether in good cause or bad, whether the subject be important or unimportant, are not characteristics peculiar to the SS; they are characteristics of the time in which we live.[98]

Following Bucheim, for later standard bearers of this approach to Holocaust history it was almost axiomatic that the Holocaust was itself an axiom of modernity – as Hans Mommsen wrote the Holocaust was a warning to 'advanced industrial societies' about their destructive potential.[99]

Such analyses thus sought to overturn enlightenment assumptions of progress, but for those historians labelled 'intentionalists' almost the precise opposite was true. For them, the 'Final Solution' appeared not to be the result of modernity and the age of reason but of barbarism and the hatreds of the past. This was the inevitable analytical consequence of the indictment of an ideology, the roots of which were often traced back into either the German or European pasts. If Hilberg and those who came after relied on the technological metaphor of the machine, these scholars used starkly different language. For Leon Poliakov for example, Hitler was the 'high Priest' of a movement which drew on 'primitive magic'.[100] Such imagery developed directly from the interpretations of Nazism as a kind of Satanic anti-religion that abounded after the war and grew out of wartime propaganda of Nazism as the inversion of Christian culture.[101] When intentionalist historiography reached its apogee in Lucy Dawidowicz's *The War Against the Jews* this particular argument had been developed, and Nazi antisemitism was portrayed as the bastard child of Christian anti-Judaism. However, the imagery of the Holocaust as a barbaric throw-back remained: 'in modern Germany', Dawidowicz argued, 'the mass psychosis of anti-Semitism deranged a whole people. According to their system of beliefs elimination of the Jews resembled medieval exorcism of the Devil.'[102]

The contrast between the two approaches was such that in the intentionalist schema modernity was even seen as the antidote to the poisonous hatred that had given birth to the 'Final Solution'. In part this reflects the desire of many intentionalist historians to see the Holocaust in the context of Jewish history. Dawidowicz wrote of 'another link in the chain of Jewish suffering', and as such related to the ideology that had ensured and conditioned that suffering.[103] In its most trenchant manifestation intentionalist historiography could even point towards the incorporation of the Holocaust into an almost whiggish history of, specifically Jewish, progress – self-evidently the utter antithesis of Arendt *et al.*'s critique of modernity. Again the example of Dawidowicz is instructive. The latter half of *The War Against the Jews* is given over to engaging with Hilberg's allegation of Jewish passivity and even complicity in the face of the Nazi onslaught. Dawidowicz demonstrates the range and depth of Jewish active resistance in her reply to Hilberg. But in doing so, as Dan Stone has argued, she inevitably valorises active resistance as a response to anti-Judaism.[104]

While Dawidowicz herself drew no political conclusions from this, Israeli scholar Leni Yahil suggested (before Dawidowicz' work was published) that such an argument allowed the Holocaust to be incorporated into a narrative of Jewish history as a progression towards the state of Israel, and specifically Israeli action in the face of ideological enemies.[105] Nora Levin's *The Holocaust* is perhaps the archetypal example of this rendering of the Holocaust inside a narrative of progress. She concludes: 'the Jewish experience in Europe was plainly finished ... For the surviving Jews of Europe ... there was no return possible ... there was only one way left: Palestine.'[106] It is not my purpose here to suggest that intentionalist historiography was the necessary bedfellow of Zionism. I only use the example of Israel to suggest the degree of intentionalist scorn for the idea that the Holocaust revealed something profound about modern states and society.

Disagreements over the relationship between modernity and barbarism betrayed the wider discourse over morality and progress which lay behind the beginnings of the intentionalist functionalist dispute. As we have already seen Hannah Arendt's investigations of the Holocaust were in essence part of a moral treatise which sought to overturn the assumption, inherent in much enlightenment thinking, that 'moral law was written on the tablets of eternity'.[107] *Eichmann in Jerusalem* argued that the Third Reich developed its own new morality which the perpetrators of the Holocaust used to evaluate their behaviour. Arendt's antagonists, both her contemporaries and more modern critics, sought to reassert moral certainties primarily of course to demonstrate that the perpetrators of the 'Final Solution' knew that their actions represented a moral transgression.

Such a discourse also revealed differences over the relationship between the historian and moral evaluation. Because, for example, Lucy Dawidowicz believed in the certainty of some moral assumptions – effectively the enlightenment values of reason – she in turn accepted that the historian could not avoid morally evaluating the pasts which they uncovered. Her investigation of the Holocaust therefore made no effort to hold up a 'neutral mirror' on the Nazi past but was an analysis 'charged with passion and moral judgement'.[108] Such a desire to reach firm judgements about the guilt of the perpetrators was, in part, the result of the judicial context in which intentionalist historiography was born. But it was also the result of a wider faith in the institutions of modernity. Demonstrating that individuals understood (in classical terms) right and wrong, implied the continuing triumph of enlightenment values of reason. If individuals had made choices to reject those values, then this did not suggest (as structuralist historians implied) any murderous potential in a world built on those values.

The functionalist scholarship which followed Arendt and Hilberg was perhaps more wary of making the kind of moral judgements that Dawidowicz endorsed. Because within structuralist thinking more generally ideas were themselves not believed to be independent of their social and political context, its historiography tended to echo Arendt's contention that morality was historically contingent. As such individual choices were of less interest to functionalist historians who wished to demonstrate the structural determinants that they believed circumscribed the moral, or otherwise, choices that individuals made. This did not mean that functionalist historiography eschewed the intentionalist desire to condemn, indeed the opposite is true. At its root the functionalist historical project was about indicting an entire system of governance as the progenitor of genocidal violence. E.H. Carr observed that there is a moral judgement inherent in historians' phraseology like the 'cost of progress', and what could be more a moral evaluation than the observation that the Holocaust was made possible by the machinery of modern, bureaucratic government?

A common belief in 'the Holocaust'

The historiography of the perpetration of the Holocaust has been built on the foundations of the bi-polar landscape described above. Although the focus of this chapter has been on the profound methodological and interpretative differences between these two approaches, they have not actually been irreconcilable and post Eichmann-trial Holocaust scholarship did inhabit some common ground.

Much early Holocaust scholarship had been concerned to view the sufferings of Jews in a wider context, within the Nazis' more general racialised vision of the future of Eastern Europe. While the scholarship that followed Arendtian universalising of Eichmann may have wished to apply the lessons revealed by the sufferings of Jews to a wider context, it did share with what became intentionalist scholarship, the desire to assert that it was the sufferings of Jews that contained the lessons for modernity. As such both intentionalists and functionalists believed that the Holocaust was, as it were, *unique*. Arch-intentionalist Nora Levin began her history of the *Shoah* with this declaration that the destruction of the European Jews was incomparable: 'The Holocaust refuses to go the way of most history, not only because of the magnitude of the destruction – the murder of six million Jews – but because the events surrounding it are still in a very real sense humanly incomprehensible.'[109] Intriguingly, functionalist

Karl Schleunes, whose *The Twisted Road to Auschwitz* was written at about the same time and reached almost the opposite conclusions, began his history in these starkly *similar* terms: 'violent death accompanying war in an age of industry and technology … had its precedents. The institutions which most appropriately symbolise the Nazi era – Auschwitz [and] Treblinka, and some 50 other concentration and extermination camps – had none.'[110]

Perhaps nothing symbolises more this collective sense that the sufferings of Jews at Nazi hands needed to be dealt with as a phenomenologically separate event than the development of the term 'Holocaust' itself which has served to separate the destruction of Europe's Jews from the course of 'normal' history. The sacrificial overtones of the term are certainly not History's usual semantic. It is impossible to fully excavate its archaeology, or to understand its precise genealogy, but it is clear that 'Holocaust' entered popular and historical discourse between the late 1950s and the early 1960s. Various scholars have observed that its first use in the *New York Times* came in May 1959.[111] Elie Wiesel has been credited with coining the term 'Holocaust', but he himself recalls only first using it in 1963.[112] While it is true that during the 1950s not a single publication on the Nazi genocide used the term in its title, historians did begin to discuss 'the Holocaust' during that decade. Leon Poliakov used the label once in his groundbreaking *Harvest of Hate*.[113] As Boaz Cohen has demonstrated, Jewish historians in Israel also used the term in the first issues of *Yad Vashem Studies*,[114] although other terms were much more common; 'the Catastrophe' was favoured in English-language publications.[115]

However it emerged, it is clear that the label 'Holocaust' helped fix the genocide of the Jews in popular memory. There is no doubt to what one is referring when one uses the word. There is seldom any need to describe the Nazi genocide of the Jews as the Jewish Holocaust. As such, the term both reflected and reinforced the sense that the genocide of the Jews stood apart. As previously noted, the term was first used consistently by Jewish scholars, and Zev Garber and Bruce Zuckerman have argued that it was adopted as the signifier of the murder of the European Jews because it implied the uniqueness of Jewish victims and thus helped relate the Holocaust to the Jewish tradition.[116] But it is worth noting that 'Holocaust' did not define the Nazi campaign against Europe's Jews using the language of the Nazis' principal victims. Judaism could (and did) apply the existing terms *Shoah* and *Khurbn* to the Nazi genocide. The term 'Holocaust', with its connotations of sacrifice and martyrdom, represented and defined the Shoah using a language that, if not specifically Christian, was at least subject to Christian interpretation too.[117] That the label was in part popularized by a publication on Edith Stein, the Catholic Church's Christian Holocaust martyr, reinforces this sense.[118] As such it is a mistake to assume that the adoption of the Holocaust as a universal signifier is a result of an ethnic campaign to Judaise historical memories of Nazi barbarism. Leon Poliakov implicitly acknowledged as much when he used the term 'holocaust' to describe the quasi-religious significance in the Nazis' own imagination of the campaign against the Jews: 'They wished to draw a veil of sacred horror, to transform it into a sanctifying and purifying mystery.'[119]

In the period following the Eichmann trial then, 'the Holocaust' emerged as a distinct subject of historical investigation. As such, often in relation to judicial investigations of the Nazi past, historians began to assert that the Nazi persecution of the Jews was a subject in and of itself that did not need to be seen solely within the context of the wider destruction politics of the Third Reich. It was not just one but two metanarratives that emerged from courtrooms however: the intentionalist thesis rooted in the history of ideas and ideology, and the functionalist thesis grounded in the sociology of the modern bureaucratic state. These were not just opposing interpretations of the Holocaust but embodied entirely different visions of the purpose and possibilities of historical enquiry. It is on this polarised terrain that the historiography of the perpetration of the Holocaust has been constructed, as the discussion in Chapters 4, 5 and 6 of this book will demonstrate.

The separation of the sufferings of the Jews as a subject of historical investigation also meant that other questions emerged in scholarship, besides just the perpetration of the genocide itself. As has been touched on in this chapter, Jewish victims of Nazi persecution also emerged as the subject of historical investigation and in some senses survivors asserted themselves as a subject for scholarly concern. Chapters 7 and 8 below will analyse such scholarship. Once the Holocaust emerged as phenomenologically distinct it became possible to ask how others had responded to this event or set of events. If there was a distinct Nazi campaign against Jews then how had the rest of the world reacted? Such questions began to be asked at the Eichmann trial and in its aftermath too. It is to the study of the witnesses to the 'Final Solution', who have become known as its bystanders, that this book now turns. Again at the centre of bystander scholarship is a set of moral and political judgments of the present rather than the past.

Notes

1 Attorney General's Opening Statement, 17 April 1961, *Trial of Adolf Eichmann*, Vol. 1, Session 6. – accessed through Nizkor. http://www.nizkor.org/hweb/people/e/eichmann-adolf/transcripts/Sessions/Session-006-007-008-01.html.

2 See for example Jeffrey Shandler, 'The Man in the Glass Box: Watching the Eichmann Trial on American Television', Barbie Zelizer, *Visual Culture and the Holocaust* (New Brunswick: NJ, 2001), pp. 91–110.

3 See Halina Birenbaum, *Hope is the Last to Die: A Personal Documentation of Nazi Terror* (New York, 1971) in which Birenbaum suggests that it was the Eichmann trial that persuaded her to tell her story. A number of publications appeared between Eichmann's capture and his trial. For example Charles Wighton, *Eichmann: His Career and Crimes* (London, 1961). It perhaps says something about prevailing attitudes to the trial and to the Holocaust that the back cover of this book proclaimed that Wighton's book was all the more important because he was 'not a Jew'.

4 Peter Novick, *The Holocaust in American Life* (Boston: MA, 1999), pp. 127-45; David Cesarani, *Eichmann: His Life and Crimes* (London, 2005), p. 325.

5 See for example David Ritter's account of this process in Australia in 'Distant Reverberations: Australian Responses to the Eichmann Trial', Tom Lawson and James Jordan (eds), *The Memory of the Holocaust in Australia* (London, 2008), pp. 51–74.

6 Dan Diner argues that Arendt sows the seeds of both the intentionalist and functionalist interpretations of the Holocaust in her *Eichmann in Jerusalem*, it seems to me that she is doing this in *The Origins of Totalitarianism* too. See Dan Diner, 'Hannah Arendt Reconsidered: On the Banal and the Evil in Her Holocaust Narrative', *New German Critique* (No. 71, 1997), pp. 177–90.

7 Tim Mason, 'Intention and Explanation: A Current Controversy about the interpretation of National Socialism', reprinted in Michael Marrus (ed.) *The Nazi Holocaust: Vol. 3.1 The 'Final Solution': The Implementation of Mass Murder* (London, 1989), pp. 3–20.

8 See Isser Harel, *The House on Garibaldi Street: The Capture of Adolf Eichmann* (London, 1975) for a somewhat sensationalist account of the plan to capture and then the abduction of Eichmann.

9 Cesarani, *Eichmann*, p. 203.

10 Rudolf Höss, *Commandant of Auschwitz* (London, 2000), p. 147.

11 For example Joseph Tennenbaum , *Race and Reich: The Story of an Epoch*

(New York, 1956), pp. 252, 339, which depicted Eichmann as an 'arch fiend of such fanatical devotion', the Nazis 'chief executioner.

12 Karl A. Schleunes, *The Twisted Road to Auschwitz: Nazi Policy Toward German Jews 1933–39* (Chicago: IL, 1970), p. 203.

13 Michael Wildt, 'Before the "Final Solution": The Judenpolitik of the SD, 1935-38', *Leo Baeck Institute Yearbook* (No. 43, 1998), pp. 263–4.

14 Hans Safrian, 'Expediting Expropriation and Expulsion: The Impact of the 'Vienna Model' on Anti-Jewish Policies in Nazi Germany, 1938', *Holocaust and Genocide Studies* (Vol. 14, No. 3, 2000), pp. 390–414.

15 Deborah Dwork and Robert Jan van Pelt, *Holocaust: A History* (New York, 2002), p. 206.

16 Cesarani, *Eichmann*, p. 77.

17 Götz Aly, *'Final Solution': Nazi Population Policy and the Murder of the European Jews* (London, 1999) p. 36.

18 *Ibid.*, pp. 96–7.

19 Cesarani, *Eichmann*, pp. 98–111.

20 *Trial of Adolf Eichmann*, Vol. 1, Session 6–8.

21 David Ben-Gurion cited in Cesarani, *Eichmann*, p. 240.

22 Cesarani, *Eichmann*, pp. 248–9.

23 See Rebecca Wittmann, *Beyond Justice: The Auschwitz Trial* (Cambridge: MA, 2005), p. 3.

24 Helmut Krausnick, 'The Persecution of the Jews', Krausnick and Martin Broszat (eds), *Anatomy of the SS State* (London, 1970). First published in German in 1965.

25 Lucy Dawidowicz, *The War Against the Jews 1933–45 – Tenth Anniversary Edition* (London, 1987), p. xxiv.

26 Mason, 'Intention and Explanation', pp. 11–12.

27 Leon Poliakov, *Harvest of Hate: The Nazi Program for the Destruction of the Jews of Europe* (New York, 1957), p. ix.

28 Jacob Robinson, *And the Crooked Shall be Made Straight: The Eichmann Trial, the Jewish Catastrophe and Hannah Arendt's Narrative* (New York, 1965), pp. 38–9.

29 Krausnick, 'The Persecution of the Jews', p. 19.

30 *Ibid.*, p. 25.

31 Nora Levin, *The Holocaust: The Destruction of European Jewry 1933–45* (New York, 1968), p. 39.

32 Krausnick, 'The Persecution of the Jews', pp. 42, 49–50.

33 Dawidowicz, *The War Against the Jews*, p. 127.

34 Krausnick, 'The Persecution of the Jews', p. 62.

35 Poliakov, *Harvest of Hate*, p. 108.

36 Krausnick, 'The Persecution of the Jews', p. 7.

37 Dawidowicz, *The War Against the Jews*, p. 160.

38 *Ibid.*, p. 195.

39 Krausnick, 'The Persecution of the Jews', p. 137.

40 Levin, *The Holocaust*, p. 184.

41 Poliakov, *Harvest of Hate*, p. 113.

42 For a much more developed but markedly similar interpretation see Peter Longerich, *Politik der Vernichtung: eine Gesamtdarstellung der nationalsozialistischen Judenverfolgung* (Munich, 1998). Now published in English as Peter

Longerich, *Holocaust: The Nazi Persecution and Murder of the Jews* (Oxford, 2010).

43 Dawidowicz, *The War Against the Jews*, p. 119. This anticipates the detailed archival work of Michael Wildt on the SD.

44 *Ibid.*, p. 198.

45 Hannah Arendt, *Eichmann in Jerusalem: A Report on the Banality of Evil* (London, 2006), p. 276.

46 Reitlinger combined his interests in Nazi Germany with a career in art history. His interest in genocide was also wider than just the Holocaust, see his *A Tower of Skulls: A Journey through Persia and Turkish Armenia* (London, 1932), especially pp. 12, 269, 298–9, for his confrontation with the memory of the Armenian genocide.

47 Gerald Reitlinger, *The Final Solution: The Attempt to Exterminate the Jews of Europe 1939–45* (London, 1961), p. 114.

48 *Ibid.*, p. 271.

49 *Ibid.*, pp. 27, 483.

50 Arendt, *Eichmann in Jerusalem*, p. 44.

51 *Ibid.*, p. 137.

52 For a discussion of the relationship between Arendt's thesis and wider social science scholarship see Michael Thad Allen, 'Grey Collar Worker: Organisation Theory in Holocaust Studies', *Holocaust Studies: A Journal of Culture and History* (Vol. 11, No. 1, 2005), pp. 27–54. See also Gerald D. Feldman and Wolfgang Seibel (eds), *Networks of Nazi Persecution: Bureaucracy, Business and the Organisation of the Holocaust* (New York, 2005).

53 Literally translated the term *Vernichtung* means to make nothing.

54 Arendt, *Eichmann in Jerusalem*, p. 146.

55 Ian Kershaw, 'Working Towards the Führer': Reflections on the Nature of the Hitler Dictatorship', *Contemporary European History* (Vol. 2, No. 2, 1993), pp. 103–18. See also Ian Kershaw, *Hitler: Hubris 1889–1936* (London, 1998), and *Hitler: Nemesis 1936–45* (London, 2000).

56 Arendt, *Eichmann in Jerusalem*, p. 215.

57 *Ibid.*, p. 279.

58 *Ibid.*, p. 276.

59 *Ibid.*, p. 33.

60 Hannah Arendt, *The Origins of Totalitarianism* (New York, 2004), pp. 11, the quotation is from p. 409.

61 *Ibid.*, p. 503.

62 Arendt, *Eichmann in Jerusalem*, p. 287.

63 Michael Thad Allen, *The Business of Genocide: The SS, Slave Labour and the Concentration Camps* (Chapel Hill: NC, 2002), pp. 8–10. For Allen's specific critique of Arendt see his 'Grey Collar Worker', and 'The Banality of Evil Reconsidered: SS Mid-Level Managers of Extermination Through Work', *Central European History* (Vol. 30, No. 2, 1998), pp. 253–94.

64 Arendt, *Eichmann In Jerusalem*, pp. 114-16.

65 Yaacov Lozowick, *Hitler's Bureaucrats: the Nazi Security Police and the Banality of Evil* (New York, 2002), p. 38.

66 Arendt, *Eichmann In Jerusalem*, p. 279.

67 Hans Safrian, *Eichmann's Men* (Cambridge, 2010). This is the translated and updated version of *Die Eichmann-Männer* (Wien, 1993).

68 Raul Hilberg, *The Politics of Memory: The Journey of a Holocaust Historian* (Chicago: IL, 1996), p. 105.
69 *Ibid.*, p. 70.
70 Raul Hilberg, *The Destruction of the European Jews* (New Haven: CT, 2003), p. 51. Please note that these specific references are to the third edition but none of the concepts that are referred to differ in any meaningful way to those introduced in the first edition published in 1961.
71 *Ibid.*, p. 132.
72 For example Hilberg discusses the construction of the death camp at Chelmno as 'strictly a local enterprise'. *Ibid.*, p. 1014.
73 *Ibid.*, p. 792.
74 See Ernst Fraenkel, *The Dual State* (Oxford, 1941); Franz Neumann, *Behemoth: the Structure and Process of National Socialism* (London, 1944).
75 Hilberg, *Politics of Memory*, p. 89.
76 Neil Gregor, *Nazism: A Reader* (Oxford, 2000), p. 194, including extracts from Peter Hüttenberger, 'Nationalsozialistische Polykratie', *Geschichte and Gesellschaft* (1976).
77 Hilberg, *Destruction of the European Jews*, p. 61.
78 See *ibid.*, pp. 615–32 for a description of this process in the Netherlands.
79 *Ibid.*, p. 946.
80 *Ibid.*, p. 1060.
81 A copy of Höppner's letter can be found in Jeremy Noakes and Geoffrey Pridham (eds), *Nazism 1919–45, Vol. 3: Foreign Policy, War, and Racial Extermination* (Exeter, 1995), p. 1103.
82 Hilberg, *Destruction of the European Jews*, p. 1065.
83 *Ibid.*, p. 1059.
84 See Krausnick *et al.*, *Anatomy of the SS State*, for a collection of these expert submissions. See also Uwe Dietrich Adam, *Judenpolitik im Dritten Reich* (Düsseldorf, 1972).
85 Schleunes, *Twisted Road to Auschwitz*, p. 2.
86 Marrus, *Holocaust in History*, p. 42.
87 Hans Mommsen, 'Hannah Arendt and the Eichmann Trial', *From Weimar to Auschwitz* (Princeton: NJ, 1991), p. 255.
88 Hilberg, *Destruction of the European Jews*, pp. 1030–44.
89 Leon Poliakov, *Harvest of Hate*, pp. 101–4; Gerald Reitlinger, *The Final Solution*, pp. 64–6.
90 Arendt, *Eichmann in Jerusalem*, pp. 117–26.
91 Hilberg, *Politics of Memory*, p. 109.
92 Nathan Eck, 'Historical Research or Slander', *Yad Vashem Studies* (Vol. VI, 1967), pp. 385–430.
93 Hilberg, *Destruction of the European Jews*, p. 246.
94 Robinson, *And the Crooked*, p. 144.
95 See Dana Villa, 'Totalitarianism, Modernity and the Tradition', Steven Ascheim (ed.), *Hannah Arendt in Jerusalem* (Berkeley: CA, 2001), pp. 124–45.
96 Raul Hilberg, 'The Significance of the Holocaust', Henry Friedlander and Sybil Milton (eds), *The Holocaust, Ideology, Bureaucracy and Genocide* (New York, 1980), pp. 101–2.
97 Hilberg, *Destruction of the European Jews*, p. 1061.

98 Hans Bucheim, 'The SS – Instrument of Domination', in Krausnick *et al.*, *Anatomy of the SS State* (London, 1968), p. 329.

99 Hans Mommsen, 'The Realization of the Unthinkable: the 'Final Solution of the Jewish Question' in the Third Reich', Marrus, *The Nazi Holocaust*, p. 249.

100 Poliakov, *Harvest of Hate*, pp. 5–7.

101 See Chapter 1 and for example Tennenbaum, *Race and Reich*, pp. 73–81.

102 Dawidowicz, *The War Against the Jews*, p. 210.

103 Dawidowicz, *The War Against the Jews*, p. 20.

104 Stone, *Constructing the Holocaust*, pp. 150–1.

105 Leni Yahil, 'The Holocaust in Jewish Historiography', *Yad Vashem Studies* (VII, 1968), p. 70.

106 Levin, *The Holocaust*, p. 710.

107 Jonathan Glover, *Humanity: A Moral History of the Twentieth Century* (London, 1999), p. 1.

108 Dawidowicz, *The War Against the Jews*, pp. 17–21.

109 Levin, *The Holocaust*, p. xi.

110 Schleunes, *Twisted Road to Auschwitz*, p. 1.

111 Isabel Woolaston, *A War Against Memory: The Future of Holocaust Remembrance* (London, 1996), p. 2; Tim Cole, *Images of the Holocaust* (London, 1999), p. 7.

112 Zev Garber and Bruce Zuckerman, 'Why Do We Call the Holocaust "the Holocaust": An Inquiry into the Psychology of Labels', *Modern Judaism* (May 1989), pp. 197–211, 202.

113 Poliakov, *Harvest of Hate*, p. 213.

114 Boaz Cohen, 'The Birth Pangs of Holocaust Research in Israel', *Yad Vashem Studies* (Vol. 33, 2005), pp. 203–43. There is a reference to 'the archives of the Holocaust' in Philip Friedman, 'Preliminary and Methodological Problems of the Research on the Jewish Catastrophe in the Nazi Period', *Yad Washem Studies* (Vol. 2, 1958), p. 133.

115 See for example Koppel S. Pinson (ed.), *YIVO Annual of Jewish Social Science, vol. 8, Studies on the Epoch of the Jewish Catastrophe* (New York, 1953).

116 Garber and Zuckerman, 'Why Do We Call the Holocaust "the Holocaust"'. Garber and Zuckerman offer a critique of Elie Wiesel's explanation of his use of the term 'Holocaust ... as the only way to preserve the specialness of the tragedy as a Jewish tragedy'. Wiesel claims the Jewishness of 'Holocaust' by relating it to the *Akedah*, the story of Abraham's sacrifice of Isaac. Isaac was to be offered as a sacrifice, a burnt offering which according to Wiesel 'is really the Holocaust ... I call Isaac the first survivor of the Holocaust'.

117 *Ibid.*, p. 206.

118 See Fabregues, *Edith Stein: Philosopher, Carmelite Nun, Holocaust Martyr* (New York, 1965).

119 Poliakov, *Harvest of Hate*, p. 213.

3

'The Deputy': bystanders to the Holocaust

Rolf Hochhuth's deliberately controversial play *Der Stellvertreter* first appeared on the Berlin stage in February 1963, less than a year after Eichmann was hanged. *Der Stellvertreter* – which can be variously translated as The Deputy, The Representative or The Vicar – was, according to both its author and producer, more than just a play, it was a moral historical treatise which indicted the recently deceased Pope Pius XII for failing to respond adequately to the tragedy of European Jews. Pius XII had, the play suggested, remained coldly and impassively silent in the face of the Nazi onslaught. In doing so he had abandoned the Jews of Europe to their fate. The content of the play was believed to hold such potential for offence that its first performance was heavily policed and notices were posted asking theatre goers to refrain from demonstration.[1]

While *Der Stellvertreter* was not a work of History, we can certainly see it as a contribution to historiography. It has been evaluated almost exclusively in historical terms and its critical reception at the time, and since, has been explicitly unconcerned with the literary or dramaturgical merits of the play.[2] Indeed Hochhuth raised, almost for the first time in the public realm, questions that have come to play a prominent part in Holocaust historiography, about wider responsibility for the destruction of Europe's Jews. What did the rest of the world do? What choices did individuals, institutions, governments, make in the face of Nazi destructiveness?[3] How far did they understand what the Nazis were doing to the Jews of Europe, and how did they react to that knowledge? How did they approach the perpetrators and how did they treat the victims? How far did they attempt to stop the destruction and what *could* they have done?

These questions have claimed a place in an historiography concerned with what have become known as the bystanders, that is the co-presents or witnesses of genocide who were neither its victims or its perpetrators. *Der Stellvertreter*, and reactions to it, introduced the ideas that have been central to this historiography. Indeed it appears that it even provided this very vocabulary. The term 'bystander' was first used in this regard in a *New York Times* editorial on the play in February 1963.[4] The play depicts an emotionless pope who despite being intimately acquainted with Jews' fate refuses publicly to condemn the Nazis, or call upon the faithful to set themselves against the slaughter. Pius XII decided, the play alleges, not to speak out in favour of the Jews because he ignored his role as the Vicar of Christ and acted as a calculating political diplomat concerned only to preserve the Church, whatever the moral cost. This silence is contrasted with that of the fictional Father Riccardo, who in the play's key scene, attaches a yellow star to his robes in order to identify himself with the suffering Jews of Rome and share their fate as people of God. Riccardo's words to Pius XII are representative of the interpretation at the heart of the play: 'A Vicar of Christ who has that [the deportation of the Jews] under his eyes and who keeps silent for reasons of state ... such a pope is a criminal.'[5]

That such an account of Pius XII was associated with the invention of the bystander in Holocaust studies is telling. The concept is inherently theological, concerned with the obligations of witness. Pius XII *should* have reacted differently because he was representative of a moral and theological tradition that required intervention on behalf of the suffering, and prioritised charity. The historiography under review in this chapter consistently follows this lead and for example, employs the image of the Good Samaritan as a common trope.[6] The contemporaries of genocide themselves at times evaluated their response to Nazi anti-Jewishness in these terms too. Richard Law, under secretary at the Foreign Office, insisted that the 'story of the Good Samaritan is still valid' when he sought to persuade the British cabinet to release some shipping for the transportation of refugees in May 1943.[7]

The theological grounding of the idea of the bystander raises problems for the historian. The application of such a fixed moral

code stretches the boundaries of a discipline which usually operates the fundamental observation that morality is contingent and
not universal. As such to impose a fixed moral code on the past,
and argue that the contemporaries of genocide *should* have reacted
differently appears peculiarly problematic, to judge the past
anachronistically using the standards of the present. And much
bystander historiography does use language which historians are
usually nervous of. It is replete with suggestions that the 'international community *failed*',[8] that the Church 'should' have shown
more concern for the Jews,[9] that the pope '*should*' have issued a
protest against the deportation of Roman Jews,[10] that the 'American response to the European Jewish catastrophe was a *dismal
failure*'.[11]

Such judgementalism is just one of the methodological difficulties of bystander historiography. It can also appear to lack
context too. Susan Zuccotti's study of Vatican reactions to the
deportation of the Jews of Rome boldly states its intention to
ignore the context in which Vatican attitudes to Jews were cast:
'the frightening events leading to war are beyond the scope of this
book, only responses to Jewish issues will be considered here'. But
surely 'Jewish issues' were bound up in the wider context of war
and occupation?[12] Bystander History can also appear to be overtly
'emotional' based on a contemporary anger and anguish at the
very fact of the death camps.[13] Such tendencies have led some critics to dismiss the field as 'wishful thinking ... history as it should
have been' articulating our contemporary anger but telling us little
about the past.[14]

This critique of bystander History is largely reducible to the
allegation that it is too much informed by the present. Historians
certainly have to be careful that they are not requiring the historical actors of the past to have responded to the events in a drama
that can only really be seen today.[15] Much bystander historiography operates a specific interpretation of the narrative of
anti-Jewish policy itself, asking individuals and institutions to have
appreciated the 'full enormity' of Nazi anti-Jewish policy.[16] Yet as
we have seen this is a sense that was constructed largely after the
event by historians, and the full enormity of anti-Jewish policy
meant something very different to the scientists of Nazi population policy in the 1950s than it did to those who perceived a unique
Holocaust by the 1970s. Indeed it could be argued that it was only

after the destruction of the European Jews emerged as a discrete event constructed in courtrooms and history books that scholars could begin to ask what responses to the Holocaust had been.

However, the central argument of this book is of course that the line between the past and the present cannot be so easily drawn, that the past is always passed through the filter of present when it is constructed as History. As such bystander historiography need not be dismissed as hopelessly problematic. It may well be that the relationship between present and past is more intimate here than elsewhere. It certainly seems the case that those of us separated from the killing fields of Eastern Europe can more easily identify with the bystanders. As Tony Kushner has argued, we do not wish to see ourselves as either the perpetrators or victims and thus the bystander represents 'us' in the past.[17] Yehuda Bauer equally implied as much when he beseeched the German Bundestag in 1998 to never, ever become a bystander.[18] Such identification inevitably renders bystander History more morally immanent than some fields of enquiry even into the Holocaust, because, as David Wyman argues, 'we were the all too passive accomplices' to the Shoah.[19]

But who exactly were the bystanders *in the past*? *Der Stellvertreter* was Deputy of us all. The Vicar of Christ stood as the conscience of all humanity, representative of all humankind who were in a sense the bystanders to Nazi persecution. But historians cannot draw the category so widely. Functionally it is not even very useful to use the idea of the bystander to encompass all who were neither perpetrators nor victims during the Holocaust. In a recent survey Victoria Barnett included the Catholic Church; Allied and neutral governments, states and societies; *and* the physical witnesses to genocide in the ordinary populations and institutions of Germany, Poland and other countries under Nazi rule. Within such a schema the inhabitants of Mauthausen were bystanders in the same way that the officials of the British Foreign and Commonwealth Office were. In Barnett's words, the behaviour of the 'international community ... to a striking degree parallels the behaviour we find among bystanders in Germany'.[20] But it seems clear that the ordinary Germans who were the witnesses to both the deportations and the death camps inhabited a different world to that of those separated by distance and experience from the oppression of the Third Reich. The ordinary

German population were in a very real sense both victims and perpetrators of a regime which did not confine its terrorism to Jews,
as well as bystanders to anti-Jewish policy.[21]

I will employ a narrower definition and will proceed in part
from Hochhuth's original vision of the bystander, and evaluate
those who are broadly comparable to Pius XII. He was not entirely
separated from the destruction of the European Jews. Physically
he was separated from the killing fields, and yet his responsibility
certainly extended to them (or at least to the Catholics resident
there) and he was well informed about the Nazi murder machine.
He also interacted with both the perpetrators and the victims of
the Holocaust before, *during* and after. In that sense he was very
similar and can be considered at the same time as bystanders such
as the governments of Allied and neutral states who experienced
through diplomacy, war and, for example, refugee policy both the
perpetrators and the victims of destruction alike.

The chapter that follows charts the history of bystander historiography through two case studies. One deals with the
historiography that more or less directly emerged from
Hochhuth's interpretation in *Der Stellvertreter* and confronts the
issue of Catholic but more particularly papal reactions to the
Shoah. Such is the ferocity of this discourse it has become known,
not unreasonably, as the 'Pius Wars'. Second I will survey the development of scholarship relating to Britain and the USA as
bystanders, which is the most voluminous aspect of bystander historiography. Ultimately, by charting the history of these
overlapping discourses, I will demonstrate the degree to which
bystander historiography is anchored in the ideological, political,
religious and even theological cleavages of the present rather than
the past. And yet this chapter also asserts the importance of
bystander History – arguing that its moral immanence gives the
discipline of History social and political purpose.

'The Pius Wars'

The documentary record of the papal reaction to the Nazi regime
was patchy when bystander historiography was born. Hochhuth's
play was not based on primary source material, but the scholars
who followed in his wake could begin to piece together the story
of the Pope's reaction to Nazi genocide from the archives. During

the 1960s Saul Friedländer and Carlo Falconi used documents orig-
inating from the Vatican found in the archival wreckage of the
Third Reich and its satellites to construct their critical histories of
Pius's involvement with the Nazi regime, as well as the records of
the Nazis' own diplomatic involvement with the Vatican. But this
was largely a one-sided documentary record because scholars were
denied access to the archives of the Holy See itself. As such Saul
Friedländer could, for example, know what the German Foreign
Office was attempting to do in its relations with the Vatican but
not vice-versa. 'The historian,' Friedländer pleaded at the end of
his study, 'is reduced to the hope that the essential documents that
he lacks, and particularly the documents of the Vatican archives,
soon will be published so that the events and personages can be
brought into proper perspective.'[22]

Despite these gaps in the documentary record, there was still
enough material to construct a comprehensive picture of 'events'.
One of the central allegations – that Pius XII had failed to speak
out about the Nazi regime – could be easily tested, as his public
statements were, self-evidently, a matter of public record. Pius's
Christmas message of 1942 was the only time that he 'spoke out'
against the treatment of 'hundreds of thousands of people, who
through no fault of their own and solely because of their nation
or their race, have been condemned to death or progressive extinction'.[23] This oblique statement, which made no reference to either
the specific perpetrators or victims of the Nazis destruction policies, was his only public statement on the 'Final Solution',
something which allowed Falconi to refer to the 'fact' of Pius XII's
'silence'.[24] Pius did later make a secret statement to the College of
Cardinals which made reference to those who 'because of their
nationality or their race, are ... doomed to extinction' and argued
that protest on their behalf was at best futile and at worst could
endanger them further, but this had also become a matter of public record by the time Friedländer called for the opening of the
Vatican archives.[25]

In part in response to the allegations of silence, the Vatican did
begin to make archival material available from the Second World
War period. Between 1965 and 1981, a team of scholars published
twelve volumes of documents (in their original languages – chiefly
Latin, but also Italian, German, French, Spanish and English)
under the title *Actes et Documents du Saint Siege relatifs a la*

Seconde Guerre Mondiale.[26] These volumes of unedited material have formed the documentary basis of virtually all subsequent studies of the papal and Vatican response to the Holocaust, along with already published material such as the Vatican newspaper *L'Osservatore Romano.*

These documents, and those already available in the public domain, have helped establish a narrative of papal interaction with the Nazi regime with which virtually all scholars can agree. It goes something like this. Pius XII was head of a Catholic Church whose communicants included both the perpetrators and the victims of Nazi violence which created a dilemma when responding to such violence. The Church also had a problematic theological relationship with Jews and Judaism which further confused the range of responses to Nazi persecution. That said, Pius XI had condemned Nazism and the racially inspired persecution of Jews prior to his death in 1939. His most famous, and public, condemnation of Nazism, the encyclical *Mit Brennender Sorge* (with burning concern) was published in 1938. It had in part been written by his secretary of state Eugenio Pacelli, who would become Pius XII. Pacelli had been papal nuncio in Berlin and had been responsible for negotiating the concordat with the Nazi regime. These negotiations, reflecting Vatican policy as a whole towards dictatorial regimes, gave Pacelli a sense that the best way to do business with the Nazis was through ongoing and active diplomacy. This diplomacy continued in the context of a world war in which the Vatican stayed steadfastly neutral.

As well as keeping up diplomatic relations with the Nazi state, we also know that the German ambassador to the Vatican, von Weizsacker, warned his political masters in the autumn of 1943 that if the Jews of Rome were deported Pius XII would publicly protest. We do not know whether this warning was at the behest of the German ambassador or the Vatican, but we do know that in the event Pius XII did on this occasion remain silent.[27] We know that some Jews fleeing the deportation found shelter in the Vatican, but again we do not know at whose behest. We know also that the Vatican provided financial assistance to the Roman Jewish community at this time.[28] We know that the Pope did protest, and instructed his nuncio to protest, to the Hungarian government about the deportation of Jews there in the spring and summer of 1944.[29]

Conversely we also know that Pius XII supported, if critically, the murderous fascist regime in Croatia under Ante Pavelic and that the Pope received Pavelic in the Vatican. We know that after the war accused war criminals (both Germans and other fascists) found refuge and safe passage to South America through the Vatican, and specifically through the German priest Alois Hudal who operated so-called 'rat lines'. Hudal helped various luminaries to freedom, including Pavelic, Adolf Eichmann, Josef Mengele and the former commandant of both Sobibor and Treblinka, Franz Stangl.[30]

This narrative of events suggests a somewhat contradictory relationship between the Vatican and the Nazis, and perhaps because of this ambivalence the intellectual battle over the meaning of these events has been ferocious. Perspectives now range from literally those who wish to declare Pius XII a saint to those who are willing to argue that he approved of, if not the means, then the religious, political and demographic impact of the Nazi campaign against a Jewish people that he largely despised.

Scholars located closer to the beatification end of this historiographical spectrum commonly allege that the critical view of Pius XII comes not from the historical record but from Hochhuth's dramatic invention.[31] Yet there had been a sense that there were unresolved questions about Pius XII amongst Holocaust historians since as early as 1950. Leon Poliakov argued that Pius had never clearly condemned the 'criminal policy of the Third Reich' during its lifetime.[32] Indeed Poliakov went on to outline, but deliberately refused to comment upon, the Vatican's stated approval for some measures against Jews which separated them, economically at least, from the rest of society. Hochhuth transformed Poliakov's gentle questioning into the insistent condemnation of *Der Stellvertreter*. At the same time the Vatican itself was beginning in the process of an unprecedented self-reflection. This included recasting the Church's relationship with the Jews, leading to *Nostra Aetate*, published under the auspices of the Second Vatican Council. This revolutionised Catholic teaching about the Jews not least by denying for the first time that the Jewish community bore an historic responsibility for the death of Christ.

What *Der Stellvertreter* had done then was contribute to a new context in which public revision of Catholic attitudes and actions towards Jews was commonplace, and it is in this context that the historians who followed in Hochhuth's wake were writing. Saul Friedländer, before the Vatican documents had been available, argued that papal silence had been the result of a fatal combination of the Pope's Germanophillia and anti-communism. Pius XII 'feared a Bolshevisation of Europe more than anything' and as a consequence he was unable unequivocally to condemn Hitler's regime and its treatment of Jews. Friedlander suggests that Pacelli ultimately saw the Hitler regime as the lesser of two evils.[33]

Because of Vatican II, some Catholic historiography could also be critical of Pius. John Morley's history of papal diplomacy during the Second World War was written using the Vatican's published volumes, and was self-consciously a part of the second Vatican council's effort to reconceive their historic relationship with Judaism.[34] Morley, a Catholic Priest, argued that neither the Pope nor his nuncios 'manifested any consistent humanitarian concern' on behalf of the Jews of Europe. This was, in part because they defined their obligations as first and foremost to the faithful and in part because they came to understand their own roles politically and diplomatically rather than in moral and humanitarian terms. For Morley, this was (and you will note the language) a 'dual failure'.[35]

Ironically *Der Stellvertreter* perhaps had a more direct influence over that historiography which sought to defend Pius XII, than that which criticised him. Pinchas Lapide sought to expose Hochhuth's charges to scrutiny in the light not of Catholic teaching as Morley later did, but the Jewish tradition. Lapide suggested that the haven given to some Jews in Rome was enough to exonerate Pius XII, because the 'Talmud teaches us that "whosoever preserves one life, it is accounted to him by scripture as if he had preserved a whole world"'.[36] British Catholic Anthony Rhodes' argument that Pius XII had protested to the Hungarian government was also made as a deliberate engagement with Hochhuth's picture of silence.[37]

These gentle opening skirmishes of the 'Pius Wars' in which he was both castigated and exonerated were largely based on the same documentary evidence as well as the same narrative of events. Morley and Rhodes both utilised the Vatican's published sources, but came to starkly different conclusions. It is often claimed, as Friedländer did in his original contribution to the debate, that the controversy could be somehow solved by the release of some further documentary evidence.[38] Yet this seems unlikely, because of the common documentary base that all scholarly perspectives share. Even dramatic changes in the available evidence seem to have little impact on extant perspectives. Pius XII has often been accused of deliberately suppressing an encyclical commissioned by his predecessor that explicitly condemned Nazi antisemitism. It was thus imagined that the discovery of this encyclical might prove active collusion with the Nazi regime. Yet when the 'hidden encyclical' did come to light in the 1990s, all that was revealed was a document that was deeply ambivalent about Jews. It condemned Nazi antisemitism but also appeared to endorse some sense of the importance of separating Jews from the rest of society. Scholars could be no clearer about why, either positively or negatively, Pius XII had not gone ahead with its publication. Had he done so, however, it could easily have been interpreted as another example of the oblique ethereal language adopted by the Holy See. It would have added little clarity to any Catholic searching for a guide as to how they should react to Nazi antisemitism.[39]

There have been other efforts to expand further the scope of documents available. In the late 1990s a team of scholars under the umbrella of the International Catholic-Jewish Historical Commission were briefly commissioned to identify remaining questions concerning the Vatican response to the Holocaust. Their task was to return first to the twelve published volumes and then, if necessary, to the archives themselves. The Commission was established as a part of the reconciliatory work done by the Holy See in the lead up to the millennium and was designed to pursue a 'healing of memory' between Catholics and Jews. However, the millennium reconciliations seemed to have little impact on the culture of archival secrecy at the Vatican. The head of its press office had declared in 1998 that 'there was nothing to add – repeat nothing – to what is already published'.[40] Perhaps inevitably the Commission did identify some outstanding questions that it wished to pursue in the archives, but unfettered access was not granted and it was therefore disbanded.[41]

Part of the problem was that the International Catholic-Jewish Historical Commission had been attempting to do its work in the midst of a second, and much more toxic, wave of the 'Pius Wars'. One result of Pope John Paul II's programme of reconciliation at

DEBATES ON THE HOLOCAUST

the millennium was the publication of *We Remember: A Reflection on the Shoah*. This statement, prepared by American cardinal Edward Cassidy, instead of encouraging reconciliation with regard to the controversy over the Vatican and the Holocaust led to a flurry of publications which adopted much more entrenched positions than had thus far been typical. *We Remember* acknowledged that individual Catholics had been blinded by their own anti-Judaism and as such had failed to respond adequately to Nazi persecution of the Jews. At the same time it was kind both to Christianity as a whole and especially both to the institutional Church and its leader. Although the Church was besmirched by an historic anti-Judaism, *We Remember* suggested that this set of religious prejudices, while mistaken, had been quite different to the political antisemitism which gave rise to the Holocaust. Those Christians who confused racial and religious anti-Judaism had therefore been acting despite rather than because of their Church. Catholic rescuers of Jews are the only Christians that *We Remember* argued had been acting truly in accordance with the dictates of their faith. This band of the righteous included Pius XII who had not been limited by the Church's historic and mistaken teachings and had been a dedicated opponent of the Nazi regime. Indeed such had been the depth of his opposition to Nazism, Pius XII had been responsible for saving hundreds of thousands of Jewish lives.[42]

The claim that Pius was a rescuer inspired indignation. Susan Zuccotti argued that there is no evidence that Pius directed the 'rescue' of Roman Jews in 1943. In the aftermath of the deportation of the Jews of Rome in October 1943, an unspecified number of Jews did find refuge in Church buildings and institutions. However, Zuccotti claimed that those rescued prior to October 1943 benefited from the individual charity of the priests, monks and nuns who allowed them in. Those Jews who assumed that they had benefited from the interventions of the Pope did so in a state of 'benevolent ignorance' in which their gratitude to the Church as a whole was mistakenly directed to Pius XII as its symbol.[43] Indeed Zucotti alleged there is rather more evidence that the Pope was nervous of the presence of Jews inside the Vatican itself.

Michael Phayer's contributions to the 'Pius Wars' highlight the Pope's nervousness. Phayer's Pius XII is first and foremost a diplomat, whose actions were shaped by his obsessive anti-communism rather than any particular engagement with Nazism. This led him actively to conceal what he knew of what was to become the 'Final Solution'.[44] Phayer's latest intervention claims some new documentary sources – the declassified records of the American intelligence services. Yet the picture remains the same – of a Pope whose anti-communism clouded his moral vision to such an extent that it was more important to cling to diplomatic relations with Germany in the face of the genocide of the Jews, than it was to articulate anguish at this obvious violation of God's teachings.[45]

Phayer's analyses again demonstrate that new documentary sources, or indeed even just a return to those already extant, are unlikely to provide the ground for a truce in the 'Pius wars'. In his first monograph Phayer firmly accused Pius XII of silence, but in the second (and on the basis of the same sources) Phayer has, and he acknowledges this, shifted ground considerably. Indeed he now believes that 'Pius unmistakably denounced genocide' in his Christmas message of 1942.[46] Of course, the word genocide is used quite deliberately here – this was no denunciation of the Judeocide, after all it did not mention either Germans or Jews – but it was, Phayer claimed, an attempt to articulate the Church's opposition in general to the atrocities performed by the Nazi state.[47]

Perhaps the most controversial response to *We Remember* came from British Catholic academic John Cornwell. *Hitler's Pope* depicted a diplomatic pontiff unable to respond adequately to the 'Final Solution'. Cornwell argued that a toxic combination of Germanophilia and an obsessive rendering of Russian communism as the anti-Christ meant that Pius XII was unable clearly to condemn the genocide of the Jews, and indeed any other of the Nazis' murderous occupation policies, because he wished above all else for the defeat of communism. This rendered the Pope mute as a moral voice in the 1930s, and as such he was precisely the incumbent of the Vatican whom Hitler would have chosen. This meant, to return to the book's rather dramatic title, he was *Hitler's Pope*.[48]

Cornwell also suggested, and despite his claims this was again on the basis of no new evidence, that Eugenio Pacelli associated Judaism and Bolshevism which further blunted his ability to confront Nazi persecution.[49] In doing so Cornwell rejected perhaps the most controversial argument proposed in *We Remember* that antisemitism played little role in determining a Catholic response to the Holocaust, other than preventing some Catholics from distinguishing the racial antisemitism of the Nazis. In part because antisemitism is just too broad a concept, previous studies of the Vatican response have avoided it. Of course churchmen held negative attitudes towards Jews and Judaism, but this did not make them enthusiastic supporters of Nazi racism. As such when Cornwell employed the concept of antisemitism he broke new ground, and paved the way for a new wave of scholarship that portrayed Pius XII in precisely those terms.

Prior to *We Remember* many scholars had acknowledged that Jews and Judaism were negatively evaluated in the Vatican. But the suggestion of Cornwell, James Carroll, David Kertzer and most vociferously Daniel Goldhagen, that Catholic antisemitism ensured Catholics and indeed Pius XII were, if not supporters of the Nazi genocide, unable to set themselves unambiguously against it, is quite different.[50] Goldhagen's *A Moral Reckoning* goes as far as to say that Pius XII shared Nazi conceptions of the Jews and this is why he did not protest publicly against persecution or murder.[51] For Goldhagen, antisemitism is a much more monolithic concept than most scholars would allow, and this therefore makes his Pius XII a supporter of genocide. 'The fourth central feature of antisemitism' Goldhagen claimed, 'is the tendency among antisemites toward violence and even mass murder against Jews'.[52] Radical Jewish theologian Richard Rubenstein went even further than Goldhagen, suggesting that Pius XII 'silence' is only explicable if one understands that he believed that the demographic removal of the Jews was 'in the best interests of an endangered Christianity'.[53] Rubenstein claimed that Pius XII 'regarded the elimination of Jews as no less beneficial than the destruction of Bolshevism'.[54]

In response to such criticisms there has also been a new wave, since *We Remember*, of much more sympathetic scholarship too. Scholars such as Pierre Blet (one of the editors of the volumes of documents produced by the Vatican), Jose Sanchez, Patrick Gallo and Ronald Rychlak have all produced monographs aimed at rehabilitating Pius XII's image. At the most extreme end, Ralph McInerney has produced a book which aims specifically in undoing the 'infamous calumny' done in the 'defamation of Pius XII' one of the few 'unalloyed heroes of World War II'.[55]

In many ways the narrative offered by such scholarship is familiar. While Pius XII's defenders routinely argue that he did not remain silent about the sufferings of Jews, they acknowledge that he spoke only obliquely and quietly. According to Pierre Blet he made 'clear references' to the 'Final Solution', not least in his message of Christmas 1942, but only 'for those who were willing to listen' to his voice.[56] Blet admits that this message was not enough for those who wished the Pope would abandon his deliberate neutrality. John Pawlikowski, a Catholic Priest at the forefront of Catholic-Jewish relations who has attempted to steer a middle course in the polarised debates, also dismisses the very idea that Pius remained silent, while acknowledging that he did not speak very loudly at all.[57] Eugene Fisher goes somewhat further and argues that Pius XII 'never wavered from staunch opposition to Nazism'.[58]

Most of Pius's defenders suggest that instead of speaking loudly, and again this is a familiar argument, he chose to pursue diplomacy as the best solution to the crisis engulfing the world, and not just the Jews. Jose Sanchez concludes that Pius XII was faced, through no fault of his own, with an impossible dilemma during war. He found perhaps the only route out of that dilemma – maintaining the silence of neutrality in public while working behind the scenes for the practical alleviation of the privations of the suffering.[59]

If the picture of a diplomatic pontiff is familiar, then the idea that he was motivated by a desire to alleviate the suffering of the persecuted is not. And it is here, in the arguments surrounding both the motivation and the consequence of Pius XII's silent diplomacy, that scholars who wish to defend his record are really set apart. Pierre Blet argues unambiguously that Pius XII 'employed all the means at his disposal' to intervene on the behalf of, to rescue and ultimately to attempt to save, the stricken Jews of Europe.[60] Patrick Gallo argues that Pius XII devoted himself to the cause of peace, and used his diplomacy to that end. He was a 'positive and activist force. He attempted to bring an end to war and gave aid and comfort to the persecuted.'[61]

How is it then that we have such opposing pictures of Pius XII emerging from the same documentation, and despite an almost universally agreed record of events? They cannot simply be explained by the contradictions in the historical record of relations between the Holy See and the Third Reich. On one level these are disagreements about what is admissible as historical evidence. Pierre Blet would claim that only the sympathetic are faithful to the documentation. Indeed Blet argues that 'there is only one way of returning from fiction to reality, from legend to history, and that is by going back to the original documents, for those directly reveal what the pope did and said'.[62] But such devotion to strict empiricism dismisses at a single stroke one of the questions that has most preoccupied scholars, the question of what Pius XII did *not* say, or did *not* do. Why for example did he not draw attention to the fact that it was, more often than not, Jews who had been consigned to death? Why did he not protest at the deportation of the Jews from Rome? These *are* legitimate historical enquiries, yet the answers to them cannot be found by simply returning to the documents.

The only manner in which these silences can be investigated is by attempting to recreate the ideational and ideological world in which Pius XII and other Vatican officials operated. Confronting the fundamental questions of *why* what was said was said; and *why* what was not said, was not said. In these terms this is not a move away from the documents into legend, but is to practise History and the attempt to recreate a complex picture of the past as opposed to mere chronicle.

Evaluation of Pius XII's response to the Holocaust requires some understanding and interpretation of the purpose of the pope, the Vatican, and his Church in the world.[63] And indeed it is these different political, moral and indeed theological judgements about the purpose of the Church that can often determine the differing interpretations. As such these are not necessarily judgements about the past at all. Pierre Blet and Michael Phayer would not disagree for example that Pius XII's was chiefly a diplomatic response. However they would differ fundamentally as to the worth of that diplomacy and the degree to which it fulfilled the obligations and indeed purpose of the Church.

It seems that those scholars who are critical of Pius operate a definition of the purpose and scope of the Church (and thus the institution of the papacy) which required Pius to have gone beyond diplomacy. For Victoria Barnett, Christianity is essentially an ethical discourse on love, and therefore the 'behaviour of the churches during the Holocaust is a scandal that challenges both Christian credibility and its very belief' because they failed consistently to articulate the injunction to love above all else.[64] Carlo Falconi argued that a diplomatic papacy, and therefore one that was concerned chiefly by the political power of the Church, was a 'dangerous contradiction to all religious movements and of a Christian Church'.[65] John Morley, a self-proclaimed supporter of Vatican II, claimed that the chief purpose of the Church should be humanitarian, and thus a Church that did not live up to these values could be reasonably argued to have failed.[66] Susan Zuccotti and Daniel Goldhagen have argued similarly that the Church had a moral mission that extended to all mankind, a claim that it made for itself, and thus can be evaluated as a moral institution which therefore failed to live up to this (self-proclaimed) duty.[67]

John Cornwell's *Hitler's Pope* is perhaps the thesis most self consciously shaped by a contemporary vision of the Church and thus the papacy. Cornwell argues that Pius XII's moral and spiritual understanding of the Catholic community, led to a political handling of the Church which not only conditioned an inadequate response to Jewish suffering but also undermined the very fabric of the Church itself. Pius XII's vision of the Church and indeed the world was one in which individual Catholics could abandon social responsibility. Cornwell, on the other hand, holds a different vision of the 'pilgrim Church', where communities and the faithful are empowered and indeed seek to shape the world in which they live. It is this 'pilgrim Church' which he sees as the ideal of the Catholic community.[68]

Those scholars who have lined up to defend Pius XII simply believe in a different purpose for the Church and its leader, often arguing that the protection of the faithful was its very first and most fundamental purpose. That led in turn to an obligation to protect the Church itself, as the only vehicle through which the faithful (and indeed anyone else) could find salvation. As such Pius XII was not duty bound to speak out and thus endanger himself, rather his duty was to protect himself and his Church (and thus remain silent).[69] Patrick Gallo claims that this line of argument is to accept the contextual realities of the time, because the Church was a political institution. But in doing so he also seems to accept that this *should* be the purpose of the Holy See in the world.[70] After all, John Cornwell would not disagree that this is a realistic interpretation of the way that Pius XII responded to the Holocaust, he just argues that the pope has other obligations too.

The antagonists in the 'Pius Wars' also operate different, indeed opposing, interpretations of the Holocaust and its place in the history of the twentieth century. Daniel Goldhagen, for example, bases his *A Moral Reckoning* on the fundamental observation that antisemitism led to the Holocaust. As a purveyor of anti-semitism, the Church naturally enough becomes, in Goldhagen's understanding, part of the social and political structures which produced the Holocaust. In such an interpretation the 'Final Solution' is understood not as the result of a seamless bureaucracy or the peculiar structure of the Nazi state, nor is it the result of the pressures of conformity inherent in modern society. Instead the Holocaust is explained as the ultimate act of an *anti-modernity* of bestial hatreds and centuries-old prejudices.

All Pius XII's critics or detractors would appear to agree with the fundamentals of such an interpretation. Susan Zuccotti finds the Vatican unable to condemn the emerging Holocaust because they were too closely tied into the ideational structures which, in part, underpinned the motivations for the 'Final Solution'. That worldview was one which saw the need in particular for the separation of Jews and Christians, but also more generally the pushing back of the tide of modernity and the restoration of tradition. John Cornwell's analysis of the establishment of the Concordat essentially proposes the same argument, that the Church became allied with all forms of authoritarianism against the forces of decadence – most symbolised, of course, by communism. Even John Pawlikowski, argues that the Church was hamstrung because it set its face against modernity, and saw that Nazism also did the same.[71]

Yet for the defenders of Pius XII, the Holocaust is the ultimate example of the dangers of modernity – demonstrating just how right Pius XII was. This is not a radical critique of the structures of modern society such as that pioneered by Hannah Arendt and then Zygmunt Bauman, but a much more conservative vision of the dangers of relativism and the perceived decadence of the root-less and traditionless modern world. What better example of this rejection of tradition, and indeed Christianity, it is argued, than Nazism, which specifically required a revolutionised moral and ethical framework and set itself as the enemy of Christianity. For Eugene Fisher, for example, it is entirely nonsensical to indict Catholicism in any explanation of the Holocaust, precisely because the Church had so vehemently opposed the developments of modernity.[72] Ralph McInerney agrees, arguing that the Church (in its opposition to abortion for example) has set itself against modernity's 'culture of death'. The Holocaust was also a modern crime, a result of this culture of death – and as such was necessarily opposed by the Church and its leaders. In essence this is also the position put forward by *We Remember*, in its separation of the apparently gentle prejudices of medieval past from the visceral, social and political hatreds of the modern world.

It is clear then that the 'Pius Wars' have been fought on top of a gulf of understanding that goes much deeper and wider than the issues at hand. Protagonists in this discourse have antagonistic views on (among other matters) the moral and political purpose of the Church and ergo its theological realities. As well as differing views of the present, the antagonists appear to hold entirely different conceptions of the past and particularly of the significance of the *Shoah* within that past. As such, the debate on the Holocaust and the Catholic Church which Rolf Hochhuth began in *Der Stellvertreter* reveals the degree to which historiographical dispute can mask some much more profound social, political and moral disagreements.

The Allies and the Holocaust

Arthur Morse's sensationalised 1968 study of Allied reactions to the Holocaust was in part inspired by his understanding of the 'silence' of Pius XII. Morse alleged that the governments of the USA and Britain also apathetically looked on *While Six Million Died*.[73] A controversy as elongated, and at times as bitter, as the 'Pius Wars' has followed.

The central question for much of this historiography has been, as Yehuda Bauer phrased it, 'when did they know?'.[74] When did the Allies know that the Nazis were planning, or indeed enacting a plan, to annihilate the Jews of Europe? Documentary evidence was at first, as with the Vatican, patchy. Governments were slow to disclose files. All British government documents are normally subject to the thirty-year rule and indeed many of the records of the British Foreign Office remain closed for reasons of national security. This documentary deficit is reflected in some of the first contributions to this historiography. Andrew Sharf's study of what the British press knew of the Nazi genocide was the first of Britain as bystander, and could be pieced together from already available material but, crucially, could tell us little about perspectives from inside government.

However, the question of when the Allies 'knew' of the Holocaust is far from simple, regardless of the documents available. After all the question of when the 'Final Solution' began remains contested to this day. Historians can easily locate the traces of genocide in the press reports or government documents of the late 1930s and 1940s, but this does not go very far in demonstrating *knowledge*. An article in *History Today* in 1999 proclaimed that the British *knew* of Auschwitz in early 1942 not, as had up until that point been assumed, in 1944.[75] But what did it mean to know of Auschwitz in 1942? After all, it is clear that Auschwitz did not assume its central place in the 'Final Solution' until much later, after the death camps of Aktion Reinhard had ceased to operate. Further, Auschwitz has only assumed its metonymic status as representative of the Holocaust *since* 1945. As such, I ask again what could the British government *know* of Auschwitz in early 1942? They may have been exposed to its name, they may even have been told that people, even Jews, were being murdered there. But that knowledge is very different to understanding, *knowing*, about Auschwitz in the way that we do today.

As such, just as documentary material from the Vatican needs always to be considered in context, so does the material that has slowly been released from government archives since the end of the Second World War. More and more documents become available, but they often serve to complicate. The intercepts of the British and American intelligence communities have recently been released. These documents, which are the intercepted signals of the Order Police (*Ordnungspolizei*) and *Einsatzgruppen* in the field in 1941 and 1942 are important because they have revealed much about the activities of those groups in the perpetration of the 'Final Solution'. But, the information they contained could be contradictory. We cannot therefore assume they were as useful to the intelligence community in developing a picture of the 'Final Solution' as they are to us, or that the information would be put together in the same way we would.[76]

As such the story of Allied understanding of the Holocaust, and the historiography which charts it, cannot just be told through a history of when documents became available revealing the traces of genocide, because these do not actually reveal what was *understood*. However, what the documents that have been progressively released since the end of the war have provided is a basis for a narrative of the Allied response to the Nazi persecution and murder of Europe's Jews over which, just like with scholarship on the Church as bystander, there is widespread agreement.[77]

Prior to war and the 'Final Solution', what were to become the Allies have been scrutinised for their response to the refugee crisis provoked by Nazi anti-Jewish legislation. While there is disagreement as to why, and indeed what this means, it is universally acknowledged that governments changed little about their refugee policies as a response to Nazi persecution. The USA continued to operate a quota-based immigration system which made no special dispensation for the Jewish victims of Nazism.[78] The British, too, operated barriers to Jewish immigration from Germany, including the introduction of more stringent visa restrictions after the *Anschluss* which were then eased after *Kristallnacht*.[79] The Evian conference is often used as a symbol for the response to the refugee crisis, in that the conference participants met on the understanding that they would not be required to make policy changes.[80] This disinclination to change policy reveals a reluctance to provide a haven for Jewish refugees from Nazism in Britain and the USA, based, in large part, on cultural and economic fears as to their ability to absorb large numbers and the assumption that the provision of a universal haven for the persecuted would only lead to the expulsion of more Jews.[81] That said, it is also universally acknowledged that after *Kristallnacht* extraordinary measures were taken, for example in the shape of the *Kindertransport* programme which brought several thousand Jewish children to Britain.[82]

Regarding the war itself, historians have largely concentrated on both the continuing policies of the Allies towards refugees from Nazi Europe – notwithstanding the increased difficulties of escape – and on their willingness, or otherwise, to enact schemes of rescue. Britain worked, for example, to make Jewish emigration to Palestine *more* rather than less difficult, because this was believed to be the best way of maintaining security in the region.[83] Knowledge of the 'Final Solution' did, although originally suppressed,[84] eventually force the Allies into a public acknowledgement, on 17

December 1942, that the Nazis were attempting the extermination of the Jews of Europe.[85] Despite this, however, it is widely accepted that rescuing the Jews of Europe was never one of the major priorities of war, although it was often argued (self-evidently) that the defeat of Nazism was understood as the best way to ensure Jews' liberation:

> For the Soviet Union, Great Britain and the United States, the rescue of Jewry was not a priority ... all three were concerned with the war ... the entire territory behind enemy lines was viewed primarily as a complex of production, mobilisation and supply. Very little else invited Allied curiosity. The veritable decimation of populations subjugated by Germany and its partners was at best a subordinated interest ... the currency of the Second World War was the bullet, shell and bomb; those who did not have these means were the war's forgotten poor. With weapons one could obtain praise and often additional arms; with plight one could buy neither care nor help.[86]

Despite this widely accepted narrative, the historiography of the Allies and the Holocaust remains sharply divided. Again, it has been traditionally split between those who wish to indict Allied failure in the face of the moral challenge of the Holocaust, and those who have sought to rehabilitate the Allies from what is perceived as both a scandalous attack and an attempt to find moral equivalence between Nazism and the liberal democracies which defeated it.

Andrew Sharf's study of the British press response to the Holocaust was published in 1964 and was the first to consider the British context. Arthur Morse's *While Six Million Died* was the first to highlight the US response, and studied government policy. Although at times sensationalist and methodologically problematic, these two works really established many of the central features of the historiographical landscape. Sharf's observation that British journalists filtered their understanding of Jewish suffering, and thus the manner in which they communicated it, through domestic concerns continues to underpin much contemporary scholarship.[87] The argument that members of the fourth estate feared Nazi antisemitism because it would produce unwanted Jewish refugees, and that during the war they feared schemes to rescue the Jews of Europe for precisely the same reason, also remains a key contention.[88] At the same time Sharf presaged the argument of A.J. Sherman that Britain's was not an entirely negative record, and that refugee policy had been 'comparatively ... generous' in that more refugees had reached British shores than had reached the US.[89]

Morse was the first to label the Allies 'bystanders', with all the pejorative implications that label has, and as such his work was from the outset invested with a moral indignation. Arguing that the US government had adopted a 'co-ordinated policy of inaction' toward the Jews,[90] Morse reported a 'core belief that rescue was incompatible with the Allies principal war aims'. He recorded the attempts of officials such as Breckenridge Long and Cordell Hull to prevent Jewish immigration to the USA, even after they were clearly aware of the Nazis' intention to destroy all Jews. His clear implication was that by avoiding schemes of rescue, by 'abandoning' the Jews, more were condemned to death than might have otherwise been the case.[91] This was, Morse insisted, an abandonment of the liberal traditions on which the US had been built.[92]

Scholars who followed attempted more complex explanations as to why the British and the Americans had sought to avoid both rescue and therefore large-scale Jewish immigration, without ever challenging the fundamental assumption that such actions represented a betrayal of the liberal traditions of both nations. Henry Feingold's *The Politics of Rescue* demonstrated that rescuing Jews was of no concern at all to the Roosevelt White House as well as the State Department.[93] David Wyman's two studies of American indifference at a policy level adopted Morse's contention that the Jews of Europe had been actively abandoned by US officials, and continued Feingold's interrogation of the president. Wyman suggested that officials in the State Department simply did not see the Jews of Europe as within their sphere of obligation. Their vision of the world was determined by a powerful nativism, that even saw Jewish immigrants as a danger to American society.[94] Wyman's conclusions have cast a long shadow. More recently scholars have studied those officials responsible for policy on the ground, and found a similarly toxic combination of indifference and hostility to potential Jewish immigrants, or to put it another way, to the Nazis' Jewish victims.[95] This indifference to the plight and indeed the fate of the Jews of Europe, Wyman suggested, rendered the US government 'the all too passive accomplices' in Nazi genocide.[96]

Bernard Wasserstein and Martin Gilbert reached similar conclusions regarding Britain, presenting a pitiless picture of ministers and officials attempting to prevent Jewish immigration to Britain and British-controlled territories in the face of Nazi terror. Wasserstein particularly focused on the White Paper of 1939 which restricted Jewish immigration to Palestine and symbolised the victory of strategic over humanitarian priorities in policy making.[97] The White Paper formed the basis of Palestine policy throughout the war. Gilbert demonstrated that it was used to argue against pursuing offers to ransom Jews in 1944. Officials suggested that if negotiations were successful this would have lead to large-scale immigration to Palestine, in contravention of the White Paper.[98] By concentrating on the future Israel, Wasserstein set the policies of the British state in the context of attitudes to the wider 'Jewish problem'. Although Wasserstein did find individual instances of anti-Jewish prejudice, not least Foreign Secretary Anthony Eden's now famous quip that 'I prefer Arabs to Jews',[99] he did not however seek to explain the lack of British sympathy through antisemitism. In part it was engendered by the inevitable 'xenophobia and hysteria' of war. However, in the main Wasserstein cited a culture of 'bureaucratic indifference' whereby officials were separated by an imaginative gulf from the Jews of Europe, and where crucially they could not entirely see the consequences of their actions. In proposing such an argument Wasserstein demonstrated the long shadow that Hannah Arendt's thesis of the banality of evil has cast over Holocaust studies in general.

Gilbert, Feingold, Morse, Wasserstein and Wyman essentially shared the thesis that the liberal traditions of Britain and the USA had *failed* in the face of the challenge of the Holocaust. Writing in the 1990s, Tony Kushner led a new generation of Anglo-Jewish historians, no less critical of Allied policies, but who would argue that this was not a failure of liberalism at all, but a *consequence* of its own inherently exclusionary tendencies.[100] Kushner's *The Holocaust and the Liberal Imagination* explained the failure to provide either a haven or rescue for Jews as a consequence of the modern liberal nation-states' inability to cope with Jewish and indeed any ethnic difference. As such there was an essential ambivalence about Anglo-American responses to the Holocaust, which combined a genuine anguish at the plight of the victims with a fear that those victims would destabilise Britain and the

USA if they were allowed unfettered access. Hence the oft-repeated argument of officials that large-scale Jewish immigration would bring antisemitism in its wake. Such was this fear of Jewish particularity that across British society there was a reluctance to acknowledge that Jews were suffering as Jews at Nazi hands; instead the Third Reich was seen as a universal threat which, of course, then justified the argument that victory in war was the only conceivable form of rescue. This tendency to universalise the Third Reich, and thus deny the particularity of the Jewish experience endured in the post-war world too.[101]

Yet as Kushner argued, there were also activists calling for a different approach to the 'Jewish problem' before, during and after the war. Both Britain and the USA had active protesting constituencies who put pressure on government, for example, to attempt schemes of rescue – including the opening of all borders to any Jews who could escape. These pro-rescue voices were as much part of the liberal response to the Holocaust as government intransigence.[102] Yet these were men and women who were able imaginatively to understand the Jews' plight in a way that government bureaucrats could not. Take James Parkes, an Anglican Priest who berated his fellow Christians to understand that Jews were being attacked as Jews by the Nazis and that the challenge for all men in the light of the death camps was to rethink and reconceive their relationship with Jews and Judaism. For his fellow Christians that meant abandoning the desire to convert Jews and indeed the assumption that Jews held an incomplete understanding of God's revelation. For society as a whole it meant embracing Jewish particularity rather than requiring assimilation. That Parkes was so well ignored by his fellow Christians only serves to illustrate the enduring validity of Andrew Sharf's observation that the Holocaust was understood through extant ways of thinking and Kushner's sense of the marginality of such radicals within liberal societies.[103]

That liberalism almost prescribed an inadequate response to the crisis of European Jewry was also the main thesis proposed in Richard Bolchover's study of the British Jewish community and the Holocaust. Bolchover found a community, and especially its leadership, which strove to demonstrate its own liberalism and thus its assimilation with the British way of life. Remarkably the Jewish leadership, Bolchover argued, was also ambivalent about schemes of rescue, lest legions of foreign Jews destabilise both the Jewish community, its relationship with society as a whole and thus social cohesion.[104] At the same time this led Jews to conceive of the conflict with the Third Reich in universal terms, as an 'attack on civilisation as a whole, not an explicit war against the Jews'. Inevitably then, Bolchover argues, many Jews supported the notion that victory was the only form of liberation and rescue.[105]

Perhaps the most recent and the most forceful contribution to the field is Louise London's exhaustive study of *Whitehall and the Jews*. London repeats the arguments first developed by Wyman *et al.* that the reason schemes of rescue, or negotiations over Jewish lives, were not pursued vigorously by the Allied governments was because of a fear not of their failure but of their *success*. As the Home Secretary Herbert Morrison wrote to his counterpart at the Foreign Office in July 1944, 'it is essential that we should do nothing at all which involves the risk that the further reception of refugees here might be the outcome'.[106] Ultimately *Whitehall and the Jews* goes further than many bystander histories by explaining that the inherent inability of nation-states to provide succour for the Jewish victims of Nazism was a result of the same 'Jewish problem' that haunted the Nazi imagination. Those British officials who wished to keep Jews from Britain understood the nation as an homogenous ethnic unit. Jews threatened that homogeneity. As such London suggests that while the method of the Nazi solution to the Jewish problem was alien to British policy makers and bureaucrats, their goal of a singular ethnic state was not – indeed it was the goal they sought too.

The suggestion that the Allies and the Nazis shared a conception of a Jewish problem has manifold implications – both in terms of the worth and the limitations of bystander historiography. First it locates the Holocaust very firmly in a global historical context, suggesting that it is in part the result of ideological and bureaucratic tendencies that are located throughout modernity. The bystanders thus become part of the study of the destruction process itself because they helped 'create a world in which genocide was possible'.[107] This is a challenging argument, but for many scholars encapsulates the flaws of bystander historiography too. At face value the argument that the Allies were the *passive* accomplices of Nazi genocide is logically indefensible as by definition the Allies *actively* opposed and indeed defeated the very

perpetrators of that genocide. Some critics of bystander historiography allege, therefore, that instead of recognising this essential
fact, historians of the bystanders are attempting to prove that the
Allied nations were themselves, if only in part, responsible for the
'Final Solution'.[108]

Other objections to bystander historiography have included the
idea that it represents 'wishful thinking'.[109] Lucy Dawidowicz
dismissed *The Abandonment of the Jews* precisely because there
were, she argued, so few opportunities for rescue, Michael Marrus
likewise.[110] Along these lines a rather ritualised debate has
emerged over the totemic issue of whether or not the Allies could,
should, could not or should not, have bombed Auschwitz, or the
train lines leading to it. David Wyman had suggested that the
bombing of Auschwitz would have given hope to Jewish victims
and disrupted the technical capabilities of the Nazi murder
machine. Famously US bombers did attack the Auschwitz site, but
only to bomb the IG Farben plant at Monowitz. For Wyman this
was a rather symbolic indication of the priorities of war.[111] The
debate that has followed has pursued two main avenues: first,
whether the bombing of Auschwitz was a technical possibility, and
second, whether or not it *would* have made a difference. For critics
the answer appears self-evident – 'any Allied option to frustrate
the Holocaust from the air was [and therefore remains] illusory, a
fact so unmistakably obvious to contemporary commanders that
it was take for granted and warranted little policy discussion'.[112]

William Rubinstein combined these criticisms of bystander historiography in the most sustained attack on the field in *The Myth
of Rescue*. First, he takes what he sees as the mistaken attempt to
widen responsibility for the 'Final Solution' as the starting point:

> it cannot be emphasised too strongly that the responsibility for the
> Holocaust lies solely and wholly with Adolf Hitler, the SS and their
> accomplices, and with no-one else. In searching for a rational expla-
> nation of modern history's greatest crime, it is important that we do
> not assign guilt to those who were innocent.[113]

And second, countering what he sees as the counter-factual arguments of Wyman *et al.*, Rubinstein set out to demonstrate that the
Allies *could not* have rescued any more Jews from the Holocaust.
Indeed he argues that they did what they could, and in pursuing
military victory the Allies ensured the survival of the remnant of

Jewish Europe by liberation. For Rubinstein the idea that the democracies did little in the face of the refugee crisis of the 1930s is nonsensical – Jews did leave Germany and Austria, Jews did find haven in Britain and the USA. The idea that Jews could have been rescued from Nazi Europe stretches the boundaries of credulity even further. Jews were slated for extermination and thus were not able to escape. As such the argument that the Allies should (or indeed could) have provided a haven for Jews is seen as absurd – Jews did not perish in Nazi Europe because they had nowhere else to go, they died because of a genocide which would not let them go: 'the Nazis and the Nazis alone, bear total responsibility for erecting these barriers to Jewish emigration, obviously in preparation for genocide.'[114]

How then do we account for the sharpness of this interpretative divide, especially over what is after all an agreed narrative of events? This is once again a discourse about the past concerned with the present. It is, as I said at the beginning of the chapter, about us and about the extent of our responsibilities to one another. From the outset these histories have had a clear political purpose. Andrew Sharf's study was conceived under the auspices of the Institute for Race Relations and was thus designed to shed light on the role of race in British society and culture. The very first criticisms of US policy responses were also based on a very clear sense of what America should represent in moral political terms. The tradition of sanctuary of the US as a haven was 'despoiled' according to Arthur Morse in response to the Holocaust. This was, as was observed at the time, part of an attempt to indict a 'a generation of Americans' and can thus be read as part of the culture wars of the 1960s, concerned as much about the future as it was the past.[115] David Wyman shared Morse's outrage, arguing that a sense that the US had 'failed the test of civilisation' during the Nazi era had informed policy to give sanctuary to Indo-Chinese 'boat people' at the end of the 1970s.

More recent bystander scholarship is also self-consciously rooted in the present. Kushner's critique of liberalism, and identification of the difficulty that the nation-state has in coping with ethnic differentiation, can be applied today. Indeed, Kushner's own recent summary of bystander scholarship tellingly contains a quotation from Rabbi Hugo Gryn which states that 'asylum issues are an index of our spiritual and moral civilisation'.[116] Louise London's critique of British refugee policy in the past is also a part of an ongoing discourse on British refugee and asylum policy in the present. As London has argued, the politics of asylum in the present is often surrounded by invocations of Britain's proud tradition of providing refuge for the oppressed and specifically the Jews of Europe. London's demonstration of the emptiness of that myth therefore has a present day political purpose.[117]

London and Kushner's opponents may claim more political neutrality, but this is hardly the case. Rubinstein's defence of British and American immigration restrictions is based on his clearly articulated belief that nation-states *should* limit the number of refugees who cross their borders. Rubinstein does not deny that British immigration policy in the 1930s attempted to limit entrance to those that were economically useful. Indeed he believes that this was (and is) a political necessity.[118] Pamela Shatzkes, whose book *Holocaust and Rescue* borrows from Rubinstein's thinking, also seems politically to approve of the British government's reasons for operating a parsimonious refugee policy which was '*inevitably* indifferent to the fate of a foreign ethnic minority at a time of national emergency'.[119]

Bystanders and the discipline of History

The political, theological and moral immanence of bystander historiography is commonly identified as its central, even fatal weakness. Michael Marrus has even questioned whether this is history-writing at all.[120] However I would like to argue almost precisely the opposite, that it is in this immanence, in the reality that the bystander debate is a discourse about now, that we may find (as one of the original reviewers of *Der Stellvertreter* put it) the 'meaningfulness of history'.[121] The final section of the chapter seeks to bring the two case studies together to reveal first the degree to which the cleavages in bystander historiography are also defined by different approaches to the past and then discusses the possible worth of these approaches for Holocaust studies and the discipline of History in general.

There can be no doubt that bystander History at times indulges in an extraordinarily unsophisticated discourse. Proclamations that one or other argument represents the 'truth' are common. Elie Wiesel's introduction to *The Abandonment of the Jews* asks readers 'What was the truth?' before promising them 'read David Wyman's courageous, lucid, painful book and you will learn it too'.[122] William Rubinstein equally suggests that his opposing argument represents the single reality, declaring that he would be 'genuinely surprised if any reasonable person were not persuaded' by his version of the past.[123] Such rhetoric is unhelpful, especially when applied to an area of historiography which perhaps more than any other challenges the idea of a singular monolithic historical truth – with interpretations so dependent on extraneous ideologies. Representing bystander History in such binary and Manichean terms also obscures its worth, because it seems to embrace simplicity rather than nuance.

Much the same can be said for the common calls within bystander historiography for a strict empiricism, a return to the documents as a way out of the fog of controversy. As if by returning 'to the documents' somehow an unalloyed, objective, reality about the past will be found. Such simplicitism ignores the importance of context in History and indeed implicitly denies the agency of the historian. Some bystander historians do wish to deny the agency of the historian and thus their own agency too. The most common accusation levelled, for example, at those who have produced critical histories of Pius XII is that they lack the detachment required by historical discourse, that they fail to find the objectivity needed to represent the past on its own terms.[124] Such a noble dream may be laudable, but the idea that the defenders of Pius XII themselves make no moral or political judgements about the past is, as we have seen, nonsense.

The idea that a return to the documents could somehow hold the solution, solve the problem and find the truth also appears to betray an assumption about what is significant in the past. It requires that History must be the history of action, of what happened and cannot, and perhaps can never be, the history of inaction, of what did not happen. On the surface that appears to be an inherently reasonable position. Of course History must be an account of what happened, rather than what did not. The latter it could be argued is about fiction, the former about reality. Yet bystander History demonstrates that if historians confine themselves just to action in the past they limit their possible understanding of that reality.

To explain further, those historians who offer what we might call sympathetic bystander studies – arguing that the Church or Allied governments did all they could – focus broadly on *action*. Pius XII, therefore, was not 'silent' because at Christmas 1942 he spoke out, or the importance of the *Kindertransport* to Britain lies in the fact that it saved 10,000 Jewish children – as such it cannot be argued that Britain did not provide a haven for Jews, because Jews reached its shores. However the important message of what might be called critical bystander studies is that what did not happen can be illuminating too, and perhaps even more importantly that inaction can be the result of an *active* choice. As such what Pius XII did *not* say when he named neither the German perpetrators of atrocity nor its Jewish victims was a choice which requires explanation. That the *Kindertransport* saved only the lives of Jewish children who were seen as easily assimilable is important because Britain, quite deliberately, did not provide a haven for their parents whose presence was seen as undesirable. This inaction was again the consequence of an active choice. These observations are perhaps most important when discussing the idea of rescue. Rubinstein argues that rescue could not possibly have been successful, that it could not have saved more Jews. As such in a vision of history where action is all important, rescue becomes an irrelevance. But the central question remains why did Britain and the USA *not* act, why did they *not* employ significant schemes of rescue. This history of inaction is again crucial, because as the likes of David Wyman and Louise London have demonstrated, the Allies actively avoided schemes of rescue because they feared their possible success.

This debate over whether or not inaction can be a matter of active choice, is not just an abstruse philosophical question. It is after all the core of the Good Samaritan concept that informs so much of bystander History, and thus has a very clear social and political application. If History as a discipline cannot explore such moral and philosophical questions as these, and that seems to be the implication of those historians who dismiss our right to explore what did not happen and why, then it becomes legitimate to ask what is the use of the discipline at all? By challenging History to become able to reflect on what did not happen as well as what did, critical bystander History attempts to find a moral and ethical value for the study of the past. We in the present are able to reflect on the consequences of not acting, of not speaking out. At the same time it is a clear lesson for historians that to pursue the reasons why individuals did not do certain things can be more illuminating than investigating what and why they did.

It is not just in advocating a history of inaction rather than action that bystander History can also require a much more challenging methodology for historians. Some of its practitioners boldly proclaim their right or obligation to judge the past too, their ability to declare what the Catholic Church or the Allies *should* have done. Daniel Goldhagen argues forcefully that his right to judge the past is based on a sense of universal moral truths 'that are applicable to any persons and any deeds during any time'.[125] David Wyman asserted his right to condemn the actions of the US government refusing to 'excuse [the] people of the past from moral responsibility for their actions'. Wyman can do this because 'the Americans of half a century ago were not members of some distant culture with *different basic values and standards from our own in regard to human responsibility*'.[126] In making such an assertion Wyman denies that there is a meaningful distinction between past and present. In doing so he required that historians do no less than rethink one of the building blocks of their discipline.

The critics of bystander History, from the sober to the hysterical return time and again to this issue of the distinction between past and present, and in doing so reject Wyman's call to judgement as unfounded 'historical moralism'.[127] And there is no doubt that such judgmentalism *is* problematic because the morality that Daniel Goldhagen finds to be universal is surely contingent. However whilst it may be problematic to draw such exact equivalence between past and present, it is also problematic to attempt to draw such firm boundaries between the two, as it is to entirely dismiss the role of moral and indeed political judgement in History.

First it is notable that some of those who deny the historians' right to judge the bystanders have no such qualms about applying precisely such judgment to the perpetrators of atrocity themselves. Indeed as we have seen in previous chapters the historiography of the 'Final Solution' itself has been built on precisely such moral outrage. Lucy Dawidowicz for example, denied David Wyman's right to judge the US while asserting that her own history of the Holocaust was a moral history that made no efforts at objectivity – objectivity being impossible in the face of such an obvious moral transgression as the 'Final Solution'. Bystander History simply does the same but applies that moral outrage inwardly because the bystander represents us.

Second, bystander History, like so much historiography, is defined by an interaction between past and present. It takes our own disgust at the death camps and asks how individuals in the past reacted to it. It is in this sense an historical project entirely filtered through another set of historical observations regarding the Holocaust itself, and thus suggests a complex interaction of past and present. An interaction which applies in other spheres of historiography, indeed Holocaust historiography, yet without attracting much controversy at all.

But this interaction between past and present can still tell us something about the past. First, that individuals and institutions struggled to assimilate knowledge and understanding of what we call the Holocaust is a vital observation, despite its being informed by a present conception of the genocide of the Jews.[128] The idea that the *Shoah* changed everything is rhetorically familiar – but that it did not force Christians to reconceive their relations with Jews; that it did not engender the Vatican to abandon its diplomatic approach to international moral problems; that it did not force nation-states to re-evaluate their own approaches to refugee policy; that it did not force bureaucrats of the Foreign Office and the State Department to adopt a more humanitarian attitude, is telling. The rhetoric of change is overblown, empty even; in fact the Holocaust and knowledge of it changed little in the bystanders' approach to and understanding of their world.[129] Bystander History can therefore be used to puncture some important myths, versions of the past that are, as it were, active in the present. This is especially the case with national mythologies. The idea of Britain and the USA's good war, fought on the side of right, is challenged by the picture of an inadequate response to the crisis of European Jewry.[130]

The Church's relationship with the Holocaust, whether the subject of condemnation or praise, can tell us a great deal about the Church as an institution in the world. Placing judgement to one side, the Vatican's diplomatic response to the crisis of European Jewry reveals the Church as first and foremost a political institution. This is not an unimportant observation. Regardless of whether Britain and the USA *should* or *could* have provided more comprehensive refuge for the Jews of Europe, that they acted in the manner that they did reveals something about modern liberalism and the ability of the nation-state to reconceive itself in the face of an humanitarian emergency. As such, albeit under the heavy influence of the present, to ask how societies in the past responded to the Holocaust reveals a good deal about how those societies worked and the assumptions around which they operated.[131]

Primarily however, historians of the bystanders are interested in uncovering the global context in which the Holocaust occurred. By exposing the 'bystanders' to moral and political judgement it could be argued, albeit to adopt a cliché, that historians are seeking to *learn* from the past. As such they are using the moral and political judgements they make about the past in order to try to shape the future. If, as David Wyman alleges, knowledge of the inadequacy of the response to the Holocaust dictated a different American political response to the refugee crisis of the late 1970s, then this suggests that bystander History can have an important moral and political purpose in the present. As I said above, John Cornwell's attempt to indict Pius XII as *Hitler's Pope* is in part a contribution to a discourse concerned with the future direction of the Catholic Church.

Outside Holocaust studies, Genocide scholars are increasingly aware of genocide as a fact of the international system.[132] Such an observation has an ethical commitment to genocide prevention at its core. Arthur Morse asked in the very first book-length study of the bystanders, 'if genocide is to be prevented in the future, we must understand how it happened in the past'.[133] Part of that understanding requires engaging with the context provided by the bystanders. As such bystander studies could and should, when applying judgement, have such a political purpose as its inspiration. Far from a betrayal of the discipline of History as some critics allege, this is an effort to make History an active force in humanisation of global politics and society.

But I should end on a note of caution. Much bystander History essentially rests on the idea that the Holocaust contained unique challenges. If then the lesson that we take from this is that genocides or humanitarian crises must look like the Holocaust before we act, then the study of the bystanders could become the spur to inaction rather than action. It is easy to imagine an argument constructed that the West need not intervene, need not provide succour for victims, because this or that crisis is not like the Holocaust. Western failure in the face of the Rwandan genocide was often implicitly justified or, at least explained by, the spurious notion that that genocide was inspired by some form of primitive tribalism.[134] As such the clear implication was that as it was not a crime of Western modernity, then the West need not be concerned. Ironically in such circumstances the study of the bystanders, which I have argued here has a moral and political value, could become something which encourages us to continue to walk by on the other side of the road.

Notes

1 *The Times*, 10 May 1963.
2 For a contemporary arts review see *The Times*, 26 September 1963. See a collection of critical responses Eric Bentley, *The Storm Over the Deputy* (New York, 1964).
3 Robert Davis, 'The possibility of individual choice', *Storm Over the Deputy*, p. 96.
4 *New York Times*, 28 February 1963. It has been claimed that the term was first used by Michael Marrus – David Cesarani and Paul Levine, 'Introduction', *Bystanders to the Holocaust: A Re-evaluation* (London, 2000), p. 1 – but this is wrong.
5 Quoted in Pinchas Lapide, *The Last Three Popes and the Jews* (London, 1967), p. 230.
6 See for example David Wyman, *The Abandonment of the Jews: America and the Holocaust 1941–45* (New York, 2007), p. xix; Bernard Wasserstein, *Britain and the Jews of Europe 1939–45* (Oxford, 1988), p. 356.
7 Richard Law's memo from the Bermuda conference which was submitted to the War Cabinet May 3 1943 (ref. WP (43) 191), National Archives, Public Record Office, FO 371 / 36731.
8 Victoria Barnett, *Bystanders: Conscience and Complicity During the Holocaust* (Westport: CT, 1999), p. 53.
9 John F. Morley, *Vatican Diplomacy and the Jews During the Holocaust 1939–43* (New York, 1980), p. 195.
10 Susan Zuccotti, *Under His Very Windows: The Vatican and the Holocaust* (New Haven: CT, 2002), p. 97.
11 Wyman, *Abandonment of the Jews*, p. 342.
12 Zuccotti, *Under his Very Windows*, p. 25.
13 Jose M. Sanchez, *Pius XII and the Holocaust: Understanding the Controversy* (Washington: DC, 2002), p. vii.
14 John Conway, review of Tom Lawson, *The Church of England and the Holocaust* (Woodbridge, 2006), *Reviews in History*, December 2006, http://www.history.ac.uk/reviews/paper/conway.html.

15 Pope Paul VI implied this when he attacked Hochhuth as being 'insufficiently endowed with historical discernment'. The subjects of history cannot be expected to have understood the world in the way that we require of them now, especially when they were operating in, to continue with the example of Pius XII, the context of a world war in which the very survival of himself, his office and his church was under threat. See *The Times*, 28 June 1963.

16 See for example Robert W. Ross, *So it was True: The American Protestant Press and the Nazi Persecution of the Jews* (Minneapolis: MN, 1980), p. 164.

17 Donald Bloxham and Tony Kushner, *The Holocaust: Critical Historical Approaches* (Manchester, 2005), p. 183.

18 Yehuda Bauer, *Rethinking the Holocaust* (New Haven: CT, 2002), p. 273.

19 Wyman, *Abandonment of the Jews*, p. xix.

20 Barnett, *Bystanders*, p. 53.

21 Bloxham and Kushner, *The Holocaust*, p. 178.

22 Saul Friedländer, *Pius XII and the Third Reich* (London, 1966), p. 237.

23 *Ibid.*, p. 130.

24 Carol Falconi, *The Silence of Pius XII* (London, 1970), p. 17.

25 Friedländer, *Pius XII and the Third Reich*, p. 143.

26 Pierre Blet, *Pius XII and the Second World War: According to the Archives of the Vatican* (London, 1999), p. xiii.

27 Michael Phayer, *Pius XII, the Holocaust and the Cold War*, p. 78.

28 Ronald J. Rychlak, *Hitler, the War and the Pope* (Colombus: OH, 2000), p. 205.

29 Cornwell, *Hitler's Pope*, pp. 324–5.

30 Phayer, *Pius XII, the Holocaust and the Cold War*, pp. 173–207. On Stangl see Gitta Sereny, *Into that Darkness: From Mercy Killing to Mass Murder* (London, 1974), pp. 289–90.

31 Jose M. Sanchez, *Pius XII and the Holocaust: Understanding the Controversy* (Washington: DC, 2002), p. 26; and Patrick J. Gallo, *Pius XII, the Holocaust and the Revisionists* (Jefferson: NC, 2006), p. 4.

32 Leon Poliakov, 'The Vatican and the Jewish Question: the record of the Hitler period and after', *Commentary* (November 1950), p. 441.

33 Friedländer, *Pius XII and the Third Reich*, p. 237.

34 Morley, *Vatican Diplomacy and the Jews*, p. 4.

35 *Ibid.*, p. 208.

36 Lapide, *Last Three Popes*, p. 268.

37 Anthony Rhodes, *The Vatican in the Age of the Dictators* (London, 1973).

38 John K. Roth and Carol Rittner, 'What We Must Remember', *Pope Pius XII and the Holocaust* (London, 2002), p. 278.

39 See Georges Passelcq and Bernard Suchecky, *The Hidden Encyclical of Pius XII* (New York, 1997), p. 166. See also Michael R. Marrus, 'The Vatican on Racism and Antisemitism 1938–39: A New Look at a Might-Have-Been', *Holocaust and Genocide Studies* (Vol. 11, No. 3, 1997), pp. 378–95.

40 Blet, *Pius XII and the Second World War*, p. xiv.

41 See www.jcrelations.net/en/?item=1770.

42 The full text of *We Remember: A Reflection on the Shoah* is available on the Vatican website – http://www.vatican.va/roman_curia/pontifical_councils/chrstuni/documents/rc_pc_chrstuni_doc_16031998_shoah_en.html

43 Zuccotti, *Under His Very Windows*, p. 301.

44 Michael Phayer, *The Catholic Church and the Holocaust, 1930–65* (Bloomington: IN, 2000), p. 51.
45 Phayer, *Pius XII, The Holocaust and the Cold War*, p. xii.
46 *Ibid.*, p. 53.
47 Harold Tittman reports, for example, Pius' incredulity at the suggestion his intervention was oblique. Harold H. Tittmann, *Inside the Vatican of Pius XII: The Memoir of an American Diplomat During World War II* (New York, 2004), p. 123.
48 John Cornwell, *Hitler's Pope: The Secret History of Pius XII* (London, 1997)
49 *Ibid.*, p. 75. Cornwell describes Pacelli's use of antisemitic stereotypes in 1920s Munich as 'repugnant and ominous'.
50 Goldhagen and Cornwell are discussed below. See also David Kertzer, *Unholy War: The Vatican's Role in the Rise of Modern Anti-Semitism* (London, 2002); James Carroll, *Constantine's Sword: The Church and the Jews, A History* (New York, 2001).
51 Daniel Goldhagen, *A Moral Reckoning: The Role of the Catholic Church in the Holocaust and its Unfulfilled Duty of Repair* (London, 2002), p. 48.
52 *Ibid.*, p. 73.
53 Richard Rubenstien, 'Pius XII and the Shoah', Roth and Rittner, *Pius XII*, p. 196.
54 Quoted in Joseph Bottum, 'The End of the Pius Wars', Gallo, *Pius XII, the Holocaust*, p. 184.
55 Ralph McInerney, *The Defamation of Pius XII* (South Bend: IN, 2001) – this is a quotation from the back cover.
56 Blet, *Pius XII and the Second World War*, p. 283.
57 John T. Pawlikowski, 'The Papacy of Pius XII: The Known and the Unknown', Roth and Rittner, *Pius XII*, p. 57.
58 Eugene Fisher, 'What is Known Today: A Brief Review of the Literature', Roth and Rittner, *Pius XII*, p. 87.
59 Sanchez, *Pius XII*, p. 172.
60 Blet, *Pius XII and the Second World War*, p. 167.
61 Gallo, *Pius XII, the Holocaust*, p. 4.
62 Blet, *Pius XII and the Second World War*, p. 1.
63 Eva Fleischner, 'The Spirituality of Pius XII', Roth and Rittner, *Pope Pius XII*, p. 126.
64 Barnett, *Bystanders*, p. 138.
65 Falconi, *The Silence of Pius XII*, p. 98.
66 Morley, *Vatican Diplomacy and the Jews*, p. 4.
67 Zuccotti, *Under His Very Windows*, p. 319; Goldhagen, *A Moral Reckoning*, p. 88.
68 This is made clear in John Cornwell, *The Pope in Winter: The Dark Face of John Paul II's Papacy* (London, 2005) which is a critique of the pontificate of John Paul II from the same direction.
69 Sanchez, *Pius XII and the Holocaust*, p. 14.
70 Gallo, *Pius XII, the Holocaust*, p. 5.
71 John T. Pawlikowski, 'The Papacy of Pius XII: The Known and the Unknown', Rittner and Roth, *Pius XII*, pp. 46–69.
72 Fisher, 'What is Known Today', p. 74.
73 Arthur D. Morse, *While Six Million Died* (London, 1968).

74 Yehuda Bauer, 'When did they Know?', *Midstream*, April 1968, pp. 51–8.

75 Barbara Rogers, 'Auschwitz and the British', *History Today* (Vol. 49, No. 10, 1999), pp. 2–3.

76 Nicholas Terry, 'Conflicting Signals: British Intelligence on the 'Final Solution' through Radio Intercepts and Other Sources', *Yad Vashem Studies* (Vol. 32, 2004), p. 353.

77 Most of these references to the agreed narrative come from William D. Rubinstein, *The Myth of Rescue: Why the Democracies Could not Have Saved More Jews from the Nazis* (London, 2000). This is because Rubinstein set out to deliberately overturn much of the extant scholarship in this area. As such where he agrees this narrative it can be fairly suggested to be accepted across the historiographical spectrum.

78 Rubinstein, *The Myth of Rescue*, p. 33.

79 Louise London, *Whitehall and the Jews 1933–48: British Immigration Policy and the Holocaust* (Cambridge, 2000), pp. 58–60.

80 Tony Kushner, *The Holocaust and the Liberal Imagination* (London, 1994), p. 50.

81 Rubinstein, *The Myth of Rescue*, p. 41.

82 *Ibid.*, p. 19.

83 *Ibid.*, p. 102.

84 *Ibid.*, p. 86.

85 *Ibid.*, p. 126.

86 Raul Hilberg, *Perpetrators, Victims, Bystanders: The Jewish Catastrophe 1933–45* (New York, 1992), p. 249.

87 This is in effect the key argument of Lawson, *The Church of England and the Holocaust*.

88 Andrew Sharf, *The British Press and the Jews Under Nazi Rule* (London, 1964), pp. 180–5.

89 A.J. Sherman, *Island Refuge: Britain and Refugees from the Third Reich 1933–39* (Berkeley, 1973), p. 267.

90 Morse, *While Six Million Died*, p. 129.

91 *Ibid.*, p. 28.

92 *Ibid.*, p. 98.

93 Henry Feingold, *The Politics of Rescue: The Roosevelt Administration and the Holocaust* (New York, 1970).

94 Wyman, *Abandonment of the Jews*, p. 313.

95 See Bat-Ami Zucker, *In Search of Refuge: Jews and US Consuls in Nazi Germany 1933–41* (London, 2001).

96 Wyman, *Abandonment of the Jews*, p. xix.

97 Bernard Wasserstein, *Britain and the Jews of Europe* (Oxford, 1988), p. 28.

98 Martin Gilbert, *Auschwitz and the Allies* (London, 1981), pp. 241–2.

99 Wasserstein, *Britain and the Jews of Europe*, p. 34.

100 Cesarani and Levine, 'Introduction', p.18.

101 See Joanne Reilly, *Belsen: The Liberation of a Concentration Camp* (London, 1997) which highlights the struggle that Jews had to be recognised as Jews, rather than Poles or even Germans, by the British forces that took over the running of the camp.

102 Kushner, *The Holocaust and the Liberal Imagination*, pp. 172–82.

103 For more on Parkes, see Lawson, *The Church of England and the Holocaust*, pp. 101–07.
104 Richard Bolchover, *British Jewry and the Holocaust* (Cambridge, 1993), see the conclusion for a summary, pp. 144–56.
105 *Ibid.*, p. 146.
106 Quoted in London, *Whitehall and the Jews*, p. 240.
107 Barnett, *Bystanders*, p. 59.
108 This is the argument proposed in John Fox's review of Wasserstein's *Britain and the Jews of Europe*, which appeared in *International Affairs* (Vol. 56, No. 1, 1980), pp. 143–4.
109 John Conway, review of David Wyman, *The Abandonment of the Jews*, *German Studies Review* (Vol. 8, No. 2, 1985) pp. 356–57.
110 Dawidowicz and Marrus' criticisms of Wyman are recorded in an Afterword to Wyman, *The Abandonment of the Jews*, pp. 341–53.
111 Wyman, *Abandonment of the Jews*, pp. 288–307.
112 James H. Kitchens III, 'The Bombing of Auschwitz Re-examined', Michael J. Neufeld and Michael Berenbaum (eds), *The Bombing of Auschwitz: Should the Allies Have Attempted it?* (New York, 2003), p. 100.
113 Rubinstein, *The Myth of Rescue*, p. 216.
114 *Ibid.*, p. 80.
115 Selig Adler, review of *While Six Million Died*, *American Historical Review* (Vol. 74, No. 1, 1968), p. 328.
116 Bloxham and Kushner, *The Holocaust*, p. 179.
117 See, for example, Louise London, 'Whitehall and the Refugees: The 1930s and the 1990s', *Patterns of Prejudice* (Vol. 34, no. 3, 2000), pp. 17–26.
118 Rubinstein, *The Myth of Rescue*, p. 42.
119 Pamela Shatzkes, *Holocaust and Rescue: Impotent or Indifferent? Anglo-Jewry 1938–1945* (London, 2002), p. 239.
120 Michael Marrus, 'Pius XII and the Holocaust: Ten Essential Themes', Roth and Rittner, *Pius XII*, p. 54.
121 Robert Gorham Davis, 'The Possibility of Individual Choice', *New York Times Book Review*, 1 March 1964, reprinted in Bentley, *The Storm over the Deputy*, p. 98.
122 Elie Wiesel, 'Foreword to the 1985 edition', Wyman, *Abandonment of the Jews*, p. x.
123 Rubinstein, *The Myth of Rescue*, p. x.
124 Patrick Gallo, 'Introduction', *Pius XII, the Holocaust*, p. 5.
125 Goldhagen, *A Moral Reckoning*, pp. 15, 22.
126 Wyman, *Abandonment of the Jews*, p. 345.
127 See Hugh Macleod's review of Tom Lawson, *The Church of England and the Holocaust*, *English Historical Review* (Vol. CXXIII, No. 503), p. 1089.
128 See for example Ross, *So it was True*.
129 See Laurel Leff, *Buried by the Times: The Holocaust and America's Most Important Newspaper* (Cambridge, 2005) which demonstrates how news of the Holocaust was domesticated within the ordinary approach of the *New York Times*.
130 Wasserstein, *Britain and the Jews of Europe*, p. vi.
131 Bloxham and Kushner, *The Holocaust*, p. 200.

132 Mark Levene, 'A Dissenting Voice: Or How Current Assumptions of Deterring and Preventing Genocide may be Looking at the Problem Through the Wrong End of the Telescope', *Journal of Genocide Research* (Vol. 6, No. 2, 2004), pp. 153–66.

133 Morse, *While Six Million Died*, p. x.

134 This argument was proposed in this leading article: 'Carnage in Africa', *The Times*, 11 April 1994.

4

'The Realisation of the Unthinkable': searching for the origins of the 'Final Solution'

Although by the 1970s scholars agreed that the Holocaust was a conceivable singular event, there was no consensus as to when and how that event or set of events began. In fact the question of when and how the Nazis achieved, in the words of Hans Mommsen, the 'realisation of the unthinkable' remained the subject of a sharp interpretative controversy. When Mommsen articulated his answer in the essay that gives this chapter its title in the early 1980s, giving his explanation of how the Nazis crossed the Rubicon to a policy of systematic annihilation and extermination, he was then intervening in an ongoing historiographical debate.

Mommsen asked when and how 'the unimaginable utopian dream [could] become unspeakable reality' in the Third Reich.[1] His answer was in many ways unpalatable and apparently out of step with the magnitude of the events he described. Mommsen suggested that Germany had not been led into this genocidal crusade by a visionary and charismatic leader with diabolic intentions. The 'Final Solution' had instead emerged piecemeal, related only tangentially to both the *Führer* and his ideological mania. What is more, 'Hitler gave no formal order to carry out the "Final Solution"'.[2] Instead, Mommsen's thesis was that the origin of the German descent into genocide could be found, mundanely, in the *structure* of rule that Hitler had constructed and of which he was a prisoner. This structure was not the totalitarian monolith, but the polycratic chaos observed by Neumann and Huttenberger. Echoing Karl Schleunes' conclusions that anti-Jewish policy in the 1930s had progressed not according to any plan but in the chaos of the Nazi system, Mommsen concluded that the 'Final

125 *Functionalist*

'Weak dictator thesis'

Solution' was carried by a bureaucracy that 'functioned more or less automatically'.[3]

Mommsen's striking argument implied that an event other (usually intentionalist) scholars were increasingly prepared to declare 'unique' in human history, in fact had the most banal roots – in the structure of government and administration. His argument was an intervention in already vociferous debate – a development of 'functionalist' thinking. By suggesting that even the ideological intentions of Hitler himself were unimportant in understanding the genesis of genocide, Mommsen was directly refuting those who declared the origins of the 'Final Solution' could be found in ideology – and to put it simply the Nazis' premeditated will to exterminate the Jews. This chapter analyses the ongoing discourse in which Mommsen's argument must be understood, and thus presents the narrative of Holocaust historiography up to the end of the 1980s.

During this time the debate became fixated on the apparently narrow question of the specific decision-making process behind the transition to genocide, on when (if at all) the 'Final Solution' was ordered. At first glance this may appear a narrow historiography indeed. Yet, as we saw in Chapter 2, far from narrow, this controversy concerned fundamental questions. Different philosophical approaches to the discipline of History and, as the debate has progressed, increasingly opposing political understandings of both present and past were subsumed beneath this apparently trivial enterprise. As a consequence, divergent interpretations of the Nazi state itself emerged, both in terms of how that state and society functioned, and more globally where one could situate both Nazism and especially the 'Final Solution' within wider chronologies of modern history. The question of when the 'Final Solution' began was therefore so much more than '*just* a dating game', it was a search for its origins and crucially the meaning of the Holocaust and its lessons.[4] What follows is a brief survey of this debate and its implications from the late 1970s.

The documents of destruction

What Saul Friedländer describes as 'global' interpretations of the Nazi era, struggled to explain the specific 'Final Solution'. All-encompassing efforts to understand the Third Reich, and

SEARCHING FOR THE ORIGINS OF THE 'FINAL SOLUTION'

specifically to place it into some kind of comparative twentieth-century context, seemed ill equipped to offer a compelling account of the development of Nazism's most specific and salient feature. The theory of fascism, which concentrated on structural interpretations of the various power relations between regime, party, state and people, simply could not account for why the 'Final Solution' occurred in Germany and not, for instance, Mussolinian Italy. Similarly the idea of totalitarianism, which sought comparison between dictatorial regimes of all political colours could no better explain why systematic, industrial, genocide had emerged in Hitler's Germany and not Stalin's Soviet Union. For Friedländer such a lacuna was easily explained, these global interpretations had no place for the ideological conviction that drove politics in the Nazi state – for the political antisemitism at its heart.[5]

Yet for Hans Mommsen, Friedländer's identification of the causal importance of antisemitic ideology could not represent all the answers. Ideology was important for the development of the 'Final Solution', if nothing else because it identified its primary victims. Antisemitism may have been a necessary cause, but it does not amount to a sufficient explanation. The existence of an ideology which *could* accommodate genocide does not demonstrate *how* that ideology was translated into murderous policy. There was a gap between ambition and implementation that required explanation.

In part that gap reflected a very real absence of source material.[6] Despite the many trials since the end of the war (and most notably the trial of Eichmann), sources concerning Jewish policy at the centre of government in the Third Reich remained scarce. Unlike the so-called Euthanasia Programme to murder the mentally and physically impaired, no written order for the beginning of the 'Final Solution' exists.[7] The minutes of the Wannsee protocol had been discovered in 1947, but from the outset it was clear that this meeting did not reveal specifically how the policy of genocide that it apparently discussed had been arrived at. And, making clear the ambiguity of documents, to this day the meeting at Wannsee remains disputed – and in any case it did not involve the most senior decision-makers, but their representatives. While various sources (Hitler's *Table Talk*, Goebbels' diary, personal testimonies) included references to Hitler's attitudes to anti-Jewish policy there is very little evidence of his direct personal involvement in that policy – in the shape for example of written policy directives or orders. Most importantly there exists no written records of meetings between Hitler and the two most senior figures in the SS who were ultimately responsible for the implementation (and probably design) of genocide – Heinrich Himmler and Reinhard Heydrich. As Mommsen's colleague at the IfZ, Martin Broszat wrote, we know that during the key decision-making phase in the second half of 1941 and into 1942, Himmler and Heydrich met regularly with the *Führer*. We 'know almost nothing' about what was discussed.[8]

The documentary evidence that we do have also uses quite deliberately oblique and obfuscatory language. The terms 'Final Solution', 'special treatment', 'action', 'external resettlement' all allude to genocide, but they are hardly clear. To return to the Wannsee protocol, while the written record of the meeting refers to 'evacuation' and Jews being 'transported to the East', this is only because, according to his trial testimony, Adolf Eichmann had translated the 'plain talk' of murder at the meeting into 'official language' when he prepared the minutes.[9] The inherent flexibility of such language was a consequence of both a desire for secrecy – evacuation has a literal meaning too after all – and was used to protect the protagonists from facing the reality of their murderous intentions and actions. The meanings of this language could also, crucially, change. References to the 'Final Solution' in summer of 1940 were not allusions to mass murder – at this stage the 'Final Solution' was to be emigration – references to the same phrase in the summer of 1942 were.[10]

This obfuscation has had serious consequences for historians – we just have to admit that the documents do not tell us all that we want to know.[11] Yet this ignorance is difficult to bear, and has thus often been, implicitly at least, denied in historical narratives. The search for the traces of genocide has led to extravagant claims being made about statements which, at first glance, appear if not innocent then hardly genocidal. Two examples should suffice. In his 1991 biography of Heinrich Himmler, Richard Breitman declares with certainty that by March 1941 a decision had been made that the Jews of Europe were to be murdered. His evidence? A document in which Adolf Eichmann refers to the 'final evacuation' of the Jews.[12] Some fifteen years later Bogdan Musial declared with similar certainty that he had discovered the decision to murder all the Jews of the General Government in October 1941. The evidence for this claim is a meeting at which Odilo Globocnik, SSPF Lublin, refers to Jews being 'transferred across the Bug river'.[13] Despite the certainty of historians then, these are but fragments and they are frustratingly written in code.

The testimonies of the former *genocidaires* themselves offer little more certainty. Both Rudolf Höss and Adolf Eichmann referred to being informed of a *Führer* order for the extermination of the Jews in the summer of 1941. While some historians have taken them at their word, there are many reasons to be cautious.[14] Rudolf Höss remembers being told about the order, *after* the extermination sites were operational – the first murders took place at Chelmno in December 1941, and Belzec in March 1942.[15] Eichmann's memory of being informed of a *Führer* order by Heydrich were vague, but seemed to point to the summer of 1941. He recalled that he was sent to Lublin to visit Globocnik (who would be organising the genocide there) immediately after Heydrich had informed him of the *Führer*'s historic decision. It appears more likely that Eichmann's visit to the future extermination site at Belzec took place in October rather than the summer as he recalled. There is little evidence of genocidal planning in the General Government before then. Eichmann's misdating of his trip to Lublin was typical, and as David Cesarani has summarised his account of various inspection trips to the East in 1941 and 1942 is highly suspect – manufactured by an uncertain memory attempting to evade the death penalty.[16]

Such a documentary deficit has ensured that historians can only speculate as to when, if at all, the 'order' for the 'Final Solution' was issued, and as such that the historian of this subject can only deal with the balance of probabilities.[17] Thus the language of this historiography is often markedly provisional. Eberhard Jäckel bases his analysis on the 'fact' that it is '*difficult to imagine*' (emphasis added) that the 'Final Solution' could have been 'initiated by subordinate agencies' in the Third Reich.[18] Robert Jan van Pelt is prepared to go only as far as concluding that Adolf Eichmann '*perhaps*' (emphasis added) visited Auschwitz to discuss the deportation of German Jews rather than the 'Final Solution' in August 1941.[19] Despite this provisionality, at times speculation does give way to certainty. But, somewhat contrarily, such confidence betrays the very *uncertainty* of the evidence on which interpretations are based. Peter Longerich declares that radicalising decisions on Jewish policy '*must*' have been taken in March 1942, precisely because the evidence suggests only that this is one possibility (albeit the one he takes most seriously).[20] Yitzhak Arad writes with equal surety about 'the Führer's directive to Himmler ... regarding the total physical annihilation of the Jews of the USSR [which was] issued at the planning stage of the invasion'.[21] But of course Arad has never seen such a document.

The uncertainty of the documents also allowed room for tendentious and politically inspired attempts to exonerate Hitler within mainstream historiography. The question of Hitler's role in the decision-making process was brought to the fore in the late 1970s by David Irving's thesis, put forward in his book *Hitler's War*, that the *Führer* had been *unaware* of the extermination of Jews until the middle of 1943. Before that point Irving suggested that Hitler had even attempted to rein in subordinates who were pursuing the most radical of anti-Jewish action. Indeed he argued: 'there is no evidence for the Hitler order of the "Final Solution" but the incontrovertible evidence is that Hitler ordered on November 30 1941, that there was to be "no liquidation" of Jews'.[22] Hitler's attempts to intervene failed, and the murders continued because by then they had 'gained a momentum of [their] own'.[23] Irving seemed to suggest that these revelations not only reduced Hitler's responsibility for the Holocaust but also the responsibility of ideological Nazism more generally – the murders had ultimately proceeded as a means of crisis management and the 'animal desire of the murderers to loot and plunder the Jewish victims'.[24]

Irving's thesis sparked a debate that has been important in Holocaust studies in terms of establishing Hitler's involvement, will and responsibility for anti-Jewish policy which will be reviewed below. However, more importantly it also demonstrates that, despite the uncertainty and the deliberately camouflaged language, there *are limits* to the interpretations that the documents will allow. Irving's claims were based on a deliberate manipulation (if not actual falsification) of the evidence. He focused on a single document – Hitler's instruction that a group of Jews deported from Berlin to Riga at the end of November 1941 should *not* be murdered. This instruction was recorded in Himmler's telephone log, after consultation with the *Führer* as 'Jewish transport from

Berlin. No liquidation.'[25] As such the order to halt the murders, related only to this single transport of 1500 Jews who were actually murdered on the morning of 30 November. The attempt to stop this massacre seems to demonstrate an enduring sensitivity about what could be done with *German* Jews, and far from Hitler's aloofness from the process of anti-Jewish policy his understanding of its minutiae. Yet Irving, deliberately and without regard for the 'facts', suggested that this was a general order showing Hitler's opposition to mass murder.

Irving's interpretation was clearly mendacious. In 2001 he was declared in the High Court in London to be 'anti-Semitic' and 'a racist' who treated historical evidence in a manner which 'fell short of the standard to be expected of a conscientious historian' in essence because he 'distorted the evidence'.[26] Yet as I have said, at the time, scholars did engage with Irving. Martin Broszat issued a reply to *Hitler's War* which has become the classic functionalist reading of the decision for the 'Final Solution'.[27] While Broszat rejected what might be termed the moral and political implications of the Irving thesis – he proclaimed decisively Hitler's moral responsibility for the 'Final Solution' – he did accept and indeed develop the key point, that Hitler had not issued an order for the commencement of genocide (although this is somewhat different to the claim that the *Führer* had not known about it). I will now review Broszat's argument and summarise the functionalist interpretations to which it gave voice.

Functionalism and the 'Final Solution'

Following directly the arguments of Karl Schleunes and Uwe Dietrich Adam that Nazi anti-Jewish policy had followed no clear plan during the 1930s, Broszat argued that the extermination of the Jews had not come about because of a single decision but had emerged piecemeal in a process that lasted between the summer of 1941 and 1942. In emphasising the 'Final Solution' as a process, Broszat consciously engaged not only David Irving but also Lucy Dawidowicz's argument that its origins could be sought in Hitler's 'preformed psychological motive of destruction'. Broszat argued that the process had begun with the *Einsatzgruppen* massacres, which *were* the result of a 'personal directive' from Hitler. Incremental decisions followed, all of which carried Hitler's stamp of approval. In the Autumn of 1941 it was decided to deport the Jews of Germany and the Czech protectorate, but only to an uncertain future in the East, a 'vague idea to employ Jews ... in ghettos and camps, at forced hard labour. Many of them would perish.' The ad-hoc nature of these deportations led to difficulties in local administration, not least where to house and how to feed the deported, and thus 'liquidations of the Jews began not solely as the result of an ostensible will to extermination but also as a "way out" of a blind alley into which the Nazis had manoeuvred themselves'. Once the practice of liquidation had been established in different locales it inevitably coalesced into policy as the most radical solution – what after all could be more 'final' than extermination? – and 'evolved into a comprehensive programme'. Such a programme was linked to the Nazis' ideological ambitions, but only vaguely: '[ideological] motives can be understood not only as semantic rules for the accomplishment of real ideological objectives, but rather as a conglomeration of various factors stemming from ideology, propaganda and, first and foremost, unexpected reactions of the individual which exceeded objectives set forth by racist ideology.'[28]

Functionalism rendered the history of the 'Final Solution' within the mode of modern historiography, and modern German historiography at that – suggesting that it was in part a consequence of modern social organisation thus emphasising the structural pressures on its protagonists. It also used the language of modern social science. Broszat and others used, unambiguously, their understanding of the 'Führerstaat', to explain the 'Final Solution' as the result of the peculiar structure of Nazi rule. Anti-Jewish measures 'gained momentum' through that structure which relied on ceaseless competition and internecine conflict. To quote the example used by Hans Mommsen, Reinhard Heydrich sought Hermann Göring's charge of responsibility for the 'Final Solution' at the end of July 1941 in order to extend the power of the RSHA. The Wannsee conference, the invitations for which cited Göring's directive, was then an opportunity to cement that power further and inflate RSHA prestige. On both occasions the result of Heydrich's will to power was the radicalisation of anti-Jewish policy and the spread of mass murder through the system.[29]

Hans Mommsen's interpretation was also inextricably linked to his wider thesis on the Nazi system. He proposed that Hitler

SEARCHING FOR THE ORIGINS OF THE 'FINAL SOLUTION'

was not the totalitarian tyrant of popular conception, but rather a 'weak dictator'. Mommsen viewed Hitler's aloofness from practical politics, his preference for creating multi-agency competition rather than singular direction in policy as a sign of inherent weakness rather than Machiavellian control. Mommsen's Hitler was not the author of polycratic dynamism, but was a vacillating coward unable to make decisions who created a system in which radicalism filled the vacuum left by his loss of control. Hitler was the *Führer* and therefore the myth of his power was crucial to such a system, but he was a *function* of it rather than its controlling force.[30] In terms of the 'Final Solution' Mommsen saw this vacillation in Hitler's willingness to tolerate a system in which Jews continued to be treated differently, depending under which agencies, purview they found themselves, right up until the destruction of the Third Reich itself. Throughout the period of annihilation, for example, Jews continued to be employed as slaves in the German war economy, and various agencies, at various different times after 1941, protested the economic consequences of murdering the Jewish labour force. For Mommsen this apparent contradiction could be explained by Hitler's reluctance to choose between the demands of the total war economy and the diktats of maniacal ideology.[31]

For functionalists, Hitler's statements of ideology are thus much more complex than just indicators of ideological intent. They have a general context in terms of their delivery, and they had an impact beyond their original purpose because of the system of government into which these rhetorical hand-grenades were thrown. When Hitler told the Reichstag in January 1939 that a future war would end in the annihilation of the Jews, he was therefore speaking figuratively and within the context of a mocking attack on the liberal democracies, parsimonious refugee policies, *and* delivering a rallying call to his supporters using his most familiar propagandistic tool. He was not literally demanding Jews be executed. Yet, when two years later annihilation had become a reality rather an apocalyptic vision, Hitler referred to himself as a visionary and a prophet. In those intervening two years, officials on the ground who grappled with what to do with their Jews could recall, in the absence of any firm policy directives, Hitler's vision of extermination.[32]

Underpinning all of these aspects of the functionalist thesis was an interpretation of the relationship between centre and periphery in the Third Reich, which has become absolutely key to understanding the 'Final Solution'. Whether interpreting this as a sign of weakness or otherwise, it seemed clear to functionalists that the most radical policy emerged on the periphery and not at the centre. Hitler's statements on the issues were, while apocalyptic, vague. And there exists little documentary trail to suggest that radical policy measures were born in Berlin. Although it is a slightly misleading example, the transport from Berlin to Riga at the end of November 1941 can serve as an illustration of this. Those Jews were murdered, it turned out, against the wishes of the central (and indeed highest) authorities in Berlin. There were no further murders of Jews from Central Europe until March 1942, and it was made clear to officials that such oversights should not occur again.[33] But the fact remains that the most radical means for dealing with German Jews was from November 1941 mass murder, and that was adopted as policy a few months later. The genie could not be put back in the bottle.

Functionalism offered compelling insights, but there are some uncomfortable and objective problems with the functionalist thesis. At times, partly because it adopted the language of social science, its writing has certainly lacked linguistic clarity (note Martin Broszat's reference to 'semantic rules for the accomplishment of real ideological objectives' quoted above). Such linguistic indulgence is indicative of a methodological complexity which may actually defy understanding altogether. The idea that the *structure* of Nazi rule was responsible for the radicalisation of policy is, in many ways, actually incomprehensible. *Men* murdered Jews during the Holocaust, but functionalism describes that using the metaphor of the *machine*. If the machinery of destruction functioned automatically, if the 'Final Solution' was an 'autonomous process' then one is entitled to ask who drove that process and what did they believe about it? It seems to me that Hans Mommsen's reply might be, to misuse Hannah Arendt, that 'they did not know what they were doing [and] ... they were able with strange consistency to suppress such knowledge as dawned upon them'.[34] Yet, it defies logic to argue that some of the murderers who looked their victims in the eyes before they shot them either did not know what they were doing or that they were able to suppress knowledge of their actions.

Perhaps therefore the most damning criticism of the function-alist school is the proximity of its arguments to those proposed by the perpetrators themselves. We dismiss the work of David Irving as apologia when one reads the acknowledgements to *Hitler's War* which include a note of thanks to the SS ideologue Werner Best. And, one is aware that Irving moved from denying Hitler's respon-sibility for the Holocaust to denying the Holocaust altogether. Yet according to Nicolas Berg, functionalist historians themselves had a similar 'real-world nearness to the perpetrators', for example through their questioning of the self-same Best. Jan Phillip Reemstma argues that the protagonists at Nuremberg relied on what were essentially functionalist arguments, such as Julius Streicher's claim that the language of annihilation was only figu-rative and functional and should not be interpreted literally in the light of the death camps.[35] As Michael Thad Allen has argued in relation to the 'practice of extermination through work', those involved consistently argued that their use of slaves in ultimately murderous conditions was un-ideological.[36] Similarly Adolf Eichmann's claimed psychological disengagement with the reality of his actions – a key part of the defence he offered at his trial – is very close to the suppression of knowledge described by Hans Mommsen.

This is not to say that functionalism is simply apologia in the same way that the work of David Irving is, although it may amount to a form of evasion. As Nicolas Berg points out however, and as we saw in Chapter 2, functionalism emerged in part as a reaction against (and of course in part as an element of) the trials of the 1950s and 1960s and their insistence on *personal* responsi-bility. It is therefore unsurprising that some functionalist arguments look like those of defendants who were precisely trying to argue against their own personal responsibility.[37] The idea of personal, and even legal, responsibility was, of course, at the very heart of the intentionalist alternative to the functionalist thesis.

Intentionalism and the 'Final Solution'

Eberhard Jäckel eloquently summarised the dilemma that inten-tionalist historians saw in the functionalist arguments: 'We must not ask simply whether Hitler ordered the Holocaust but whether the Holocaust was *improvised or premeditated*' (emphasis added).[38] His adoption of legalese was deliberate and recalled the origins of the intentionalist case – after all if the Holocaust were not premeditated then responsibility for it became much harder to determine. In a similar vein Israeli scholar Yehuda Bauer conceded that structural analyses might be able to illuminate (in general terms) how modern states and societies functioned, but he argued they ultimately might obscure the perpetrators of the Holocaust and the 'initiative' they showed when 'carrying out the most dev-ilish deeds'.[39] For intentionalists this was a crime committed by legally and morally responsible individuals.

Such concern for the initiative, the premeditation and thus responsibility of the perpetrators is reflected in the specific methodology of intentionalism. Intentionalist readings of the 'Final Solution' have often been contained within essentially biographical studies, or at least have viewed the decision making process through the prism of an individual. Richard Breitman placed his argument that Hitler planned the destruction of Europe's Jews from March 1941 onwards in a biography of Heinrich Himmler, whom he regarded as the 'architect of genocide'.[40] Gerald Fleming's rebuttal of David Irving, and by implication Martin Broszat, was a study of Hitler's involvement in the 'Final Solution' which proceeded from the assumption that 'the line that leads' from Hitler's antisemitic beliefs as articulated first in the aftermath of the Great War 'to the liquidation orders [he] personally issued during the war ... is a direct one'.[41] Philippe Burrin's renewal of intentionalism at the end of the 1980s was contained tellingly within a study on *Hitler and the Jews*.

The *Führer* was, self-evidently, the individual most often at the centre of the intentionalist case. In terms of Hitler's fundamental decision for the 'Final Solution', although speculation over the precise date varied, intentionalist scholars invariably placed it earlier rather than later, September 1941 being the very latest.[42] All explain that decision with reference to the fixed goal of his worldview. Sarah Gordon imagined the internal conversation of a Holocaust victim who asked 'Why must I die' as a means of explanation, her answer was that 'power was totally concentrated in one man, and that man happened to hate' Jews.[43] Echoing Lucy Dawidowicz, Gordon, Eberhard Jäckel, Gerald Fleming, Leni Yahil, Helmut Krausnick all argue that the 'plan' to murder the Jews was inherent within the decision to invade the Soviet Union (which Hitler formally authorised in December 1940).[44] Yitzhak Arad similarly saw at least the extermination of Soviet Jewry as being initiated at this time.[45] Richard Breitman argued that the goal of extermination was fixed in the planning for the invasion of the Soviet Union – although its method of execution emerged over 1941.[46]

Such nuance means that it is important that we do not caricature the intentionalist thesis – although this is the title of an important intentionalist essay, its method and arguments cannot just be reduced to the formulation 'Hitler orders the Holocaust'. For the most part these scholars accepted that there was no one single moment of decision, where the 'Final Solution' was conceptualised and then ordered. Jäckel and Yahil were representative when they argued that Hitler always intended to expunge the Jews in some form, and the 'Final Solution' itself emerged incrementally as he sought to determine both the practical method of that utopian vision, and to initiate others into this 'plan'. For Jäckel the 'Final Solution' as we know it, the industrial killing of Jews potentially at the expense of the general war effort, only crystallised in Hitler's mind when he became conscious of the likelihood of defeat. To borrow a phrase from another part of the study of the Third Reich, the war against the Jews could become the 'war that Hitler won'.[47]

When prioritising the apportioning of responsibility, intentionalism was concerned with restoring human agency to the study of the past. To this end Gerald Fleming wrote deliberately of his search for 'the beast in man', as opposed to society.[48] At the same time the intentionalist method sought the literal interpretation of language, notwithstanding the Nazis' deliberate obfuscation. As Jeffrey Herf wrote in the most recent intentionalist reading, 'in his speech to the Reichstag on January 30 [1939] Hitler made his first unequivocal public threat to exterminate (that is murder) – not merely, deport, or defeat – the Jewish race in Europe'.[49] Yet again however we should be careful not to caricature intentionalism as simplistic, as opposed to the complexity and sophistication of the functionalist alternative. After all what could be more literal an interpretation than to declare that, in the absence of the document itself, there was no order for the 'Final Solution'?

Reading language literally also operates certain assumptions as to the history of the Third Reich as well as suggesting a narrative of that history. The notion of design, of intent, is at the centre of that literal interpretation. Language was *deliberately* camouflaging, while Hitler *knowingly* sought to distance himself from Jewish policy to avoid self-incrimination. Such arguments both suggest and assume a great degree of central control within the Hitler state, in contrast to the functionalists' fragmented polycracy. At the same time, the idea of a 'plan' equally suggests control rather than chaos. It implies, where functionalism saw the 'Final Solution' born from conflict; intentionalists found it the result of conspiratorial co-operation.[50]

Like functionalism, the intentionalist thesis has objective shortcomings. As observed at the beginning of the chapter, the documentary evidence records, simply through an absence, a gap between conceptualisation or intention to murder Jews, and the implementation of the murder programme – we simply do not have any account of how and why Hitlerian rhetoric became the industrial murder of the 'Final Solution'. This does not mean that there has to be a gap, but there is no evidence to suggest otherwise, beyond the existence of the rhetoric of extermination and the gas chambers themselves. Intentionalist historians *conclude* that one led directly to the other, yet this is the premise that they start out with too. As well as being self-fulfilling there is something powerfully teleological about this lack of will to explain. The end of the story, the gas chambers, explains the murderous intent of the beginning of the story, ideological antisemitism and the rhetoric of murder. The following extended quotation from Eberhard Jäckel illustrates these shortcomings:

> My conclusion that the Final Solution was ordered by Hitler is based on three arguments. First, nobody else had ever advocated systematic killing by the state as a way to solve the Jewish question. That Hitler had done so in the 1920s is not in itself proof that he acted accordingly in the 1940s. But it is a strong indication ... Second, all participants who expressed themselves on the subject testified both during and after the war that the killings were ordered by Hitler... [and] Third, given the nature of the Nazi state and its ruler, it is difficult to imagine [otherwise].[51]

The insistence on the autonomy of individuals and their agency is also problematic. We know, and we still know this despite the decline of Marxist scholarship, that individuals do not act alone. They are subject to the pressures of their societies, and the networks and communities in which they work and live. As such, in the words of Tim Mason, 'unless the whole of modern social science represents an epochal blind alley, "Hitler" *cannot* be a full or adequate explanation' (emphasis added).[52]

Interestingly however, like functionalism the primary problem with the intentionalist reading is that it is close to the account proposed by the perpetrators themselves. If functionalists have produced a thesis which reflects Nazis post-war explanations, then intentionalism offers one close to their self-image during the Third Reich. Hitler publicly revelled in his mythical role as 'prophet', witness his recalling the 1939 call to annihilation at the Berlin sportpalast in 1942 after the extermination had begun.[53] As intentionalists themselves acknowledge, Hitler had a clear conception of the purpose and the ideals of leadership, one the central tenets of the Nazi canon was that National Socialism was above the shifting horizons of democratic politics, pursuing its world historical goals with iron consistency. As such the *Führer* himself would have approved of the thesis 'Hitler orders the Holocaust', and indeed it was the thesis he himself constructed when looking back at his prophetic past.

Beyond intentionalism and functionalism?

The differences between these two interpretative schools were stark, and the pictures of the 'Final Solution' they produced very different indeed. Consider their alternative accounts of the Wannsee conference. The conference still represents the most wide-ranging primary source account we have of genocide as *policy* in the Third Reich, it is therefore perhaps the closest (in documentary terms) we can come to the administration of mass murder. Both intentionalists and functionalists seemed to take the conference seriously, and view it as important evidence in favour of their interpretations. For Hans Mommsen the fact that Heydrich speaks in the conference minutes about slave labour *and* extermination signals that the 'Final Solution' was still provisional in January 1942. The conference represents a snap-shot of a decision-making process that is still progressing at this point, highlighting the different treatments that Jews suffered in the Nazi empire. What better evidence can there be that this was not a coherent and directed undertaking than the contradictions inherent in the vision of the 'Final Solution' laid out by its putative director at the conference table?[54]

The intentionalist picture of the same conference, based on the same documentary material is almost unrecognisable. Wannsee suggests no contradictions, it is the announcement of a genocidal policy pure and simple. The central organ of that genocidal operation, the SS, is meeting with other agencies to gain their approval and improve the already iron central control over a firmly established policy.[55] Leni Yahil too sees Wannsee as the post-hoc confirmation of a policy already set in stone, as communicated by Heydrich. Talk of slave labour suggests no contradiction – it is simply camouflage for a murder and extermination the programme which began immediately the conference ended.[56]

Yet despite the apparent gulf between these interpretations, there were points of consensus, which Christopher Browning highlighted in his efforts to find a middle way between them, a 'moderate functionalist' interpretation of the 'Final Solution'. Browning began this search for common ground in the mid-1980s, and to an extent it continues today. Before briefly summarising Browning's developing thesis, I shall explore the points of consensus he found between apparently opposing schools of thought.

Whether Hitler was weak and unable to grasp control of the 'Final Solution', or he was the inspiration and guiding hand of the entire project, neither interpretation found Hitler marginal to the destruction of the European Jews. Both Martin Broszat and Gerald Fleming, whose interpretations represent polar opposites, found Hitler lurking in the shadows of the 'Final Solution', if not connected to its minutiae then the unquestionable inspiration for destruction. Neither Broszat nor Fleming would have dissented from the simple aphorism – No Hitler, No Holocaust. Both schools also agree on the importance of war as the radicalising agent in the Nazi state. Disagreements as to the nature of that radicalisation are profound – ranging from those that saw a centrally directed race war with the 'Final Solution' always planned to be at its heart; to the argument that the 'Final Solution' was an opportunistic strike against the Jews as the Third Reich was at its most powerful seized with the euphoria of a prospective National Socialist Europe in which there could be no Jews;[57] or even a Third

Reich facing the despair and desolation of military defeat which turned upon its eternal enemy the Jew in a final apocalypse.[58] However the central idea that one could not entirely separate the 'war against the Jews' from the military conflict was uniformly accepted.

Both interpretative camps sought to concede ground to the other too. After the functionalist critique, even the most intentionalist of scholars could no longer argue that there had been a single decision which brought the 'Final Solution' into being. Fleming, Yahil, Jäckel and Breitman all recognised that there was a decision-making process around the 'Final Solution' stretching from the plans to invade the Soviet Union to the Wannsee conference and, especially for Yahil, beyond. While intentionalists see that process as having been centrally directed, Broszat *et al.* were able to give much more priority to the influence of the periphery and thus the emergence of murderous policies on the ground. These scholars, although pointing to the antisemitic consensus surrounding Nazis, also conceded that the system was beset by conflict. And despite the emphasis on ideology and individual responsibilities, intentionalist scholars could not entirely avoid the language with which functionalists had successfully characterised the 'Final Solution'. Witness Yitzhak Arad's references to the 'delineation of functions [within the] machinery of destruction for the extermination of Lithuanian Jewry'.[59]

Both approaches seemed to have the same essential short-coming too: because they represent attempts at complete explanations neither could fully account for the internal contradictions of the 'Final Solution'. Both showed similar discomfort when dealing with the issue of Jewish slave labour for example. As we have seen the fact that the armed forces, industry and the SS itself continued to exploit Jews as slaves in the midst of the campaign for extermination confirmed for many functionalists that the 'Final Solution' could not be explained by ideological will alone. Yet the murderous conditions in which slaves were kept and employed can be explained by little else but primacy of ideology.[60] Yet for intentionalists the enduring presence of Jewish workers, and indeed the vociferous arguments voiced by many within the Nazi state in favour of retaining Jewish slaves in the war economy, hardly accorded to an ideological 'Final Solution' pursued with murderous efficiency from the centre. To account for this, Leni Yahil, like other intentionalist scholars, employed what she called the 'doctrine' of 'extermination through labour', whereby slave labour was explained as another method of murder to account for this apparent gap.[61]

Christopher Browning's attempt to steer a middle course was therefore, at least in the explanation of the origins of the 'Final Solution', made in the awareness that neither of the extant alternatives offered a logically coherent account. Browning's moderate functionalism was worked out in a series of essays, beginning with a reply to Martin Broszat in which he argued that Hitler had sought a plan for a 'Final Solution' to the Jewish Question in July 1941, as suggested by Göring's authorisation to Heydrich at the end of that month.[62] Prefiguring Yahil's thesis of a year-long process of decision-making, Browning then saw the Nazi state progress incrementally towards the 'Final Solution' through a series of key decisions – such as that to deport German Jews in September 1941.[63] Although Browning does concede that policy emerges piecemeal, with for example local improvisations over ghettoisation, this was a process that was often triggered by impulses from the centre, not least the decisions to deport more Jews further East. Browning's synthesis also accepted the inherent murderousness of plans for the invasion of the Soviet Union – but argued that any decisions taken in this context applied only to Soviet Jews. By July when the murder of all Soviet Jews by the *Einsatzgruppen* was underway, a general 'Final Solution' was sought. The movement of Euthanasia personnel into the General Government in October 1941 demonstrated that the planning process had come to an end and that the murder of Jews in lethal gas chambers had become the 'Final Solution' requested in July. From that point on the programme underwent only technical refinement.

By attempting synthesis Browning suggested, perfectly reasonably, that neither intentionalism nor functionalism captured the essence of the Nazi state. The state was polycratic, policy did develop on the periphery; but it was also a state defined by an ideological centre which sought control over key policies. The 'Final Solution' as the leitmotif of the Third Reich was one of these. As well as attempting synthesis, in looking at the movement of personnel Browning also slightly extended the documentary basis of this debate. But ultimately he was still unable to overcome the absence of definitive answers. Browning's language remained provisional. One of his first articles on the subject declared (without irony) 'my conclusion is ... Hitler ordered, or to be more precise, incited or solicited, the preparation of an extermination plan'.[64] And Browning's efforts to link Hitler to the 'Final Solution' are ultimately speculative too. For what Hitler was thinking he argues, look at what Himmler was doing.[65]

The modernity and or uniqueness of the 'Final Solution'

Ultimately I suspect Browning's attempt to achieve consensus over when the decision for the 'Final Solution' occurred was fruitless because this was always a debate about the origins of genocide in its broadest sense. The dating of a 'Final Solution' order was a way into a much wider question of the meaning of the Holocaust and its location (or otherwise) in the broader sweep of modern history. Intentionalists saw the 'Final Solution' as a hangover from a more barbaric past. Note this characterisation of Himmler the 'architect of genocide' – 'Himmler's mind was ... not a twentieth century mind. His character was feudalistic, Machiavellian, evil.'[66] As a consequence intentionalists often explained the 'Final Solution' as the opposite of the defining features of the twentieth century. If human history after the Enlightenment had been defined by reason, then the 'Final Solution' went against the grain, it was an example of utter *irrationality*.[67]

An irrational 'Final Solution' was the consequence of an ideology, which predominated even when threatening the objective needs of the state. Hence the diversion of resources from the actual war to the (ideological and in many ways imaginary and irrational) war against the Jews. Such ideas also fed into claims as to its uniqueness. If the Holocaust could only be explained with reference to the particular and incomparable ideology of Nazism, an ideology which uniquely required a people, the Jews, expunged from the face of the earth then it was, as it were, *sui generis*. As Leni Yahil explained 'this cataclysm stands out among the revolutionary events of the twentieth century as a focal phenomenon from both the broad human and the specifically Jewish point of view.'[68] The uniqueness claim also had a very specific present-day political context – in that it was first articulated after the crises faced by the state of Israel from the mid-1960s onwards.[69] As such it also had a political purpose to alert the world to the unique dangers of an *enduring* antisemitism.[70] It is no coincidence that intentionalism is enjoying something of a renaissance in the early twenty-first century in which existential threats to Jews and the state of Israel seem to pervade.

Such an emphasis on barbarism also impacted the images of the Holocaust conjured by intentionalist historians. These accounts were much more likely, perhaps self-evidently, to focus on the profound violence at the heart of the 'Final Solution'. After all many found the *Einsatzgruppen* massacres to be its first manifestation as policy, rather than the first moves to industrial murder in the death camps of Operation Reinhard. Daniel Goldhagen's *Hitler's Willing Executioners*, first published in 1996, represents the apogee of this tendency and indeed his book was criticised for, in its graphic descriptions of violence, peddling the 'pornography of horror'.[71]

Functionalism proposed an entirely different picture of the 'Final Solution', often concentrating for its imagery on the production lines of the 'death factories' which defined the 'machinery of destruction'. Such imagery proposed an alternative prescription of the relationship between the Holocaust and the twentieth century, which also had profound political implications. Instead of seeing the 'Final Solution' as an aberration, the inverse of rational modernity, functionalism was much more likely to view it, in the Arendtian tradition, as its consequence.[72]

Zygmunt Bauman's *Modernity and the Holocaust*, published in 1989, represents the most developed thesis in this area. While Bauman is a sociologist the argument he proposed was forged in the wake of both functionalist historiography and acted as a further critique of intentionalism. That critique attempted to reclaim the Holocaust from the exclusive ethnic ownership implied in the uniqueness argument, suggesting that while a 'Jewish tragedy' it was not 'just a Jewish problem'. The Holocaust was not *just* a 'Jewish problem' precisely because it was not just the consequence of antisemitism, not just the consequence of impulses evident in the Third Reich. In fact the Holocaust was also shaped by, and prosecuted using, 'the powerful instruments of rational and effective action that modern development itself brought into being'. Far from an aberration, for Bauman, the 'Holocaust is the *truth* of modernity'.[73]

Bauman's thesis rested on two key observations. First that the 'Final Solution' required the defining features of modern state and society in its carrying out. It relied on state power, and on the mechanisms of state bureaucracy. Those mechanisms were uniquely able to ensure the smooth functioning of the 'Final Solution' because, reliant on the division of labour, they were able to protect individuals from the murderous reality of their tasks. The modern state had not eliminated violence, far from it, but it was a mechanism for keeping violence from sight even from its perpetrators. Indeed the gas chambers at Auschwitz may have been the ultimate example of this. 'Rage and fury' Bauman wrote, are 'pitiably primitive and inefficient as tools of mass annihilation'. Of course such an argument borrowed much from Hannah Arendt. Second, and this was to attempt to meet the intentionalist argument head on, Bauman pointed to the inherent modernity of Nazi ideology, despite the widespread assumption that Nazism had set itself against the modern world, in for example its rejection of the ideals of the French Revolution. Technology obsessed, Nazism undertook (through the 'Final Solution') a grand social engineering project which attempted to recast society in its own image, an image based on the (albeit spurious) science of racial hygiene.[74]

Bauman's thesis demonstrated clearly the powerful political implications of functionalist historiography. Remember for example the tendency of intentionalist historians to find the modern state of Israel as the antidote to the Holocaust. Nora Levin made such a connection explicitly in her book published at the end of the 1960s and Leni Yahil did the same in her history of the Holocaust published at the end of the 1980s.[75] Bauman's sociological exploration of the implications of functionalism, which concluded that the Holocaust reveals the crisis and the murderous potential of modernity itself (not its discontents as it were), was necessarily profoundly troubling for such a position. Bauman suggested to the citizens (and scholars) of the modern West that the darkness revealed by the Holocaust was not a darkness alien to our own worlds, but *of* our world. The Holocaust was not a poison for which modernity had the antidote, but a mirror in which we should really see ourselves.

The Holocaust as product

Bauman's modernity thesis reflected a general tendency, born of functionalism, that the Holocaust could be seen as the product of larger, more profound historical forces. In such a formulation it was self-evidently regarded as a mistake simply to explain the origins of the Holocaust with reference to ideological anti-semitism.

Some scholars simply sought to place that ideology in a wider context. As part of his attempt to avoid over ethnic identification with the Holocaust, Arno Mayer argued that anti-communism was actually the central ideological urge of the Nazi regime and that Jews were literally the victims of the war against the Soviet Union. The 'Final Solution' was a consequence of the failure to win that war and the 'incipient debacle' of the Third Reich.[76] Henry Friedlander asked that we see the Holocaust a consequence of the T4 Euthanasia Programme against the mentally and physically handicapped in Germany. The murder of the unfit had demonstrated the limits and the extent of what was possible to the Nazi regime, both in terms of the willingness or otherwise of the general population to acquiesce in a programme of killing and in their technical capability of enacting mass murder.[77] Others have suggested that the Euthanasia Programme came from the same ideological impulse as the 'Final Solution', as a primarily defensive economic measure aimed at freeing the economy from the burden of 'useless eaters'.[78]

The idea that the Holocaust was the consequence of economic thinking was perhaps the most provocative. That the 'Final Solution' was objectively irrational, driven either by an irrational ideology or an automatic bureaucracy, was broadly accepted by most scholars. Even functionalists who argued that it depended on rational procedures and organisation for its implementation agreed that ultimately, in the context of war, the programme represented an irrational nonsense. But Götz Aly and Susanne Heim argued quite differently: not only was the Holocaust the product of the modern state – it was also the consequence of a rational vision of economic modernisation. Alarmingly, they suggested, it was the product of fundamentally familiar, utilitarian, thinking.

Aly and Heim argued that the 'Final Solution' was part of a much broader vision for the reorganisation and (and this is a key phrase in understanding the intellectual heritage of their arguments) the *modernisation* of the Eastern European economy. What is more they suggested that these economic plans had been worked out not by the ideologues at the helm of the Nazi movement but by a cabal of functionaries and civil servants, removed from the centre of political power who they termed the 'planning intelligentsia'. Although Aly and Heim placed themselves within the functionalist school, there was a role for ideological antisemitism in their narrative of the genesis of the 'Final Solution' too.

Nazi racial thinking expanded immeasurably the limits within which the economic planners could explore solutions. When Dr Fritz Arlt (head of the Department of Population Management and Welfare in the General Government) recommended the removal of the Jewish commercial class from the economy in order to stimulate urbanisation of the Polish peasantry in 1940, he anticipated the murderousness of his Nazi masters. Antisemitism was the means here to the ends of economic change. 'The policy of mass murder was not primarily motivated by racist or terrorist ideology, but was an instrument designed to speed up the industrialisation and the agrarian rationalisation of the General Government as an "emerging country".'[79]

The authors themselves recognised the limits of their thesis. While arguing that the apparently irrational and frenzied attack on Hungarian Jewry, commonly regarded as having been the death throes of the contracting Nazi regime, was in fact an attempt to solve problems of German food supply, they state candidly 'we cannot adduce any proof for our alternative hypothesis'.[80] Indeed they offer very little evidence for the actual impact of the planners they studied on policy decisions. Yet like Bauman they posed a singularly difficult question for scholars and citizens of the modern West: is there an inherent genocidal potential in the modern practice of 'structural, planning and development policy'?[81]

Like their functionalist forebears, those who sought to link the Holocaust and modernity relied on a vocabulary which conjured the images of the modern world. Metaphors of the machine, of the factory, were common. All such rhetoric reflected a very specific construction of a *clean* modernity where reason and rationality have triumphed, and banished the blood and the guts of barbarism. Perhaps however, such scholars have again accepted the Nazi characterisation of the 'Final Solution' – that it was based on the triumph of hygiene, that its perpetration was ultimately a refined industrial process. Indeed, the rhetoric with which Bauman *et al.* expressed their arguments was in some ways borrowed from the Nazi lexicon, the idea of 'cleansing' territories of Jews.[82] But such vocabulary conceals, ultimately, a lie.

First, not all the victims of the Holocaust were processed through the crematoria of Birkenau or Treblinka. Were those that lay face down in a pit which contained their dead and dying families before being shot in the back of the neck like the 33,000 victims of Babi Yar, really the victims of a genocide which bore the hallmarks of a peaceful, clean and rational modernity? Or were they the victims of a bestial, bloody and disgusting hatred? Second, while it is possible to describe the death camps as places of smooth, factory-like operations – the victims disembarked the train which had arrived (on time) at the camp at Birkenau, before being processed and led to their deaths, a death that was administered through the application of poison gas – does this really capture the reality of a place that one of its own medical staff described as the 'arsehole of the world'?[83] Does it really capture the reality of a death in which the corpses commonly ended piled in a human pyramid? Corpses which had to be wrenched apart, before the gold was extracted from their bleeding mouths, and which were cremated in ovens or just in large pits dug in the ground by their co-religionists? Meanwhile the chamber in which death had been administered had to be cleaned of the blood and excrement that the dead had expelled.

Clearly the Holocaust was neither a reflection of either just modernity, or just primal barbarism. It was a variegated and varied process, to which both models applied – sometimes, as the above description suggests, in the same place and at the same time. Nazism was obsessed with modernity and modernisation, yet it was also an attack on the values and achievements of modernity. These contradictions cannot be explained away by claims to have discovered its essence. As such neither the intentionalist nor the functionalist model was (to borrow their vocabulary) a total or sufficient explanation. Yet both were necessary.[84]

Conclusion

The 'intentionalist' 'functionalist' controversy developed the two Holocaust metanarratives that were established during the 1960s. Both perspectives suggested that the Holocaust was singularly explicable – the result of either ideological intention or peculiar bureaucratic structure. This debate became narrowly focused on the idea of when the 'decision' for the 'Final Solution' was taken. But this is no narrow historiographical controversy. Albeit conducted between broadly liberal scholars, the disagreements are profound and concern both approaches to History as a discipline and crucially where to situate the 'Final Solution' in the broader sweep of history. Ironically it would be seismic shifts in that broader sweep of history, with the collapse of communist rule in Eastern Europe, which would challenge and indeed develop the insights of both these approaches. It is to the scholarship of the post-Cold War world that this book now turns.

Notes

1 Hans Mommsen, 'The Realisation of the Unthinkable', Michael Marrus (ed.), *The Nazi Holocaust Vol. 3* (London, 1989), p. 224.
2 *Ibid.*, p. 236.
3 *Ibid.*, p. 250.
4 Michael Thad Allen, 'Not Just a "Dating Game": Origins of the Holocaust at Auschwitz in the Light of Eyewitness Testimony', *German History* (Vol. 25, No. 2, 2007), p. 162.
5 Saul Friedlander, 'From Anti-Semitism to Extermination: A Historiographical Study of Nazi Policies Towards the Jews: An Essay in Interpretation', *Yad Vashem Studies* (Vol. 16, 1984), p. 16.
6 Philippe Burrin referred to 'great gaps in the documentation' in his *Hitler and the Jews: The Genesis of the Holocaust* (London, 1994), p. 20.
7 Although it is overwhelmingly unlikely such a document ever existed, the nature of the Euthanasia order offers some insight into the manner in which the 'Final Solution' might have developed as policy. The order was post-dated, legally confirming the murderous enterprise that had been underway for some months.
8 Martin Broszat, 'Hitler and the Genesis of the Final Solution: A Reply to David Irving', *Yad Vashem Studies* (Vol. 13, 1979), p. 98.
9 David Cesarani, *Eichmann: His Life and Crimes* (London, 2005), p. 115.
10 Götz Aly, *Final Solution: Nazi Population Policy and the Murder of the European Jews* (London, 1999), p. 3.
11 Mark Roseman, *The Villa, the Lake, the Meeting: Wannsee and the Final Solution* (London, 2002), p. 35.

12 Richard Breitman, *The Architect of Genocide: Himmler and the Final Solution* (London, 1991), p. 156.
13 Bogdan Musial, 'The Origins of Operation Reinhard: The Decision Making Process for the Mass Murder of the Jews in the General Government', *Yad Vashem Studies* (Vol. 28, 2000), pp. 113–53 reprinted in David Cesarani (ed.), *The Holocaust: Critical Concepts in Historical Studies* (London, 2004), p. 183.
14 Eberhard Jäckel, 'Hitler Orders the Holocaust', Marrus, *The Nazi Holocaust*, p. 61.
15 Robert Jan van Pelt and Deborah Dwork, *Auschwitz 1270 to the Present* (New Haven, 1996), pp. 279–80.
16 Cesarani, *Eichmann*, pp. 98–105.
17 Christopher Browning, 'The Decision for the Final Solution', *Fateful Months: Essays on the Emergence of the Final Solution* (New York, 1985), p. 8.
18 Jäckel, 'Hitler Orders the Holocaust', p. 66.
19 Van Pelt and Dwork, *Auschwitz*, p. 280.
20 Peter Longerich, 'The Wannsee Conference in the Development of the Final Solution', in Cesarani (ed.), *The Holocaust*, p. 142 – originally published as *HET Research Papers*, 1:2, 1999–2000.
21 Yitzhak Arad, 'Alfred Rosenberg and the Final Solution in the Occupied Soviet Territories', *Yad Vashem Studies* (Vol. 13, 1979), p. 285.
22 David Irving, *Hitler's War* (London, 1977), p. xiv.
23 *Ibid.*, p. 332.
24 *Ibid.*, p. xiv.
25 Christopher Browning (with Jürgen Matthäus), *The Origins of the Final Solution: The Evolution of Nazi Jewish Policy September 1939–March 1942* (Lincoln: NE, 2004), p. 396.
26 Charles Gray, *The Irving Judgement* (London, 2001), paras 13.101, 13.106, 13.51.
27 The origins of functionalism are discussed in Chapter 2.
28 All quotations taken from Broszat, 'Hitler and the Genesis of the Final Solution', pp. 73–115.
29 Mommsen, 'Realisation of the Unthinkable', pp. 240–7.
30 For a discussion of the Mommsen thesis and its location in the historiography see Ian Kershaw, *The Nazi Dictatorship: Problems and Perspectives of Interpretation,* 4th edn (London, 2000), pp. 69–92.
31 Mommsen, 'Realisation of the Unthinkable', pp. 251.
32 See Hans Mommsen, 'Hitler's Reichstag Speech of 30 January 1939', *History and Memory* (Vol. 9, Nos 1–2, 1997), pp. 142–61.
33 Donald Bloxham, *The Final Solution: A Genocide* (Oxford, 2009), p. 215.
34 Mommsen, 'Realisation of the Unthinkable', p. 225.
35 Cited in Nicolas Berg, *The Invention of "Functionalism": Josef Wulf, Martin Broszat and the Institute for Contemporary History (Munich) in the 1960s* (Jerusalem, 2003), p. 10.
36 Michael Thad Allen, 'The Banality of Evil Reconsidered: SS Mid-Level Managers of Extermination Through Work', *Central European History* (Vol. 30, no. 2, 1998), p. 258.
37 Berg, *Invention of Functionalism*, p. 34.

38 Ebprhard Jäckel, 'Hitler Orders the Holocaust', *Hitler's Weltanschauung* (Middletown: CT, 1972), p. 54.
39 Yehuda Bauer, 'Trends in Holocaust Research', *Yad Vashem Studies* (Vol. 12, 1977), pp. 11, 19.
40 See Breitman, *The Architect of Genocide*, p. 156.
41 Gerald Fleming, *Hitler and the Final Solution* (London, 1985), p. 2.
42 See Hans Günther Adler, *Der verwaltete Mensch. Studien zur Deportation der Juden aus Deutschland* (Tübingen, 1974); Burrin, *Hitler and the Jews.*
43 Sarah Gordon, *Hitler, Germans and the Jewish Question* (New Jersey, 1984), p. 316.
44 See for example Jäckel, 'Hitler Orders the Holocaust'; Gordon, *Hitler, Germans and the Jewish Question*, p. 127; Leni Yahil, *The Holocaust: The Fate of European Jewry* (Oxford, 1990), p. 253; Fleming, *Hitler and the Final Solution*, p. 66; Helmut Krausnick and Hans Heinrich Wilhelm, *Die Truppe des Weltanschuungskrieges: Die Einsatzgruppen der Sicherheitspolizei und des SD 1938–1942* (Stuttgart, 1981), pp. 162–3, this reference is taken from Browning, *Origins of the Final Solution*, p. 491.
45 Yitzhak Arad, *Belzec, Sobibor, Treblinka: The Operation Reinhard Death Camps* (Bloomington: IN, 1999), p. 3.
46 Breitman, *The Architect of Genocide*, p. 32.
47 Robert Herzstein, *The War that Hitler Won: The Most Infamous Propaganda Campaign in History* (London, 1979).
48 Fleming, *Hitler and the Final Solution*, p. xxxvi9
49 Jeffrey Herf, *The Jewish Enemy: Nazi Propaganda During World War II and the Holocaust* (Cambridge: MA, 2006), p. 5.
50 For example Arad, *Belzec, Sobibor, Treblinka*, pp. 18–19.
51 Jäckel, 'Hitler Orders the Holocaust', p. 66.
52 Mason, 'Intention and Explanation', p. 219.
53 Ian Kershaw, *Hitler: Nemesis 1936–1945* (London, 2000), pp. 459–95.
54 Mommsen, 'Realisation of the Unthinkable', p. 248.
55 Bretiman, *Architect of Genocide*, p. 229.
56 Yahil, *The Holocaust*, p. 318.
57 Browning, 'Beyond "Intentionalism" and "Functionalism"', p. 121
58 Broszat, 'The Genesis of the Final Solution', p. 162.
59 Yitzhak Arad, 'The Final Solution in Lithuania in the Light of German Documentation', *Yad Vashem Studies* (Vol. 12, 1976), p. 238.
60 Ulrich Herbert, 'Labour and Extermination: Economic Interest and the Primacy Weltanschauung in National Socialism', *Past and Present* (Vol. 138, No. 1, 1993), pp. 144–95.
61 Yahil, *The Holocaust*, p. 385.
62 Christopher Browning, 'A Reply to Martin Broszat Regarding the Origins of the Final Solution', Marrus, *The Nazi Holocaust*, p. 169.
63 Yahil, *The Holocaust*, pp. 319–20.
64 Browning, 'A Reply to Martin Broszat', p. 169.
65 Christopher Browning, 'Beyond Intentionalism and Functionalism: The Decision for the Final Solution Reconsidered', *The Path to Genocide* (Cambridge, 1992), p. 121.
66 Breitman, *Architect of Genocide*, p. 6.
67 See for example Jacob Robinson, 'The Holocaust', Yisrael Gutman and Livia

Rothkirchen (eds), *The Catastrophe of European Jewry: Antecedents – History – Reflections* (Jerusalem, 1976), p. 252.

68 Yahil, *The Holocaust*, p. 3.

69 Gavriel D. Rosenfeld, 'The Politics of Uniqueness: Reflections on the Recent Polemical Turn in Holocaust and Genocide Scholarship', *Holocaust and Genocide Studies* (Vol. 13, No. 1, 1999), p. 35.

70 The idea of uniqueness also sparked a noisy, often polemical debate about the merits of comparing genocides. Ultimately this debate became extremely polarised and unhelpful. Those scholars who claimed the Holocaust to be unique often accused those who sought comparison of relativising Jewish suffering in order to either downplay its significance or worse still obscure it altogether. They were faced by other scholars who in turn accused those who wanted to find the Holocaust unique of downplaying or indeed denying the suffering of other peoples by refusing comparison in order to protect Jewish power in the present. See Alan S. Rosenbaum (ed.), *Is the Holocaust Unique? Perspectives on Comparative Genocide* (Philadelphia, 2009) for a number of essays from each position. Ultimately this debate shed little light on the Holocaust, and is as such not surveyed at any length here.

71 Y. Michal Bodemann, 'Pornography of Horror?', *The New York Review of Books* (Vol. 44, No. 6, 1997).

72 This is not to say that functionalists recognised no irrationality in the 'Final Solution'. The argument that the process became an end in itself pointed to a nihilism that was at least ultimately irrational. However functionalism in its emphasis on structure at least allowed the possibility that the 'Final Solution' was a consequence of rationality. See Mason, 'Intention and Explanation', p. 216.

73 Zygmunt Bauman, *Modernity and the Holocaust* (Cambridge, 1989), pp. x, xiv, 6.

74 These arguments are found throughout but the specific quotation is from Bauman, *Modernity and the Holocaust*, p. 90. Bauman does not have the field all to himself here, but his is the most enduring argument. See also Wolfgang Sofsky, *The Order of Terror: The Concentration Camp* (New Jersey, 1997). Jeffrey Herf also offers a different and intentionalist version of Nazism's relationship with modernity, which he describes as 'reactionary modernism' arguing that Nazi modernism was irrational and backward looking and as such offered a different prescription of modernity to the modern west. See Jeffrey Herf, *Reactionary Modernism: Technology, Culture and Politics in Weimar and the Third Reich* (Cambridge, 1986), pp. 189–216.

75 Yahil, *The Holocaust*, p. 11.

76 Arno J. Mayer, *Why did the Heavens not Darken? The Final Solution in History* (London, 1990), p. 279.

77 See Henry Friedlander, *The Origins of Nazi Genocide: From Euthanasia to the Final Solution* (Chapel Hill: NC, 1995), p. xiii. Friedlander argues that the Euthanasia programme served as a model for all Nazi killing operations thereafter.

78 See Michael Burleigh, *Death and Deliverance: "Euthanasia" in Germany 1900–1945* (Cambridge, 1994) which throughout highlights the unique combination of economic and racial thinking that underpinned the premeditated Euthanasia campaign in the Third Reich.

79 Götz Aly and Susanne Heim, *Architects of Annihilation: Auschwitz and the Logic of Destruction* (London, 2002), p. 184.
80 *Ibid.*, p. 251.
81 *Ibid.*, p. 295.
82 Bauman, *Modernity and the Holocaust*, p. 106.
83 From the diary of SS Dr Kremer, Ernst Klee, Willi Dressen and Volker Reiss (eds), *"The Good Old Days": The Holocaust as Seen by its Perpetrators and Bystanders* (New York, 1991), p. 259.
84 This is an argument also put forward by Michael Thad Allen in 'Modernity, the Holocaust and Machines Without History', *Technologies of Power: History, Authenticity, Knowledge and Machines* (Cambridge: MA, 2001), pp. 175–214.

5

'National Socialist Extermination Policies': the end of the Cold War and the breakdown of Holocaust metanarratives

When the communist bloc disintegrated from the end of the 1980s, *everything* changed. The American sociologist Francis Fukyama claimed at the time that the collapse of the Berlin Wall represented the 'end of history', the triumph of liberal capitalism.[1] It appears now that Fukyama was very wrong. The certainties of life in a bipolar Cold War world disappeared at the end of the 1980s, something to which the confusion of our current times are a continuing testament. But Fukyama was not just wrong about the present and future. What 1989 and the progressive dismantling of communist Europe changed more than anything, was the past.

Across continental Europe the contexts in which recent history had been understood were transformed. In the Baltic states, in Hungary, Romania and (what was to become) the former Yugoslavia, the roles ascribed to long since dead leaders were almost immediately revolutionised. Men like the Croatian Ante Pavelic, who in the previous half-century had been decried as murderous fascist collaborators removed by the liberating communists, were suddenly rehabilitated as nationalist heroes. And it was not just in public History that the past was transformed, academic narratives were also revolutionised, none more so than accounts of the 'Final Solution' and the Holocaust. During the 1990s a group of younger German scholars working in the archives of the former communist bloc challenged the metanarratives which had dominated the study of the Holocaust since the 1960s. The theses of intentionalists and functionalists could not always bear the weight of detailed archival scrutiny, and as such these 'total' or 'global' explanations of the Holocaust began to break down. These historians produced a number of *local* studies of *National*

Socialist Extermination Policies, which suggested that local contexts were as important in the study of the 'Final Solution' as the central directors of the Nazi regime. This chapter analyses this new historiography.

However, the nature of these changes in the study of the Holocaust raise peculiar problems for a book which proceeds from the assumption that historiography is as much shaped by the present as the past. 1989 did not transform the 'Final Solution' because Marxist-Leninist interpretations were discredited – after all a convincing Marxist interpretation of the Holocaust has never really been produced and the field has been dominated by broadly 'liberal' theses.[2] Instead, the discovery of large numbers of new *documents* produced new perspectives on the history of the 'Final Solution'. The new historiography was constructed using the documents unearthed in the liberalisation of the archives of the former Soviet Union. As such, when thinking about the emergence of the 'Final Solution' as policy, it has ultimately been the documents (or their absence) that have set the limits of interpretation.

But this does not mean that I am suddenly trying to construct an argument in favour of positivism. The end of the Cold War has transformed the political limits of Holocaust historiography too, especially in the countries of the former Soviet bloc. One of the features of Holocaust History since 1989 has been the (re)discovery of indigenous involvement in what was previously believed to be the Nazi persecution and murder of Jews. Such developments are unthinkable without a transformation in the political contexts in which histories of the Holocaust have both been written and perhaps more importantly read. As a consequence this chapter continues the analysis of Holocaust History as a conversation between past and present – arguing that both have had a determining influence on the Holocaust histories produced.

Yet the way historians engage with documents is a central concern in this chapter. It begins with a brief narrative of the transformation of the archival base for Holocaust historiography since the collapse of the Soviet Union. I then chart the impact of this new material and the regional variation and diversity of the 'Final Solution' that have been revealed. This emphasis on regionalisation has highlighted the diversity of perpetrators too and has, in the absence of overarching communist memories of the past since the collapse of the Soviet bloc, allowed renewed focus on the relationship between non-Germans and the genocide which was after all carried out mainly outside of Germany. These histories of 'national Holocausts' are the subject of the penultimate section of the chapter. I conclude with some thoughts on the implications of this historiography for the Holocaust metanarratives reviewed in previous chapters, and more generally on the role of historical evidence or documents in modern Holocaust historiography.

The new documents of destruction

The liberalisation of the Soviet Union also led to a liberalisation of its archival holdings, as the knee-jerk secrecy of the communist regime began to fade away. This brought to light a profusion of Holocaust-related documents. In 1991 the so-called 'Death Books' from Auschwitz-Birkenau, presumably seized during the liberation of the camp, were returned to the Auschwitz museum on the site of the former concentration camp, detailing the names of some 69,000 victims.[3] But these were just one, albeit the most iconic, of the documentary discoveries. Much more significantly in February 1990 a Russian journalist reported the existence of an entire 'special archive' (Osobyi) in Moscow which contained records seized from Nazi-controlled Eastern Europe.[4] These records became available to researchers in 1991/92.

The existence of the special archive brought to light documents which had long been considered lost. The original photoplates of Goebbels' diaries and Heinrich Himmler's appointments diary for 1941 were among some of the records relating to individuals.[5] On an institutional scale, records captured from the RSHA, from the Construction Directorate at Auschwitz-Birkenau, IG Farben, the Gestapo, as well as the occupation authorities throughout Nazi-occupied Europe, all suggested that new information relating to the 'Final Solution' would be unearthed.[6]

While the documents have spawned new perspectives on the debates over the genesis of the 'Final Solution', on the decision making process, what they did not contain was a 'smoking gun'. If scholars had thought they might discover a precise order for the beginning of the 'Final Solution' then they were disappointed. It became increasingly clear in the light of such documentation that such a directive probably never existed. What the new documents have allowed, along with those held in the archives of other former communist countries or in the Baltic nations liberated from the Soviet Union, is a much more developed sense of the relationship between the satellite agencies of the Third Reich and its central authorities, and thus a much more precise picture of occupation regimes.

It is not just the documents found in the archives of the former Soviet bloc that have impacted the study of the Holocaust. The passing of time has meant that more and more Western records have been released too. In the British case the transcripts of intelligence decrypts have been made available to researchers. These are the reports made, using the Enigma code-breaking machine, of communications sent from occupation areas back to the central authorities in Berlin. Not only have these changed the understanding of what the West knew about the Nazi genocide, they also revealed new perspectives on the genocide itself, not least the extensive involvement of the Order Police in the prosecution of the 'Final Solution'.[7] As a whole the new documents discovered in the 1990s have tended to reveal the 'Final Solution' as varied and variegated process, not least because of the sheer number of different organisations involved.

Final Solutions?
Locality, region and the emergence of genocide

Overall, studies of Nazi-occupied Europe based on this new documentary evidence have shown us that individual mass murder projects in the localities 'begat the idea of genocide as much as the other way around'.[8] Thus, the regionalisation of 'Final Solution' studies has echoed and emphasised a key contention of the functionalist thesis – that genocide did not emerge solely as a result of directives from the centre, and therefore the radicalisation of anti-Jewish policy was not simply exported from Berlin. Regional administrators in the Nazi empire continually made radical proposals to the centre.[9] Yet this is not to say that functionalism simply 'won' the debate of the 1970s and 80s in the light of new documentation. After all, it has also been widely accepted that this was a system *deliberately designed* to achieve the smooth application of the most radical policies. Götz Aly describes Heydrich's empowerment of regional commanders in the invasion of the Soviet Union as the 'Heydrich System'. Heydrich had no wish to dictate unrealistic policies from Berlin and required that men in the field report back on the conditions on the ground.[10]

The importance of the regions, and also the expansion of the Third Reich, in the radicalisation of Jewish policy did not start in 1939. Hans Safrian has argued that the more aggressive emigration policies of later 1938 and 1939 were based on the 'Vienna Model' and thus exported back into the Reich from annexed Austria.[11] But it is perhaps in the emergence of genocide in the Warthegau that the importance of regional impulses in driving genocide is seen most clearly, and was first revealed. Ian Kershaw's 1992 study, based on documents from Polish war crimes investigations, was a self-conscious modification of the functionalist thesis that showed both the initiative taken in the regions and the importance of central authority in moving the Third Reich along the road to genocide.[12]

Famously, in the summer of 1941 Rolf Heinz Höppner, who was head of the SD in Posen and close to the summit of regional power in the Warthegau, wrote to Adolf Eichmann asking for direction in Jewish policy. In this letter Höppner wondered whether it might just be more humane to murder the Jews incarcerated in the Łódź ghetto than see them starve to death as a result of its meagre food supply.[13] Höppner's concern reflected a general sense in the region that the ghetto had reached capacity. However in September 1941 Heinrich Himmler informed the regional leader Artur Greiser that German Jews would soon be deported to Łódź as an 'initial step' ahead of their being sent further east in the future.[14] Inside the Warthegau itself confusion still reigned. Höppner again wrote to Eichmann on 3 September asking for clarity and specifically whether or not the Jews were to be 'totally eradicated'.[15] In October, Jews outside of Łódź in the Warthegau region began to be murdered. In November Herbert Lange, who had run a special commando within the Euthanasia Programme, transferred to the region. At the beginning of December 1941 Lange's unit began to murder Jews from Łódź in gas vans at the nearby extermination site at Chelmno.[16]

Kershaw's account demonstrated that genocide developed in the Warthegau as a solution to a number of *regional* problems, not least what to do with Jews, the number of whom was increasing because of deportations from Germany. Of course, that increase, and thus that problem, was centrally imposed. As such according

to Kershaw the impetus for mass murder came from a fatal combination of direction *and* initiative. It was for example at the
behest of Wilhelm Koppe, local Higher SS and police leader
(*Höhere Schutzstaffeln- und Polizeiführer*, or HSSPF) that Herbert
Lange's unit was invited to the region. Such murderous initiative
was however taken in the full knowledge of Berlin and indeed in
the belief, on the part of local leaders, that they were acting in
accord with the wishes of central authorities and thus of Hitler
himself.[17] Greiser, Koppe and Höppner were all engaged in what
Kershaw describes as 'working towards the Führer', a system by
which individuals decided on a specific course of action in the
absence of central direction but according to the vague, and well-
known, world historical goals of the *Führer*.[18] With reference to
similarly murderous initiatives in the Ukraine, Wendy Lower has
called this a system of 'anticipatory obedience'.[19]

Kershaw's study was just the first in a series which emphasised
the local context for decision-making. Looked at collectively these
studies suggest that the 'Final Solution' gave unity to individual
(and thus in some ways separate) genocidal initiatives that
emerged on the ground across the latter half of 1941 and into
1942. Placing genocidal attacks on Jews within a local context has
also had the curious impact of returning Holocaust studies to
some of the premises which shaped it in the 1940s and 1950s (and
are the subject of Chapter 1 here), namely that the 'Final Solution
of the Jewish Question' must be seen in the context of general
Nazi occupation policies.

In terms of each locality, the picture that emerges is of a complex amalgamation of ideological mission and situational context,
driving genocidal policy. Both Dieter Pohl and Christian Gerlach
have demonstrated how mass murder (and thus genocide) emerges,
time and again, as a way out of much more mundane policy
problems. These range from problems of security and food supply
to the management of diseases.[20] The decision to murder immediately Jews discovered outside the Warsaw Ghetto was taken at the
behest of public health officials wishing to contain the epidemics
ravaging the population inside, echoing a policy that had been
employed in Łódź for over a year for the same reason.[21] Thus a step
along the road to mass murder was taken, but without ostensible
reference to any ideological premise and certainly not any central
direction and in response to an apparently unrelated problem. In

Eastern Belorussia 'economic pressure' was the key factor in the specific decision-making processes that led to individual campaigns of mass murder. There was a low demand for Jewish slaves in the region whose agricultural base had to feed the Wehrmacht as well as local populations. One way out of the problems of supply that this often engendered was simply to reduce the population and thus demand for food – which could be done by murdering Jews.[22]

Christoph Dieckmann's study of the transition to genocide in Lithuania also suggests a range of causal pressures. The murder of Jewish men in the immediate aftermath of the invasion was part of a security policy, while the transition to murdering the general Jewish population after August 1941 began as a solution to local food supply problems.[23] Local context could work in the opposite direction too, and ensure Jews were kept alive in some regions. Sybille Steinbacher has shown that in East Upper Silesia the importance of Jews in the local economy meant that they were less likely to be victims of murder before May 1943. After this point they were murdered in line with a new emphasis on security, and the Jewish threat to it, in the light of the Warsaw ghetto uprising.[24]

The idea that genocidal policies emerged from below sounds like traditional functionalist historiography, and new scholars certainly echo the observations of Broszat *et al*. However, the regionalised 'Final Solution' differs significantly from its functionalist forerunner. The new historiography does not rely on just the images of clean industrial murder that were conjured by Hans Mommsen and underpinned Bauman's thesis. Ulrich Herbert reminds us that 40 per cent of the Holocaust's victims died outside of the homicidal gas chambers and as a consequence priority has been given to explaining the emergence of more 'primitive' forms of mass killing.[25] At the same time, as Donald Bloxham has pointed out, the bureaucracies of murder constructed in Nazi-occupied Europe which have been revealed, do not much resemble the rational machinery of government described by Bauman.[26]

Dieter Pohl's account of the murder of the Jews of Stanislawow is an excellent example of both these tendencies, and thus of the complex amalgam of ideological commitment, local context, venality, corruption and brutality that drove the 'Final Solution'. These events hardly seemed to develop as a result of organised bureaucracy. Pohl reconstructs the role of the local security police commander Hans Krüger in the murder of Jews in the region from October 1941 until the end of 1942. This genocide began prior to the construction of the extermination camps, and Pohl concedes that it is impossible to see where exactly the order to murder the Jews of Stanislawow came from. But it appears that the plans of local commanders were in accord with the wishes of central policy makers. The first massacres in the region occurred just prior to the meeting between Globocnik and Himmler at which the planned murder of the Jews of the General Government may have been initiated. Instead of waiting for the more refined murder processes of the extermination camps, the deaths of Stanislawow's Jews were bloody, and brutal and involved some ingenuity and a capacity for base brutality. The 'Rudolf Mill' which was used to house and then murder the ghetto's sick is a particularly striking example of this. Krüger's small staff, which Pohl describes as a 'motley crew' were personally responsible for murdering 70,000 Jews, in concert with various other agencies including the Order Police. The men were ultimately implicated in a corruption scandal which suggested that they had stolen from their victims too. Such was Krüger's pride in his work that he was demoted because he was found to have been boasting of the murders to a local Polish woman.[27]

Pohl's uncertainty over the exact decision-making process is typical of a new historiography that is unwilling to make the kind of 'global' judgements that characterised the intentionalist functionalist controversy. Judgements as to the essence of the 'Final Solution' and where it originated are notable only by their absence. Such historiography is marked by an empiricism which at times refuses to look up from, let alone go beyond, the archival material. This is in part a consequence of the richness of the newly discovered material, but it is also a reaction against the theory-laden discourse of historians like Broszat and Mommsen.[28] It is also striking that, following the pioneering work done by Browning and Kershaw, this is a very German historiography.[29] It has been carried out largely by a generation of German scholars, and in reacting against the impersonal abstractions of functionalism is a rejection of a previously dominant social scientific historical discourse in Germany. It is thus an historiography which is also much more concerned than its predecessor with personal responsibility. There is no doubt that the regionalisation of 'Final

Solution' studies has shown that genocide emerged in different contexts for a variety of different reasons, and at the behest of different individuals and institutions. The new German historiography seeks to name (and shame) them all.

What is sometimes missing is that these 'Final Solutions' emerged *at the same time*. In the absence of a *Führer* order, prevailing wisdom now suggests first, that there were any number of discrete decisions for individual murder projects (that ultimately make up the 'Final Solution'); and second, that these were taken in a spirit of co-operation and exchange between centre and periphery. As such the 'Final Solution' is no longer seen as the result of either ideology or structure; competition or co-operation; but a toxic combination of all. As Walter Manoschek wrote about the murder of the Jews in Serbia, 'the first phase of the extermination programme depended neither on the existence of a comprehensive order for Jewish extermination nor on Hitler's approval'.[30] At the same time military authorities in Serbia were left in no doubt as to the prevailing attitudes in Berlin. When Adolf Eichmann was asked what should be done with Serbian Jews in September 1941 he answered simply, 'shoot them'.[31]

National Holocausts

Although some of the scholars who have produced this regionalised picture of the 'Final Solution' may have been unwilling to relate the meaning of their empirical work more widely, new perspectives have emerged. The regionalisation of the study of the Holocaust, the discovery of 'Final Solutions' as it were, has raised anew the question of the relationship between local populations and authorities with the politics of annihilation throughout Nazi Europe. In doing so, especially in central and eastern Europe, the Holocaust has been cast into debates about national character and belonging – about what it means to be Polish or Hungarian for example. In part this is because the Holocaust often challenges mythical versions of the war experience which have been important building blocks of a post-war identity. If the deportation and destruction of Jews from the Polish and Hungarian countryside was not simply the result of German orders but can be cast in domestic histories too, then the idea, for example, that 'the Hungarians' or 'the Poles' resisted the tyrannical German occupation becomes difficult to sustain. Crucially, it appears to have been the ending of the Cold War and the collapse of communist regimes that has forced this re-examination of national memories. This process has happened in Germany too, not least because the idea that the 'Final Solution' was a regionalised, varied and variegated process (or processes) has necessarily expanded the community of perpetrators under investigation.

Attempts by German historians to broaden understanding of the perpetrator community had actually begun in the late 1970s with the investigation of the criminal responsibilities of groups traditionally not associated with Nazi criminality – chiefly the *Wehrmacht*. The regular armed forces had been remembered as, if anything, the victims of the Nazi state. As such historical investigations which suggested otherwise meant the violation of an important national myth.

In the immediate aftermath of war, the historiography of the *Wehrmacht*'s involvement with the Nazi regime was dominated by its surviving generals. Erich von Manstein was typical of this. Manstein had been commander of the 11th Army on the Eastern front, and had enthusiastically encouraged his troops to take the harshest reprisals against Jewish civilians in the genocidal atmosphere of November 1941.[32] Manstein had been tried for war crimes and sentenced to eighteen years' imprisonment by a British court in 1949. But before, during and after his trial a vociferous and international band of protestors had publicly opposed the suggestion of his criminality. Instead they suggested that Manstein had simply been an 'honourable soldier', ideologically separated from the Nazi regime and fighting a legitimate war against the Soviet Union.[33] Post-war military historiography confirmed such a view, with British military historian Basil Liddell Hart's *The Other Side of the Hill* cementing the position of the German army as distanced from the Nazi regime, and indicating the influence of a transnational conservative historiography that praised the army.[34] Allen Welsh Dulles, who had been head of the Office of Strategic Services (OSS) in Bern during the Second World War,[35] produced a history of military resistance to the Nazi regime which did much the same. It was into such an atmosphere that Manstein, released from prison in 1952 in the light of the Cold War, produced his own sanitised version of his (non) Nazi past. *Lost Victories* suggested that the army had been hamstrung in their war with the (now enemy of the West) Stalin by Hitler's interference and indeed an SS bent on destruction rather than military success.[36] Manstein went to be an adviser to the post-war *Bundeswehr*.

Manstein symbolises a powerful narrative – not least because it provided an alibi to ordinary German soldiers serving in the armed forces. German society as a whole could take comfort from such 'war stories' as evidence of their victimisation both at Hitler's hands and then at the hands of the Soviet Union, by whom many had been taken as Prisoners of War.[37] As a consequence when historians sought to puncture this powerful mythology and highlight ordinary German soldiers' complicity in the barbaric atrocities of war on the Eastern front by producing social, rather than military histories of war, they inevitably attracted controversy. One of the first, and most controversial, was Christian Streit's *Keine Kamaraden* which explored German soldiers' murderous treatment of Soviet POWs. Streit has been followed by (amongst others) Helmut Krausnick who exposed further the relationship between the *Wehrmacht* and the SS *Einsatzgruppen*, Jürgen Förster, Omer Bartov and Hannes Heer who collectively have affected a gradual transformation, in historiography at least, of the image of the *Wehrmacht* from 'honourable soldiers' to *Hitler's Army*.[38]

This transformation of the status of the *Wehrmacht* in historiography was made immeasurably easier by the discovery of archival material, not least the personal photographs of ordinary German soldiers, in the former Soviet Union after the end of the Cold War.[39] Yet it has still proved publicly very difficult. Many of those photographs were put on display in a touring exhibition in Germany in the mid-1990s, 'The Crimes of the Wehrmacht', which drew outraged reactions from veterans groups, public representatives and indeed politicians. From the outset the exhibition was recognised as 'violat[ing] a taboo' and was even banned from some towns and cities. Why? Precisely because it forced Germans to reconceive their relationship with the Holocaust. 'The exhibition … forced its way into the heart of the legend, and exposed the "terrible truth" that the Holocaust took place … in the territories occupied by Wehrmacht troops, and with their energetic participation.'[40]

It is not just in Germany that historiography which suggests a varied 'Final Solution' has proved painful. In post-communist

Poland at the beginning of the twenty-first century controversy erupted in a debate which clearly shows that there too, there was a profound relationship between historical memories of the Holocaust and the changing political circumstances of the post-war world. The unprecedented discussions prompted by Jan Thomas Gross' small book, *Neighbors*, did not just involve historians or scholars but the Polish media, the Catholic Church and indeed the political establishment, in wide-ranging discourse concerned ultimately with what it meant to be Polish in the modern world.

The story of Gross' book, and the events it describes and the way in which they have been remembered, captures in microcosm Poland's relationship with the Holocaust since 1945. *Neighbors* rediscovered the murder of approximately 1600 Jews in Jedwabne, a small town in the Eastern part of Poland that had been occupied by the Soviet Union in 1939 and then was invaded by the Nazis in the summer of 1941. In the immediate aftermath of the invasion, Jews in Jedwabne were subject to violence and harassment, at the hands of 'hoodlums' in the local Polish population. Although the violence for a time subsided, on 10 July – at the behest of the Germans – it reached a new and terrible ferocity. 'Local hooligans', with the encouragement of the town's mayor, subjected Jedwabne's Jews to a series of brutal humiliations: 'beards of old Jews were burned, newborn babies were killed at their mothers' breasts, people were beaten murderously and forced to sing and dance.' Ultimately, with the town surrounded by German forces so that no-one could escape, the remaining Jews in the town, sought out by Polish volunteers, were forced into a barn that was 'doused with Kerosene' and set alight. While impossible and unthinkable without the presence of German troops, the Jews that died in that barn died at the hands of *Polish* men.[41]

Gross's allegation was clear. The destruction of the Jews in Jedwabne was a part of the genocide of Polish Jews, but this was not something that happened independent of the rest of the Polish community carried out by alien Nazi invaders. Ordinary Poles were not only intimate witnesses to this bloody and bestial violence, there were, in this case, its perpetrators too. As such Poles could not simply regard themselves as having been victims and martyrs of the Nazi murder machine.

But Gross also made clear that he had *re*discovered the murder of Jedwabne's Jews. In the immediate aftermath of war it was widely accepted that the Jews had been murdered by their neighbours. Indeed in 1949 twenty-two Polish men had stood trial for the crime, and it was the records of this trial and investigation that had provided much of the source material for Gross's study. So what had happened to the memory of the murdered Jews of Jedwabne, and thus the Holocaust, in the intervening years? Why did Gross's book about an event that was in the public domain cause such controversy?

The guilty men in Jedwabne served short sentences before returning to the town.[42] And while Gross alleges that the residents of Jedwabne knew very well what had occurred there, the rest of Polish society was keen to forget. The enthusiastic reception that the German armies had received from Poles in the formerly Soviet occupied areas did not fit with a dominant understanding of the war in which the Poles had been the primary victims of the Nazi sadists, liberated by the Red Army. Indeed, according to Gross, both Jews and those who had helped Jews during the Nazi occupation faced hostility in post-war Poland – not least because they reminded some Poles of their collaboration with the Nazi regime there.[43] By 1948 the communist consolidation of power in Poland was complete, and a narrative of Polish and communist martyrdom clearly established. The concentration camp at Auschwitz I was chosen very specifically as a memorial site because it was a site of Polish and communist as well as Jewish suffering. The Soviet state exported its own form of anti-Judaism during the 1950s, which had also had little or no place for memories of Jewish suffering, especially not at Polish hands. The erasure of Polish complicity in the massacre at Jedwabne was completed in the 1960s when a memorial was erected commemorating the Gestapo murder of 1600 Jews there. Towards the end of the 1960s the Polish state indulged in its own anti-Jewish campaign – symbolised for our purposes by the limiting of the activities of the JHI in Warsaw. Symbolically Jan Gross left Poland for the USA in 1968 too, following his involvement in student protests.[44]

Although the massacre at Jedwabne was remembered in the town's Yizkor book published in 1980 (in the USA and Israel), for the most part inside Poland it was forgotten or at least not discussed.[45] And although during 1980s there was a limited scholarly rethinking of Poland's wartime past, and calls for Poland to engage with the darker aspects of its wartime story could be heard, these were mainly from scholars like Gross who were now working outside of Poland. After the fall of communism however, there was a free and public space in Poland within which such arguments could be debated. As such, because the straitjacket of communist narratives had been removed, Gross's book and the furious reactions to it were competing to provide a new (or just protect the old) narrative in order to fill the void.

The first and most outraged reactions were from the political right, especially in the press, where Gross was explicitly attacked for suggesting that Poles were somehow guilty. Ironically many right-wing responses were tinged with more than a little anti-Judaism, not least from Polish historian Thomasz Strzembosz who alleged that the ignored context for the Jedwabne massacre was that Polish Jews had welcomed the Soviets after 1939. This had amounted, he claimed, to a national betrayal.[46] The leader of the Polish Catholic church also insisted that Polish-Jewish relations during the Second World War should always be considered in the light of Jews' economic advantages, 'strange customs' and support for communism.[47] According to Joanna Michlic such was the 'psychological need to see the Polish community as virtuous' that some critics of Gross were left only to 'hope' that their belief that it was the Germans that carried out the massacre would be proved right by some as yet undiscovered documentary evidence.[48]

The hope was a forlorn one, and there was no new documentary evidence. Although Gross's use of evidence and attitudes to source material was questioned, nothing in the course of the debate was really uncovered which materially disrupted his interpretation that the responsibility for the murders lay with Poles rather than the German forces. Bogdan Musial, a German-Polish historian who had allied himself with critics of the 'Crimes of the Wehrmacht' exhibition in Germany in the 1990s when he attacked their mistaken labelling of some photographic evidence, attacked Gross for making basic factual errors. But despite any mistakes that Musial found, the Polish government-sponsored commission appointed to review the massacre in the light of the scandal – the Institute of National Remembrance (*Instytut Pamięci Narodowej*, or IPN) which had been created to review, commemorate and compensate for the crimes of the Nazi and communist eras – declared in 2002 that there was no evidence of German involvement in the murders at Jedwabne.[49]

At the same time as the phobic reactions reviewed above, there was another response to Gross's book in Poland – an agonised self-reflection. This was symbolised most eloquently at the commemoration of the sixtieth anniversary of the massacre when the Polish President, Aleksander Kwaśniewski, acknowledged the 'pain and the shame' engendered by knowledge of Polish mistreatment of Jews, which must, he argued, exist *alongside* memories of Polish suffering. It may be that it is in this contradiction and complexity that the legacy of *Neighbors* lies. In the aftermath of the debate a more complex historiography of Poland's Holocaust is emerging. For example alongside Gross's identification of Polish perpetrators, Gunnar S. Paulsson has argued that the incidence of Jews being aided by Poles in Warsaw during the Nazi occupation is much higher than had been originally thought. The numbers of Jews hiding in Nazi-occupied Warsaw, supported by the Polish population, amounted to an underground 'secret city'.[50] If we consider such rescuers alongside the bloody and bestial perpetrators of anti-Jewish violence shown to us by Gross, it is clear then that there is no single Polish experience of Nazi anti-Judaism, no one label – be it perpetrator, rescuer, victim, or bystander – that can be applied.

The painful process of placing the Holocaust inside national histories has not been confined to Poland. As communist regimes collapsed throughout Eastern Europe then revision of the past soon followed. Historical commissions to investigate the relationship between local populations and Nazi violence were established in countries like Lithuania, Latvia, Estonia and Croatia.[51] Western scholars, given access to Eastern archives for the first time, have invariably painted a picture of local collaboration and co-operation in the murder of Jewish populations. The genocide in Lithuania, for example, began with pogroms carried out by local militias turning on their Jewish populations, and was latterly systematised using amongst others local volunteers in murder battalions.[52] In Latvia the role of local police serving under Nazi control has been highlighted.[53] In the Ukraine, local volunteers have been identified as playing 'an indispensable role in the killing process. In terms of police manpower involved in the atrocities in these areas, they outnumbered their Nazi German colleagues.'[54]

But at the same time as rediscovering local involvement in

genocide, the nationalist leaders who encouraged such co-operation with the Nazis have also been, in the post-Cold War
nationalist revival, often feted as heroes. Take Romania as an
example. The new historiography of Romania's Holocaust points
to the enthusiastic collaboration of its leader, Ion Antonescu, in
the deportation and destruction of the Romanian Jewish community, especially the communities of Bukovina and Bessarabia –
where indigenous persecution of Jews in 1940/41 exceeded even
Nazi brutality towards Jews in Poland.[55] Yet Antonescu has also
been rehabilitated in the post-communist era. One of the first acts
of the new Romanian parliament was to hold a minute's silence in
Antonescu's memory.[56]

While the examples of Antonescu and indeed the Polish perpetrators of the Jedwabne massacre are extreme, they do point to
the difficulty of integrating the Holocaust into national histories
in the aftermath of the Cold War. During the communist period
history-writing had often contributed to a pervasive culture of
victimhood – where populations remembered their own suffering
at Nazi hands. Communist movements also invariably encouraged
the memory of indigenous or communist resistance to Nazi rule.
I will now look in slightly more detail at the development of Holocaust historiography in Hungary, as it provides a useful case study
in the relationship between history-writing and the 'politics of
memory' and the problems of domesticating the Holocaust after
the Cold War.

In Hungary, like Poland, there had been some interest in the
persecution of the Jews immediately after 1945 – during the democratic interregnum before the communist takeover in 1948. War
crimes trials especially encouraged reflection on the co-operation
of indigenous politicians with the Hungarian Holocaust. The
three key officials in the Hungarian government as far as the
deportation of Jews had been concerned, László Baky, László
Endre and Andor Jaross, were all executed after standing trial in
April 1946.[57] This interest also manifested itself in some histories
of the treatment of the Jews, the most notable of which by István
Bibó insisted that Hungarians bore some responsibility for the
'Final Solution' there and highlighted the 'necessity of national
self examination' after the destruction of some 400,000 Hungarian
Jews.[58]

However during the communist era, the importance of the

destruction of Jews in histories of the Hungarian war was downplayed and that self examination never came. In its stead came
myths of Hungarian victimhood and most importantly Soviet
liberation. The amnesia around the destruction of the Jews was,
according to Randolph Braham, a consequence of the generally
anti-Jewish attitudes of the Soviet bloc especially after the
establishment of the state of Israel in 1948. Although there were a
few Hungarian publications during the 1970s, especially on antisemitism and thus the prehistory of the genocide, in the main the
history of the Hungarian Holocaust was left to scholars outside
Hungary until the 1980s.[59]

Yet even those scholars, of which Braham was the most prominent, did not at first seek to explain the Holocaust as an element
of *Hungarian* history. Braham published both documentary
readers and historical narratives at the beginning of the 1960s
which found the 'Final Solution' in Hungary the result of a Nazi
blueprint for genocide, more or less personally implemented by
Adolf Eichmann. That such histories used largely German sources
and indeed were produced in the context of the Eichmann trial,
means that such an interpretation is not surprising. It might also
be that this is a further example, from a Western perspective, of
the influence of the Cold War on the understanding of the
Holocaust. After all, the totalitarian paradigm insisted on the
ability of dictatorial states to impose themselves wholesale on their
populations and that of their satellites. When applied to the past
such an interpretation saw the Nazi totalitarian juggernaut arrive
in Budapest in March 1944 and let loose their now perfected
machinery of destruction.[60]

At the beginning of the 1980s Braham himself was at the forefront of an historiography which began to investigate more closely
Hungarian involvement in the 'Final Solution'.[61] Scholars inside
Hungary soon followed suit, especially around the occasion of
the fortieth anniversary of the genocide when conferences and
scholarly publications highlighted indigenous co-operation with
the Nazis.[62] Since the fall of communism this historiography
has gathered further momentum – both inside and outside
Hungary. Recently Judit Molnar and Tim Cole have suggested,
through studies of local bureaucracy, that Hungarian officials
exceeded Nazi demands as far as Jewish policy was concerned.[63]

Two Hungarian historians, Gábor Kádár and Zoltán Vági,

have proposed that it is in the area of Aryanisation that the Holo-caust in Hungary can be considered genuinely Hungarian. Aryanisation policies in Axis Hungary ensured that the *Hungarian* state, in its widest definition, was 'in practice ready' for the plun-dering of Jews which accompanied their deportation and murder in 1944. That plunder took place in the chaos unleashed in the aftermath of the Nazi whirlwind (the 'Final Solution' on Hungar-ian soil lasted just over 100 days) – and was in part a consequence of a wider vision of economic restructuring in Hungarian society and in part simply rapacious looting. It is in the economics of genocide that the Holocaust can also be situated in a much wider context of Hungarian history. Not only did successive administra-tions employ limited Aryanisation prior to 1944 and as such establish the principle of expropriation, but the successor regimes after the end of the war failed to make good losses to surviving Jews or indeed the families of the dead. This absence of restitu-tion, and indeed the expropriation of restitution payments coming from West Germany by the communist state in the 1960s and 70s, represent for Kádár and Vági a continuity of Jewish suffering at Hungarian hands.[64]

In highlighting the economics of genocide Kádár and Vági bring scholarship on Hungary's Holocaust in line with other mod-ern Holocaust historiographies – as such 'national' Holocaust scholarship of this kind is not just a discourse in the politics of identity. Götz Aly and Christian Gerlach have also written an his-tory of the Holocaust's 'final chapter' which stresses the economic imperative for the Hungarian genocide. Both the occupiers and the Hungarian state, according to this interpretation, were in thrall to the idea of Jewish wealth and thus saw the destruction of Hun-gary's Jews as an act of larceny first and foremost.[65] The narrative of 'national Holocaust' scholarship is familiar then – progressing from assumptions as to the ideological imperative behind the 'Final Solution', to explanations which root the Holocaust in the mundane, grubby politics of enrichment.

But in Hungary however, the new historiography which emphasises domestic responsibility has to compete with quite dif-ferent narratives in the public arena. In the aftermath of the communist era, the 'Jewish Question' has re-emerged, with debates over the loyalty of Jews as citizens of the Hungarian nation. In 1993 the decision was taken to repatriate and re-inter the remains of Hungary's wartime national leader Admiral Horthy. Horthy and his milieu may have been indicted as, at least in part, responsible for the destruction of the Jews in historiography – but in public discourse he was being reinstated as a national hero. According to David Cesarani, Jewish groups who protested such a decision were dismissed as being nationally disloyal.[66] At the same time there has been an upsurge in nationalist historiography in Hungary – ranging from the celebration of Horthy as a the man who stopped the Holocaust (because of his decision to prevent the deportation of the Jews of Budapest) to outright Holocaust denial.[67] As such it appears that the corollary of the re-examination of national myths using the Holocaust has been the aggressive restatement of those myths themselves.

Western Europe has been witness to a similarly painful process of accommodating the Holocaust within national narratives too – although this has occurred over a much longer time frame. Coming to terms with the Holocaust past has been stretched over the period since 1945 rather than since 1989 – but it is still a process that has been involved in a discourse about the present and about national belonging. Consider the example of the Netherlands. In the immediate post-war period there, historiography was dominated by the idea of resistance, and the opposition of the Dutch population to Nazi rule. The history of the sufferings of Dutch Jewry was doubly marginalised in such narratives. First, because the Jews had, as it were, not fought back and in the shape of the Jewish Council had to an extent attempted to ameliorate the experience of occupation through co-operation with the Nazi authorities. And second because the persecution of Dutch Jewry rather undermined the myths of resistance by revealing at the very least the passivity of many non-Jews in the face of persecution.[68]

The Dutch Jewish community was itself undergoing an agonising conversation in the immediate post-war period about the extent of its leaders' complicity with Nazi occupation authorities – and the history-writing produced in this period reflected this, rather than ignore the relationship between the persecution of Jews and Dutch society more generally.[69] And the most famous Holocaust narrative of all, Anne Frank's diary, encouraged the idea that the persecution of the Jews did not require any self-examination for society in general – after all the Franks had been hidden from the Nazis by heroic acts of Christian charity. As such Anne's story bolstered rather than undermined the myths of Dutch resistance.[70]

The first substantial challenge to the view that the persecution of Dutch Jewry was 'not properly Dutch history' because it did not 'arise from Dutch circumstances' came with Jacob Presser's monumental history – first published in 1965 under the title *Ondergang,* or Destruction.[71] Perhaps because it was a part of the official history of the war emerging from the State Institute for War Documentation, Presser's study caused a sensation. Through investigating the murder of Dutch Jewry, Presser began to revise the pervasive myths of the Dutch war experience – contributing to the Netherlands' own version of the generational culture wars of the 1960s. Co-operation and complicity for the first time became part of a public discourse about the war that had hitherto been dominated by the idea of resistance.[72]

Remarkably for a work written in 1965, Presser's remains the most complete study of the Holocaust in the Netherlands. This does not mean that no historians have followed Presser – but none have attempted a monographic study in quite the same way and more recently there has been a tendency toward studies which ask why the death toll amongst Dutch Jews was so high in comparison with other Western European nations.[73] In essence this scholarship is a continuation of the search for a functional national identity in the light of the Holocaust, a process which Presser began. Underpinning such work is the question what went wrong in the Netherlands, what did the Holocaust reveal about Dutch society and social relations?[74] As such Presser's book has ensured, and contemporary historiography seems to suggest that this remains the case, that the Holocaust has become a kind of moral touch-stone in Dutch national life; a prism through which Dutch national identity has been critiqued and is being reconstructed, used in moral education in the Netherlands – in order to investigate the extent and the limits of one's moral responsibilities to fellow citizens.[75]

The list could go on. Scholarship on the 'Final Solution' in France has a similar narrative. In the aftermath of war French memories of war were dominated by the idea of resistance; the collaboration of the Vichy regime had been somewhat erased from national memory, a tendency famously described by Henry Rousso as the 'Vichy syndrome'.[76] The persecution of the Jews sat awkwardly within such a narrative because, once again, it revealed a more complex relationship between the French and the German occupiers than simply suppression and resistance. A certain amnesia around the specificities of the Jewish experience in Vichy and occupied France was typified by Alan Resnais' 1955 film *Nuit et Bruillard* (Night and Fog) which makes clear references to both deportations and the extermination process, but which makes no mention at all of the Jewishness of the victims of these phenomena.[77]

It suffices to say that amnesia has, for both domestic and foreign historians, now passed. In terms of public narratives, a series of painful war crimes trials in the 1980s forced confrontation with the role of Vichy in the deportation of French Jews. In scholarly terms, the indigenous nature of much Vichy antisemitic legislation was exposed by 'historians from the other side of the Atlantic' who showed that Franco-German 'co-operation in the persecution of the Jews was particularly extensive'.[78] Michael Marrus wrote as early as 1994 that the idea that French historians had struggled to come to terms with Vichy was now not the case.[79] Since that point there have been further narratives of Jewish suffering produced, none of which avoid the question of French responsibility, albeit often written by scholars who have left or are outside France.[80]

I wish to conclude this section by reflecting that Holocaust History in the West since the collapse of communism is markedly a post-Cold War affair too. As such it is not just in the East that global political winds have transformed the focus of both public historical narratives and indeed historiography itself. As many scholars have pointed out, the marked upsurge in interest in the Holocaust since the Berlin Wall fell is in part the consequence of the disappearance of present-day enemies through which those in the West could define themselves. As the communist East dissolved, and before fundamentalist 'Islamic' terrorism had really asserted itself, it was the Nazis who provided the 'other' by which Western nations and indeed international organisations defined who they were.[81]

Final Solutions? Central authorities and decision-making

The regionalisation of Holocaust studies may have highlighted the peculiar role that Holocaust History can play in the creation of national identities throughout Europe. The new documents revealed by the end of the Cold War may have shifted the study of the 'Final Solution' from Berlin to the killing fields themselves, but this does not mean that debate over the emergence of genocidal policy at the centre has entirely disappeared. Just as regional studies have tended to place the 'Final Solution' within the context of Nazi occupation policy more generally, so too have studies of central agencies made a plea for contextualisation. Götz Aly has argued that the 'Final Solution' needs to be seen as an offshoot of comprehensive race and resettlement policies which included the movement of ethnic Germans and Poles.[82] The 'Final Solution', Aly argues, emerges from the ashes of the failure of much more grand population policy projects. Such an argument restores Himmler's position as Reich Commisar for the Strengthening of Ethnic Germandom to the centre of Holocaust studies for the first time since Robert Koehl's 1950 study.

Attempts to reconstruct the genesis of local murder projects can also be related back to the 'Final Solution' as a whole, and even if mass murder did 'begat genocide' this simply sparked the beginning of an effort to wrought a general 'Final Solution' as policy from the chaos. It is notable however that when historians return the focus to Berlin, their language displays the mixture of provisionality and misplaced certainty that defines scholarship on the 'Final Solution'. This provisionality demonstrates the limits of the new historiography, or at least the documents on which it is based. Bogdan Musial writes of the 'decision' with regard to the General Government: 'Himmler *probably* received Globocnik's letter shortly after October 1. Yet the decision was of such fundamental political importance that Himmler *must* have presented Globocnik's proposal – *doubtless* seconding it – to Hitler' (emphasis added).[83]

At first glance there is now, at least over some issues, consensus. As well as the idea that policy was at times driven forward in the regions, few historians, if any, would disagree with the claim that it 'was certain … there was no voluntaristic decision on the systematic, industrialised mass murder of the European Jews'. Instead it emerged piecemeal as a solution to various problems including those imposed by the murder process itself such as how to murder more quickly and with more regard for the sensitivities of the killers.[84] At the same time crucial central decisions were made, each of which had the effect of radicalising policy in more general terms. Because of our awareness of those central decisions however the idea that Hitler ordered the 'Final Solution of the Jewish Question' in July of 1941 (as reflected in Göring's order to Heydrich) is no longer a tenable interpretation.[85] Instead it is almost universally accepted that the descent to genocide can only be explained as a decision-making *process* involving a high degree of exchange between centre and periphery.

The first central decision concerned the extension of the remit of the itinerant killing squads on the Eastern front, from a security policy based on mass murder to genocide. Jürgen Matthäus has recently argued that the relationship between centre and periphery in this case needs to be reconsidered, and that a (centrally) 'controlled escalation' accounts for the development in policy. Put colloquially the Reich leadership were unaware how far they could expect their political aspirations to be translated into mass violence in the field, and as such the development from mass murder was the result of an incremental process as horizons broadened and awareness that almost anything was possible dawned.[86] The understanding of what was possible came from the field however, as Konrad Kwiet has demonstrated with reference to Lithuania. General massacres there were sanctioned *after the fact* by the head of *Einsatzgruppe A*, Franz Stahlecker, and Heinrich Himmler, but had been carried out at first on the initiative of local commanders.[87] As massacres occurred from then on Himmler facilitated the spread of murder throughout the system at the pace he desired. As such at times he acted as a spur – issuing direct orders – at times he acted as a brake to prevent the outbreak of anarchic or uncontrolled violence. In doing so, and thus in facilitating the spread of mass murder both vertically and horizontally through the Nazi system, Himmler maintained control over a process which he did not always initiate.[88]

Christopher Browning's total history of the *Origins of the Final Solution* attempted to be the last word in this debate. It was published by *Yad Vashem* as part of their planned 'comprehensive history' of the Holocaust. Browning suggested that in the aftermath of the completion of the decision-making process for the murder of Soviet Jewry, a new decision-making process was inaugurated with regard to the rest of Europe's Jews, symbolised by Göring's 31 July directive to Heydrich.[89] Although others would reject Browning's analysis here, it is largely accepted that the decision to deport German Jews in September 1941 is part of this second phase decision-making process. But even this incremental decision was not 'voluntaristic', and was made in response to growing pressure within the regime. Gauleiter Kaufman of Hamburg had written to Hitler on 15 September 1941, in order to request deportation of his Jewish population to provide space for air-raid victims.[90] These transports would be made into regions where genocide already represented policy in the former Soviet Union and in the Wartheland where, as we have seen, it soon would in response to those transports. As such the act of deportation may well have been effectively genocidal (as suggested by a number of scholars), but it is largely agreed that at the time they were not actually part of a systematic genocidal vision.

Bogdan Musial has attempted to pinpoint another incremental decision, that is the move to the annihilation of the Jews of the General Government. Again Musial sees this as the result of a process of exchange – he believes it was proposed by SSPF Lublin Odilo Globocnik and then approved by Hitler. Heinrich Himmler then worked with Globocnik on the development of the technical details of this plan in October 1941, identifying the site of the extermination facilities at both Belzec and Sobibor.[91] Dieter Pohl, Christian Gerlach and Peter Longerich have all argued rather differently that the original plans of both Globocnik and Himmler were for the murder of the Jews of Lublin that were then extended to the rest of the General Government.[92] However we can say with certainty that the principle that this was a separate process has been widely accepted.

There is also widespread agreement over when the decision-making process came to an end. Christopher Browning, Peter Longerich and Christian Gerlach all agree for example that by the spring of 1942 the preparations were complete and as such the 'Final Solution' as we know it had taken shape. As Josef Goebbels recorded in his diary on 27 March, 'A judgment is being carried out against the Jews that, indeed barbaric, is fully deserved. The prophecy that the Führer made is beginning to come true in the most terrible manner.'[93] In April 1942 construction began on the extermination site at Treblinka, signalling the practical extension of the mass murder programme to encompass all of Poland's Jews. On 4 July 1942 the first selection took place at Auschwitz-Birkenau.[94]

Despite this consensus, disagreements persist about when the decision – in terms of the practical intention to pursue an indiscriminate effort, by whatever means, to remove the Jews from the face of the earth – was taken. *This is due to the simple fact that the documents alone cannot provide the answer.* For Browning October 1941 still represents the moment when an operational vision of genocide existed amongst the Reich leadership. Although that vision still required dissemination throughout the Nazi system, and still had not acquired concrete form, there was nonetheless no going back. The policy of emigration had officially ended on 18 October 1941, Jews in the Soviet Union were being exterminated, and the extermination of Polish Jews had been agreed in principle, and German Jews were being transported East.[95] Browning acknowledges that the 'Final Solution' was still defined by contradictions after this point, but this is just evidence of the experimentation inherent in the implementation of policy.

Michael Thad Allen has used the documents of the construction directorate at Auschwitz, and evidence from Soviet trial testimony, to attempt to place the camp within this chronology too. Perhaps surprisingly, Auschwitz has remained on the periphery of debates about the origins of the 'Final Solution'. Robert Jan van Pelt's argument that it developed alongside genocidal policy and did not assume a central role in the 'Final Solution' until the early part of 1942 has, until relatively recently, held sway.[96] While the idea that face-to-face killings could be local initiatives, homicidal gas chambers are usually associated with central direction precisely because they are the instruments of industrial, directed genocide. Thad Allen argues that on the contrary they were developed on the ground in the latter part of 1941 – just at the time that Browning suggests that planning for genocide had been unleashed. Zyklon B gas chambers were the result of enthusiastic engagement on the part of lower-level designers inside the construction office itself. Thus industrial killing emerges from the ground up too. What Thad Allen is unable to do however is link such activity definitively with the 'Final Solution' at a time when the labour pool for Birkenau was still envisaged as Soviet

POWs and Auschwitz also had a role in the successor to the T4 Euthanasia Programme codenamed 14f13.[97]

Uniquely, Christian Gerlach has argued that amongst this fluid exchange of ideas it is actually possible to pinpoint the moment of dissemination of a fundamental decision to pursue the 'Final Solution' as comprehensive policy. For Gerlach the lack of uniformity in Jewish policy in the autumn of 1941 signals that October cannot be the beginning of a general genocidal intent. Intriguingly, he focuses on the Riga transport that David Irving used to deny Hitler's involvement in the 'Final Solution' as evidence of this – demonstrating in documentary terms how far Holocaust historiography *hasn't* travelled. However, Gerlach's thesis is actually based on a key documentary discovery from the Soviet special archives too, the previously missing 1941 appointments diary of Heinrich Himmler. This records an 18 December meeting between the head of the SS and his *Führer* and notes 'Jewish Question/ to be exterminated as partisans'. For Gerlach this tiny fragment indicates that the decision *in principle* to murder Jews was taken around this time. Such a view gives ideology a key role in explaining the movement of Hitler towards the 'Final Solution' because it was on the 8 December 1941, with the entry of the US into what was now a genuinely 'World War', that Hitler's prophecy was fulfilled. Gerlach goes on to argue that Hitler presented this fundamental decision to the upper echelons of the Nazi movement on 12 December 1941 when he met with his *Gauleiter*. And indeed this meeting certainly acted as a spur to genocidal activity. Hans Frank returned from this Berlin meeting and famously declared to the officials of the General Government that he had been told that they would have to liquidate their Jews.[98]

Gerlach's thesis seems to depart however from the principle of adherence to the documents that have underpinned much of the new historiography, including his own work. He can after all only *infer* that Hitler announced a fundamental decision on 12 December 1941. Peter Longerich's accounts of central decision-making on the other hand, which suggest the move to indiscriminate murder came only in April and May 1942, follow the documents to, perhaps, their logical conclusion. Longerich rejects inference and assumption, asking only what the documents can definitely tell us. As such the contradictions in policy which Browning sees as experimentation and simply the time that it takes for the idea of genocide to spread, are for Longerich evidence that a single-minded genocidal policy did not yet exist. And this is literally true – after all it simply *is* the case that German Jews were not murdered immediately on arrival in Łódź or Minsk in the latter part of 1941; that Hans Frank's speech of 16 December suggested that he at least had no conception as to how the liquidation of the Jews of the General Government might be achieved; that Jews continued to be employed in slave labour, and indeed that Heydrich spoke in terms of labour deployment at the Wannsee conference. It is literally the case that the process which became Aktion Reinhard involved all of the Jews of the General Government only when Treblinka was constructed and the Jews of Warsaw were within its range; and that German Jews deported to Łódź only began to be murdered in May of 1942.[99]

But ultimately, despite an apparent commitment to empiricism, and perhaps this is the historian's dilemma – in the end Longerich has to rely on inference too. Because ultimately the contradictions did, slowly, begin to fade (even if they never disappear) and the 'Final Solution' assumed a coherence. The Nazis did pursue Jewish communities wherever they were, trains did begin to roll across the continent, heading first from Slovakia to Auschwitz-Birkenau and Sobibor in July 1942. At this point, because the contradictory evidence runs out, Longerich is forced to infer precisely the certainty that we saw in the previous chapter betrays uncertainty: 'at about the same time ... the major decisions on radicalising the entire murder programme *must* have been taken'.[100] No evidence required.

But pinpointing the specific origins of the 'Final Solution' as policy is only one, very small, part of Longerich's history of the Holocaust which attempted to offer a new grand narrative in the wake of the evident failure of intentionalism and functionalism. The concluding part of this chapter will attempt to place Longerich's concept of a 'annihilation policy' within an analysis of the breakdown of metanarratives.

The breakdown of grand narratives

What the regionalisation of the studies of the 'Final Solution' have ultimately demanded is that we set the history of the Holocaust firmly within the broader history of the Third Reich. This is of course the mirror image of the process by which the Holocaust was made by historians, which required removing it from its wider context and demanding that the 'Final Solution' be recognised as phenomonelogically separate. The implication of this separation was, as we have seen, that the 'Final Solution' had coherent logic and meaning. Often that meaning was sought in ideology, but even when it was sought in the structure of government and administration it was still *singularly* conceived – concerned only with antisemitism, anti-Jewish policy. As such although at first it appears that regional studies of the 'Final Solution' undermine the totality of that concept, in fact they actually require that concept to be much more broadly conceived.

Local (and I use the term local here in its regional and institutional sense) studies seem to suggest, however, that the 'Final Solution' did not have a *single* meaning, if indeed it had a meaning at all. Take the work of Götz Aly as an example and the two significant theses that he has contributed to contemporary Holocaust studies. If the 'Final Solution' emerged as a consequence of grand economic restructuring on the one hand, and the wreckage of much more ambitious population policy on the other – the murder of Jews has at the same time two very different meanings. This was because the Third Reich had different ideological missions according to the staff of different agencies. For the 'planning intelligentsia' it was concerned with and offered the opportunity for economic transformation, for the staff of the Race and Resettlement Office it offered the opportunity to bring ethnic Germans 'home to the Reich' and to create a new national and population settlement in Eastern Europe.

For the managers of the Nazis' colonial empire in the East who were ultimately the subject of these regional studies, their active participation in the 'Final Solution' had different meanings too. For public health officials in the Warsaw ghetto the murder of Jews was a way of controlling epidemics; for the army commanders concerned to feed their troops and the local populations in Belorussia during the long winter of 1941 the murder of Jews offered a way out of a food crisis. For the managers of Operation Reinhard that 'Final Solution' was one part of a much wider project to construct racial utopia.[101] For the commanders of the military in Serbia it was a rational aspect of security policy in the midst of a dangerous and volatile partisan conflict. For the

DEBATES ON THE HOLOCAUST

military high command in Western Europe too the 'Final Solution' offered a way of managing the local population, and demonstrating the severity of the occupation regime.[102]

I suggested in the previous chapter that one of the shortcomings of the intentionalist and functionalist thesis was the inability of either metanarrative to account convincingly for the enduring fact of Jewish slave labour within the Nazi system. Put simply if the 'Final Solution' was a coherent project with a coherent meaning, *why* did Jews continue to be exploited for their labour *after* the move to genocide had taken place? But once it is accepted that the 'Final Solution' is multivalent, then such problems melt away. Mark Roseman's analysis of the Wannsee conference is instructive here. Roseman regards Wannsee as postdating the transition to an explicitly genocidal policy and yet he accepts that the labour discussed by Heydrich was a reality – references to road-building alluded to the construction of the road across the Ukraine, *Durchgangstrasse* 4.[103] Michael Thad Allen has described how the WVHA set about exploiting slave labour, transforming Jews into the means of production, not in conflict with the goals of the 'Final Solution' but as a part of its complexity.[104]

A diverse historical phenomena requires a diverse explanation and it is an emphasis on context and complexity which has sought to replace essentialist explanations of the Holocaust. The new historiography of the Holocaust, despite disagreements over detail, suggests that the 'Final Solution' emerged from the ashes of *many* of the utopian dreams of the Third Reich (even if it itself represented the route to utopia on its own for some). All the population policy plans, the plans toward economic reconstruction, or simply the chaos of colonial administration, coalesced into a 'Final Solution' that was an expression of the 'annihilation policies' of the Third Reich. To this end Peter Longerich states:

> the systematic murder of the European Jews cannot be fully explained as the result of the individual decisions of the dictator, nor was it primarily the result of an acquisition of independence by an irrational ideology which was blind to reality, nor can it be solely traced to the activity of an overheating, cumulatively, self-radicalising bureaucracy. It was instead the result of a consistently pursued policy of the Nazi leadership that was adapted to external circumstances in the various phases of the 'Third Reich'. Only if the annihilation policy is seen as

an integral part of National Socialist war policy, as a major factor alongside strategic, military-economic and alliance policy considerations, can its role within the history of the Nazi regime be assessed.[105]

It perhaps should be noted that some years earlier Raul Hilberg had similarly argued that the Nazis pursued the destruction of the European Jews as a state might the prosecution of a modern war; it was a collective expression of the entire organised community.[106]

And what of the role of Hitler himself? That Christian Gerlach was able to associate Hitler unambiguously with articulating a fundamental order for the 'Final Solution', rightly or wrongly, highlights the degree to which the functionalist caricature of an absent or weak Hitler has not endured. Although it has remained impossible to link Hitler definitively to many decisions, it has proved more difficult to separate him from them. Perhaps most famously David Irving discovered this when took his project to disassociate Hitler from the 'Final Solution' to the High Court in London.[107] In post-Cold War historiography Hitler has been found permanently lurking in the shadows around the essential points of decision-making in this process. This observation holds as true for before 1939 as after – Hitler's central role in *Kristallnacht* has been revealed for example.[108] Perhaps Götz Aly has best summed up this new consensus when he wrote that Hitler 'cannot be described as … [an] inexorable giver of orders, but as … a politician who gave his people free rein and encouraged them to develop the imagination to make the apparently impossible possible and backed them unconditionally.'[100]

Ideology and the idea of 'Final Solutions'

But what of the role of ideology within this new, implied, grand narrative which emphasises the complexity and diversity of the 'Final Solution'? At the beginning of the twenty-first century it is clear that there is an emerging critique that suggests that the will to exterminate and indeed pathological fear of Jews need once again to be awarded a greater causal role. Despite their protestations to the contrary, there is a nagging sense that the German empiricists who identified the variety of *National Socialist Extermination Policies* downplayed the ideological drive behind them. Saul Friedländer's monumental two-volume study of the

Holocaust and its prehistory self-consciously asserts that his interpretation is 'manifestly incompatible' with the broad implications
of a new historiography which does not give enough attention to
'ideological-cultural factors as the prime movers of Nazi policies'.[110] Jeffrey Herf has similarly demanded the reintegration of
ideology into the history of the Holocaust. Adopting a perspective
that Herf describes as 'modified intentionalism', he asserted,
'When Hitler and his accomplices took the step from persecution
to mass murder in the midst of World War II, they said they did
so in retaliation against the international Jewish conspiracy they
held responsible for starting and escalating a war of extermination
against Germany'.[111]

The emphasis on context, and the suggestion that there was
often a utilitarian motive for mass murder central to much of the
work reviewed in this chapter, is of course a long way from the
idea that Hitler simply ordered the Holocaust in line with a pre-
existing ideological desire to exterminate Jews. In the words of
Sybille Steinbacher, 'anti-Jewish policy was in no sense steered
toward mass murder in carefully prepared, increasingly radical
phases'.[112] Yet while at first glance the document-centred approach
of Gerlach *et al.* may indeed suggest an even further diminution
of ideology within the causal matrix, I am not convinced that this
is actually the case. By emphasising that genocides emerged as a
response to local crises, historians are simply reporting documents
which refer to killing Jews in the name of food policy, or in the
name of security. These were the immediate pressures which
pushed local administrations, or indeed military commanders,
across the Rubicon to genocide. But, as Christian Gerlach himself
concedes, the identification of Jews as the potential victims for
radical economic policy is an inherently ideological act reliant on
antisemitism and the assumptions bound up in it.[113] The decision
to murder Jews as useless eaters operates around the idea that Jews
cannot be genuinely productive members of the economy. The
murder of Jews in Serbia may have been the result of security fears,
but the assumption that Jews represented a security risk is underpinned by a phobic antisemitism.

Thus there is a clear, and indeed enhanced role for ideology
within this post-Cold War historiography. Underpinning all the
decisions taken at a local level is a default and murderous antisemitism which assumes that Jewish lives have no value and in

some ways (for example with reference to infectious disease) that a region's Jews posed an existential threat. The idea that Hitler's state provided a vacuum of vague ideological ambitions which officials were invited to fill with policy at the very least implies a crucial and determining role for ideology. That said, by highlighting that the impulses leading to a murderous Jewish policy were rather wider than just racial policy in its strictest sense or for its own sake, historians have demonstrated that antisemitism was *more* rather than less fundamental. Antisemitism appears as the basis of all politics and administration rather than one aspect of it.[114] As Michael Thad Allen suggests, such observations may be best explained as highlighting the importance of ideologies rather than a single, antisemitic, ideological impulse.

Such ideas are not incompatible with the idea that the policy of the 'Final Solution' was not driven by central authorities, who were actually co-ordinating and seeking to control a complex process emerging on the periphery in response to different problems. Indeed it is certainly not at odds with the thesis proposed by Herf that through propaganda the state gave meaning – through casting the war as an apocalyptic conflict between Germany and Jewry – to the process that they called the 'Final Solution'.

If this consensus can be constructed, why is this gulf opening in Holocaust historiography? The insistence on the role of ideology is also the result of another debate in Holocaust historiography which has occurred alongside the post-Cold War German historiography described in this chapter. Crudely put, this discourse involves the analysis of the individual perpetrators of the Holocaust and their motivations, and it stands in contrast to the conservative, almost positivist historiography of regionalised Final Solutions. It is highly theorised and has been profoundly affected both by the politics of the late twentieth and early twenty-first centuries, and by the theoretical discourse surrounding the postmodern challenge to the discipline of History. This is the subject of the next chapter.

Conclusion

Post-Cold War Holocaust History reveals historical enquiry in all its complexity. The discovery of new documents in the archives of the former Soviet Union has shown that ultimately the limits, and indeed the extent of an historiography, are set by the documentary base with which historians work. However clearly historians are prisoners of their own time, they are bound, and limited, by their sources too. Holocaust historiography after 1989 is a field transformed, but not (or at least not with this particular facet of it) by the application of new theoretical perspectives or a new politics, but a massive enlargement of the documentary resources at historians' disposal. That source base was changed by massive shifts in global politics no doubt, and that alone is evidence that History is an ongoing conversation between present and past. Thus the present quite clearly can limit how much of the past we can see. But once the political obstacles to the documents had been removed they have been interpreted in a conservative manner with, perhaps, too great a respect for literally what they do and do not say. This is not to say that such endeavour cannot be cast as part of an historiographical tradition – the historiography reviewed in this chapter represents a German engagement with the past. However it is sobering for us to be reminded, even within the context of a book which is essentially arguing that History is a discourse created in the present, that such a discourse involves engagement with the past and the documents which represent for us its surviving fragments.

One of the impacts of this new material has been to move the focus of Holocaust History away from Berlin, to the killing fields themselves. But in doing this historiography has also been revealed as a discourse in which the present is all important too. Throughout Eastern Europe the new politics of the post-Cold War era has revealed new pasts, and the Holocaust has been an issue that has proved particularly difficult to come to terms with – especially where it has challenged national identities. If the discourse around the massacre at Jedwabne tells us anything, it is that History (whatever the role of documentary evidence) is about now as well as then.

Notes

1 Francis Fukuyama, *The End of History and the Last Man* (London, 1992), pp. xi–xxiii.
2 For a discussion of Marxist Holocaust scholarship in the GDR see Konrad Kwiet, 'Historians of the German Democratic Republic on Antisemitism and Persecution', *Leo Baeck Institute Yearbook* (21, 1976), pp. 173–98.

3 Teresa Swiebocka, 'Archival Collections at the Auschwitz-Birkenau State Museum', which can be viewed on-line at www.rtrfoundation.org/webart/chappolteresa.pdf, accessed 10/11/2008.

4 Patricia Kennedy Grimsted, 'Russia's Trophy Archives – Still Prisoners of World War II', which can be accessed from the Open Society Archives Website, www.osa.ceu.hu. Accessed 10/10/2008.

5 Himmler's appointments diary was subsequently edited for publication: Peter Witte *et al.* (eds), *Der Dienstkalender Heinrich Himmlers 1941/42* (Hamburg, 1999).

6 On the discovery of the documents see George C. Browder, 'Captured and Other Nations Documents in the Osobyi (Special) Archive, Moscow', *Central European History* (Vol. 24, No. 4, 1992), pp. 424–45 and 'Update on the Captured Documents in the Former Osobi Archive Moscow', *Central European History* (Vol. 26, No. 3, 1993), pp. 335–42.

7 Richard Breitman, *Official Secrets: What the Nazis Planned, What the British and Americans Knew* (New York, 1998), pp. 4–5.

8 Mark Roseman, *The Villa, the Lake, the Meeting: Wannsee and the Final Solution* (London, 2002), p. 5.

9 Dieter Pohl, 'War Occupation and the Holocaust in Poland', Dan Stone, *The Historiography of the Holocaust* (London, 2004), p. 99.

10 Götz Aly, *Final Solution: Nazi Population Policy and the Murder of the European Jews* (London, 1999), p. 250.

11 Hans Safrian, 'Expediting Expropriation and Expulsion: The Impact of the 'Vienna Model' on Anti-Jewish Policies in Nazi Germany', *Holocaust and Genocide Studies* (Vol. 14, No. 3, 2000), pp. 390–414.

12 Ian Kershaw, *Hitler, the Germans and the Final Solution* (Jerusalem, 2008), p. 19.

13 Christopher Browning (with Jürgen Matthäus), *The Origins of the Final Solution: the evolution of Nazi Jewish Policy September 1939–March 1942* (Lincoln: NE, 2004), p. 321.

14 Aly, *Final Solution*, p. 228.

15 Browning, *Origins of the Final Solution*, p. 322.

16 Ian Kershaw, 'Improvised Genocide: The Emergence of the 'Final Solution' in the Warthegau', *Transactions of the Royal Historical Society, 6th Series, Vol. 2* (London, 1992), pp. 51–78.

17 Kershaw, *Hitler, the Germans and the Final Solution*, p. 20.

18 Ian Kershaw, 'Working Towards the Führer: Reflections on the Nature of the Hitler Dictatorship', *Contemporary European History* (Vol. 2, No. 2, 1993), pp. 103–18.

19 See Wendy Lower, *Nazi Empire Building and the Holocaust in Ukraine* (Chapel Hill: NC, 2005), pp. 6–10 and '"Anticipatory Obedience" and the Nazi Implementation of the Holocaust in the Ukraine: A Case Study of Central and Peripheral Forces in the Generalbezirk Zhytomyr, 1941–44', *Holocaust and Genocide Studies* (Vol. 16, No. 1, 2002), pp. 1–22.

20 Dieter Pohl, 'The Murder of the Jews in the General Government', Ulrich Herbert (ed.), *National Socialist Extermination Policies: Contemporary German Perspectives and Controversies* (Oxford, 2000), p. 92. This summarises the thesis put forward at much greater length in Dieter Pohl, *Nationalsozialistische Judenverfolgung in Ostgalizien 1941–1944* (Munich, 1996).

21 On Warsaw see Christopher Browning, *The Path to Genocide: Essays on Launching the Final Solution* (Cambridge, 1992), p. 157; Pohl, 'The Murder of the Jews', p. 87.

22 Christian Gerlach, 'German Economic Interests, Occupation Policy, and the Murder of the Jews in Belorussia, 1941–43', Herbert, *National Socialist Extermination Policies*, p. 227. This is a summary of the thesis proposed in Christian Gerlach, *Kalkulierte Morde: Die deutsche Wirtschafts- und Vernichtungspolitik in Weißrußland 1941–44* (Hamburg, 1999).

23 Christoph Dieckmann, 'The War and the Killing of the Lithuanian Jews', Herbert, *National Socialist Extermination Policies*, pp. 258–62, 66; Götz Aly, *Hitler's Beneficiaries: Plunder, Racial War and the Nazi Welfare State* (New York, 2006), p. 174.

24 Sybille Steinbacher, 'In the Shadow of Auschwitz: The Murder of the Jews of East Upper Silesia', Herbert, *National Socialist Extermination Policies*, p. 292. Jews were being murdered there from May 1942, but the order for the destruction of all Jews in the area came in May 1943. Steinbacher's thesis is expanded in *'Musterstadt' Auschwitz: Germanisierungspolitik und Judenmord in Ostoberschlesien* (Munich, 2000).

25 Herbert, *National Socialist Extermination Policies*, p. 36.

26 Donald Bloxham, 'Organised Mass Murder: Structure, Participation and Motivation in Comparative Perspective', *Holocaust and Genocide Studies* (Vol. 22, No. 2, 2008), p. 211.

27 Dieter Pohl, 'Hans Krüger and the Murder of the Jews in the Stanislawow Region (Galicia)', *Yad Vashem Studies* (Vol. 26, 1998), pp. 239–64.

28 For an attempt to locate this historiography in a 'German tradition' see Wulf Kansteiner, 'The Rise and Fall of Metaphor: German Historians and the Uniqueness of the Holocaust', Alan S. Rosenbaum (ed.), *Is the Holocaust Unique? Perspectives on Comparative Genocide* (Philadelphia: PA, 2009), pp. 271–94.

29 Pohl makes this point in 'Hans Krüger', p. 239.

30 Walter Manoschek, 'The Extermination of the Jews in Serbia', Herbert, *National Socialist Extermination Policies*, p. 182.

31 Menachem Shelach, 'Sajmiste – An Extermination Camp in Serbia', *Holocaust and Genocide Studies* (Vol. 2, No. 2, 1987), pp. 244–5 for a discussion of this exchange.

32 Manfred Messerschmidt, 'Forward Defense: The "Memorandum of the Generals" for the Nuremberg Court', Hannes Heer and Klaus Naumann (eds), *War of Extermination: The German Military in World War II 1941–1944* (Oxford, 2000), pp. 391–2.

33 See for example Reginald Paget, *Manstein: His Campaigns and his Trial* (London, 1951).

34 Basil Liddell Hart, *The Other Side of the Hill: Germany's Generals, their Rise and Fall and their Own Account of Military Events 1939–45* (London, 1951).

35 OSS was the forerunner of the CIA, of which Dulles became head in 1953.

36 See Erich von Manstein, *Lost Victories* (London, 1955).

37 Robert Moeller, *War Stories: The Search for a Usable Past in the Federal Republic of Germany* (Berkeley: CA, 2001), p. 6.

38 Christian Streit, *Keine Kameraden: Die Wehrmacht und die sowjetischen Kriegsgefangenen 1941–45* (Stuttgart, 1978). For a study related explicitly to

the emergence of the 'Final Solution' see Christian Streit, '*Wehrmacht, Einsatzgruppen*, Soviet POWs and Anti-Bolshevism in the Emergence of the Final Solution', David Cesarani (ed.), *The Final Solution: Origins and Implementation* (London, 1996), pp. 103–19. See Jürgen Förster, 'The Relation Between Operation Barbarossa as an Ideological War of Extermination and the Final Solution', Cesarani (ed.), *Final Solution*, pp. 85–102; Omer Bartov, *The Eastern Front: German Troops and the Barbarisation of Warfare* (London, 1986) and *Hitler's Army* (Oxford, 1991). For a survey of the most recent historiography see Heer and Naumann, *War of Extermination*.

39 Volker R. Berghahn, 'Preface', Heer and Naumann, *War of Extermination*, p. xii.

40 Hannes Heer, 'The Difficulty of Ending a War: Reactions to the Exhibition "War of Extermination: Crimes of the Wehrmacht 1941 to 1944', *History Workshop Journal* (Vol. 46, Autumn 1998), pp. 187, 190.

41 Jan Thomas Gross, *Neighbors: the Destruction of the Jewish Community in Jedwabne, Poland* (Princeton: NJ, 2001), this description is taken from the testimony of Szmul Wasersztjan, eyewitness to the pogrom, which is quoted in full on pp. 16–20.

42 Gunnar S. Paulsson, *Secret City: The Hidden Jews of Warsaw 1940–45* (New Haven: CT, 2002), p. 245.

43 Jan Thomas Gross, *Fear: Anti-Semitism in Poland After Auschwitz* (Princeton: NJ, 2006), p. 247.

44 Joanna Michlic and Antony Polonsky (eds), *The Neighbors Respond: The Controversy over the Jedwabne Massacre in Poland* (Princeton: NJ, 2004), p. 26.

45 Joanna Michlic, 'Coming to Terms with the 'Dark Past': The Polish Debate about the Jedwabne Massacre', *Analysis of Current Trends in Antisemitism* (Vol. 21, 2002), p. 8. For a translation of the memorial book see http://www.jewishgen.org/Yizkor/Jedwabne/Yedwabne.html, accessed 14/07/09.

46 Tomasz Strzembosz, 'Collaboration Passed Over in Silence', Michlic and Polonsky, *The Neighbors Respond*, pp. 220-37.

47 Michlic, 'Coming to Terms with the 'Dark Past", p. 18.

48 Michlic was describing the work of Tomasz Szarota, *ibid.*, p. 29. See also Tomasz Szarota, 'Jedwabne without Stereotypes', Michlic and Polonsky, *The Neighbors Respond*, pp. 371–85.

49 Ultimately the IPN findings and all available material were published. See Jan Thomas Gross, 'Critical Remarks Indeed', Michlic andPolonsky, *The Neighbors Respond*, pp. 344–68.

50 Paulsson, *Secret City, passim.*

51 For a discussion of this see Martin Dean, 'Local Collaboration in the Holocaust in Eastern Europe', Dan Stone, *Holocaust Historiography*, pp. 120–40.

52 This is also an historiography which has been heavily influenced by war crimes trials programmes in the West (especially the USA and Australia) where individuals who emigrated from especially the Baltic states have been investigated since the 1980s for their links to Nazi crimes. For example Michael MacQueen, who was the historian of the Office of Special Investigations in the US Department of Justice, wrote the 'inescapable fact' of the Holocaust in Lithuania was that the majority of the killings were carried out by Lithuani-

ans. See his 'The Context of Mass Destruction: Agents and Prerequisites of the Holocaust in Lithuania', *Holocaust and Genocide Studies* (Vol. 12, No. 1, 1998), p. 27.

53 See Andrew Ezergalis, *The Holocaust in Latvia: The Missing Centre* (Riga, 1996), pp. 53–4. That Ezergalis' history might be difficult in terms of Latvian national identity is confirmed on p. xxi where he discusses that this is the first history of the Holocaust there by a Latvian: 'although some of my country-men will disown me for having written this work.'

54 Martin Dean, *Collaboration in the Holocaust: Crimes of the Local Police in Belorussia and Ukraine, 1941–44* (London, 2000), p. viii.

55 See for example Radu Ioanid, 'The Holocaust in Romania: The Iasi Pogrom of June 1941', *Contemporary European History* (Vol. 2, No. 2, 1993), pp. 119–48.

56 Tony Judt, *Postwar: A History of Europe Since 1945* (London, 2005), p. 824.

57 On the peoples courts in Hungary see László Karsai, 'The People's Courts and Revolutionary Justice in Hungary, 1945–46', István Deák, Jan T. Gross and Tony Judt (eds), *The Politics of Retribution in Europe: World War II and its Aftermath* (Princeton: NJ, 2000), pp. 233–50.

58 For a discussion of István Bibó's essay see Attila Pók, 'Germans, Hungarians and the Destruction of Hungarian Jewry', David Cesarani (ed.), *Genocide and Rescue: The Holocaust in Hungary 1944* (Oxford, 1997), pp. 147–58.

59 Randolph Braham, 'Hungary', David Wyman (ed.), *The World Reacts to the Holocaust* (Baltimore: MD, 1996), pp. 210–12.

60 See for example Randolph Braham (ed.), *The Destruction of Hungarian Jewry: A Documentary Account* (New York, 1963).

61 Randolph Braham, *The Politics of Genocide: The Holocaust in Hungary* (New York, 1981) – this remains the standard account.

62 See for example Elek Karsai, 'Deportation and Administration in Hungary' and Bela Vágo, 'The Hungarians and the Destruction of the Hungarian Jews', Randolph L. Braham and Bela Vágo (eds), *The Holocaust in Hungary: Forty Years Later* (New York, 1985).

63 See Tim Cole, *Holocaust City: The Making of a Jewish Ghetto* (London, 2003), p. 67. Cole also describes Molnar's work.

64 Gábor Kádár and Zoltán Vági, *Self Financing Genocide: The Gold Train, the Becher Case and the Wealth of Hungarian Jews* (Budapest and New York, 2004).

65 Christian Gerlach and Götz Aly, *Das letzte Kapitel: Der Mord an den un-garischen Juden* (Stuttgart, 2002)

66 David Cesarani, 'Introduction', *Genocide and Rescue*, p. 6.

67 See Ivan T. Berend, 'The Revival of Anti-Semitism in Post-Communist Hun-gary: the early 1990s', and Michael Shafir, 'Hungarian Politics and the Post 1989 Legacy of the Holocaust', Randolph L. Braham and Brewster S. Cham-berlain, *The Holocaust in Hungary: Sixty Years Later* (Boulder: CO, 2006), pp. 167–76, 257–90.

68 For a discussion of post-war historiography see Deborah Dwork and Robert Jan van Pelt, 'The Netherlands', David Wyman, *The World Reacts to the Holocaust*, pp. 56–8. For example the most extensive history in this period was called 'Suppression and Resistance', J.J. van Bolhuis *et al.* (eds), *Onder-drukking en Verzet: Nederland in oorlogstijd* 4 Vols. (Amsterdam, 1949–54).

69 See for example Abel Herzberg, *Kroniek der Jodenvervolging 1940–45* (Amsterdam, 1956). See Chapter 7 for a more detailed discussion of this.

70 For a discussion of this issue see also Bob Moore, *Victims and Survivors: The Nazi Persecution of the Jews in the Netherlands* (London, 1997), p. 2.

71 Jacob Presser, *Ondergang. De vervolging en verdelging van het Nederlandse jodendom 1940–45* (Amsterdam, 1965). English translation published in 1968, *Ashes in the Wind: The Destruction of Dutch Jewry* (London, 1968).

72 Dwork and van Pelt, 'Netherlands', p. 64.

73 Moore, *Victims and Survivors*, p. 9.

74 See for example J.C.H. Blom, 'The Persecution of the Jews in the Netherlands: A Comparative Western European Perspective', *European History Quarterly* (XIX, 1989), pp. 333–51; and Pim Grffioen and Ron Zeller, 'Anti-Jewish Policy and Organisation of the Deportations in France and the Netherlands, 1940–1944: A Comparative Study', *Holocaust and Genocide Studies* (Vol. 20, No. 3, 2006), pp. 437–73.

75 Dwork and van Pelt, 'Netherlands', p. 64.

76 Henry Rousso, *The Vichy Syndrome : History and Memory in France Since 1944* (Cambridge: MA, 1991).

77 Alan Resnais, *Nuit et Brouillard* (1955).

78 Renée Poznanski, *Jews in France During World War II* (Hanover: NH, 2001), Poznanski is referring to the work of Michael Marrus and Robert Paxton. See their *Vichy France and the Jews* (Stanford: CA,1981).

79 Michael Marrus, 'Coming to Terms With Vichy', *Holocaust and Genocide Studies* (Vol. 9, No. 1, 1995), p. 23.

80 See for example Susan Zucotti, *The Holocaust, the French and the Jews* (New York, 1993); Poznanski, *Jews in France*.

81 Richard Evans, 'Prologue – What is History? – Now', David Cannadine (ed.), *What is History Now?* (London, 2004), pp. 1–18.

82 Aly, *Final Solution*, p. 4.

83 Bogdan Musial, 'The Origins of "Operation Reinhard": The Decision-Making Process for the Mass Murder of the Jews in the General Government', *Yad Vashem Studies* (Vol. 28, 2000), pp. 113–53.

84 Aly, *Final Solution*, p. 253.

85 Roseman, *The Villa, the Lake, the Meeting*, p. 36.

86 Jürgen Matthäus, 'Controlled Escalation: Himmler's Men in the Summer of 1941 and the Holocaust in the Occupied Soviet Territories', *Holocaust and Genocide Studies* (Vol. 21, no. 2, 2007), pp. 218–42.

87 Konrad Kwiet, 'Rehearsing for Murder: The Beginning of the Final Solution in Lithuania in June 1941', *Holocaust and Genocide Studies* (Vol. 12, No. 1, 1998), p. 4.

88 Matthäus, 'Controlled Escalation', p. 233.

89 Browning, *Origins of the Final Solution*, p. 314.

90 Peter Witte, 'Two Decisions Concerning the "Final Solution to the Jewish Question": Deportations to Lodz and Mass Murder in Chelmno', *Holocaust and Genocide Studies* (Vol. 9, No. 3, 1995), p. 324.

91 Musial, 'The Origins of Operation Reinhard', p. 27.

92 See for example Peter Longerich, 'The Wannsee Conference in the Development of the Final Solution', in David Cesarani (ed.), *The Holocaust: Critical*

Concepts in Historical Studies (London, 2004), p. 131. – originally published as *HET Research Papers*, 1:2, 1999–2000.

93 Browning, *Origins of the Final Solution*, p. 428.

94 Longerich, 'The Wannsee Conference and the Development of the Final Solution', p. 143.

95 Browning, *Origins of the Final Solution*, p. 370.

96 Robert Jan van Pelt and Deborah Dwork, *Auschwitz 1270 to the Present* (New Haven: CT, 1996)

97 Michael Thad Allen, 'Not Just a 'Dating Game': Origins of the Holocaust at Auschwitz in the Light of Witness Testimony', *German History* (Vol. 25, No. 2, 2007), pp. 162–91.

98 Christian Gerlach, 'The Wannsee Conference, the Fate of German Jews, and Hitler's Decision in Principle to Exterminate all European Jews', *Journal of Modern History* (Vol. 70, December 1998), pp. 759–812.

99 Longerich, 'The Wannsee Conference and the Development of the Final Solution', pp. 137–43.

100 *Ibid.*, p. 142.

101 Michael Thad Allen, *The Business of Genocide: The SS, Slave Labour and the Concentration Camps* (Chapel Hill: NC, 2002)

102 See Ulrich Herbert, 'The German Military Command and in Paris and the Deportation of French Jews', *National Socialist Extermination Policies*, pp. 128-62.

103 Roseman, *The Villa, the Lake and the Meeting*, p. 78.

104 See Allen, *The Business of Genocide*.

105 Longerich, 'The Wannsee Conference', p. 145. This thesis was first outlined in Peter Longerich, *Politik der Vernichtung: Eine Gesamtdarstellung der nationalsozialistischen Judenverfolgung* (Munich, 1998). Longerich's English language history of the Holocaust will be published in 2010: Peter Longerich, *Holocaust: The Nazi Persecution and Murder of the Jews* (Oxford, 2010).

106 Raul Hilberg, *The Destruction of the European Jews* (New Haven: CT, 2003), p. 1060.

107 Richard Evans, *Telling Lies About Hitler* (London, 2002), pp. 77–111.

108 Stefan Kley, 'Hitler and the Pogrom of November 9/10 1938', *Yad Vashem Studies* (Vol. 28, 2000), pp. 87–112.

109 Aly, *Final Solution*, p. 257.

110 Saul Friedländer, *The Years of Extermination: Nazi Germany and the Jews 1939–1945* (New York, 2007), p. xvii.

111 Jeffrey Herf, *The Jewish Enemy: Nazi Propaganda During World War II and the Holocaust* (Cambridge: MA, 2006), p. 264.

112 Sybille Steinbacher, 'In the Shadow of Auschwitz: The Murder of the Jews of East Upper Silesia', p. 277.

113 Gerlach, 'German Economic Interests, Occupation Policy, and the Murder of the Jews', p. 229.

114 Of course this was not necessarily a new argument, Raul Hilberg had made a similar argument in his *The Destruction of the European Jews*.

6

'Ordinary Men':
rethinking the politics of perpetrator history

The idea that the 'Final Solution' was varied and complex now represents received wisdom. Contrary to what might be expected however, awareness of the diversity of the decision-making process has not really supported explanations of the Holocaust which rely on the abstractions of social and bureaucratic structure. If anything it has undermined them. After all, as we have seen the more diverse the origins of the 'Final Solution', then the greater number of individuals and agencies that were involved in its prosecution and the more diverse the contexts and situations within which mass murder was carried out. As Holocaust History has focused on those different institutions and individuals then the question of agency and *intention*, of what motivated so many men to commit what appear so obviously heinous crimes, has returned, perhaps inevitably, to the fore. But whereas previously such questions were really only asked of the ruling cabal, now the foot-soldiers of Nazism have become the focus of a developing social history of the perpetrators of the Holocaust. To put it bluntly, why did ordinary Germans *choose* to murder ordinary Jews?

Christopher Browning's *Ordinary Men*, first published in 1992, both epitomises and in many ways prompted this turn to the agency of individual perpetrators active in diverse institutions of the Third Reich. *Ordinary Men* is a study of a group of Order Police men, Reserve Police Battalion 101. Reserve Police Battalion 101 was stationed in the Lublin area, but had been recruited and formed in Hamburg. Although the Order Police had been progressively militarised during the Third Reich (Browning compares them with US National Guard Units) and came (like all policing after 1936) under the aegis of the SS, the men who served in them were not necessarily the ideological warriors of Nazism. Service in the Order Police Reserve battalions offered the chance to be stationed near to home and the prospect of avoiding frontline postings. It also was an alternative for men who were too old to be considered of worth to the armed forces.[1] After 1939 Order Police battalions were often transferred to the occupied territories, charged with the task of pacifying their locale. That task included from 1942, more and more, the murder of local Jewish populations or their deportation to concentration and death camps. These men may thus not have been ideological Nazis, but they became the agents of the 'Final Solution' itself.

Reserve Police Battalion 101 also stood out in particular because prior to their first involvement in a mass killing, they were expressly offered the *opportunity to withdraw*. At Józefów on the morning of 13 July 1942, the men, having been informed that their task that day was to murder the town's Jewish population, were told by their commanding officer that anyone wishing to be assigned other duties just needed to identify themselves. Such a possibility of non-participation meant that by definition the men of Reserve Police Battalion 101 were *volunteers*. They had chosen in the face of an alternative to participate in a bloody and brutal mass execution. The agency, or otherwise, of this choice required explanation. Why did they do it?

Browning's account of that choice was controversial. Using the testimonies of 125 of the men given in police custody or trial, he argued that their motivations were complex. Some were simply ideological Nazis, and some were motivated by a base sadism; yet the majority's choices were determined as much by situational (i.e. environmental, communal, social) contexts and pressures and not simply ideological animus towards Jews or blood-lust. Ultimately for Browning there could be no single explanation of perpetrator behaviour. His emphasis on complexity demands the following lengthy illustrative quotation from the conclusion:

> most of all one comes away from the story of Reserve Police Battalion 101 with great unease. This story of ordinary men is not the story of all men. The reserve policemen faced choices, and most of them committed terrible deeds ... those who killed cannot be absolved by the notion that anyone in the same situation would have done as they did. For even among them, some refused to kill and others stopped killing. Human responsibility is ultimately an individual matter ... but despite

this their story does have a great resonance mainly because within virtually every social collective, the peer group exerts tremendous pressures on behaviour and sets moral norms. If the men of Reserve Police Battalion 101 could become killers under such circumstances, what group of men cannot?[2]

Although *Ordinary Men* was a micro-history of a very small group of perpetrators, Browning's final rhetorical question demonstrates that this was a local history concerned with the most universal of questions. The chapter that follows is therefore an attempt to put micro-studies of the *Ordinary Men* of the Holocaust into both political and methodological context. I want to demonstrate that, despite the new empiricism reviewed in Chapter 5, Holocaust History continues to be primarily concerned with moral and political questions regarding the relationship between the Holocaust and modern state and society, and with the moral and ethical basis of modernity. At the same time the 'voluntaristic turn' is also a response to and consequence of the postmodern challenge to established historical methodologies, although some scholarship in the area displays little sign of these origins.[3] It is to this historiographical context that I turn first.

The *Historikerstreit* and the *Alltagsgeschichte*: the contexts for a new history of destruction

Before the late 1980s studies of perpetrator motivation had been very narrowly focused, concentrating on the symbolic leaders of the Nazi movement. Although something of an extreme caricature, the tendency towards psychological biographies of Hitler is illustrative here. Efforts to locate why Hitler hated the Jews, to pinpoint the moment of his conversion to antisemitism were typical – usually citing occasions of psychological distress as some kind of trigger point. This in turn was typical of an approach to both biography and studies of Nazism, which drew heavily upon classical psychology. In terms of Nazi violence they came together to produce a picture of the perpetrators as dysfunctional and disturbed. The history of the perpetrators did not really extend much beyond this approach, and indeed it did not need to according to the psycho-biographers. For Robert Waite, Hitler's dysfunction 'produced the greatest deliberate mass murder of history'.[4] Although there were persistent calls to widen the social history of the Holocaust, it seems that this usually envisaged the history of the victims being added, not the further investigation of the perpetrators.[5]

The use of psycho-historical approaches did spawn some limited considerations of the motivations of individual perpetrators, perhaps harking back to the Freudian origins of Holocaust studies. Gitta Sereny's investigation of Franz Stangl, who was Commandant of both Sobibor and Treblinka, is at root a work of psychoanalysis – which searched for the 'essence' or 'mysterious core' of the human condition.[6] Sereny's Stangl has much in common with Arendt's Eichmann, in that he portrays himself as an enthusiastic cog in the machinery of murder which somehow freed him of moral responsibility for his actions.[7] Sereny's account also had some similarity to Robert Jay Lifton's attempt to understand *The Nazi Doctors*. Sereny portrayed a man struggling to reconcile the ordinary and extraordinary elements of his life story. Lifton similarly emphasised the psychological distance that many of the perpetrators achieved from their crimes. Explicitly attempting to discern a 'psychology of genocide', Lifton gave a two-pronged analysis of the role of medical professionals in both the Euthanasia programme and the genocide of the Jews. First he argued that National Socialism achieved a medicalisation of society which allowed doctors to domesticate their murderousness with the vocabulary of healing or cleansing. And second he proposed the concept of 'doubling' whereby perpetrators divided their selves 'into two functioning wholes' which did not impinge upon each other. The 'Auschwitz self' could deal in death without affecting the medical or personal self, which continued to explore the sustaining of life and to lead 'normal' professional, social and familial lives. In the main this 'doubling' allowed the perpetrators of violence to avoid guilt because of the separation of their two selves.[8] One of the key assumptions of the Lifton approach, which has been attacked more recently, was the idea that the perpetrators had to overcome an innate moral repugnance to their deeds – as such Lifton echoed Arendt's thesis that the perpetrators did not identify with their crimes.

On the whole histories of the perpetrators of the Holocaust were limited and thus any investigation of motivation would have filled an historiographical gap. But the histories which did emerge were also a response to other pressures brought to bear on the study of Holocaust history, somewhat different to those that led to the regionalisation of studies of the 'Final Solution'. Although the expanding documentary base of Holocaust studies after 1989 has extended the number of perpetrators who could be investigated, and especially the agencies they worked for, the turn to individual motivation has not entirely relied on 'new' or rediscovered archival sources. Much of this scholarship has simply involved returning to extant records with a new eye. The case of Reserve Police Battalion 101 is again instructive here – both *Ordinary Men* and Daniel Goldhagen's reply *Hitler's Willing Executioners* were based on sources emanating from the men's arrest and trial in Hamburg in the late 1960s. It was not therefore the documents that had changed, but the questions asked of them.

In part, this shift was a consequence of the *Historikerstreit* or historians' dispute which took place largely in the pages of German newspapers and journals during the 1980s. The dispute emerged as a response to the then German Chancellor Helmut Kohl and his historical adviser Michael Stürmer seeking to rethink the location of the Third Reich, and thus the Holocaust, in German national History. Stürmer argued that the history of the Third Reich should be placed within a wider context, and by doing so, that it might be able to support a more positive national identity through emphasising for example the (West) German transition to democracy.[9] Conservative German historians such as Andreas Hilgruber and Ernst Nolte enthusiastically heeded this call to arms, arguing both that the Holocaust should not be allowed to cast a shadow over the entire German twentieth century; and at the same time that it should not be wrenched from historical continuity and proclaimed a uniquely, terrible crime (and thus an event through which all history should be filtered). Nolte's claim that the Soviet Gulag was 'more original' than Auschwitz is often used as a shorthand for this position – implying (in an echo of the Nazis themselves) that the Nazi genocide had been a response to Soviet terror and thus that German nationalism had not committed the original offence.[10] The response to this apologia was led by left-leaning social philosopher Jürgen Habermas, who argued conversely for the centrality of the crimes of National Socialism in the creation of German national identity. Auschwitz stood as a permanent and functional limitation on German nationalism for Habermas – reminding Germans of the need for a 'constitutional patriotism' which cemented ties with the West and emphasised the importance of the rule of law.[11]

It is widely asserted that this discourse was, in the end, of little interpretative value, other than showing baldly the links between History and politics.[12] And indeed arguments like Hilgruber's, that the destruction of the European Jews and the destruction of the German Reich were somehow comparable, have had little enduring impact. Yet underneath the political rhetoric, the call for the 'normalisation' of the history of the Third Reich which under-pinned German politicians' original intentions, did impact Holocaust studies. In a much more thoughtful argument than those of Stürmer *et al.*, Martin Broszat issued 'a plea for the historicisation of the history of the National Socialism' in 1985 which accepted that for those who lived through it, the Third Reich *was* situated in the continuity of the twentieth century, and thus this was a past like any other and could be treated as such by historians.[13] In many ways Broszat was simply articulating what his own Bavaria project had been doing since the late 1970s, study-ing the everyday life of Germans during the Third Reich which had emphasised that 'below the barbarism and horror of the regime were patterns of social "normality" which were, of course, affected by Nazism in various ways but which pre-dated and survived it'.[14]

Broszat's plea was heavily criticised, most notably by Saul Friedländer as a short route to the trivialisation of the Holocaust era.[15] For him, if Auschwitz was not set as the centre of the history of the Third Reich then it risked disappearing from view. The significance of the Third Reich lay not in the continuities of indi-viduals' everyday lives from the Weimar era to the Federal Republic but in what set the era apart – the genocide of the Jews.

Despite this, however, the idea of 'normalisation' provided a crucial context for the studies of perpetrator motivation which are now vogue. Broszat's Bavaria project essentially applied the methodology known as the *Alltagsgeschichte* or History of Everyday Life to the Third Reich. This method (sometimes also called micro-history, especially in an Italian context) seeks to 'enter the inner world of popular experience in the workplace, the family and household' and reconstruct not only 'ordinary' people's lives but also their hopes, fears and feelings.[16] The *Alltagsgeschichte* thus sought to break down the barriers between the public and the private. In the context of the Third Reich, it sought the relationship between the 'everyday and the exceptional'.[17] Thus by focusing on the normal, the abnormal – like Auschwitz – might be better understood, *not* simply ignored. Such an approach fundamentally rejected the ideas of historical psychoanalysis which had previously dominated perpetrator studies, that they led a 'double' existence and sought instead to see the murderers' lives as an integrated if frequently contradictory whole.

The History of Everyday Life is postmodern history in action. It has thus been through the *Alltagsgeschichte* that the postmodern critique has had one of its most positive influences on Holocaust History. By deconstructing images and language it applies the techniques of literary analysis in reconstructing and deconstructing the ideational worlds of people in the past, and thus allows for the interplay between past and present. It is also allows for, indeed encourages, imagination.[18] At the same time, the inevitable focus of the History of Everyday Life is on difference, on the lack of homogeneity in the past because by its very nature it must focus on the multiplicity of experiences. At its most radical the *Alltagsgeschichte* therefore denies the utility of 'total' theories or explanations – such as those traditionally used by social historians, be they materialist or otherwise – and embraces, indeed celebrates, the diversity and perhaps even the chaos of the past, pointing not to history but histories.[19] Although some historians of Nazi Germany have dismissed such an approach as history by anecdote which, by emphasising the sheer number of narratives in the past, renders the historian simply a storyteller, the History of Everyday Life underpins many of the major achievements of modern Holocaust History. By focusing on the everyday, historians have been able first to ask what the relationship was between German society and the 'Final Solution' prosecuted (secretly) in its name. After the regionalisation of Holocaust studies had demonstrated how those enacting the 'Final Solution' were also, very often, the ordinary Germans of that society, not some removed and distant ideological elite, then the *Alltagsgeschichte* could also help illuminate how the perpetrators of violence itself conceived of their crimes.

Alltagsgeschichte and German responses to the Holocaust

As was discussed in Chapter 1, the study of domestic German attitudes to Jews and Judaism within Holocaust studies was first
conceptualised as the study of antisemitism, in terms of delineat-
ing the causes or pre-history of the 'Final Solution'. Because of
this, such investigations often stopped in 1933 – implying that the
Hitler dictatorship was the culmination of German antisemitism.
Of course such an approach left the question of how German society responded to Nazi antisemitic policy, and ultimately the 'Final
Solution', unasked and thus unanswered. This is not surprising.
The study of public attitudes or public opinion in any society, past
or even present, is difficult; an exercise in 'nailing jelly to the wall'.
In terms of the past, only traces of public attitudes can be found
in the source material – especially in societies where surveying
public opinion was not routine. Entering *private* conversation, and
this is what the historian of general attitudes must do, is especially
fraught. As far as the history of the Nazi state is concerned it is
potentially even more problematic – because this was a police state
in which public attitudes were heavily censored and thus the
expression of dissenting opinions took on a new and possibly
lethal potential.

Despite the challenges, increasingly cultural historians do feel
able to stray into the private sphere. Even if we cannot enter the
lost world of the family kitchen, we can begin to glimpse how that
world was understood by looking at the ways in which it was
constructed in the public realm – by deconstructing wider sources
such as advertising or popular media. This kind of approach is
more fruitful in the study of the Third Reich than for less extreme
societies. During the Nazi era, it can be argued that the state
sought to *eliminate* the autonomy of the private sphere and it
certainly sought to make private actions publicly significant.
Consider the example of women and childbirth. The Nazis sought
both to remove women from the workplace, from the public
sphere, and to increase the birth rate and thus intervene in the
private. As such the private sphere became public, in that women
enacting this return to the private realm were certainly characterised as doing public works at the same time. Alongside this
encouragement of procreation, the Nazis also sought to affect the
population negatively too – the Law for the Elimination of Hered-
itarily Diseased Progeny attempted to limit those groups allowed

to have children through forced sterilisation. As such in the Third Reich, the private act of having children and indeed the whole private world of the family became ideologised. While we cannot say that all those German women who returned to the home and had children consciously revelled in their role as the 'Mothers of the Fatherland', what we can say is that their private behaviour did have a public significance, that the private had thus become public too.[20] Stories such as Edith's from Wesel demonstrate just how complex the matter could be. Edith's mother received the 'Mother's Cross' as a reward for her fertility after the birth of a fourth child. After receiving the award, which declared her private behaviour to be a public virtue, Edith's mother buried it in her garden. She thus privately rejected her new public role.[21]

There is also potentially much more source material for the study of public opinion in the Nazi era than there might be in more normal societies. Far from being contemptuous of public attitudes (as the mythical totalitarian image might suggest) the Nazis were obsessed with public opinion which was regularly surveyed, at a local and national level, using the instruments of repression themselves. As such historians have at their disposal literally hundreds of thousands of reports which attempted to tell the regime how its public were feeling about any number of issues.[22] At the same time, opposition organisations also sought to survey public attitudes during the Nazi era. The Social Democratic Party in Exile had a network of informants reporting on attitudes to the regime, within which its leaders searched for the glimmers of hope for the non-Nazi future.[23] Other institutions which shaped opinion also offer a valuable perspective, most notably the churches.[24]

Not that this source material is without its problems and limitations. Public opinion reports produced by the SD do not represent a precise window on public opinion, but are a complex amalgam of different pressures. They must in some way relate to what people reported on were thinking, but they also reflect the sensibilities of the individual author, the institutional priorities of the SD and perceptions of what the central authorities wanted to hear. They also reflect, self-evidently, what the regime wanted to know. Take the example of reports on public reactions to the application of the Yellow Star decree to German Jews in September of 1941. SD reports stated that Germans were calling for more radical policies and thus the removal of Jews. Such observations can be interpreted in any number of different ways, and the idea that Germans wished for more radical policies and that this reflected an enthusiasm for Nazi anti-Judaism is only the most obvious. It is also possible to argue that Germans objected to the public display of anti-Judaism that the star represented and thus wanted the Jews removed in order to expunge this public reminder of their own knowledge and complicity. It is equally plausible that the SD projected their own desire for radicalism into the reports, or that the SD projected their own sense of what central authorities wanted to know about reactions to the Jews. The list could go on. As such whatever the different perspectives on the attitudes of wider society to Jewish policy, it can never represent a trade in certainty, which for some historians means that it will remain forever elusive.[25]

Despite this uncertainty there have been continual efforts to characterise the relationship between the Germans and the 'Final Solution' since the 1970s. Prior to Broszat's Bavaria project these were largely less than systematic attempts to tackle the problem on a general level.[26] What the Bavaria project did (and this is perhaps best symbolised for our purposes by the work of Ian Kershaw who worked under its auspices),[27] was allow reactions to Jewish policy to be placed in the context of people's everyday lives and therefore identify the relationship between the 'normal' and the 'abnormal'. This also meant that the local and regional heterogeneity of attitudes could be laid bare – breaking down the stereotypical view that 'the Germans' did not know. After all this was just the study of one, very distinctive, region.

The micro-history enacted by the Bavaria project established an idea of diversity which is now embedded in all approaches to this question. The simple truth that the population was variegated, divided between an enthusiastic Nazi core, pliable majority (over whose attitudes there remains some dispute) and dissenting periphery is largely universal. It is also widely accepted that this applied across the social spectrum, that class was no insurance against Nazi attitudes. So although there is evidence that workers in the Third Reich retained a sense of class identity, the idea that they were the eternal victims of the Nazi state and could never identify with Nazi goals is simply not the case.[28] Indeed studying the workers using the *Alltagsgeschichte* perspective has revealed how even those who might have defined themselves in opposition to the Nazi regime had imbibed the regime's racial assumptions. Alf Lüdtke cites an exchange in Viktor Klemperer's diary as evidence of this tendency. A factory worker who had befriended Klemperer, and even brought him food, asked him one day 'Albert says your wife is German; is she really German?'[29]

Klemperer's friend Frieda clearly did not think too much about her own attitudes to Jews and their relationship with Germans, despite her relationship with one of the victims. It was Ian Kershaw's work that first highlighted how little attention Germans gave to the Jewish question, and as such how far the abnormal failed to disrupt the normal lives of individuals in the Third Reich. Only vague knowledge of the extermination of Jews abounded in German society according to Kershaw, and thus the true significance lay in how little the Jews (either positively or negatively) mattered to ordinary Germans. In a memorably pithy phrase Kershaw alleged that the 'road to Auschwitz was built by hate but paved with indifference.'[30] Germans were largely so engaged with other pressures in their own lives, which in wartime meant their own suffering, that Jews simply didn't impinge on their consciousness at all.

That the idea of indifference was so problematic for other scholars highlights once again how far Holocaust History can be a discourse about much more than just the sufferings of Jews. One of the critics of Kershaw's thesis, Otto Dov Kulka, had also attacked the idea of 'normalising' the history of the Third Reich in the first place. For Dov Kulka and also David Bankier the idea of indifference implied too little *moral* responsibility on behalf of the German population. Working from the same sources, Dov Kulka and Bankier sought to identify Germans' 'passive complicity'.[31] The silence surrounding Jews was evidence not of indifference but of a basic consensus over Jewish policy, a consensus which only began to break down when the fortunes of the Nazi regime changed and antisemitism became feared as the motivation for retribution.[32] You will note there was no disagreement that silence surrounded the Jewish experience, only over what that silence might mean. Jeffrey Herf also suggested in his analysis of propaganda that the regime used antisemitism to tie the population to their own criminality, to create a kind of community of fate. Herf argues that propaganda, although short on detail, advertised the 'Final Solution' to the population, rendering it a kind of 'open secret'.[33]

There is a disagreement here about the extent of ideological conformity and conviction. Kershaw finds silence to be indifference, Dov Kulka and Bankier interpret silence as assent. Part of the problem, and again this is familiar, is that actually neither concept can account for all, nor could any other single explanation suffice.[34] Sometimes silence undoubtedly meant indifference, sometimes assent, sometimes a complex combination of the two.[35] Consider the doleful example of Lilli Jahn.[36] Lilli, a German Jew, was married to a non-Jewish physician, Ernst Jahn. In October 1942, Ernst divorced his wife and the mother of his children, largely it seems because of the social humiliation and economic hardship that his marriage represented in the Nazi era and because he had fallen in love with another woman. Ernst was aware what this might mean for Lilli. Lilli was arrested, moved around various work camps and was ultimately transported to Auschwitz where she died. Ernst does not appear to have been an ideological antisemite, he had married a Jew, yet he was it appears so inured to Jews' fate, that he was able to allow and actually facilitated his wife and mother of his children being taken away.[37] Such an action seems so actively morally repugnant that the concept of indifference is somehow not enough. But it is a story so complex that it is clear that simply labelling Ernst complicit does not suffice either.

What is clear from Lilli's example is that, whatever the extent of their ideological conviction, ordinary Germans had a functional relationship with the organs of state terror and thus the persecution of the Jews even in their everyday lives. Ernst did not choose to send Lilli to Auschwitz, he chose to divorce her. But in the nightmare of the Third Reich that ordinary, in a way private, decision had extraordinary public consequences. Similarly, Robert Gellately and Eric Johnson have recently demonstrated just how far the institutions of terror were a part of everyday life for Germans. According to Gellately, the Gestapo was an underfunded and undermanned organisation which rather than keeping the population in check, relied on that population for information to carry out its work. The majority of investigations for crimes such as race defilement came from denunciations, and there is some evidence that such allegations were frequently made maliciously in order to solve petty, private disputes.[38] While such evidence cannot necessarily suggest support for ideological antisemitism, there is a growing sense among historians that the Nazi state was a consensual dictatorship.

The *Alltagsgeschichte* established that Germans were tied to the criminal policies of the Nazi state, whether they approved of them or not. More recently historians have begun to investigate their material links with the persecution of the Jews. Frank Bajohr's study of 'Aryanisation' in Hamburg, for example, highlights how ordinary Germans there could profit from Jews first deported to the East and then murdered. The belongings of murdered Jews were regularly sold at public auctions in the city.[39] Götz Aly has gone further, arguing that Germans were tied to occupation policies in the East and ultimately the Holocaust, because they spared them the burdens of war. Genocide directly increased the material wealth of the German population. Aly writes: 'the Nazi leadership did not transform the majority of Germans into ideological fanatics who were convinced they were part of the master race. Instead it succeeded in making them well fed parasites.'[40]

Richard Evans has recently argued that the consensus model of the Third Reich underplays the violence and terror of the regime.[41] But on the whole fears that the 'normalisation' of the history of the Third Reich would trivialise have not been realised. Indeed the opposite has happened and the profound relationship between the normal and the abnormal has been revealed.

Alltagsgeschichte and German perpetrators of the Holocaust

As Browning acknowledged when applying the *Alltagsgeschichte* method, there was little that was 'everyday' about the men of Reserve Police Battalion 101. They operated in a world where 'normality itself had become exceedingly abnormal'.[42] But Browning did not therefore seek explanation *only* in the abnormality of their situation or beliefs, because he argued being an agent of genocide was a part of the human experience and needed explanation therefore on human terms. One is tempted to add the sheer frequency of genocidal violence in the twentieth century begs that the Holocaust cannot simply be explained in terms of the way Germans thought about Jews.[43] Browning was seeking an explanation for a specific type of Holocaust perpetrator, who saw their victim face to face, who could look them in the eye before killing them. After all, functional explanations of the Holocaust that found their inspiration in the idea of modernity may help understanding the so-called 'desk murderers', but they are of little use trying to understand and explain the violent deaths of the victims of Nazi massacre. The added fascination with Reserve Police Battalion 101 was that these were a group of men with no military experience, largely unfamiliar with the grim reality of the Nazi occupation of Eastern Europe. Crucially they were on average older, they had been schooled before the advent of the Third Reich and were 'men who had known political and moral norms other than those of the Nazis'.[44] And, of course, they chose to participate, to conform to a situation and community that required them to commit murder again and again and again.

Why? Browning suggests that war, and its attendant brutalisation can only in part explain the men's behaviour. On that July morning when they were initiated into murder, most of the reservists of Reserve Police Battalion 101 had not been brutalised. They may have been frightened and bewildered by their posting and the war that surrounded them, but they had not been exposed to the extremities of the Eastern Front. All the subsequent actions of Reserve Police Battalion 101 could potentially be explained by the brutality of their experiences, but not that first day. But antisemitism cannot alone explain it either. The men had received a rudimentary ideological education, but none discussed antisemitism in their own efforts to explain their behaviour. Of course Browning does not naively accept this silence, the men must at the very least have accepted the Nazi idea that their victims were the enemy, and indeed he acknowledges the commitment to that ideal that some of the men's actions seem to manifest. The practice of 'Jew Hunts', for example, which betrayed 'an existential condition of constant readiness and intention to kill every last Jew who could be found.'[45] But Browning's entire approach to Holocaust History has always been that antisemitism alone is not a sufficient explanation.

Ultimately then he was left to seek explanations in the everyday, confirming the view of sociologists that there is a violent potential in all situations of both authority and group identity, a potential immeasurably amplified by the context of war.[46] The idea that peer pressure and group dynamics can in part explain why very few men availed themselves of the opportunity not to take part in the first massacre in July 1942 is grotesque, but for Browning unavoidable. The 'cost of not shooting' he explains 'was to separate themselves from their comrades and expose themselves as weak'.[47] To take part in a massacre may seem to us the ultimate transgression, but the moral norms for Reserve Police Battalion 101 were fundamentally different. At the same time the men were loyal to one another, they may have been able individually to avoid involvement in the 'dirty work' of killing Jews, but the unit as a whole still had to discharge this duty. Equally, while they may have been able to withdraw from shooting without punishment, that is not the same as their being aware that no negative repercussions would follow. As one of the men who did not take part in the killing explained, he, because he was older, did not have a career to worry about.[48] Browning's emphasis on context was later negatively confirmed through a study of the police of East Upper Silesia. These men were stationed in their own community, and were therefore not an isolated group of individuals operating far from home and thus whose moral boundaries were dictated only with reference to one another. The Jewish population were familiar, still often employed in private industry and not marked with the Yellow Star like the rest of the Jews in Poland. As a consequence the interaction between the police and the Jews was very different, despite the police receiving regular ideological training. Even in the midst of deportations, there were cases of fraternisation between Jews and the police.[49]

Yet the *Alltagsgeschichte* approach has not been without its critics, largely because it fails to give priority to ideological antisemitism in tracing the symbiotic relationship between Germans and the elimination of Jews. Germans may have profited from the murder of Jews, they may thus have been complicit in it, but for the mass of the population the removal of Jews does not appear in such histories as an ideological imperative.

Daniel Goldhagen's *Hitler's Willing Executioners* was in essence a criticism of the everyday life approach from that direction, and a reply to Browning's *Ordinary Men* (hence the subtitle *Ordinary Germans and the Holocaust*). Goldhagen called emphatically for ideological antisemitism to be put back in to the history of both German society and the Holocaust and in the history of the perpetration of the 'Final Solution'.[50] His argument is well known, and was widely criticised.[51] Simply put Goldhagen proposed that 'eliminationist antisemitism' was an axiom of German culture prior to 1933, and that after that point this genocidal attitude drove Germans in a 'Final Solution' that was in essence their shared project. 'Ordinary Germans' according to Goldhagen were not indifferent to the removal of Jews, but enthusiasts for it. He framed this argument using some theoretical approaches from social anthropology which allowed him to interpret the silences around Jews as evidence not of their marginal place on the horizons of most Germans but indicative of their centrality.[52]

The idea that silence could mean indifference was, according to Goldhagen, based on a flawed conceptual model – that Germans, as citizens of a modern twentieth-century nation-state, were like us.[53] They were not, and what set them apart was a society-wide, irrational obsession with the Jews. In a conscious reversal of the historian's usual methods which harked back to the original intentionalist reading, the evidence for this claim was the Holocaust itself. What Goldhagen then sought was empirical evidence to disprove this hypothesis, whereas most historians would, of course, work the other way around. At the time Goldhagen's work, although it received a great deal of attention, was widely dismissed by historians; applying one of the more memorable epithets Ruth Bettina Birn compared it to a 'bad historical novel'.[54] And it seems it has little to tell us about the complex relationship between wider German society and the Holocaust, because of its insistence on simplistic monocausality.

Unsurprisingly *Hitler's Willing Executioners* offers a rather different account of perpetrator motivation too. Intriguingly though, Goldhagen also focused on the same group of perpetrators in Reserve Police Battalion 101. If Browning's men were reluctantly initiated into mass murder that summer morning in Józefów; then Goldhagen's Reserve Police Battalion 101 reached a state of grace that same morning. They took 'open joy' in the mass slaughter which was (and the image conjured here is important) 'their *baptismal* moment as genocidal executioners'.[55] Goldhagen's men were not reluctant killers pressured into committing acts which ordinarily they would have believed beyond the pale, progressively brutalised by the circumstances which bound them together, on the contrary they were 'ideological warriors' who 'in slaughtering Jews ... believed themselves to be performing heroic deeds'.[56] They were thus 'Ordinary Germans' giving violent expression to their 'eliminationist' culture which was their 'motivational mainspring'.[57]

So how can we explain the differences between these two accounts of the same group of individuals based on the same sources? First and foremost it is their alternative disciplinary approaches which are crucial. Browning is an historian, using the methods of the *Alltagsgeschichte* to attempt to 'rethink' the men of Reserve Police Battalion 101, to put back together their mindset in order to see the extent and the limits of their mental horizons. In doing so Browning attempts to understand what the crimes they committed meant to the men themselves. Browning relies on the inductive reasoning at the heart of the historians' discipline, looking forward from the evidence to find an explanation. Goldhagen is a political scientist who rejects this method and relies instead on an interpretation of the methods of social anthropology.[58] Thus the murder of Jews by Reserve Police Battalion 101 stands as evidence of their genocidal antisemitism. Goldhagen then works backwards from this hypothesis asking whether there is any evidence to *disprove* such a hypothesis. At the same time he declared that the evidence from the men was largely inadmissible because it was necessarily given in an attempt to avoid legal responsibility. The men's silence on antisemitism, however, reflects not its marginality but its very centrality – a shared assumption that was, as it were, beyond discussion.

Goldhagen's attempt to reconstruct the interior lives of the men of the Reserve Police functioned around a rather cavalier attitude to historical evidence. Many of the men of Battalion 101 were Catholics. Goldhagen declares therefore that they must have related their actions as *genocidaires* to their faith. Indeed he goes as far as to suggest that they did this in the confessional: 'some of the men went to Church, prayed to God, contemplated eternal questions ... took communion and went to confession.' Such events are an important part of the argument that the motivations for killing Jews were ideological, that it represented the right thing to do for the reservists, because these were morally active men who considered their actions in that way. Yet the only evidence for such claims was that the times of church services in the region were advertised to the men.[59]

Overall, although Goldhagen rejected the methods of the 'life history' approach, what his debate with Christopher Browning did represent was the beginning of a shift in the focus of Holocaust historiography to the individual perpetrators of destruction or, to use Goldhagen's phrase, 'Hitler's Willing Executioners'. These men have more and more come to predominate in Holocaust historiography – in part because of the changing political contexts of the post-Cold War world.

The politics of modern perpetrator history

Despite being dismissed by scholars, Goldhagen's thesis had a much greater resonance with what might be called the wider reading public in both the USA and Western Europe and can genuinely be regarded as a best-seller. In Germany Goldhagen was feted – he conducted a triumphant book tour, and was even awarded the 'democracy prize' by a left-wing journal for highlighting the inherent dangers in German nationalism at a time when a newly reunified Germany was feeling its way in the world.[60] Why did such a gulf exist between the public and academic reception of this history?

First, Goldhagen was riding the crest of a wave of interest in the Nazi period (which can be evidenced by the sheer number of books, television documentaries, films, museums) in which the Nazis were adopted as the antithesis of the West in the absence of any tangible present-day political enemies. As Fukuyama argued in his *End of History* thesis, modern liberal democracy appeared 'safe from any external enemies'.[61] In the absence of enemies in the present, many turned to the past. Perhaps the so-called 'year of the Holocaust', 1993, symbolises this more than anything else. Steven Spielberg's *Schindler's List* was released and ensured that many more people than ever before were forced to confront the *Shoah*. At the same time, after many years in the planning, the United States Holocaust Memorial Museum (USHMM) opened in Washington.[62] Both of these artefacts seemed to suggest a new role for the Holocaust. The USHMM is located on the Mall at the symbolic heart of American democracy and is a kind of anti-museum to all that the modern USA (and the West in general) is not, and indeed has fought against.[63] Similarly Spielberg's film offers a potentially comforting version of the Holocaust. The figure with which audiences can most identify is Schindler himself, who is in effect a modern capitalist. Although he is at first seduced by Nazism, he is ultimately redeemed and the values that he represents are shown to be the opposite of the murderous and irrational will to genocide.[64]

Such a tendency was, of course, the very opposite of the idea that the genocide of the Jews was somehow the result of a form of modernity, and as such an historiography dominated by a social science-based approach which claimed just that was ripe for public revision because it was out of step with prevailing historical memories. The ascendancy of liberalism in the aftermath of the Cold War also had an influence. The ideas of freedom of conscience and the freedom to choose appeared to be the mantras of the new age. The politics of the new Right in the 1980s (most commonly identified with Margaret Thatcher and Ronald Reagan), which ultimately felt itself to have defeated the Soviet era, preached individualism and individual responsibility. Such politics involved a knowing rejection of the idea of the importance of the collective and the community which underpinned much modern social science. That notion of responsibility is key here, because the growing sense that individuals were free to make choices demanded that they were then morally responsible for those choices and crucially that they could have made different ones. Goldhagen's study of the perpetrators operates this as one of its key assumptions and was thus both culturally and politically timely.

Genocide had also very publicly returned to the international agenda in the 1990s, which undoubtedly added to the atmosphere in which Goldhagen's history was successful. The campaigns against Tutsis by Hutu militia and populations in Rwanda in 1994, and against Bosnian Muslims by Serb forces across the mid-1990s, brought 'ethnic cleansing' and mass murder to the forefront of the conscience of the West, indeed images of genocide were projected on to TV screens. And these images, indeed these genocides, apparently in purely chronological terms more modern than the *Shoah*, looked nothing like the clean industrial murder perpetrated by 'desk murderers' that the Holocaust represented in the popular imagination. Brutal, bloody, even primal, genocide became associated not with the clean processes of a modern 'garden culture',[65] but with bestial and bloody hatreds and violence. Perhaps the Holocaust required a history to reflect these changing perceptions too.

Goldhagen's history certainly both met and reflected these changing political circumstances. And despite being dismissed by historians at the time, Goldhagen's book has not been forgotten as simply presently and politically expedient. Although the conclusions of the study were, and remain, too simplistic and as such his monocausal explanation is still anathema, *Hitler's Willing Executioners* has had an enduring impact on the field as a whole.[66] In part this is because the political context into which this study was pitched has not gone away. As a consequence the insistence that the perpetrators of the Holocaust were morally conscious volunteers, motivated by an identification with their tasks has itself become a form of received wisdom in recent years, part of what has been described as 'an emerging consensus' on perpetrator motivation.[67] It will be argued here that such a consensus continues to reflect the kind of political priorities that made Goldhagen's thesis attractive in the first instance, although now in circumstances changed immeasurably by the perceived threat to the Western world from fundamentalist terrorism.

Not that I am suggesting that all modern perpetrator histories took their lead from Goldhagen. Ulrich Herbert's study of Werner Best, the former SS intellectual and the Plenipotentiary for Denmark, was far more important in establishing the centrality of ideological motivation in terms of the history of the upper echelons of the RSHA.[68] Although Best's ideology could in no way be reduced to antisemitism, Herbert's biography seemed to reintroduce the concept of ideology to German Holocaust scholarship – arguing that the generation of men who led the SS and the RSHA were motivated by a specific worldview.[69] But what Goldhagen and Browning collectively did was to demonstrate that it was possible to drill down through the elites of organisations and attempt to understand the motivations of the individuals below them. As a consequence there are now a number of prosopographical studies of perpetrator groups, which have attempted to illuminate the mid-ranking perpetrator beyond the aphorism that they were 'cogs in the machine'. Notwithstanding the tendency of each historian to extrapolate from his own case study to an explanation of all perpetrators, this has constructed a picture of diverse ideological motivation to sit alongside the diverse regional picture of the 'Final Solution'.[70]

Micro-studies of perpetrator motivation have extended to the so-called 'desk murderers' too. Michael Thad Allen's investigation of the Economic and Administrative Main Office of the SS (*Wirtschafts Verwaltungshauptamt*, or WVHA) is perhaps the best example of this tendency because he identifies diverse ideological constellations within the different groups of the *same* organisation. As such what drove the political soldiers of the Inspectorate of Concentration Camps (*Inspektion der Konzentrationslager*, or IKL) was, according to Allen, different from the ideas that drove the Construction Office. To the inspectorate, extermination was always an end in itself, while Hans Kammler's construction office managed to synthesise extermination and slave labour in an overall vision of racial superiority. As a consequence Allen denies the simple formulation antisemitism equals genocide, but does see mass murder chiefly as the outcome of a 'plexus' of mutually reinforcing ideologies.[71] What is more, Allen is candid that his search for individuals' murderous motivation is, in part, also an assertion of their moral responsibility too: 'any assertion that the crimes of National Socialism were perpetrated by ideologically neutral bureaucrats, mere cogs in a machine, necessarily ignores the activist spirit of these men and foregoes all moral judgement of their ideas and actions.'[72]

Michael Wildt has similarly animated the history of the upper echelons of the RSHA. Again Wildt rejects simply indicting antisemitism in favour of a more complex 'unlimited, radical ideology ... [an] unbound connection between ideology and politics' which drove the men he characterises as the 'Generation of the Unbound'. Crucially Wildt rejects the dichotomy between the itinerant men of the killing fields and the 'desk murderers' of the SS institutions. Those in the leadership corps of the RSHA were *both*. Whether working behind a desk in Berlin, or elsewhere in Nazi occupied Europe – or commanding one of the *Einsatzkommando* in the field, these men were consciously attempting to transform the world in their image. What is more they were deliberately given the flexibility to interpret their orders and translate them into policy by Reinhard Heydrich. 'The description of a group of people to be murdered was only a kind of general guideline.'[73]

I want however to focus on one particular work in this area, Yaacov Lozowick's history of Eichmann's Gestapo office IVB4, *Hitler's Bureaucrats*, which places less emphasis than either Wildt or Allen on the power of institutions. Lozowick's study is particularly important for a number of reasons. First, because it is consciously presented as contributing to this new consensus, and his description of that consensus gives some indication of the influence of Goldhagen: 'that a very large number of Germans were predisposed to carry out a policy (or policies) built on killing those who obstructed the Aryan progress towards its glorious destiny.'[74] Second, Lozowick is concerned with a bureaucratic institution, and indeed the institution which most symbolises the 'desk murderer' model which he deliberately attempts to overturn. And finally because Lozowick's thesis is the most clear example of an history resting on the politics and morality of choice, as such it offers a stark indication of the role that current politics can play in shaping the perspectives of Holocaust History now.

Lozowick's conclusions about the Jewish 'desk' of the Gestapo headed by Adolf Eichmann were unequivocal. These men were the active agents and implementers of the 'Final Solution'. They did not get the chance to shape policy at a state level, but they did in terms of its implementation. In doing so they displayed considerable zeal for their task. This was no directed or self-functioning bureaucracy; it relied on the innovation of its agents. For example, letters signed by SS leaders such as Himmler, Heydrich and latterly Kaltenbrunner which appear to move policy along and thus suggest the direction of the machinery of destruction from the top, were actually written and produced on the initiative of men of much lower rank. So when Gestapo head Ludwig Muller informed Himmler that there would have to be a cessation in transports in December 1942, he was actually passing on the instructions of Eichmann's subordinates, his deputy Rolf Günther and transportation expert Franz Novak. Therefore, 'concerning one of the most important elements in determining the rate of deportation of the Jews to their deaths, it was not Himmler who dictated to his subordinates, but rather his subordinates who notified him of a fact that was not even open for discussion'.[75]

Hitler's Bureaucrats also rejected the idea that Eichmann's men were so immersed in the new morality of the Third Reich that they lost the capacity to distinguish between right and wrong. Office

IVB4 provided support for the Blobel commando, who were responsible for covering up Nazi crimes by, for example, destroying evidence of mass graves. Lozowick suggested that any attempt to erase the memory of the 'Final Solution' was an acknowledgement that it represented a moral transgression. The officers of IVB4 were also active in the non-Nazi world too. Witness their attempts to affect the deportation of the Jews of France, for which they had to 'fight for position, threaten even plead' with recalcitrant French officials. The implications of this interaction with the non-Nazi world are clear for Lozowick, 'they cannot have done so without understanding the nature of their mission and without understanding that their interlocutors thought their actions repugnant ... they were bureaucrats of evil'.[76]

In adopting the language of good and evil so unapologetically in his descriptions of Eichmann and his men, Lozowick suggests that these are objective categories. Such an approach to morality contrasts with Hannah Arendt's, but is hardly unknown in Holocaust studies, where the discourse of evil has been common. Remember Lucy Dawidowicz and Nora Levin's histories of the late 1960s and 1970s; witness too Yehuda Bauer's outspoken attack on Arendt's banality thesis from 1977: 'Evidently evil, or the embodiment of evil – the demonic man-devil – is not banal at all ... these are not mediocre postal clerks or robots; they ... [had] the capacity for taking initiative and for independent thought, for the purpose of carrying out the most devilish deeds.'[77] And the idea that the Holocaust is an event of such scale that it requires theological explanation is common within Holocaust studies.[78] Lozowick embraced such a tradition when he argued that 'evil' was the defining characteristic of the men of Eichmann's Jewish desk, defining evil as active malevolence – a knowing choice between 'right' and 'wrong'. In doing so he consciously rejected Browning's suggestion that the perpetrators of the Holocaust were 'ordinary men', as their meaning and significance could only be found in this extraordinary characteristic.[79]

By using 'evil' as an explanatory concept in this way Lozowick's history also reflected his own ideological position. Indeed it is almost a theology. At the centre of this was the idea of choice, because for Lozowick 'choice' represented the essence of the human condition. Consider the last lines of the article 'Malice in Action' in which he attempted to summarise his thesis: 'as it is written: "And you will be like Gods knowing both good and evil". *Man's greatness lies precisely in that faculty for choice: even though individuals cannot control the historical circumstances governing their lives they have the abiding ability to choose between good and evil'*[80] (emphasis added). This is a political and theological commitment to choice, applied to the past, but made in the present.

Lozowick articulated this theology more fully in another book, the title of which, *Right to Exist: A Moral Defense of Israel's Wars*, is an apt summary of its content. This second book offers a much clearer insight into Lozowick's moral, political and disciplinary approach, and therefore the context in which he cast Holocaust historiography. For the central premise of *Right to Exist* is also the unarticulated premise of *Hitler's Bureaucrats* too, that:

> there is ... an objective truth that can be known ... [and that] Morality too is universal; while not everyone will agree about what is moral in every circumstance, anyone potentially can identify it. Truth and morality are not owned by any group, although it is conceivable that some individuals or groups will be more moral than others. *But this will be something that anyone can test empirically, if one is honest about it.*[81] (Emphasis added)

And what is that universal morality? 'At the heart of all morality is choice.'[82]

Lozowick's 'theology' of choice has a clear political context too, specifically within the Arab-Israeli conflict but at the same time linked to a much wider understanding of world affairs. If the post-Cold War period originally offered certainty, then nothing could be further from the truth today. The second intifada in Israel/Palestine, the terrorist attacks of 11 September 2001, the resultant war in Afghanistan, the USA / UK invasion and subsequent occupation of Iraq in 2003, the terrorist attacks in London in July 2005, the ongoing instability in Pakistan, the quest for nuclear technology in Iran, and the regional aggression of Russia, all seem to point to an inherent confusion and uncertainty. Yet at the same time these events have often been publicly understood by politicians and intellectuals using a very simplistic vocabulary, which comes close to Lozowick's theology of choice. The discourse of liberal triumph and individual choice that seemed ascendant when the Berlin Wall fell and history was originally declared at an end is therefore used to interpret this uncertain world too. Especially in the USA, neo-conservatism relied on the rhetorical tools of the 'axis of evil' and the 'war on terror' to present the world in Manichean terms, as a choice between 'good' and 'evil' in a clash of civilisations. The then British Prime Minister Tony Blair perhaps encapsulated this approach with his continual justification of the US/UK invasion of Iraq in 2003 as 'the right thing to do'.[83]

The impact of such thinking on Holocaust historiography extends much further than just the work of Yaacov Lozowick. If violence and extremism is a matter of active choice, then it can be explained purely with reference to the realm of ideas and we are thus returned to the intentionalist formulation that antisemitism equals genocide. Such a formulation also means that the Holocaust can be instrumentalised within present-day political disputes too, just as the original claims of uniqueness instrumentalised it in the 1970s. Jeffrey Herf's new history which explains the Holocaust through antisemitism, does just that when it argues that the 'Final Solution' is a warning about the power of antisemitism as an idea. Herf invokes the contemporary antisemitism of particularly the Arab world when he writes 'in the first decade of the twenty-first century the demented discourse of radical anti-Semitism and totalitarianism has returned in different idioms and cultural contexts. It would be complacent to assume that variants on the narrative explored in this work will not play a part in the future as well.'[84]

The Holocaust and the idea of political religion

Although Herf and Lozowick's theses come close to simply being a restatement of the intentionalist case, they have actually contributed to and coalesced within a further and developing metanarrative for Nazism: the idea that National Socialism was a 'political religion', and thus the Holocaust was a product of this secular faith. Unlike previous metanarratives however, this concept can render Nazism and the Holocaust both comparable *and* unique.

The idea that Nazism was a political religion is not novel, and certainly not confined to the post-Cold War era. Even before Hitler's takeover of power, conservatives had identified that the danger of Nazism lay in its religiosity, that it was in the words of Franz von Papen a 'faith rooted in politics' rather than a 'politics rooted in faith'.[85] It was also common during the Nazi era to read, especially outside Germany, that Nazism and Soviet communism were religious movements which threatened to usurp Christianity itself.[86] Eric Voegelin, the German political philosopher who fled the Third Reich for the USA, was 'one of the first to recognise the historical significance of this phenomenon' in his 1939 treatise *Die Politischen Religionen*.[87]

Although in the post-war period it was central to the idea of totalitarianism,[88] it was not until the late 1970s however that the concept became important specifically within the historiography of the Holocaust. Uriel Tal, who had previously concentrated on Christian-Jewish relations in the nineteenth century, outlined the 'political theology' of Nazism in two influential lectures given at the University of Tel Aviv. According to Tal, Hitler believed Nazism to be a 'substitute for religion' which sought the 'attainment of irrational goals by rational means'.[89] Tal's thesis was thus also the beginnings of an explanation for the 'irrational' Holocaust. The Jew occupied a central role in the Nazi 'political theology', the 'political myth' around which all Nazism's ideas of transformation and salvation 'spun'.[90] The solution to the Jewish Question, Tal suggested, would ultimately become the principal mechanism for 'transfiguration' in the Nazi religious mindset.

Heavily influenced by Tal, Saul Friedländer stated at the beginning of the 1980s that the concept of 'political religion' offered the best hope of an overarching interpretative framework in which Nazism might be understood.[91] Ultimately he would develop this into the thesis of 'redemptive antisemitism', the central explanatory concept of his recent two-volume history of the Holocaust which suggests that it was through antisemitism, the persecution and ultimately the murder of the Jews, that Nazism led Germans to eternity. Friedländer argued that the Jew was presented to the German people as an article of faith by the Nazis, a metahistorical concept and an immutable evil which could only really be understood in religious terms. The outcome of the struggle between good and evil, Aryan and Jew, would be 'perdition or redemption'.[92]

The 'political religion' case thus rests essentially on two separate but overlapping observations. The first is that the Nazi movement and the state it produced looked rather like a religious movement and a fundamentalist theocracy. This observation accepts that the Third Reich was a state and society built on some form of consensus, alongside coercion. It also accepts some aspects of the totalitarianism thesis. Nazism sought dominion over the whole of Germans' lives, transforming as we have seen even women's bodies into a public space. The state sought to regulate amongst other things the religious lives of individuals, as well as their work and leisure time. They replaced religious rites of passage with National Socialist equivalents, and sought to inculcate young Germans with a new morality both inside and outside of formal education. At the same time the Nazi movement staged grand rituals in the performative aspects of the dictatorship – like the Nuremberg rallies – which can be interpreted not just as expressions of power but mechanisms through which the German people were integrated into the Nazi state, by which they could feel they belonged. At these same rituals the high priests of the Nazi movements, the leaders of institutions such as the SS, were displayed to the population. And at the head of this movement stood the messianic *Führer*, who (and in the case of Riefenstahl's *Triumph of the Will* this is literally true) descended from on high. The similarities to a religion are thus clear.

The second essential element of the 'political religion' thesis concerns the way in which Germans, in this formulation the faithful, related to ideology or to the teachings of this new religion, as they carried out its work or attempted to reshape the world in its image. The argument is thus proposed that the millenarian rhetoric of the Nazi movement offered ordinary Germans eternity. Germans were told repeatedly how they could ascend to their rightful place as the chosen people and in essence live forever – by rendering the world *Judenrein* as this would ensure the security and prosperity of the German *Volk*. As such, when 'ordinary Germans' were engaged in the murder of Jews they were not simply acting in accordance with a new politics, but they were in thrall to a new faith and in this they achieved an attendant state of ecstatic grace.

Although the idea of Nazism as a 'political religion' as expressed by Tal and Friedländer is much more developed than when it was first articulated, it still shares some of the implications of the conservative commentaries of the 1930s. Not least the notion that Nazism and the culture that it spawned and thus produced the 'Final Solution' was a rejection and a fundamental break from the traditional mores of the Judeo-Christian world. As such the 'Final Solution' is rendered somewhat unfamiliar to us in the Western world in this model. Yaacov Lozowick similarly suggested that the Holocaust was the product of an irrational and alien culture fundamentally different to our own.[93]

In this the idea of 'political religions' is a contribution to the ongoing discourse regarding the relationship between the Holocaust and modernity. If modernity is equated with rationality, then the Holocaust represents its antithesis in this formulation because of its irrationality. It may have been, as Uriel Tal points out, accomplished by rational means, but it was determined by the dictates of faith rather than politics. Yet the relationship between modernity and the Holocaust is more complex here than it may first seem. In his wide-ranging discussion of political religions Michael Burleigh seems to imply, for example, that Nazism as a political religion was a *secular* faith, a replacement for the traditional religiosity. Indeed Burleigh states unambiguously that the Holocaust was the 'devil's work'.[94] In that sense the Holocaust appears not as the negation of the modern world, but its product – the consequence of the modernity's negation of traditional religiosity. This argument displays clearly the long roots of the political religion thesis, as it was precisely the point that was being made by conservative Christians in the 1930s and 1940s. Nazism was the product of secular modernity. As George Bell, the wartime Bishop of Chichester wrote, the 'supreme remedy for National Socialism' was 'the Christian gospel'.[95]

Highlighting the gulf between Nazism and Christianity has been a staple of the historiography of Nazi treatment of the German churches too.[96] But there is a clear case being made in modern historiography that the relationship between Nazism and Christianity was not just one of Manichean opposition. If Nazism and thus the 'Final Solution' developed in a purely secular space, then what of the links between that politics and the religion it usurped? Richard Steigmann-Gall has recently demonstrated that Nazism owed a great deal to Christianity.[97] Equally as Neil Gregor has pointed out, that Nazism looked like Christianity may say more for the enduring influences of Christian discourse in secular modernity than anything else.[98] Susanne Heschel's recent portrait of the *Aryan Jesus* makes clear how far some Christians went to find accommodation with Nazism.[99]

It is not just by suggesting a firm dividing line between Christianity and Nazism that contemporary expressions of the 'political religion' concept seem to echo their political forebears from the 1930s. In the 1940s the idea that Nazism was a modern, secular religion demanded comparison with the Soviet Union. During the *Historikerstreit* the idea of a European civil war was revived in an explanation of both Nazi Germany and the Soviet Union.[100] And in the early twenty-first century the idea of the 'political religion' aims to situate Nazism and the Holocaust similarly in a comparative context. When Michael Burleigh first articulated his version of the thesis it was aimed at (in the aftermath) the end of history demonstrating the moral rectitude of Western liberalism, and the faiths important to it. This was done by looking backwards, and by comparing Nazism and Soviet communism again as two 'political religions' which sought to usurp faith and reason with fanaticism and violence.[101]

Casting Nazism as a 'political religion' is thus to embrace a comparative framework. But this framework can encompass more than just Nazism and Soviet communism, and comparisons are now being sought in the recent past and present too. We have already seen that Jeffrey Herf sought to view Nazi antisemitism through the prism of Middle-Eastern antisemitism today. Yaacov Lozowick suggests the terrorists of the twenty-first century are ideological actors like the Nazis, and are comparable too. 'September 11 had echoes of Nazism in being so stark that terms like good and evil demand to be applied' he wrote.[102] The delegates to the 2003 Annual Scholars Conference on the Holocaust were welcomed with the warning that they met at a time of war, at the beginning of a new century haunted by the spectre of a new totalitarianism 'Islamism', comparable with the Nazi and Soviet versions which had blighted the previous hundred years. And indeed Burleigh's 'political religions' project has ultimately become a comparative history of violence and extremism across the modern world.[103] Crucially it is a history that has continued to find the seeds of violence in the *alternatives* to the Judeo-Christian West.

There is no doubt that the 'political religion' concept is illuminating – especially in terms of understanding the relationship between the perpetrators of the Holocaust and their crimes. There is no doubt that the violence of the Holocaust needs to be accounted for. After all it was one of the defining features of the Nazi movement throughout its history.[104] As such the idea that violence, and especially violence against Jews, offered the perpetrators some kind of fulfilment in the new Germany is important and cannot be avoided. The prevalence of violence in modern society also demands that the Holocaust be cast in a comparative context. But casting the Holocaust in such a context can very quickly become an exercise in triumphalism. If Nazism was a political religion, if the 'Final Solution' the result of the tyranny of faith and the defeat of reason, then the Western historian is simply reduced to using the Holocaust to identify and understand its *enemies*.

Colonialism and genocide

At the same time as Nazism has been depicted as a 'political religion', an alternative metanarrative has recently developed (or has at least become more visible) which seeks to associate popular participation in the Nazi genocide to the study and understanding of Western modernity or, to put it bluntly, *ourselves*. This scholarship seeks to take up Hannah Arendt's challenge to understand the links between National Socialist violence in Eastern Europe and the violence which *Western* nations visited upon their colonies in the past.

The links between colonialism and genocide have usually been drawn inside critiques of Western modernity and the political impacts of the spread of western power. Arendt's *Origins of Totalitarianism* may have been at root a response to Auschwitz, but it was also an indictment of the failings of Western historical development, hence her attempt to link British imperialism and Nazi violence.[105] Jean Paul Sartre declared colonialism to be inherently genocidal in a 1968 essay 'On Genocide', the wider purpose of which was to indict US policy in Vietnam.[106] Aimé Césaire similarly argued in *Discourse on Colonialism* that the Nazis were simply visiting colonial dominion on the European continent.[107] And in terms of the Holocaust, Donald Bloxham has argued that historians on the communist side of the Iron Curtain were much ahead of their Western counterparts in identifying the importance of a general colonial vision in determining the murder of Europe's Jews.[108]

It is only recently that Western historians of the Holocaust have become much more alive to the explanatory potential in understanding the Nazis as an, albeit extreme, manifestation of colonial mindsets. Again this has been the result of a willingness to engage critically with the violence of Western pasts – and not least because of an understanding that genocide was not something invented by the Nazis. Raphael Lemkin, the author of genocide as an historico-legal concept, was particularly concerned about the genocide of indigenous peoples at the hands of settler colonialism – and had planned to include an account of the destruction of Tasmanian aboriginals in his history of genocide.[109] This greater willingness to label the destruction of indigenous peoples as 'genocide' in recent scholarship has thus been to follow in Lemkin's footsteps.

The determinants of this recognition of colonial criminality were many and various, and too complex to be dealt with here. It suffices to say that the gradual diminishing of Western colonial power in the aftermath of the Second World War, ensured the beginning of a kind of post-colonial accounting.[110] In the settler colonies themselves, such as Australia, campaigns for the rights of surviving indigenous peoples became bound up with investigations of the iniquity of the colonial past. And as the present became increasingly multi-cultural then this was reflected in studies of the past. Equally attempts to pursue reconciliation with indigenous populations in the present led inevitably to the question of past crimes. Indeed the 1997 official report on stolen aboriginal children in Australia, *Bringing them Home*, used the term genocide to describe Australian policy towards aboriginal communities.[111]

If Western societies have a history and heritage of genocide, then a new context for the study of Nazi genocides emerges. Alison Palmer argued in her *Colonial Genocide* that understanding the genocide of Queensland aboriginals in the nineteenth century can aid understanding of the Holocaust because it changes our perception of the idea of genocide itself. Settler colonists in nineteenth-century Australia acted in the absence of strong state power, and indeed a specifically genocidal will.[112] The notion that genocide must therefore be a state crime (or at least directed by the state) is thus open to challenge. And of course regional studies of

National Socialist extermination policies have demonstrated precisely that they too could emerge in the absence of central state direction. Indeed Christian Gerlach suggests that because of this the concept of genocide should be replaced by the notion of 'extremely violent societies'. Genocide, because of its legal origins, implies too great a role for the state. Gerlach hopes that his model for extremely violent societies might also shed light on the popularity of such violence, and indeed the sheer number of its perpetrators.[113]

But casting the Nazis in a colonial context is not just a comparative project – it also provides a valuable context for understanding the Holocaust itself. According to scholars such as Jürgen Zimmerer and Wendy Lower, the Nazis were a product of a colonial mindset. The Nazis were 'born into a European world of empire' and their policy of expansion into Eastern Europe 'rest[ed] on fundamentally similar concepts of space and race' to those that underpinned colonial expansion.[114] *General Plan Ost*, the Nazi project for the transformation of Eastern Europe and particularly the Ukraine was, at root, a colonial vision – albeit one which combined a vision of economic exploitation with the notion of Germanisation and settlement. The new detailed empirical histories of Nazi occupation regimes have demonstrated that it is not just ideologically that the Nazi project can be understood as 'colonial', but also because of their small, chaotic administrations which appear much like the colonial out-riders of Arendt's original thesis.[115]

Wendy Lower's study of the Ukraine has revealed the degree to which the Nazis themselves understood their colonial heritage. Ukraine was to be transformed, according to Adolf Hitler himself, into a German 'garden of Eden' in which the solder-peasant tilled the soil and defended Germany against the Asian hordes to the East.[116] Lower argues that:

> one finds in Hitler's, Himmler's and Rosenberg's imaginings of the new Aryan paradise references to the North American frontier, the British Empire in India, and the European exploitation of Africans in the late nineteenth century. In Heinrich Himmler's SS propaganda publication, *Der Untermensch*, one reads about the life and death struggle between Germans and Jews alongside Nazi claims to Eastern European territory depicted as 'black earth than could be a paradise, a California of Europe'.[117]

Yet, according to Lower, the position of Jews in the Nazi colonial mindset is, if not unique, then novel and thus requires explanation. The nature of the Nazi colonial project was fought over – between settlers and those who wished to concentrate only on economic dominion. Yet a prerequisite of both exploitation and Germanisation was the removal of Jews – and thus murderous antisemitism became the ultimate articulation of Nazi empire-building.

Of course the idea that Nazi policy in Eastern Europe represented an example of colonialism is far from universally accepted. Indeed it is an idea that can offend many groups. To some scholars who continue to proclaim the uniqueness of the Holocaust, then comparison with colonial genocide is anathema because it seems to lessen the particularity of Jewish suffering.[118] And of course, that colonialism could in itself be genocidal is a challenge to modern Western states because it disrupts the notion of their benign histories. The nations of North America, Western Europe and Australasia all 'profited enormously from imperialism' and indeed some 'owe their very existence to projects of settlement'.[119] And if National Socialist violence, and indeed Nazi genocides, can be located in the continuum of modern Western history then we are faced with something profoundly disturbing. Instead of being the antithesis of Western traditions, the Holocaust becomes, if not its product, then in some senses its consequence. Understanding the Holocaust as an example of colonial violence thus 'calls into question the Europeanisation of the globe as a modernising project'.[120]

Conclusion

Modern Holocaust historiography still wrestles with the perpetrators of the 'Final Solution' then. And although many historians still claim to have found the single key to the puzzle, it seems clear that there is no one 'perpetrator type' and thus no workable *single* explanation for their violence and their motivation. It is equally clear that it is not adequate simply to state that there are a number of easily separable perpetrator types. 'Desk murderers' could also be itinerant face-to-face killers just the same.[121] Close scrutiny of that scholarship seems to point to one ineluctable conclusion. If History is a discourse, a discussion between past and present – then the present plays a crucial and at times determining role.

This present is manifested in theoretical reflections upon the discipline of History, and in global politics too. As such our under-standing of the perpetrators of the Holocaust, and the society that supported them, has been immeasurably enriched by the applica-tion of the techniques of the *Alltagsgeschichte*. This is a development that came out of both a specific political context in the *Historikerstreit* and the postmodern challenge to the discipline of History and thus the provision for histories rather than the sin-gular history. Far from challenging the utility of History, such scholarship has demonstrated the degree to which ordinary Ger-mans were tied to the 'Final Solution' and therefore the extent to which our changing present has therefore illuminated the past yet further.

Ultimately the discourse on what motivated those ordinary German perpetrators of the 'Final Solution' returns us to a debate that has dominated Holocaust historiography since its painful birth. Christopher Browning's *Ordinary Men* suggested that in studying the perpetrators of the Holocaust we were really looking into a mirror, which reflected a human potential for violence. The men of Reserve Police Battalion 101 may have been placed in an extraordinary situation, but once in that context, their behaviour patterns are depressingly familiar, even if their product was geno-cide. For his detractors Browning offered a moral escape for the perpetrators, lessened their culpability and failed to capture what made them extraordinary, what made them evil. The use of the concept of evil is important because it symbolises how scholars such as Goldhagen and Yaacov Lozowick, to name the two con-sidered in most detail here, have treated the Holocaust not as a mirror but as a window through which we can see the genocidal 'other'. With the advent of the idea of 'political religions' that win-dow allows us, I suggest, to see and understand our present-day discontents too. For scholars pursuing the links between colonial genocide and the Holocaust, the *Shoah* is much more about 'us'. In this debate, on both sides, history and politics collide. For good or ill, the Holocaust thus becomes reduced to the terrain on which a much wider debate about who and what we are is conducted. Holocaust scholarship 'brings to the fore the most fundamental of questions: the character of humanity as a species, history as progress, the ethical basis of societies and the honour of civilisa-tions and nations.'[122]

Perhaps the greatest irony of modern scholarship on the murder of Europe's Jews, is that it seems to have returned to its origins. If the pioneers of Holocaust History sought to separate the *Shoah* from more general historical narratives – of especially of the general violence of the Second World War – then modern Holocaust scholars have returned to the study of context. Which context to place the Holocaust in remains a point of conflict – whether it is best studied as the expression of a totalitarian state and society, of a murderous secular religion, the consequence of Western modernity's racial thinking more generally, of attempts to racially or economically rebuild society – but the sense that the perpetration of the Holocaust cannot be explained independently has returned to the fore.

Notes

1 Christopher Browning, *Ordinary Men: Reserve Police Battalion 101 and the Final Solution in Poland* (London, 2001), first published in 1992, pp. 3–8.

2 Browning, *Ordinary Men*, p. 188.

3 I have borrowed this phrase from Neil Gregor, 'Nazism – A Political Religion? Rethinking the Voluntarist Turn', Gregor (ed.), *Nazism, War and Genocide: Essays in Honour of Jeremy Noakes* (Exeter, 2005), pp. 1–21.

4 Robert G.L. Waite, 'Adolf Hitler's Anti-Semitism: A Study in History and Psychoanalysis', Michael Marrus, *The Nazi Holocaust: Vol. 2 The Origins of the Holocaust* (London, 1989), p. 359. This was originally published in B.B. Wolman (ed.), *The Psychoanalytic Interpretation of History* (New York, 1970).

5 For an example of the attempt to deal with the perpetrators of the 'Final Solution' and their motivation see Leni Yahil, *The Holocaust: The Fate of European Jewry* (Oxford, 1990). Yahil asserts the importance of bottom-up social histories of the Holocaust but does not really include perpetrator communities.

6 Gitta Sereny, *Into That Darkness: From Mercy Killing to Mass Murder* (London, 1974), p. 367.

7 *Ibid.*, pp. 362–6. Ultimately, on the day before he died, still claiming that his conscience was clear, Stangl did accept that he had some share of guilt for what occurred.

8 Robert Jay Lifton, *The Nazi Doctors: Medical Killing and the Psychology of Genocide* (New York, 1986), pp. 417–500.

9 See for example Michael Sturmer, 'History in a Land without History' in James Knowlton and Truett Cates (eds), *Forever in the Shadow of Hitler: Original Documents from the Historikerstreit, the Controversy Surrounding the Singularity of the Holocaust* (Princeton: NJ, 1993), pp. 16–17. See also Richard Evans, *In Hitler's Shadow: West German Historians and the Attempt to Escape from the Nazi Past* (London, 1989) and Charles Maier, *The Unmasterable Past: History, Holocaust, and German National Identity* (Cambridge, 1988) for an analysis of the whole debate.

10 See Andreas Hilgruber, *Zweirlei Untergang: Die Zerschlagung des deutschen Reiches und das Ende des europäischen Judentums* (Berlin, 1986); Ernst Nolte, *Der europäische Bürgerkrieg 1917–1945: Nationalsozialismus und Bolschewismus* (Frankfurt, 1987), 'The Past that will not Pass', 'Between Historical Legend and Revisionism? The Third Reich in the Perspective of 1980' and 'Standing Things on Their Heads: Against Negative Nationalism in Interpreting History', all in Knowlton and Cates (eds), *Forever in the Shadow of Hitler.*

11 Jürgen Habermas. 'A Kind of Settlement of Damages: The Apologetic Tendencies in German Historical Writing' in Knowlton and Cates, *Forever in the Shadow*, pp. 34–44.

12 See for example Dan Stone, *Constructing the Holocaust* (London, 2003), pp. 190–1.

13 Martin Broszat, 'A Plea for the Historicization of the Holocaust', Peter Baldwin (ed.), *Reworking the Past: the Holocaust and the Historians Debate* (Boston: MA, 1990), pp. 77–87.

14 Ian Kershaw, *The Nazi Dictatorship: Problems and Perspectives of Interpretation* (London, 2000), p. 222.

15 See Martin Broszat and Saul Friedlander, 'A Controversy about the Historicization of National Socialism', *New German Critique* (No. 44, Spring/Summer 1988), pp. 85–126. This is reprinted in Simone Gigliotti and Berel Lang (eds), *The Holocaust: A Reader* (Oxford, 2005), pp. 264–300.

16 For a brief and accessible introduction to *Alltagsgeschichte* see Geoff Eley, 'Foreword' and Alf Lüdtke, 'Introduction: What is the History of Everyday Life and Who are its Practitioners?', Lüdtke (ed.), *The History of Everyday Life: Reconstructing Experiences and Ways of Life* (Princeton: NJ, 1995).

17 This is the title of an essay by Ian Kershaw. See Ian Kershaw, *Hitler, the Germans and the Final Solution* (Jerusalem, 2008), p. 4 for a narrative of Kershaw's approach to these questions.

18 See Paul Steege, Andrew Stuart Bergson, Maureen Healy and Pamela E. Swett, 'The History of Everyday Life: A Second Chapter', *Journal of Modern History* (No. 80, June 2008), pp. 358–78, esp. p. 375.

19 For a critique see Georg G. Iggers, *Historiography in the Twentieth Century: From Scientific Objectivity to the Postmodern Challenge* (Middletown: CT, 1997), pp. 101–17.

20 Women's roles in the Third Reich, and specifically whether, in their cooperation with Nazi natalism, they can be seen as the victims or the perpetrators of the Nazi state. For a summary of the debate see Adelheid von Saldern, 'Victims or Perpetrators? Controversies about the Role of Women in the Nazi State', David F. Crew (ed.), *Nazism and German Society* (London, 1994), pp. 141–65. In the same volume see Gisella Bock, 'Antinatalism, Maternity and Paternity in National Socialist Racism'. Also by Bock, 'Ordinary Women in Nazi Germany: Perpetrators, Victims, Followers and Bystanders', Dalia Ofer and Leonore J. Weitzman (eds), *Women in the Holocaust* (New Haven: CT, 1998), pp. 85–100. For an alternative perspective which emphasises the complicity of German women see Claudia Koonz, *Mothers of the Fatherland: Women, the Family and Nazi Politics* (New York, 1987) and Chapter 8 below.

21 This story was relayed to me by a relative of Edith who wished her and her family's identity to remain anonymous. I am very grateful for her permission to use it in this form.

22 A collection of these reports has recently been published and an English translation is anticipated. See Otto Dov Kulka and Eberhard Jäckel (eds), *Die Juden in den gehelmen NS-Stimmungsberichten 1933–45* (Düsseldorf, 2004).

23 For the public opinion reports of the Social Democratic Party in Exile see Erich Rinner (ed.), *Deutschland-Berichte der Sozialdemokratischen Partei Deutschlands (Sopade) 1934–1940* (Frankfurt, 1980).

24 See Wolfgang Gerlach, *And the Witnesses were Silent: The Confessing Church and the Persecution of the Jews* (Lincoln: NE, 2000).

25 For a discussion of the range of different interpretations, which ends with the observation that the limits of the source material mean that there are sufficient ambiguities to ensure that the debate will never be resolved, see Kershaw, *Hitler, the Germans and the Final Solution*, pp. 4–11.

26 See for example Marlis G. Steinert, *Hitler's War and the Germans: Public Mood and Attitude During the Second World War* (Athens: OH, 1977).

27 Ian Kershaw, *Popular Opinion and Political Dissent in the Third Reich: Bavaria 1933–45* (Oxford, 1983).

28 For discussions of the role of labour in the Third Reich see the collection of pioneering essays in Tim Mason, *Nazism, Fascism and the Working Class* (Cambridge, 1995), and Alf Lüdtke, 'What Happened to the "Fiery Red Glow"? Workers' Experiences and German Fascism', *The History of Everyday Life*, pp. 198–251.

29 Alf Lüdtke, 'German Work and German Workers: The Impact of Symbols on the Exclusion of Jews in Nazi Germany', David Bankier (ed.), *Probing the Depths of German Antisemitism: German Society and the Persecution of the Jews* (Jerusalem, 2000), p. 298.

30 Kershaw, *Popular Opinion and Political Dissent*, p. 277. Kershaw also discusses these issues, and objections to his thesis in *Hitler, the Germans and the Final Solution*, pp. 5–11.

31 See Otto Dov Kulka, 'The German Population and the Jews: State of Research and New Perspectives', Bankier, *Probing the Depths*, pp. 271–81, for his summary of the debate thus far.

32 David Bankier, *The Germans and the Final Solution: Public Opinion Under Nazism* (Oxford, 1992), p. 140.

33 Jeffrey Herf, *The Jewish Enemy: Nazi Propaganda During World War II and the Holocaust* (Cambridge: MA, 2006).

34 Frank Bajohr, 'The "Folk Community" and the Persecution of the Jews: German Society under National Socialist Dictatorship, 1933–45', *Holocaust and Genocide Studies* (Vol. 20, No. 2, 2006), pp. 183–206.

35 Kershaw, *Hitler, the Germans and the Final Solution*, p. 11.

36 This analysis of the story of Lilli Jahn is heavily influenced by Robert Jan van Pelt and Deborah Dwork's interpretation in 'A Distant Shore: the Holocaust and Us', *Holocaust Studies: A Journal of Culture and History* (Vol. 11, No. 1, 2005).

37 See Martin Doerry (ed.), *My Wounded Heart* (New York, 2002) for the story of Lilli Jahn.

38 See Robert Gellately, *The Gestapo and German Society: Enforcing Racial Policy 1933–45* (Oxford, 1992), and *Backing Hitler: Consent and Coercion in Nazi Germany* (Oxford, 2001); also Eric Johnson, *The Nazi Terror: Gestapo, Jews, and Ordinary Germans* (New York, 2000); see also Christl Wickert, 'Popular Attitudes to National Socialist Antisemitism: Denunciations for "Insidious Offences" and Racial Ignominy', Bankier, *Probing the Depths*, pp. 282–95.

39 Frank Bajohr, *Aryanisation in Hamburg: The Economic Exclusion of the Jews and the Confiscation of their Property in Nazi Germany* (Oxford, 2002).

40 Götz Aly, *Hitler's Beneficiaries: Plunder, Racial War and the Nazi Welfare State* (New York, 2006), p. 324.

41 Richard Evans' three-volume history of the Third Reich is a recent attempt to reassert the terroristic elements of Nazi rule. See Evans, *The Coming of the Third Reich* (London, 2003), *The Third Reich in Power* (London, 2005), *The Third Reich at War* (London, 2008).

42 Browning, *Ordinary Men*, p. xvii–iii. See also Ernst Klee, *Those Were the Days: The Holocaust Through the Eyes of the Perpetrators and Bystanders* (London, 1991) which sought a similar juxtaposition of normality and abnormality.

43 Mark Levene, 'Why is the Twentieth Century the Century of Genocide', *Journal of World History* (Vol. 11, No. 2, 2000), pp. 305–36.

44 Browning, *Ordinary Men*, p. 48.

45 *Ibid.*, p. 132.

46 See Stanley Milgram, *Obedience to Authority* (London, 2004) this was first published in 1974. Browning's critics often point to his invocation of Milgram as evidence of his ignoring the role of ideology, but Milgram acknowledges ideology as an important justification for action, see p. 189; Philip Zimbardo, *The Lucifer Effect: How Good People Turn Evil* (London, 2007) – again this is a book based in large part on experiments from the 1970s.

47 Browning, *Ordinary Men*, p. 87.

48 *Ibid.*, p. 75.

49 Christopher Browning, *Nazi Policy, Jewish Workers and German Killers* (Cambridge, 2000), pp. 143–69.

50 Daniel Jonah Goldhagen, *Hitler's Willing Executioners: Ordinary Germans and the Holocaust* (New York, 1996).

51 For critiques of Goldhagen and narratives of the debates that his work provoked see Robert R. Shandley, *Unwilling Germans: The Goldhagen Debate* (London, 1998); Norman Finkelstein and Ruth Bettina Birn, *A Nation on Trial: The Goldhagen Thesis and Historical Truth* (New York, 1998); Geoff Eley (ed.), *The Goldhagen Effect: History, Memory and Nazism – Facing the German Past* (Ann Arbor: MI, 2000).

52 For an analysis of Goldhagen's method and its relationship to social anthropology see Mark Ward Sr, 'The Banality of Culture? Reassessing the Social Science of the Goldhagen Thesis on its Own Terms', *Holocaust Studies: A Journal of Culture and History* (Vol. 14, No. 1, 2008), pp. 1–34.

53 Goldhagen, *Hitler's Willing Executioners*, p. 28.

54 Ruth Bettina Birn, 'Historiographical Review: Revising the Holocaust', *Historical Journal* (Vol. 40, No.1, 1997), p. 212.

55 Goldhagen, *Hitler's Willing Executioners*, pp. 213, 220.

56 *Ibid.*, p. 248.

57 *Ibid.*, p. 280.

58 Goldhagen relies very heavily on one book: Dorothy Holland and Naomi Quinn (eds), *Cultural Models in Language and Thought* (Cambridge, 1987). For a critique of his application of those methods see: Ward Sr, 'The Banality of Culture?', pp. 1–34.

59 Goldhagen, *Hitler's Willing Executioners*, p. 266.

60 Mitchell G. Ash, 'American and German Perspectives on the Goldhagen Debate', *Holocaust and Genocide Studies* (Vol. 11, No. 3, 1997), p. 407.

61 Francis Fukuyama, *The End of History and the Last Man* (London, 1992), p. xxi.

62 See Michael Rothberg, *Traumatic Realism: The Demands of Holocaust Representation* (Minneapolis: MN, 2000), p. 181.

63 See Tim Cole, *Images of the Holocaust* (London, 1999), p. 158.

64 For an analysis of *Schindler's List* see M.A. Bernstein, 'The *Schindler's List* Effect', *The American Scholar* (No. 63, 1994), pp. 429–32.

65 Zygmunt Bauman, *Modernity and the Holocaust* (Cambridge, 1989), p. 92.

66 Ian Kershaw accepts that Goldhagen has had a lasting impact, in a way that he had thought would not be the case. See Kershaw, *Hitler, the Germans and the Final Solution*, p. 17.

67 George Browder, 'Perpetrator Character and Motivation: An Emerging Consensus?', *Holocaust and Genocide Studies* (Vol. 17, No. 3, 2003), pp. 480–97.

68 Ulrich Herbert, *Best: Biographische Studien über Radikalismus, Weltanschauung, und Vernunft 1903–1989* (Bonn, 1996).

69 For a brief explanation of Best's concept of 'heroic realism' which was important in motivating these men see Ulrich Herbert, 'Ideological Legitimization and Political Practice of the Leadership of the National Socialist Secret Police', Hans Mommsen (ed.), *The Third Reich Between Vision and Reality* (Oxford, 2001), pp. 95–108.

70 See Donald Bloxham, 'Organised Mass Murder: Structure, Participation and Motivation in Comparative Perspective', *Holocaust and Genocide Studies* (Vol. 22, No. 2, 2008), pp. 203–45, for a discussion of this tendency to extrapolate out from individual case studies.

71 Michael Thad Allen, *The Business of Genocide: The SS, Slave Labour and the Concentration Camps* (Chapel Hill: NC, 2002), p. 11.

72 Michael Thad Allen, 'The Banality of Evil Reconsidered: SS Mid-Level Managers of Extermination Through Work', *Central European History* (Vol. 30, No. 2, 1997), p. 294.

73 Michael Wildt, *Generation of the Unbound: The Leadership Corps of the Reich Main Security Office* (Jerusalem, 2002), this is a summary of the thesis contained in Michael Wildt, *An Uncompromising Generation: The Nazi Leadership of the Reich Main Security Office* (Madison: WI, 2009).

74 Yaacov Lozowick, *Hitler's Bureaucrats: The Nazi Security Police and the Banality of Evil* (London, 2002), p. 60.

75 *Ibid.*, p. 107.

76 *Ibid.*, pp. 232–3.
77 Yehuda Bauer, 'Trends in Holocaust Research', *Yad Vashem Studies* (Vol. 12, 1977), p. 11.
78 See for example Richard L. Rubenstein and John K. Roth, *Approaches to Auschwitz: Revised Edition* (Louisville: KY, 2003), Ch. 12 for a discussion of religious responses within Holocaust studies.
79 Lozowick, *Hitler's Bureaucrats*, p. 274.
80 Yaacow Lozowick, 'Malice in Action', *Yad Vashem Studies* (Vol. 27, 1999), p. 330.
81 Yaacow Lozowick, *Right to Exist: A Moral Defence of Israel's Wars* (New York, 2003), p. 23.
82 *Ibid.*, p. 30.
83 See for example *The Independent*, 7 March 2007.
84 Herf, *The Jewish Enemy*, p. 277.
85 Quoted in Uriel Tal, *"Political Faith" of Nazism Prior to the Holocaust* (Tel Aviv, 1978), p. 7.
86 See Tom Lawson, *The Church of England and the Holocaust: Christianity, Memory and Nazism* (Woodbridge, 2006), passim, for a discussion of this interpretative tendency.
87 Uriel Tal, *Structures of German Political Theology in the Nazi Era* (Tel Aviv, 1979), p. 21.
88 See for example Jacob Talmon, *The Origins of Totalitarian Democracy* (London, 1952).
89 Tal, *Structures of German Political Theology*, p. 10.
90 Tal, *"Political Faith"*, p. 22.
91 Saul Friedländer, 'From Anti-Semitism to Extermination: A Historiographical Study of Nazi Policies Towards Jews and an Essay in Interpretation', *Yad Vashem Studies* (Vol. 16, 1984, p. 49.
92 Saul Friedländer, *Nazi Germany and the Jews Vol. 1: The Years of Persecution* (London, 1997), p. 99.
93 Lozowick, *Hitler's Bureaucrats*, p. 279.
94 Michael Burleigh, *Sacred Causes: Religion and Politics from the European Dictators to Al Qaeda* (London, 2006), p. 282.
95 George Bell, 'A Letter to my Friends in the Evangelical Church in Germany', *The Church and Humanity* (London, 1946), pp. 183–95.
96 See for example John S. Conway, *The Nazi Persecution of the Churches* (London, 1968).
97 Richard Steigmann-Gall, *The Holy Reich: Nazi Conceptions of Christianity* (Cambridge, 2003), pp. 1–12.
98 Gregor, 'Nazism: A Political Religion?', pp. 11–12.
99 Susanne Heschel, *The Aryan Jesus: Christian Theologians and the Bible in Nazi Germany* (Princeton: NJ, 2008).
100 Tom Lawson, 'The Myth of the European Civil War', Richard Littlejohns and Sara Soncini (eds), *Myths of Europe* (Amsterdam, 2007), pp. 275–86.
101 Michael Burleigh, *The Third Reich: A New History* (London, 2001), p. 16.
102 Lozowick, *Right to Exist*, p. 297.
103 The latest manifestation of this is Michael Burleigh, *Blood and Rage: A Cultural History of Terrorism* (London, 2008).

104 See Bernd Weisbrod, 'Violence and Sacrifice: Imagining the Nation in Weimar Germany', Mommsen, *The Third Reich*, pp. 5–22; Richard Evans, *The Coming of the Third Reich* (London, 2003), pp. 229–30.

105 See Chapter 1 and Pascal Grosse, 'From colonialism to National Socialism to postcolonialism: Hannah Arendt's Origins of Totalitarianism', *Postcolonial Studies* (Vol. 9, No.1, 2006), pp. 35–52.

106 Jean Paul Sartre, 'On Genocide' cited in Ward Churchill, 'Genocide by Any Other Name: North American Indian Residential Schools in Context', Adam Jones (ed.), *Genocide, War Crimes and the West* (London, 2004), pp. 108–09.

107 Aimé Césaire, *Discourse on Colonialism* (New York, 1972), p. 14 also cited in Dan Stone, *Constructing the Holocaust* (London, 2003), p. 54.

108 Donald Bloxham, *The Final Solution: A Genocide* (Oxford, 2009), p. 308. See for example Czeslaw Madajczyk, 'General Plan East: Hitler's Master Plan for Expansion', *Polish Western Affairs* (Vol. 3, No. 2, 1962), pp. 391–442 which recognises that the intensification of murder of Europe's Jews occurred under work towards *Generalplan Ost*.

109 Ann Curthoys, 'Raphael Lemkin's Tasmania: an introduction', and Raphael Lemkin (Ann Curthoys, ed.), 'Tasmania', both in A. Dirk Moses and Dan Stone (eds), *Colonialism and Genocide* (London, 2007), pp. 66–100.

110 For an analysis of the impact of decolonisation on History see Robert J.C. Young, *White Mythologies* (London, 2004) especially the new introduction 'White Mythologies Revisited', pp. 1–31.

111 For a discussion of the development of the concept of genocide in Australian history and memory see A. Dirk Moses, 'Genocide and Settler Society in Australian History', *Genocide and Settler Society: Frontier Violence and Stolen Indigenous Children in Australian History* (New York, 2004), pp. 16–28.

112 Alison Palmer, *Colonial Genocide* (Adelaide, 2000), pp. 200–11. Isobel Hull similarly argues that the separation of the colonial troops and their commanders from Berlin is important in forcing the development of violence against the Herero in German South-West Africa into a genocidal 'final solution'. Isabel V. Hull, 'Military Culture and the Production of "Final Solutions" in the Colonies: The Example of Willhelminian Germany', Robert Gellately and Ben Kiernan (eds), *The Specter of Genocide: Mass Murder in Historical Perspective* (Cambridge, 2003), pp. 141–62.

113 Christian Gerlach, 'Extremely Violent Societies: an alternative to the concept of genocide', *Journal of Genocide Research* (Vol. 8, No. 4, 2006), pp. 455–71.

114 David Furber and Wendy Lower, 'Colonialism and Genocide in Nazi Occupied Poland and Ukraine', A. Dirk Moses (ed.), *Empire, Colony, Genocide: Conquest, Occupation, and Subaltern Resistance in World History* (New York, 2008), p. 373; Jürgen Zimmerer, 'Colonialism and the Holocaust: Towards an Archaeology of Genocide', Moses, *Genocide and Settler Society*, p. 53.

115 Hannah Arendt, The Origins of Totalitarianism (New York, 2004), pp. 242-86.

116 Wendy Lower, *Nazi Empire Building and the Holocaust in the Ukraine* (Chapel Hill: NC, 2005), p. 24.

117 *Ibid.*, p. 19.

118 This is discussed in Paul Bartop, 'The Holocaust, the Aborigines, and the

Bureaucracy of Destruction: An Australian Dimension of Genocide', *Journal of Genocide Research* (Vol. 3, No. 1, 2001), pp. 83–5.

119 A. Dirk Moses, 'Conceptual Blockages and Definitional Dilemmas in the Racial Century: Genocides of Indigenous Peoples and the Holocaust', Moses and Stone, *Colonialism and Genocide*, p. 150.

120 Jürgen Zimmerer, 'Colonialism and the Holocaust', p. 51.

121 Bloxham and Kushner, *The Holocaust*, p. 152, which makes the point that there is no one 'emblematic' perpetrator.

122 Ann Curthoys and John Docker, 'Defining Genocide', Dan Stone (ed.), *The Historiography of Genocide* (London, 2008), p. 34.

7

'Like Sheep to the Slaughter': debates on Jewish responses to Nazism

Thus far, the victims of the Holocaust have been somewhat absent from this book. We have seen much of what historians have had to say about the Nazis who engineered Jews' destruction, but little has been passed on Jewish responses to Nazi annihilation policies. But of course, there is an historiography which relates to the Nazis' Jewish victims, even if it is not as voluminous as might be expected.[1] As such, their absence in the preceding chapters reflects the divisions of Holocaust historiography – between those interested in the persecutors and those concerned with their victims. While it is too crude to say this is simply a divide between German and Jewish historiographies, there is no doubt that, at least at first, the historiography of the victims *was* dominated by Jewish and increasingly Israeli scholars. And, notwithstanding the exaggerations of the misleading 'silence model', it is also the case that the history of Jewish reactions to Nazi policy was, in terms of Western scholarship, a marginal affair. In the late 1940s and 1950s it was played out in Jewish journals, the publications of Jewish organisations, or within Jewish communities more generally.

The starting point for this historiography is however, the victims themselves during the years of the Holocaust. Some went to great lengths to document their suffering and thus to ensure that the history of their communities under the Nazi yoke was written. The young historian Emmanuel Ringelblum is the most prominent example. Consider his attempt to document the deportation of Jews from Warsaw's *Umschlagplatz* which began on 22 July 1942. Recording the events in his diary, Ringelblum's anger is palpable. Of course, his fury is directed at the Germans. But he attacks his fellow Jews too. He is aghast at the 'incomprehensible brutality' of the Jewish Ghetto Police who administered the *Aktion*, and excoriates the mass for not fighting back, for not resisting. 'Why have we allowed ourselves to be led like sleep to the slaughter' he cried.[2] Ultimately he laments 'now we are ashamed of ourselves, disgraced in our own eyes and in the eyes of the world, where our docility earned us nothing'.[3] Ringelblum demanded that the only escape from this shame was active and symbolic resistance. He was also a member of the Jewish Fighting Organisation which directed the Warsaw ghetto uprising in the spring of 1943.

Ringelblum's despair at Jews passively walking to their doom 'like sheep to the slaughter' was widely held. After all it confirmed caricatures of the Jewish Diaspora, held even in the *Yishuv*, the Jewish community of Palestine.[4] And it is an idea, or perhaps it is an allegation, that shaped debates on the communal Jewish response to Nazi persecution for, at the very least, the first three decades after the Holocaust and beyond. In a sense it defined this historiography. Not that the notion of Jews' submission has gone unchallenged. The idea of passivity has been noisily countered with celebrations of Jewish heroism and resistance. As such historiography has both repeated Ringelblum's claims of Jewish inaction, and indeed interwoven them with darker suggestions of collaboration; or such ideas have been attacked and dismissed as offensive. Debates have been vociferous, even angry, and have been conducted both inside and outside academia – in the first years of the Israeli state the issue of Jewish reactions to Nazism was a constant public concern too.[5]

Ringelblum is not just representative of this discourse because he offered the most well-known articulation of a despair at Jews' passivity. He also represents for our purposes the source material which has informed much of this historiography – surviving records and most importantly diaries which were concealed during the Nazi era and recovered in the aftermath of war. As the leader and inspiration behind the clandestine Warsaw ghetto archival project *Oneg Shabbat*, Ringelblum was thus responsible for not only the preservation but also the production of much of the raw material on which histories of the Jewish victims of Nazism have been based.

The source material plays an important role in this historiography. In fact it plays a role beyond that which might normally be expected. The diaries produced under the umbrella of *Oneg*

Shabbat, and the research the organisation carried out, as well as those records produced independently or elsewhere in Poland, began to ask the questions that would dominate historical research into the victims and their response to Nazism. Why did Jews not resist, or in what ways *did* they resist? What motivated armed insurrections like the Warsaw ghetto uprising that were doomed to failure? What did Jewish leaders do or not do, in relation to both their communities and the Nazis? How far did Jewish leaders co-operate or even collaborate? How were Jewish leaders regarded by the population? What was the role of the Jewish ghetto police? How did these ghettos function as Jewish societies, and what were the divisions within them? Did the ghettos have a class structure? What was the extent of religious and cultural life in the ghetto?

As such the diaries which posed such questions were much more than just personal records, they were efforts at exegesis or interpretation of the ghetto communities, and they have been treated as such since they were unearthed in the post-war world. Dawid Sierakowiak's diary might serve as an example here. Dawid was a teenager in Łódź when the Nazis invaded Poland. He recorded a diary throughout the life of the ghetto, in which he discussed his growing disgust at his father and enduring love for his mother at the same time as his contempt for the Jewish leadership. As such it was much more than just an account of his late adolescence in the Łódź ghetto. Even his feelings towards his parents were bound up with their differing reactions to the experience of persecution. The diary is, therefore, an interpretation of precisely the same issues that exercised Ringelblum, including the question why did the Jews not resist – a question he asks most insistently of himself. Sierakowiak counsels against easy answers; for him personally it appears that the effort to stay alive consumed all his energy. For others the answer was complex, and he tried to avoid generalisation commenting simply that it was 'interesting what different kinds of people there are in the ghetto'.[6]

This is an historiography shaped by material produced by the subjects themselves then – even an entire monograph by Ringelblum, *Polish Jewish Relations Between the Wars*, survived and was published after the war.[7] This material has also been considered more 'reliable' than simply the memories of survivors that had not lay untouched under the rubble, but had been shaped and reshaped in the post-war world.[8] It was also, after 1945, an historiography practised by many who were survivors themselves – although Ringelblum himself died in Trawniki in 1944, nearly all of the major contributors discussed below are 'survivor historians' – such as Rachel Auerbach, Israel Gutman and Josef Kermish. Peculiarly then, historical debates about Jewish responses to Nazism are witness to a distinct blurring of the boundaries between document and history, between witness and historian.

This chapter will begin by charting the emergence of this material – literally its discovery and publication in the post-war world. I will argue that such primary material at times took the place of histories of Jewish behaviour. Indeed, the necessity of the historian was often denied in the presentation of documents that it was claimed could provide an 'open line' to the past.[9] That said, there were debates surrounding Jewish behaviour which reflected upon the questions first established by the ghetto chroniclers. The narrative of these debates, and their emergence from a much wider public discourse on the Holocaust especially in Israel, will then form the basis of the latter sections of the chapter. Although this is an historiography which perhaps inevitably involves Jewish scholars and centres upon Israel, it has not developed entirely separately to the historiography of the perpetrators and the links between the two will also be suggested. Overall it is my aim to show, once again, that Holocaust historiography is a moral political discourse, with debates about Jewish resistance in the past as much a discussion about post-war Jewish identities in the present.

The academic discourse on whether Jews resisted or accepted their fate is ongoing, hence this chapter does not have strict chronological boundaries, but it should be acknowledged that these questions received most scholarly attention between the war and the end of the 1970s. After this point, histories of the victims became much more concerned with testimony and individual memories than with macro questions of *Jewish* behaviour. History and historians also became more concerned with the experience of the concentration camps, whereas for the most part the debates reconstructed here concentrated on the ghettos.

The documents of Jewish life in the ghettos and camps

Ringelblum began to collect material relating to the Jewish experience under Nazi occupation in 1939. At that time he was involved in the provision of welfare, administering aid to stricken Jews. His notes on his experiences formed the basis of the diary that was posthumously published by the Jewish Historical Institute in Warsaw from 1948, and ultimately in book form in 1952, as *Notes from the Warsaw Ghetto*. From May of 1940 Ringelblum's project began to involve others, especially in the production of diaries. By the middle of 1941, the archive began to direct individuals to survey and collect material around specific themes such as 'Youth and Children', 'Education and Study' or 'Jewish Women'.[10] Ultimately the archives were interred before the final liquidation, buried in milk churns under what became the rubble of the destroyed ghetto. They were recovered by the JHI in the aftermath of war, although some material was lost. Two caches of documents were exhumed, the first in September 1946 and then a further batch in December 1950.[11] Some of those involved in the recovery and later the publication of the material such as Rachel Auerbach (who went on to head the testimony section of *Yad Vashem* in Jerusalem), had also been active in the ghetto archive itself.

Material recovered from the ghettos and camps was progressively published from 1945 onwards. In Poland especially diaries were published very quickly.[12] But this material does not just represent the raw material, the documentation on top of which an historiography was built, but its exegesis too. As a consequence it has been very common for such evidence to be presented alone, accompanied by very little analysis or interpretation – or even accompanied by a denial of the very necessity of the kind of contextual interpretation that might be expected of historians. And in the first years after the war, historiography which sought to combine such material, to weave evidence together to create both narratives of, for example, ghetto life or to offer any general interpretation of the significance of the ghetto and of Jewish behaviour within it, is notable only by its rarity.

This is not to say that material was published without external intervention, in fact quite the opposite is true – but those interventions were often disguised. Perhaps the most famous of all Holocaust diaries, the diary of Anne Frank, is evidence of this.[13] Anne's diary was heavily edited before publication. References to her teenage sexuality and to her problematic relationship with her mother were excised. Owing in part to this judicious editing of the material by Anne's father, early critics were able to impose an extraordinary narrative of hope rather than tragedy, anger and loss, on the diary. Frank's narrative quickly became seen as a celebration of the human spirit, of how despite everything people were good.[14] Emanuel Ringelblum's *Notes from the Warsaw Ghetto* were originally published in 'mutilated' form too – edited to remove references to negative relations between Poles and Jews suffering under Nazi occupation.[15]

Despite such editing, where the diaries and ghetto materials were published it was invariably claimed that they offered an objective account of Jewish life under Nazi rule. In Europe and beyond, surviving remnants of Jewish communities contributed to memorial *Yizkor* books in an effort to preserve the past that the Nazis had destroyed – over 400 were produced, each detailing the life and destruction of an individual community, between 1945 and the early 1970s. These memorials contained little analysis but they were efforts at interpretation. However, they were presented as simply 'tangible representations' of a world that had been destroyed, as a remnant of the past surviving and able to speak to the present.[16]

More overtly scholarly publications made very similar claims. Ringelblum himself confided that his diary was 'particularly important … as expressions of what the surviving remnant of the Jewish community thought about their everyday problems'. Despite being a diary, Jacob Sloan who edited it for publication, insisted that Ringelblum's work was not about him but 'about the Ghetto'. What is more, according to Sloan, events were presented without artifice, in other words the diary offered a window on the ghetto:

> things are said straight out without embellishment – and, thus nakedly stated, they stand out in larger than life size. There was no need to add dramatic quality to the ghetto: it had its own rising and falling, its own tension. Incidents and characters were all at hand; nothing needed to be invented. The catastrophe followed on its own inexorable movement. No pace had to be introduced.[17]

This tendency to deny the necessity of interpretative scholarship, of History, has continued since these original publications. Josef Kermish's edited collection of documents from *Oneg Shabbat*, first published in 1986, asserts the objectivity of the documents and their ability to 'tear away the veil' that the Nazis themselves constructed over the 'Final Solution' and see clearly the ghetto at work.[18] Alan Adelson's collection of documents from Łódź similarly declares that it brings to the reader voices 'from *then*, unmediated by time'.[19] According to the introduction, Michal Grynberg's collection of testimonies recovered by the JHI in Warsaw in the aftermath of war, first published in Polish in 1988 and in English in 2003, is important precisely because they are presented without analytical commentary: 'the documents confront the reader with personal and emotional realities often lost in the scholarly presentations.'[20] This is true of manuscripts from other Holocaust spaces too. The three manuscripts buried by individuals who served in the *Sonderkommando* in Auschwitz-Birkenau (the group of prisoners employed to service the gas chambers and the crematoria) which were uncovered there between 1945 and 1962 are another useful example. The diaries of Zalman Gradowski, Leib Langfuss and Zalman Lewenthal were all published after they had been recovered, but were not subject to scholarly analysis – in terms of systematically asking what they revealed about the experience of being a Jew in Auschwitz – until the 1990s.[21]

As a result, it is possible to offer a narrative of the development of victim historiography which simply charts the publication of important diaries or contemporary documents, as if the historian was not necessary in this regard. The life of the *Sonderkommando* was first revealed by the diaries that were found in the rubble of the crematoria and then published. Avraham Lewin's ghetto diary revealed the experience of an orthodox religious Jew under the Nazi yoke,[22] Janusz Korczak's diary reflects on the dilemmas of public service in a doomed community.[23] Vladka Meed's record of life inside the ghetto and then in hiding, illuminated the experience of women and the extent of co-operation both in the ghetto and between Poles and Jews.[24] Calel Perochodnik's haunting account of life in the Jewish Police laid bare the compromises inherent in attempting to serve both the community, the Nazis and one's own family.[25]

But, such documents are themselves efforts at interpretation and as such require unpacking.[26] As Zoë Waxman suggests in her history of Holocaust testimonies, ghetto diaries – however affecting – *cannot* be regarded as simply windows on experience. They do refract experiences, they are mediated through and constructed by their authors in the precisely the same way that a post-war memoir or oral testimony might be. The writers of *Oneg Shabbat* were from the outset involved in a conscious act of resistance against the Nazi desire to erase all vestiges of the Jewish past.[27] Efforts to assert the richness of ghetto life should be seen in this light. Ringelblum *et al.* were also part of an historiographical tradition, emerging from an incredibly rich Polish-Jewish historiography between the wars which attempted to assert the diversity and energy of Polish Jewish life. Records of life under Nazi occupation are thus examples of a continuing tradition in Polish-Jewish cultural life and should be read contextually.[28]

According to Waxman, ghetto diarists were also attempting to mediate, interpret and articulate precisely what it meant to be Jewish in the ghetto and beyond. The diary of the young orthodox Rabbi Shimon Huberband is a particularly rich example here. When published his diary was presented as being distinguished by 'a remarkable objectivity', and avoiding 'tendentiousness and any detail which would reflect a personal bias or subjective approach'.[29] Despite being assured that Huberband had 'no vested interest other than the truth', the journal contains reflections on the divisions in ghetto society with which he struggles to come to terms, and which he filters through his own religious and cultural convictions. Huberband reflects at length on the 'Moral Decline of the Jewish Woman' for example, observing that in spite of the suffering some women flaunted wealth in the Warsaw ghetto, a wealth that might even have been bought at the price of sexual relations with German men. Such a prospect is simply too much for Huberband who confides that 'the illusions of Jewish unity and Jewish compassion have been broken. One must only add ... I am ashamed.'[30]

Such observations therefore tell us more about the author, and indeed the development of cultural tensions within the ghetto, than Huberband himself would have claimed or desired. Historians would not accept simple declarations as to the 'truth' of historical evidence in any other context, and therefore they should not do so here either. However, the tendency to treat the material from the ghettos as historiographical acts in themselves – that require no further contextualisation or interpretation by historians – *is* perfectly understandable. After all the authors regarded themselves as the first historians and interpreters of the ghetto. And as such they attempted to go about their work with scientific precision. Josef Kermish reported in his edited collection of *Oneg Shabbat* material that Ringelblum always 'had several authors write about the same events' in order to achieve objectivity. Such claims create a daunting legacy for future historians and their ability to challenge any of the conclusions of the witnesses.

That the scholars responsible for the recovery and presentation of the material were themselves survivors compounds this. For example, Philip Friedman describes how he himself, Nachman Blumenthal, Abba Kovner, Josef Kermish and Isaiah Trunk (amongst others) all returned to Warsaw after the war and ultimately helped establish the JHI which would bring the efforts of *Oneg Shabbat* to wider public attention.[31] These survivor historians then became the custodians of the evidence bequeathed by the ghetto, often by persons who did not survive. As such the material achieved a canonical status, and gained the double authority of having been written at the time, confirmed by historians who were themselves witnesses. Such authority could hardly be challenged by scholars who had not been subject to the ravages of life under Nazi rule. As Hermann Langbein wrote in his account of resistance in Auschwitz in the 1980s, and his sentiments could be applicable to the other circles of the Nazi hell, 'someone who has never experienced the world of the Nazi camps can never understand'.[32] Langbein wrote from the 'privileged' position of having led Jewish resistance inside Auschwitz. Perhaps inevitably then historians were muted by the reinforced authenticity of such material. As Geoffrey Hartman observes of a collection of documents from Łódź: 'the record of this individual and communal effort to survive is overwhelming. One becomes ashamed of one's own voice.'[33]

Hartman, writing in the mid-1980s, was actually calling for historians to overcome this reluctance and engage with the issue of interpretation. But when one considers the peculiar moral and historical problems raised by the recovered accounts of the victims of Nazism, scholarly silence is all the more explicable. Although the most extreme, consider the *Sonderkommando* in Auschwitz-Birkenau. Ber Mark's original publication of the three manuscripts insists that these witnesses just be left to speak for themselves. 'Let us hear [their] words' he asks.[34] What Mark wished to avoid was the easy judgement of men who performed a task which placed them at the very borders of human experience. The *Sonderkommando* were selected for their role within the machinery of extermination. To refuse meant death. If they chose to stay alive and serve in the *Sonderkommando*, they were then responsible for the functioning of the gas chambers and the crematoria (although Zyklon B was always administered by the SS) – and they thus played a significant role in the extermination process itself. They were not only its witnesses but its workers – entering the death chambers in order to remove the bodies, which they then burnt but only after checking for and removing any valuable materials – most notably gold teeth. They received greater rations than the normal prisoners, from whom they were separated to sustain them in their grisly task. To discover members of one's own community, or even own family, amongst the dead appears to have been common.

To describe the function of the *Sonderkommando* in this manner hardly evokes or conveys the profundity of the experience, the revolutionised moral world that these men inhabited. As I write these words I feel acutely the shame that Hartman described at the inadequacy of one's own voice. One is thus drawn inevitably back to the diaries of the men themselves to try and access such an experience. Yet precious little of the diaries is given over to the description of this horror. Zalman Gradowski bequeathed two manuscripts, the first discovered in 1945 the second in 1947. The first account contains a description of life before and his journey to Birkenau, but apart from recording that he wrote these words as a *Sonderkommando* there is no description of these tasks. His work is prefaced by an ironic warning to the reader, the 'citizen of the free world' that if they are to go with him on this journey they will experience things that will transform their understanding of their fellow man, that they will be forced to confront a reality that as yet they cannot imagine: 'tell ... your friends and acquaintances, that if you never return, it will only be because your blood has frozen in your veins and ceased to flow, on beholding the fearsome horrors of the slaughter of innocent helpless children, the children of my tortured people.'[35] Yet the horror of that slaughter, to which Gradowski was witness, is not described.[36] Leib Langfuss's description of the sufferings of women transferred to Birkenau at the beginning of 1944 only takes us to the moments before their extermination by gas because at that point Langfuss reports, 'I sneak away quickly. I did not see the rest of the events for on principle I was never present when the Jews were being rushed to their death, as it might have come to pass that the SS would force me to carry out their murderous purposes.'[37]

As Nathan Cohen argued in his analysis of the diaries, one is forced to conclude that even these testimonies themselves 'fall short of revealing the whole truth' of the *Sonderkommando*.[38] Not least because all of the testimonies offer different interpretations as to the meaning of the *Sonderkommando* and the 'Final Solution' more generally. Gradowski is struck by the implications of his task for modernity: 'animals have been restrained by civilisation – their hooves have been dulled and their cruelty greatly curbed – man has not, but has become a beast. The more highly developed a culture, the more cruel its murderers, the more civilised a society, the greater its barbarians; as development increases, its deeds become more terrible'. Leib Langfuss's account however, dwells much more on the sadism and barbarous behaviour of the perpetrators.[39]

Recently Gideon Greif has attempted an historical analysis of the *Sonderkommando* based on both the recovered manuscripts and the oral and written testimonies of those who survived. In it he follows Ber Mark's original warning not to morally evaluate the *Sonderkommando*: 'let no-one judge another guilty who does not know the taste of hopelessness in the depths of extinction.'[40] As a consequence Greif paints a picture of the *Sonderkommando* as inanimate, as having become machines. By doing so he denies that the individual members of the *Sonderkommando* maintained a moral identity, arguing, in effect, that they lost their sense of humanity. He therefore cannot be accused of passing judgement on those who necessarily had not and could not make moral choices. Yet at the same time Greif argues that the *Sonderkommando* used a sense of comradeliness and mutual support to survive – something which at the very least suggests the endurance of some traditional moral precepts inside the *Sonderkommando* compound.[41] The tension in Greif's analysis reflects a tension in the accounts of the *Sonderkommando* themselves – as such the victims' material may be able to speak for itself, but the voices that we hear appear to be conflicting and contradictory.

Resistance? Conflict and controversy
in accounts of victim behaviour

None of this reluctance to engage the surviving fragments of the
ghettos and camps means that there were no historical narratives
of victim behaviour in the immediate aftermath of war, or that
there was no dissent or disagreement as to how to interpret that
behaviour. In part Ber Mark's warning not to judge the *Sonderkommando* was made because from the very moment the war
ended, and perhaps even before, judgements had been pronounced
on the way Jews had acted, on the decisions of communal leaders,
and on the moral choices that individuals had made, particularly
in the ghetto.

These judgements meant that when the Jewish past was considered the rich panorama of the Jewish wartime experience was
often reduced to the single question, first raised in the ghetto itself,
about Jews' resistance or otherwise and whether, in fact, Jews had
co-operated in their destruction. To this end, in the immediate
aftermath of war, inside occupied Europe, Jewish communities
established 'honour courts' in which those accused of collaborat-
ing with the Nazis were tried – from ghetto policemen to former
members of the Jewish councils or *Judenräte*. Such courts provided a narrative of collaboration to add to, and in part explain
and excuse, the passivity of the masses that had so aggrieved
Ringelblum.[42] They also continued judgements that had been
made on communal leaders by the ghetto chroniclers themselves –
Ringelblum had dismissed Adam Czerniakow, the leader of the
Warsaw *Judenrat*, as a weak man.[43]

In the fledgling state of Israel such accounting against those
who had collaborated with the Jews' tormentors continued. The
'Nazis and Nazi Collaborators Law' was passed in the *Knesset* in
1950, and a series of trials of former Jewish policemen and *Kapos*
(privileged concentration camp prisoners) were enacted under its
auspices between 1951 and 1964. More famously, Rudolf Kastner
(the Hungarian Jewish leader who had been involved in ransom
negotiations with the SS and who by then had become a
spokesman for the Israeli government) was the subject of a libel
trial beginning in 1954. This followed allegations, published by
pamphleteer Malchiel Gruenwald, that Kastner had collaborated
with the destruction of the Jews of Hungary, and also sought to
save himself and his family at the expense of others. The original

judgement effectively found against Kastner and thus agreed that he had collaborated, although this was overturned on appeal in 1958.[44] The trials symbolise what a live political and cultural issue the behaviour of Jews and Jewish leaders was in Israel, and the enduring sense that diasporic Jewry had in part succumbed to the Nazis because of its own 'ghetto mentality' that encouraged at best passivity and at worst co-operation and collaboration.

Concern at the idea of passivity and even collaboration, first in post-war Europe and then in the young Israel, was matched by the joyous reception given to those that had resisted the Nazis. Indeed such celebration functioned as a counterweight to these allegations. If diasporic passivity brought shame, then the heroism of the ghetto fighters bequeathed pride and hope. Nearly every *Yizkor* book discussed Jewish resistance.[45] The celebration of ghetto fighters became a cultural norm in the fledgling state of Israel, and the first institutions for the study and memorialisation of the Holocaust, such as the Itzhak Katznelson Ghetto Fighters House, were established by surviving members of resistance movements. Indeed, Jewish resisters during the Holocaust became incorporated into the foundation myths of the state, alongside the heroic fighters of the *Yishuv* who had fought the British for independence.[46]

As such, a Manichean picture of Jewish behaviour in the Holocaust emerged in nascent Israel, split between the easy condemnation of those who 'collaborated' and the even easier celebration of those who 'resisted'. There was little consideration of the moral complexities and compromises involved in *either* active rebellion, passive compliance or indeed the broad spectrum of activity that might be called collaboration. Nor therefore was there any space for the complex and contradictory memories of individuals that might fit neither or both of these models.[47] The moral condemnation of those who collaborated was a feature of early historiography too – in part of course because it grew out of the memoir and diary tradition from wartime where such judgements abounded.[48] Evaluations of the *Judenrat* leaders were often stark. As Dan Michman has demonstrated, the work of Philip Friedmann on this topic was more critical of the Jewish councils than is usually acknowledged. He decried those leaders like Chaim Rumkowski in Łódź and Jacob Gens in Vilna who assumed that they could save their communities by making them productive in the Nazi image. Friedmann alleged that these 'pseudo-saviours of the ghettos were, consciously or unconsciously, influenced by the great 'messianic' craze of the fascists, and aspired to be saviours of their people in ways that were devoid of the Jewish spirit.'[49]

As was noted in Chapter 1, the celebration of the symbolic moments of resistance such as the Warsaw ghetto uprising was also common in early historiography. Again this is not surprising considering that many of the scholars were themselves survivors of resistance groups. Celebration was not entirely without its nuances either. For example some of the original publications on the Warsaw ghetto uprising sought to demonstrate links between the Jewish and communist resistance movements in Poland in line with the prevailing political winds.[50] Philip Friedman's early history alternatively claimed that the significance of the doomed fight for the Warsaw ghetto was as a symbol of man's ability to fight against totalitarian tyranny, which Robert Rozett argues was a clear effort to claim the legacy of the ghetto fighters for resistance *against* communist oppression.[51] Indeed resistance scholarship throughout Europe, concerned with any opposition to the Nazis, was often defined by the effort to draw links between those who had opposed the Nazis in the past and those who controlled the political present. The original focus of *Yad Vashem* was also as much towards resistance as it was towards catastrophe, again reflecting the influence of the survivor historians from Warsaw who gravitated there,[52] and that the legal obligation of *Yad Vashem* was to commemorate all 'the members of the Jewish people who fell, *fought and rebelled against the Nazi enemy*' (emphasis added).[53] Some of the studies of Jewish resistance which it then published adopted a rhetorical and heroic vocabulary.[54]

During the early 1960s three scholars from outside Israel inflamed this historiography with theses on Jewish behaviour which should be seen, in part, as replies to this heroic tradition. Raul Hilberg and then Hannah Arendt put forward accounts of Jewish behaviour which provoked furious reactions. First Hilberg argued that there was very little significant Jewish resistance, and in fact the reaction pattern of Jews was defined by an ingrained passivity that had characterised Jewish responses to persecution throughout the Diaspora. The 'Jewish victims' he wrote 'were caught in the straitjacket of their history' and they 'plunged themselves physically and psychologically into catastrophe'.[55] Hilberg essentially repeated the Ringelblum thesis, but added an interpretation of the *Judenräte* as part of the machinery of destruction. He was joined in this by survivor psychologist Bruno Bettelheim who argued in 1960 that Jews 'could at least have marched as free men against the SS, rather than first to grovel, then wait to be rounded up for their own extermination and finally walk themselves to the gas chambers'.[56] Hannah Arendt then extended this vision of compliance with an allegation of the Jewish Councils' active complicity, which she alleged magnified the number of victims claimed by the Nazis.

Of course these claims were not new – indeed they were all part of a Jewish and now Israeli discourse that had been ongoing since the war itself. But they did bring such arguments to wider attention, and as such presented the image of Jewish passivity to the wider world too. Scholarly reactions to this caricature were furious – especially those emanating from *Yad Vashem*, typified by Nathan Eck's rubbishing of Hilberg's work as 'slander'.[57] Hannah Arendt's suggestion that the co-operation of the Jewish Councils meant that it was impossible to draw a clear distinction between victim and perpetrator left Jacob Robinson 'aghast'.[58] 'It is', Robinson wrote, 'difficult to conceive a statement more offensive in respect to the dead.'[59]

The historiography of the Jewish Councils, which emerged in part, but not entirely, as a response to the Hilberg/Arendt thesis will be discussed in the following section of this chapter. First, I would like to analyse the response to Hilberg's suggestion that resistance was neither widespread nor historically significant. As with all studies of 'resistance' during the Second World War it is first important to understand what is meant by the term. In Hilberg's case the answer is clear. Resistance was defined as armed insurrection. This is evident from this negative appraisal of the Jews: 'the documentary evidence of Jewish resistance, overt or submerged, is very slight ... [they] had no resistance organisation, no blueprint for armed action, no plan even for psychological warfare.'[60] In turn Hilberg only understood its importance in formal military terms. As such, because Jewish resistance did little or nothing to disrupt either the German war machine, or indeed their war against the Jews, it 'shrinks into insignificance'.[61]

On its own terms Hilberg's argument is almost irrefutable – the Jews did lack an homogenous resistance, and in purely military terms outbreaks of resistance did have little or no impact. As such he did not deny the fact of local or sporadic Jewish armed resistance, just its importance. Yet attempts to refute Hilberg were invariably crudely aimed at countering the allegation that the *Jews had not resisted at all*, an allegation he had not really made. A number of anthologies were thus published which attempted to document the fact of that resistance – to show, using the title of Yuri Suhl's collection, *They Fought Back*.[62] But such anthologies did little to counter Hilberg's central contentions – which could only really be done by proposing either a different definition of resistance, or by using a different barometer of its significance. Intriguingly, the idea that part of the purpose must always be to prove the very existence of Jewish rebellion has never really left resistance historiography. Hence in one of the most recent histories of *Jewish Resistance During the Holocaust*, published in 2004, James Glass argues that it is the very fact of resistance which is the most significant. But in doing so he also proposes a quite different scale of value by which to gauge the importance of rebellion to Hilberg. Glass suggested that the failure of Germans, and other Europeans under the Nazi yoke to resist demonstrated how far 'the ground of sanity and insanity had shifted'. The 'Final Solution', which under normal circumstances would have simply been considered madness became accepted as a rational state policy. But within this atmosphere of madness Jewish resistance 'reminded the world and posterity that sanity and courage had not been completely annihilated'.[63]

By looking to posterity Glass invoked an indicator of significance that had long been employed in the historiography of the Warsaw ghetto uprising. Remember Ringelblum had called for *symbolic* resistance in October 1942. And finding significance in non-military terms was a necessity. After all any claims that the resistance in the ghetto either disrupted Germany's war or its 'Final Solution' would be delusional. After Hilberg, scholars such as Israel Gutman (himself a veteran of the uprising) reiterated the arguments of the original historiography that had pointed to the *symbolic* importance of Jewish heroism in Warsaw. The fact of Jewish resistance was significant precisely because it overturned the passive reaction pattern of the Jews. As such its importance lay not in its negligible impact on Nazi Germany, but on its legacy for the future. Thus the uprising was 'literally a revolution in Jewish history' which rejected the diasporic tradition of compliance and co-operation, and asserted Jewish power. These were also the terms on which the men of the Jewish Fighting Organisation in Warsaw themselves understood their doomed struggle – as the leader of the ghetto fighters Mordechai Anielewicz famously proclaimed: 'Jewish armed resistance and retaliation have become a reality. I have been witness to the magnificent heroic struggle of the Jewish fighters.'[64] The status that the memory of the ghetto fighters enjoyed in Israel in the aftermath of the war, and continue to enjoy, rather confirms the suggestion that their significance was symbolic rather than practical or military.

Such a narrative was not confined to the men of Warsaw. Scholarship on resistance in the concentration and death camps makes similar claims for the symbolic importance of insurrection. Yitzhak Arad declared that the uprisings in Sobibor and Treblinka were 'successful' because as an 'act of revolt they wrote an important page in the history of Jewish fighting during World War II'.[65] Herman Langbein, too, declared that resistance in Auschwitz was important because it demonstrated that even in such an extreme environment an 'inhumane regime … although it can murder people, cannot completely stamp out human impulses on the part of others'.[66] Even the original scholarship on the *Sonderkommando* found those men significant because of their role in uprisings at Auschwitz-Birkenau.[67] Perhaps the fact of *Sonderkommando* resistance made Jews' involvement in the destruction process bearable too. It is worth noting that in many ways such arguments, by implication, concur with Hilberg's passivity thesis – in that by declaring the fact of Jews fighting back to be symbolically important they imply that previously Jews *had been* submissive. As such despite the furore that Hilberg caused, his arguments really reflected those already proposed within the Jewish and then Israeli tradition.

The very definition of resistance Hilberg proposed was open to challenge. As we have already noted, the ghetto chroniclers regarded their collecting of material as an act of defiance against the Nazi plan to extirpate Jewish civilisation. At the very least they would preserve its memory. Using this, any refusal to comply with the fell designs of the Nazis could be included in a much wider definition of resistance. Philip Friedman had included 'spiritual resistance' in his survey first published in 1960, suggesting that those who maintained dignity in the face of Nazi violence might be included in the annals of those who fought back. This would encompass Janusz Korczak, whose decision to go with the children of his orphanage to their deaths was thus an act of resistance, because he protected them from the gravity of the doom that had enveloped them. It could also stand as a beacon of Jewish dignity to contrast the gloom cast by Nazi barbarousness. Thus non-violence could be as heroic and cast as much light for the future as the heroism of those who took up arms.[68]

A conference on resistance at *Yad Vashem* in 1968 employed this more elastic definition to include all forms of Jewish non-conformity to the 'evil design of the Nazis'.[69] This would then include the maintenance of a distinct Jewish culture and religious practice. The refusal (for example in the ghetto) to submit to despair, and indeed in the context of the 'Final Solution', the very act of staying alive were thus resistant. Therefore the organisation of welfare and Jewish cultural life in the ghettos could also be resistance – which was ironic because such things were administered by the *Judenräte* that other scholars wished to dismiss as collaborators. Such a definition raises the possibility that the debate with Raul Hilberg might have been more a matter of semantics than anything else. Hilberg did not deny that the Jewish Councils performed such a role, he chose however to describe such activities as 'alleviation' rather than resistance, the attempt to lessen the burdens of Nazi rule on the wider population.

The Hebrew term *Amidah*, translated as 'taking a stand' or steadfastness, was used from the end of the 1960s to conceptualise this wider definition of resistance, most notably employed by Yehuda Bauer and Saul Esh.[70] Such developments in Jewish resistance historiography followed scholarship into resistance under the Nazi regime amongst the non-Jewish German population very closely. Martin Broszat developed the concept *resistenz*, which shadows *Amidah*, and applies to non-conformist behaviour or the refusal to allow the Nazi regime to entirely shape one's outlook and world view. Sometimes referred to as 'inner emigration', the idea of *resistenz* could encompass the continued practice of buying from Jewish shops in the 1930s or the steadfast maintenance of a class-consciousness in the face of Nazi propaganda as to the *national* community. Christopher Browning describes the overlap in these historiographies as 'ironic', but such a judgement does not seem to capture their similar purposes.[71] If *Amidah* was developed because so few Jews during the Holocaust could be described as actively resistant, *resistenz* certainly allowed a less gloomy picture of German society in the Nazi era – where resistance was almost non-existent but non-conformity endemic.

Amidah was a secular term, but it is a concept that was also used to relate ideas of Jewish resistance to religious traditions. Shimon Huberband had used the concept *Kiddush Hashem*, a term for the sanctification of God's name and central to Jewish martyrology, to give a religious significance to the events that engulfed him. Jews who died as Jews at Nazi hands had performed *Kiddush Hashem* according to Huberband, dying in the name of Judaism. But for many the idea that submission to the Nazis had a religious purpose was too much, the destruction on too great a scale, for *Kiddush Hashem* to apply. Resistance scholars, most notably Esh and Nathan Eck, sought to transform the concept into *Kiddush Ha-Hayim* or the sanctification of life.[72] This then awarded the efforts to stay alive a religious purpose too, and echoed the idea of *Amidah*. Alternatively Konrad Kwiet has argued that suicide must be included in the definition of resistance, that death itself is a form or rebellion.[73]

Just as the idea of *resistenz* has been rejected by some scholars of Nazi Germany, so some Holocaust historians rejected *Amidah* as just too elastic – because it seemed to imply that all Jewish reactions to Nazism were resistance, from collaboration to armed insurrection, from death to life. For Joan Ringelheim the term resistance 'becomes neutralised' by what she describes as 'such slippage'. As a consequence all Jews become both martyrs and heroes – and the very purpose of historical scholarship, differentiation and understanding or interpretation, is denied.[74]

Debates as to what constituted resistance are much more than just interpretative conflicts about the past. By definition the vast majority of Jews under Nazi rule did not take up arms. Extending the definition of resistance awarded a dignity and perhaps even a heroism to those that did not resist as well, and more importantly to their *memory*. It thus provided a mechanism by which the Holocaust could be remembered without the shame that Emanuel Ringelblum had felt at Jewish passivity. The following example should suffice. Raul Hilberg used the testimony of Herman Graebe to demonstrate the 'compliance' of Jews even 'in front of the grave'.[75] Graebe described the execution of the Jews of Dubno on 5 October 1942, and in particular the relationship between a boy and his father as they walked to their death:

> The father was holding the hand of a boy about ten years old and was speaking to him softly; the boy was fighting his tears. The father pointed to the sky, stroked his head, and seemed to explain something to him.

For Nathan Eck, and it is difficult to disagree with him, to dismiss this tender exchange as compliance was not adequate, and did not serve the memory of this unnamed man and his child properly, did not capture the bravery of this act of compassion which was at the very least an 'expression of lofty spirit and human dignity'.[76] *Amidah* provided a mechanism for rescuing this boy and his father, if not from death then from the easy criticism of the choices that they made in such horrific circumstances.

Extending the definition of resistance to encompass behaviour other than armed insurrection has also encouraged historians to consider the complex moral choices and compromises that were involved. James Glass's history points to the ambivalence of some aspects of using violence against the Nazis especially when that violence was without hope of success, in terms of the defeat of the Germans. First of all, to take up arms required a fundamentally new moral world and as such the resistor had to relearn moral positions in which killing became an imperative, the route to an exalted posterity.[77] Individual decisions to join resistance groups also had moral consequences that were not always unambiguous. Young men who escaped the ghetto to join bands of partisans for example, made the active choice to leave the ghetto behind. In doing so they by necessity abandoned 'weaker' members of the population and indeed their families, who not only could not survive in the forest but would not, as burdens, have been welcome in such an environment.[78] They also left the ghetto weaker. These are moral problems that are still being worked through, that have a cache in the present as well as the past. Nazi reprisal policy meant that killings of Germans by partisans were avenged, several times over, by killings of Jews. Thus partisan forces not only theoretically but physically endangered the ghetto population left behind by their revenge attacks against the Nazis. Such fighting may have been heroic, the symbol of Jewish self-defence, but it may also have been reckless and compounded Jewish suffering too.[79]

This is not the place to adjudicate in such matters. The real significance in debates over the nature of Jewish resistance, as to what resistance actually means, is that they signal that scholarship developed nuances from its beginnings in first post-war accounting and then the efforts just to demonstrate, somewhat crudely, that the Jews did fight back. As a consequence we can now point to a complex historiography. Once a more wide-ranging definition was in play then the geography of Jewish resistance could become more diverse too – with historians turning away from just Eastern Europe. An historian from the German Democratic Republic (GDR), Helmut Eschwege, demonstrated the enduring politics of resistance scholarship in the late 1960s when publication of his work on the resistance of German Jews was blocked. It was published in truncated form in the West in 1970.[80] Konrad Kwiet and Eschwege then went on to be the authors of the standard work on German Jewish resistance, which points to 'cultural resistance' and non-conformity in the absence of organised active insurrection which was functionally impossible inside the dictatorship.[81] The political problems of Eschwege's study remind us that the question of the relationship between ethnic and political identity is never far from the surface in resistance studies. The only significant armed Jewish resistance organisation inside Germany, the Herbert Baum group, Konrad Kwiet suggests was inspired by communism but involved Jews.[82] More recently Marion Kaplan and Renée Poznanski have produced accounts of Jewish life in Germany and France respectively that suggest these were communities almost defined by *Amidah* and the effort to negotiate an enduringly distinct culture under extreme pressure.[83] As such, according to Robert Rozett, resistance scholarship has come a long way from the urge simply to glorify.[84]

Jewish leadership: the darkest chapter?

If the question of resistance or passivity dominated historical evaluation of wider Jewish society in the Holocaust, then it was the issue of collaboration that dominated scholarship on the *Judenräte*. The historiography of the councils was given great impetus by Arendt's sensational claims during the Eichmann Trial that the Jewish Councils amounted to the 'darkest chapter in the whole dark story'. Arendt, and Raul Hilberg whose analysis of the councils it was alleged considered them only as part of the machinery of destruction, became the target of a wave of revisionist scholarship seeking to overturn their judgements. Such scholarship was fervent, and often geared to either the moral condemnation or vindication of the ghetto leaders. The debate was thus impassioned, but perhaps shed more heat than light on the historical conundrum of ghetto society and thus victim behaviour.

When first Hilberg and then Arendt published their claims, conceptually the Jewish Councils already amounted to 'treason' in the wider Jewish and Israeli discourse on the past.[85] It is difficult therefore to see why they provoked such a furore. In part, it was because these attacks on Jewish leadership appeared to be painting in broad brush strokes, offering all-encompassing interpretations of the councils as, effectively, collaborators or quislings. Arendt's critique was also interpreted as a broadside on Jewish leadership in general, and thus the state of Israel too. But this was not just a matter of politics. The critical historiography which existed before them frequently dealt with Jewish Councils on an individual, case-by-case basis. Take Philip Friedman as an example. Throughout the 1950s Friedman published critical accounts of Moses Merin of Sosnowiec, Jacob Gens of Vilna and Chaim Rumkowski. His conclusions could be stark – these were men who failed, they were 'contemptible', they had been 'elevated to functions beyond their wisdom',[86] 'they were ruthless men who ruled, like their Nazi masters, by coercion'. Yet despite these generalisations Friedman acknowledged first that *Judenräte* leaders were 'not simple brutes or tyrants, nor were they traitors in any ordinary sense of the word', they just did not understand the gravity of the situation that engulfed them. As such Rumkowski was mistaken in his belief that he could save the Jews of Łódź, that he could be their redeemer. But, in doing so he was guilty of nothing more than short-sightedness and vanity.[87] Second, Friedman prefaced all these conclusions with the caveat that in *general* terms he could not make a judgement – the very opposite, it appears, of what Arendt sought to do.

For Jacob Robinson, and then later Lucy Dawidowicz, and Leni Yahil, all of whom attempted to situate the Jewish Councils in wider histories of the Holocaust, both Hilberg and then Arendt failed to understand the 'paradox' of the Jewish Councils. In Arendt's rush to pronounce judgement, Jacob Robinson pointed out that she ignored the 'vast welfare' functions of the Councils – that they were responsible for the distribution of food, medical care and indeed employment (which could be literally life-preserving).[88] As such she failed to recognise the essential successes of this form of Jewish self-government, but more than this, such judgementalism failed to recognise the essential tragedy of the councils' position: 'that the Jews regarded their role as fighting on behalf of the community, whereas the Germans handed them the task of enslaving that self same community.'[89] It could be argued that by being associated with Arendt on this point Hilberg has been done a disservice, and he certainly resented it.[90] He acknowledged that the *Judenräte* both 'saved and destroyed its people' in *The Destruction of the European Jews*.[91] In his presentation of Adam Czerniakow's diary (which he edited for publication), Hilberg argued that the leader of Warsaw Jewry sought constantly to alleviate the problems of the community, albeit also arguing that he lacked any strategy as to how he might *save* the community as a whole.[92]

Ultimately Arendt implied that the Jewish Councils had contributed and co-operated with the Jews' destruction. Her detractors sought to suspend such judgement, as other scholars had done before. Because Arendt's (and indeed Hilberg's perceived) judgmentalism came from *outside* the survivor community, and indeed outside Israel, it was seen as all the more problematic. After all, passing harsh judgement on Jewish behaviour during the Holocaust was almost the norm, but this was usually an internal discourse. The original historiography crafted in the ghettos was itself, as we have seen, full of harsh condemnations. The Jewish police were often the subject of stinging rebuke. Avraham Lewin bemoaned their 'sad complicity' which became 'murderous brutality'.[93] Yet these were self-evidently internal assessments. The 'honour courts' were also a communal method of censure. But Arendt's judgements came, whatever her Jewishness and her Germanness, from an American intellectual who was perceived as having no right to judge. Yehuda Bauer certainly made clear at the *Yad Vashem* conference convened in 1977 to discuss 'Patterns of Jewish Leadership' during the Holocaust, that this was an internal dialogue. Bauer attempted to draw some conclusions on the proceedings by declaring that:

> The *Judenräte* as a whole were groups of Jewish men who tried to act for the good of the community over which they were appointed according to their best understanding and under impossible conditions. *Thus the theme of our discussion is not only legitimate but extremely important for our understanding of ourselves.*[94] (Emphasis added)

Arendt and Hilberg's judgements ultimately had a positive impact on historiography, however, because they prompted much further work. That work certainly betrays their impact too, if only in its efforts to avoid their perceived mistakes. Isaiah Trunk published the first, and to this day only, comprehensive history of the *Judenräte*, in part as a response. While Trunk was deeply critical of some Jewish Councils and particularly their leaders, his study was defined by a reluctance to reach a general and all-encompassing conclusion in order to avoid wholesale condemnation. As he stated in the introduction to his massive history (the English edition runs to some 600 pages): 'it was not my intention to pronounce judgement.' Indeed the only general conclusion Trunk could really tolerate was the impossibility of generalisation. There was no homogenous entity which the historian could identify as the Jewish Councils.[95]

Trunk confined his history to the Jewish Councils of Eastern Europe, but there was an entrenched debate concerned with Jewish leaders in the West too, particularly the leaders of the *Joodse Raad*, the Jewish Council of Amsterdam. The *Joodse Raad* became a by-word for treason in post-war Netherlands, quite literally so in that the title of the council was often changed in public conversation to the *Joodse Verraad* which translates as Jewish treason. The two presidents of the council, Abraham Asscher and David Cohen, were condemned by an 'honour court' after the war and faced a trial for collaboration, which was later abandoned by the Dutch government.[96] Much of the historiography that followed has been defined by an explicit moral condemnation of the council leaders,[97] with the alternative history provided by the protagonists themselves. A.J. Herzberg, a close associate of Cohen's, wrote the most sympathetic history in 1965, offering a cautious defence of the council as an honourable failure.[98] But ultimately the council could not escape condemnation for providing the population lists which informed the deportations of Dutch Jewry, and they were censured in the official history of the Dutch wartime experience written by Louis De Jong.[99] Joseph Michmann also labelled the council leaders collaborators because of the privileges that were awarded to Asscher and Cohen, not least the protection of their families.[100]

Yet such overt condemnation seems to have caused little concern, in the way that the Hilberg/Arendt thesis did. While it can only be speculated as to why, I suspect that it is because this is the historiography of an individual case while Hilberg and Arendt offered a general, blanket thesis. Second, the leaders of the *Joodse Raad* survived and so condemnation carried none of the risks of defaming the dead that applied to other histories. Whatever the mistakes of Rumkowski and Gens, they did not survive but perished with those whom they failed to save. Asscher and Cohen were in part being asked to account for being alive.

The historiography of the Jewish Councils in some senses culminated in the 1977 *Yad Vashem* conference. Although Yehuda Bauer attempted to draw an overall and positive conclusion at the end of the conference, his optimistic assessment was not uniformly shared. Raul Hilberg repeated his conviction that the council leaders 'succumbed to an illusion' that they could offer a way out of the crisis engulfing Jewish communities, and that illusion was to continue the passive traditions of the Diaspora.[101] The survivor historian Israel Gutman insisted on contrasting the actions of the councils with the fighting men of the Jewish resistance. The latter had 'assessed the situation correctly' and thus avoided the descent into 'moral relativism'.[102]

But the majority of scholars at the conference did construct a trenchant defence of the councils overall, if allowing for criticism and condemnation of individuals. Isaiah Trunk continued to insist that generalisation was impossible. Hilberg, as a proxy for the deceased Arendt, was attacked by Eichmann's prosecutor Gideon Hausner, who insistently questioned what alternative choices the *Judenrat* leaders had.[103] Some went even further. Yitzhak Arad argued that in fact there was a logic to the choices they made, especially the belief that ghettos could be saved by proving themselves economically productive. Both Jacob Gens and Chaim Rumkowski had co-operated with deportations in Vilna and Łódź respectively in the name of productivsim. The weak and the sick were sacrificed because they could not contribute to the ghetto economy. Perhaps the most infamous example of such thinking occurred in September 1942 when Rumkowski delivered 'one of the most extraordinary speeches ever uttered by a Jewish leader in all of history' and called upon the ghetto to deliver to him those children and elderly 'whom there is no chance of being saved in any case'. Rumkowski memorably summarised his demands: 'I must cut off the limbs in order to save the body.'[104] Grotesque as such thinking appears, inside the Nazi universe it had a purpose – there were those within the Nazi regime who supported the idea of maintaining the ghettos as a part of the war economy.[105] In other words, the ghetto leaders may have failed in their efforts to save the Jews but they had acted with honour. More recent historiography has confirmed the 'logic' of this position. Browning's study of Starachowice Factory slave labour camp confirms that it was possible for Jews to purchase their lives for the price of their slavery.[106]

What the conference at *Yad Vashem* seemed to demonstrate was that historiography had settled into a kind of ritualised dichotomy. The two sides were not going to meet, but they could co-exist. And indeed it is now common to read introductions to the subject that identify the Hilberg-Arendt school and the Trunk school as the alternative positions. The conference eschewed the language of shame and moral condemnation that had criticised early reactions to the Jewish Councils and to Hilberg and Arendt in the 1960s. As a consequence the kind of judgemental history of the councils which characterised the 1950s, 60s, and 70s has rather disappeared. In its stead the focus has been on the social history of the ghettos as communities, and more recently still the history of the ghettos as 'Jewish spaces'.

The missing social history of the ghetto

I said at the beginning of this chapter that the attempt to probe the history of the ghetto on its own terms, to understand the history of this society, was notable only in its rarity. Yet it did exist. As early as 1949 the sociologist Samuel Gringauz insisted that the ghetto needed to be understood as a community and a society, and not just in the light of the extermination camps that followed.

That is the ghettos needed to be understood within *Jewish* history and not just as a part of the *Nazi* history of Jews' extermination.[107] Gringauz argued that despite the fact that the ghetto introduced a new moral environment in which survival became an overwhelming imperative, there was no 'complete suppression of cultural values' within its walls. Focusing on the ghetto at Kovno, Gringauz found an example of a *Jewish* society which contained all the social divisions that one may expect to find in any society (albeit divisions created by the unique circumstances of the ghetto itself). The endurance of cultural and religious life, the maintenance of both religious and secular education provision within the ghetto walls was, according to Gringauz, a 'cultural miracle'. The ghetto thus offered an example of a uniquely Jewish social experiment, and thus a model of the potential of Jewish society – despite the extremity of the situation surrounding the ghetto's creation and destruction.

Despite Gringauz' call for further work on the social history of the ghetto, little followed. As ever Philip Friedman also offered a model, and identified questions of social organisation and the experience of different groups within the ghettos as priorities for study, but his was an isolated voice.[108] A limited social history of camp society did emerge – following on from the psychological history that dominated in the later 1940s.[109] According to Tim Cole this erasure of ghetto society was in part the consequence of the emergence of the Holocaust as a distinct experience, which created a powerful teleology to the history of the ghettos which could only apparently be considered in the light of their tragic outcome.[110] And indeed the historiography reviewed above – which saw the ghettos either through the prism of their leaders or through those who took up arms – certainly only really considered them in the light of the 'Final Solution'. Indeed Raul Hilberg only understood the ghettos as historically significant inside the extermination process itself. In addition, a further explanation for the failure of historians to follow Gringauz and Friedman's lead was the recovery and publication of the documents from the ghetto which stood in place of historiography.

One of the consequences of the stabilisation of the judgemental historiographies of resistance and the *Judenräte* at the end of the 1970s has been that the social history of the ghetto could re-emerge, although it has done so only slowly – tentatively escaping the strictures of early historiography. Israel Gutman's history of the Jews of Warsaw attempted a general history, but unsurprisingly because of Gutman's involvement in the uprising, he allowed the idea of resistance to dominate at the beginning of the 1980s.[111] Charles Roland's history of the Warsaw ghetto is more general, and is in essence a medical history, published a decade later.[112] Following Trunk's insistent disavowal of generalisation however, histories of the ghettos as single phenomena remain rare. Gustavo Corni's *Hitler's Ghettos*, which attempted a wholesale social history of ghetto society, is perhaps the only one in English and was only published in 2002.

Perhaps symbolising the gap in historiographical terms, Corni makes the same points as to the necessity of a social history of the ghetto that Gringauz had made some half a century previously. He insists that the ghettos are an important community and society and need to be understood and investigated in those terms and not simply in the light of their outcome, or as an 'antechamber' of the extermination process.[113] Corni also, crucially, declares a willingness to consider *critically* that very first historiography of the ghettos that was constructed inside their walls by the victims themselves. These are not, he insists, clear, polished windows that allow us to see into the ghetto. They may be voices from that society but they are attempts to construct an image and interpretation of the world, and thus need to be treated as cautiously as any other primary source material, even if Corni believes them preferable to memoirs. This is not to say that Corni did not believe them to be an incredibly rich and diverse source, quite the opposite, but he does imply that historians should treat them less reverentially than has been the norm.

Corni also makes clear how problematic the attempt at a moral history of the ghetto has been, either positively or negatively, because the ghetto was a new, perhaps unique moral environment in which previous judgements did not and could not apply:

> Many risked their lives smuggling food and other precious goods. Did they deal in contraband for themselves and their families or rather in order to get rich exploiting the wretchedness of others? Everything in the ghettos was permeated by ambiguity and duplicity. Were the smugglers heroes or merely rapacious exploiters? Were the heads of the *Judenräte* careful and tenacious defenders of the community or were they opportunists, prepared to do anything in order to save themselves

and their own relations? Were the partisans really splendid heroes, the last defenders (maybe the precursors) of Jewish national pride? Or were they in fact irresponsible and did their actions endanger the whole precarious stability of the ghetto.[114]

Even more recently ghetto communities have been considered as *places* in which Jews, German occupiers and native populations all interacted. Tim Cole's history of Budapest, a *Holocaust City*, and Gordon Horowitz's history of Łódź both make the point that the Holocaust was enacted, and indeed planned, in public spaces.[115] The ghettos and their residents could be at the very least seen by the rest of the population, not to mention various economic and social relations between ghettos and the rest of the cities or regions in which they were situated. After all, people had to move to make way for Jews, while others had to occupy the buildings vacated by Jews moved to the ghetto. And indeed some people hid Jews outside the ghetto. As such an emphasis on space as well as time may well suggest the possibility of integrating histories of the victims, perpetrators and witnesses to the Holocaust. As Omer Bartov writes in his study of the disappearance of the Jewish past from the modern Ukraine, such an approach may force us to reconceive our entire understanding of the Holocaust. The idea of places like 'the ghetto' or 'the death camp' conjure images of institutions hermetically sealed from the outside world, so much so that they have become almost metahistorical spaces. But if one just stands in the landscapes where the Holocaust was enacted today, for example in the former ghettos, one is struck with just how 'intimate' they are – how close, for example, the rest of the city is. It is this intimacy which the future social history of the ghetto will have to contemplate further.[116]

Conclusion

The historiography of Jews and Jewish behaviour under the 'Final Solution' has therefore developed problematically since the end of the war. The documentary material was treated with understandable reverence, and as such this is an historiography defined almost by its absence. That said, where discourse has occurred it began as a rather ritualised moral debate around resistance or collaboration. Such an historiography was subordinate to a much wider conversation about post-war Jewish and more importantly Israeli identity. While this is politically and indeed morally understand-able, it has not been helpful in terms of developing historical understanding. The hiatus in the development of a social history of the ghettos is evidence of enough of that.

Yet despite these problems, complex historiographies have developed. And history-writing about the victims has escaped the strictures of reverence or moral condemnation. The certainties of post-war judgementalism have given way to shades of grey. And indeed it is notable that a more complex understanding of the ghetto as a society and community can also produce a more nuanced engagement with the moral problematics of the resistance movements and their relationship with the ghettos they often lived outside. Resistance cannot just be contrasted positively with a shaming and shameful passivity, and its historiography now reflects this.

There is still a lacuna in the historiographies that have been discussed in this chapter however. Although we are, through the documents themselves, brought close to individual victims and indeed can see the Warsaw ghetto through the eyes of Emanuel Ringelblum, or Auschwitz-Birkenau through the eyes of *Son-derkommando* Zalman Lewenthal; ordinary Jewish victims and especially *survivors* are absent. Much like the Histories of the perpetrators, neither the historiography of the Jewish Councils, or indeed the resistance, had any place for individuals and especially for the memories of individual survivors. How history-writing has dealt with those survivors and especially their accounts of life under Nazi rule will be the subject of the following chapter.

Notes

1 For a much fuller evaluation than is possible here see Dan Michman, *Holocaust Historiography: A Jewish Perspective* (London, 2003).

2 Jacob Sloan (ed.), *The Journal of Emmanuel Ringelblum* (New York, 1958), p. 310.

3 *Ibid.*, p. 326.

4 See Tom Segev, *The Seventh Million: The Israelis and the Holocaust* (New York, 1993), pp. 109–10 for a discussion of *Yishuv* attitudes to the Diaspora during the Holocaust. Alternatively Dina Porat argues that in fact this image did not impact the *Yishuv* response to the Holocaust. See Dina Porat, *The Blue and Yellow Stars of David: The Zionist Leadership in Palestine and the Holocaust, 1939–45* (Cambridge: MA, 1990).

5 See Anita Shapira, 'The Holocaust: Private Memories, Public Memory', *Jewish Social Studies* (Vol. 4, No. 2, 1998), pp. 40–58.

6 Alan Adelson (ed.), *Five Notebooks from the Lodz Ghetto: The Diary of Dawid Sierakowiak* (London, 1996), p. 250.

7 Emmanuel Ringelblum, *Polish Jewish Relations During the Second World War* (Evanston: IL, 1974).

8 The diary of Rabbi Shimon Huberband, a contributor to the *Oneg Shabbat* archive, is declared in its introduction to be important precisely because it is *not* a memoir. See Shimon Huberband, *Kiddush Hashem: Jewish Religious and Cultural Life in Poland* (New York, 1987), p. xxviii. Huberband's memoir was first published in the Hebrew original in 1969.

9 Geoffrey Hartman, 'Afterword', Alan Adelson and Robert Lapides (eds), *Lodz Ghetto: Inside a Community Under Siege* (New York, 1989), p. 511.

10 Samuel D. Kassow, *Who Will Write Our History? Emmanuel Ringelblum, the Warsaw Ghetto, and the Oyneg Shabes Archive* (Bloomington: IN, 2007), pp. 226–7.

11 See Josef Kermish (ed.), *To Live with Honor and Die with Honor! Selected Documents from the Warsaw Ghetto Underground Archives "O.S." [Oneg Shabbath]* (Jerusalem, 1986), p. xiv.

12 For example Tadeusz Pankiewicz, *Apteka w getcie krokowskim* (Kracow, 1947) – the diary of the owner of the Pharmacy in the ghetto in Krakow.

13 Frank's diary was first published in March 1947. A French translation appeared in 1950, and it was published for the first time in English in the USA in 1952.

14 For an interesting discussion of the narratives surrounding Frank's diary see Alexandra Zapruder (ed.), *Salvaged Pages: Young Writers' Diaries of the Holocaust* (New Haven: CT, 2002), pp. 2–6.

15 Josef Kermish, 'Mutilated Versions of Ringelblum's Notes', *YIVO Annual of Jewish Social Science* (Vol. VIII, 1953), pp. 289–301.

16 Rosemary Horowitz, 'Reading and Writing During the Holocaust as Described in Yizker Books', Johnathan Rose (ed.), *The Holocaust and the Book: Destruction and Preservation* (Amherst: PA, 2001), pp. 128–42. See also Johnathan Boyarin and Jack Kugelmass (eds), *From a Ruined Garden: The Memorial Books of Polish Jewry* (Bloomington: IN, 1998).

17 Sloan, *The Journal of Emmanuel Ringelblum*, pp. xxii, xxvi.

18 Kermish, *To Live With Honour*, p. xxxii.

19 Adelson and Lapides, *Lodz Ghetto*, p. xxi.

20 Philip Boehm, 'Introduction', Michal Grynberg (ed.), *Words to Outlive Us: Eyewitness Accounts From the Warsaw Ghetto* (London, 2003), p. 12.

21 The diaries were first published in English, with little analytical comment in Ber Mark, *The Scrolls of Auschwitz* (Tel Aviv, 1985). Nathan Cohen observes lack of analysis in 'Diaries of the Sonderkommandos in Auschwitz: Coping with Fate and Reality', *Yad Vashem Studies* (Vol. 20, 1990), p. 274.

22 Avraham Lewin, *A Cup of Tears: A Diary of the Warsaw Ghetto* (Oxford, 1988).

23 Janusz Korczak, *The Ghetto Years: 1939–42* (New York, 1978).

24 Vladka Meed, *On Both Sides of the Wall* (Tel Aviv, 1973) – first published in 1947.

25 Calel Perechodnik, *Am I a Murderer? Testament of a Jewish Ghetto Policeman* (New York, 1996) – first published in 1993.

26 See for example Dov Levin, 'How the Jewish Ghetto Police in the Kovno Ghetto Saw Itself', *Yad Vashem Studies* (Vol. 29, 2001), pp. 183–237.

27 Zoë Vania Waxman, *Writing the Holocaust: Identity, Testimony, Representation* (Oxford, 2006), p. 8.

28 Philip Friedman, 'Polish Jewish Historiography Between the Two Wars', *Roads to Extinction: Essays on the Holocaust* (New York, 1980), pp. 467–99.

29 Jeffrey Gurock, 'Introduction to the English Language Edition', Huberband, *Kiddush Hashem*, p. xxviii.

30 Huberband, *Kiddush Hashem*, p. 242.

31 Philip Friedman, 'Polish Jewish Historiography Between the Two Wars', p. 499.

32 Hermann Langbein, *Against All Hope: Resistance in the Nazi Concentration Camps* (London, 1994), p. 2.

33 Hartman, 'Afterword', Adelson and Lapides, *Lodz Ghetto*, p. 512.

34 Mark, *The Scrolls of Auschwitz*, p. 125.

35 Gradowski's first testimony is printed in Mark, *Scrolls of Auschwitz*, p. 175.

36 Gradowski does confront the gas chambers in his second manuscript.

37 Langfuss testimony is printed in Mark, *Scrolls of Auschwitz*, p. 214.

38 Cohen, 'Diaries of the Sonderkommando', p. 309.

39 Mark, *Scrolls of Auschwitz*, pp. 175–214.

40 *Ibid.*, p. 125.

41 Gideon Greif, 'Between Sanity and Insanity: Spheres of Everyday Life in the Auschwitz-Birkenau Sonderkommando', Jonathan Petropolous and John Roth (eds), *Gray Zones: Ambiguity and Compromise in the Holocaust and its Aftermath* (New York, 2005), pp. 37–50; and *We Wept Without Tears: Testimonies of the Jewish Sonderkommando from Auschwitz* (New Haven: CT, 2005).

42 In November 1948 for example Dr Ludwig Jaffe, who had been a member of the Jewish Council of Lwow, was tried in Rome and found guilty of collaboration. For a discussion of 'honour courts' see Isaiah Trunk, *Judenrat: The Jewish Councils in Eastern Europe Under Nazi Occupation* (New York, 1972), pp. 549–55.

43 Sloan, *The Journal of Emanuel Ringelblum*, p. 316.

44 For a narrative of the Kastner trial see Segev, *The Seventh Million*, pp. 273–307.

45 Abraham Wein, 'Memorial Books as a Source for Research into the History of Jewish Communities in Europe', *Yad Vashem Studies* (Vol. 9, 1973), pp. 255–72.

46 Michman, *Holocaust Historiography*, p. 217.

47 Shapira, 'The Holocaust: Private Memories, Public Memory', pp. 40–6.

48 See for example the condemnation of Jewish Kapos in Wolf Glicksman, 'Social Differentiation in the German Concentration Camps', *Annual of Jewish Social Science* (Vol. VIII, 1953), pp. 123–50.

49 Dan Michman, 'Jewish Leadership in Extremis', Dan Stone, *The Historiography of the Holocaust* (London, 2004), p. 321.

50 See Israel Gutman, 'The Genesis of Resistance in the Warsaw Ghetto', Michael Marrus, *The Nazi Holocaust Vol. 7* (London, 1989), p. 125.

51 Philip Friedman (ed.), *Martyrs and Fighters: The Epic of the Warsaw Ghetto* (New York, 1954); Rozett, 'Jewish Resistance', p. 342.

52 Boaz Cohen, 'The Birth Pangs of Holocaust Research in Israel', *Yad Vashem Studies* (Vol. 33, 2005), p. 207.

53 Benzion Dinur, 'Problems Confronting Yad Vashem in its Work of Research', *Yad Vashem Studies* (1957), p. 8.

54 See Bernard Mark, 'Problems Related to the Study of the Jewish Resistance in the Second World War', *Yad Vashem Studies* (1959), p. 41.

55 Raul Hilberg, *The Destruction of the European Jews: 3rd Edition* (New Haven: CT, 2003), p. 1118.

56 Cited in Robert Rozett, 'Jewish Resistance', Stone, *The Historiography of the Holocaust*, p. 343.

57 Nathan Eck, 'Historical Research or Slander', *Yad Vashem Studies* (Vol. VI, 1967), pp. 385–430.

58 Jacob Robinson, *And So the Crooked Shall be Made Straight: The Eichmann Trial, the Jewish Catastrophe and Hannah Arendt's Narrative* (New York, 1965), p. 147.

59 *Ibid.*, p. 142.

60 Hilberg, *The Destruction of the European Jews*, p. 1104.

61 *Ibid.*, p. 1105.

62 Yuri Suhl, *They Fought Back: The Story of Jewish Resistance in Nazi Europe* (New York, 1967). Other examples include Lucien Steinberg, *Not as a Lamb: The Jews Against Hitler* (Andover, 1974); Ruben Ainsztein, *Jewish Resistance in Nazi Occupied Eastern Europe* (London, 1974); Isaac Kowalski, *Anthology on Jewish Armed Resistance Volume III 1939–45* (New York, 1986).

63 James M. Glass, *Jewish Resistance During the Holocaust: Moral Uses of Violence and Will* (London, 2004), p. 168. For another example of the continuation of this approach see Sophie Roberts, 'Jews, Vichy and the Algiers Insurrection of 1942', *Holocaust Studies: A Journal of Culture and History* (Vol. 12, No. 3, 2006), pp. 63–88.

64 Israel Gutman, *Resistance: The Warsaw Ghetto Uprising* (Boston: MA, 1994), p. xx.

65 Yitzhak Arad, 'Jewish Prisoner Uprisings in the Treblinka and Sobibor Extermination Camps', Marrus, *The Nazi Holocaust Vol. 7*, p. 283.

66 Langbein, *Against All Hope*, p. 2.

67 Mark, *The Scrolls of Auschwitz*, passim. Although this book includes the fragments of the *Sonderkommando* diaries it is only really concerned with the *Sonderkommando*'s role in resistance.

68 Philip Friedman, 'Jewish Resistance to Nazism', *Roads to Extinction*, p. 393. This essay was first published in 1960.

69 Rozett, 'Jewish Resistance', p. 346.

70 See Dan Michman's discussion of this scholarship: Michman, *Holocaust Historiography*, pp. 217–48.

71 Christopher Browning, "'Alleviation' and 'Compliance': The Survival Strategies of the Jewish Leadership in Wierzbnik Ghetto and Starachowice Factory Slave Labour Camps', Petropoulos and Roth, *Gray Zones*, p. 27.

72 See for example Esh's use of the term in Saul Esh, 'The Dignity of the Destroyed', *Judaism* (Vol. 11, No. 2, 1962), pp. 99–111.

73 Arnold Paucker and Konrad Kwiet, 'Jewish Leadership and Jewish Resistance', David Bankier, *Probing the Depths of German Antisemitism, 1933–41* (New York, 2000), p. 373.

74 Joan Ringelheim, 'Women and the Holocaust: A Reconsideration of Research', Carol Rittner and John Roth, *Different Voices: Women and the Holocaust* (St Paul: MN, 1993), p. 390.

75 Hilberg, *The Destruction of the European Jews*, p. 1043.

76 Eck, 'Historical Research or Slander', p. 139.

77 Glass, *Jewish Resistance During the Holocaust*, p. 25.

78 Suzanne Weiner Weber, 'The Forest as Liminal Space: A Transformation of Culture and Norms during the Holocaust', *Holocaust Studies: A Journal of Culture and History* (Vol. 14, No. 1, 2008), pp. 35–60.

79 I was present at a conference in Philadelphia at which a survivor from a partisan group gave a presentation and was subsequently verbally attacked by a ghetto survivor whose mother had been murdered in a German reprisal action. The latter blamed the former for this death. Such an exchange certainly revealed that resistance was morally problematic.

80 Helmut Eschwege, 'Resistance of German Jews against the Nazi Regime', *Leo Baeck Institute Yearbook* (1970), pp. 134–80.

81 Konrad Kwiet and Helmut Eschwege, *Selbstbehauptung und Widerstand. Deutsche Juden im Kampf um Existenz und Menschenwürde, 1933–45* (Hamburg, 1984). See discussion of this work in Arnold Paucker, *Jewish Resistance in Germany: The Facts and the Problems* (German Resistance Memorial Center Pamphlet, 1990).

82 Konrad Kwiet, 'The Problems of Jewish Resistance Historiography', Marrus, *The Nazi Holocaust Vol. 7*, p. 64.

83 See Marion Kaplan, *Between Dignity and Despair: Jewish Life in Nazi Germany* (Oxford, 1998); Renée Poznanski, *Jews in France During World War II* (Hanover, 2001).

84 Rozett, 'Jewish Resistance', p. 349.

85 Michmann, 'Jewish Leadership in *Extremis*', p. 321.

86 Philip Friedman, 'Jacob Gens: Commandant or the Vilna Ghetto', *Roads to Extinction*, p. 378 – this essay was first published in 1953.

87 Philip Friedman, 'Psuedo-Saviors in the Polish Ghettos: Mordechai Chaim Rumkowski of Łódź', *Roads to Extinction*, p. 334 – this essay was first published in 1954.

88 Robinson, *And the Crooked Shall be Made Straight*, p. 162.

89 Leni Yahil, *The Holocaust: The Fate of European Jewry* (Oxford, 1990), p. 238.

90 Raul Hilberg, *The Politics of Memory: The Journey of a Holocaust Historian* (Chicago: IL, 1996), pp. 149–57, for a discussion of Arendt.

91 Hilberg, *The Destruction of the European Jews*, p. 216.

92 Raul Hilberg, Stanislaw Staron and Josef Kermisz, *The Warsaw Diary of Adam Czerniakow: Prelude to Doom* (New York, 1979).

93 Lewin, *A Cup of Tears*, p. 25.

94 Yehuda Bauer, 'The Judenrate: Some Conclusions', Yisrael Gutman (ed.), *Patterns of Jewish Leadership in Nazi Europe 1933–45: Proceedings of the Third Yad Vashem Historical Conference* (Jerusalem, 1979), p. 164.

95 Trunk, *Judenrat*, p. xvii.

96 Joseph Michmann, 'The Controversy Surrounding the Jewish Council of Amsterdam', Gutman, *Patterns of Jewish Leadership*, p. 236.

97 See for example Jacob Presser, *The Destruction of the Dutch Jews* (New York, 1969) – this is the translation of the Dutch original which was published in 1965.

98 For a discussion of Herzberg's history see Michman, 'The Controversy Surrounding the Jewish Council of Amsterdam', p. 249.

99 Louis de Jong, *Het Koninkrijk der Nederlanden in de Tweede Wereldoorlog* (Den Haag, 1969).

100 Michmann, 'The Controversy Surrounding the Jewish Council of Amsterdam', p. 251. See also Joseph Michmann, 'The Controversial Stand of the Joodse Raad in the Netherlands', *Yad Vashem Studies* (1974).

101 Raul Hilberg, 'The Judenrat: Conscious or Unconscious Tool', Gutman, *Patterns of Jewish Leadership*, p. 44.

102 Yisrael Gutman, 'The Concept of Labour in Judenrat Policy', Gutman, *Patterns of Jewish Leadership*, p. 179.

103 Gideon Hausner, Gutman, *Patterns of Jewish Leadership*, p. 59.

104 This assessment and the quotations come from Richard Rubenstein, 'Gray into Black: The Case of Mordecai Chaim Rumkowski', Petropoulos and Roth, *Gray Zones*, p. 305.

105 Yitzhak Arad, 'The Lithuanian Ghettos of Kovno and Vilna', Gutman, *Patterns of Jewish Leadership*, p. 103.

106 Browning, "'Alleviation' and 'Compliance'", pp. 29–34. See also Christopher Browning, *Collected Memories: Holocaust History and Postwar Testimony* (Madison: WI, 2003), pp. 57–69.

107 Samuel Gringauz, 'The Ghetto as an Experiment of Jewish Social Organisation', *Jewish Social Studies* (Vol. 11, No. 1, 1949), pp. 4–5.

108 Philip Friedman, 'Social Conflicts in the Ghetto', *Roads to Extinction*, pp. 131–52. This essay was first published in 1954.

109 See for example Israel Gutman, 'Social Stratification in the Concentration Camps', Michael Marrus, *The Nazi Holocaust Vol. 6* (London, 1989), pp. 952–85.

110 Tim Cole, 'Ghettoization', Stone, *The Historiography of the Holocaust*, p. 71.

111 Israel Gutman, *The Jews of Warsaw, 1939–43: Ghetto, Underground, Revolt* (Brighton, 1982).

112 Charles Roland, *Courage Under Siege: Starvation, Disease and Death in the Warsaw Ghetto* (Oxford, 1992).

113 Gustavo Corni, *Hitler's Ghettos: Voices from a Beleaguered Society 1939–44* (London, 2002), p. 332.

114 Corni, *Hitler's Ghettos*, p. 333.

115 Tim Cole, *Holocaust City: The Making of a Jewish Ghetto* (London, 2003); Gordon Horowitz, *Ghettostadt: Lodz and the Making of a Nazi City* (Cambridge: MA, 2008).

116 Bartov uses the term intimate: Omer Bartov, *Erased: Vanishing Traces of Jewish Galicia in Present Day Ukraine* (Princeton: NJ, 2007), p. xvii.

8

'Holocaust Testimonies':
the ruins of memory and Holocaust
historiography

According to Lawrence Langer's *Holocaust Testimonies*, history-writing has failed the victims and survivors of the Holocaust. They were either forgotten in narratives concerned only with the perpetrators; or worse still they were marginalised by a mode of historiography which attempted to make the fundamentally disrupting stories of survivors safe for the post-war world. In such historiography, victims were turned into either martyrs or heroes (or indeed traitors or collaborators), a discourse which Langer found repugnant. The inherent desire to pass judgement, either positive or negative, on a moral universe literally unimaginable to those outside it was itself morally unacceptable. Far from allowing easy narratives of heroism and despair, Langer argued that the stories of victims and survivors suggested infinite complexity and nuance, manifold 'versions of the truth', that forced us to consider not the meaning but the 'meaninglessness' of the *Shoah*.[1]

Langer was suggesting that the discipline of History – with its inherent desire for generalisation – was ill-suited to giving voice to victims and survivors, that it could not incorporate them into its narratives because of the infinite variety of their stories. This discomfort had manifested itself first in History's neglect of survivors and their stories – they are simply absent from the vast majority of Holocaust History – and subsequently in the desire to force survivors' stories into the grand narratives of resistance and heroism. The purpose of this chapter is both to subject Langer's argument to scrutiny, to ask how History as a discipline has approached the individual victims of the Holocaust and the rich historical material that is provided by their testimonies; and second to ask, if indeed History has failed survivors and their memory, how the discipline needs to change or adapt in order to right this failure. And failure it must be – for if History is incapable of producing narratives of the Holocaust that are meaningful to its victims and which help us to understand their experiences then, to put it bluntly, what use is History?

This chapter begins by charting the use of survivor testimony in history-writing, at the same time as attempting to summarise the history of that testimony. Of course, this is in many ways the narrative of an absence, especially after the initial interest in victims and survivors shown by psychologists in the late 1940s had waned. The chapter will then very briefly relate the development of concern for 'memory' in historical studies since the late 1970s, and the consequent explosion of interest in Holocaust survivors and their stories. I will suggest that, perhaps paradoxically, this interest in the testimony and oral history of survivors has often made the Holocaust past *more* rather than less elusive – even if it has placed the survivor and the act of remembering itself at centre stage. That said, using testimony and memory has greatly enriched our understanding of the *Shoah*, not least through the application of the concept of gender to Holocaust studies – and the realisation that women and men suffered in different ways, and understood that suffering in different ways in the aftermath. Ultimately the chapter will conclude by suggesting that *if* Holocaust History is to utilise fully survivors and their memories, for which there is a clear moral as well as intellectual imperative, then it does indeed need to recast both itself as a discipline and the Holocaust that it represents, not least in the provision of a new and much less certain chronology.

The silence of survivors in historical narratives

While it is simply not the case that survivors were engulfed by a shroud of silence in the aftermath of the war, there is no doubt that *their* stories, somewhat perversely, found no place in historians' attempts to explain and contextualise *their* suffering. The pioneering work of psychologists who sought to use survivors and their memories to construct a picture of life in the concentration camps, and thus of human behaviour *in extremis*, was not built upon. David Boder's study *I Did Not Interview the Dead* remained the only major published study of survivor memory in the 1940s and 1950s.[2] Indeed according to Tony Kushner, because they ignored the victims those historians who were interested in the Holocaust in the 1940s and 1950s were part of a world that told 'survivors to forget and get on with re-building their lives'.[3] Although organisations like the Wiener Library and *Yad Vashem* continued to collect testimonies and the stories of survivors during this period, it appears historians simply did not know what to do with them.

Why did historians neglect the survivors and their memories which could have provided such rich evidence? In the main it was because an historiography that was in so many ways born from attempts to prosecute the crimes of National Socialism was inherently mistrusting of a body of evidence that could be seen, because of the vagaries of memory, to be inherently unreliable. Shoshana Felman and Dori Laub claim that Western 'legal, epistemological and philosophical' traditions prioritise being there and the first-hand witness.[4] But the International Military Tribunal at Nuremberg and the historiography it spawned prioritised the fragments of the past, documents that were physical remnants, over people who were there. Even that historiography which sought explicitly to investigate and illuminate the experience of the victims was much more comfortable with the kind of eye-witness observations contained in the ghetto diaries than it was with the memories of survivors – which had been subject to the ravages of time. Benzion Dinur agonised in one of the very first publications emanating from *Yad Vashem* that one of the great problems confronting the Holocaust historian was that there was so little evidence from the victims and survivors, apart from the memories of individuals – the authenticity of which could not be guaranteed.[5] And of course the group of victims who might have been able to bear witness to the true extremity of the Jewish experience during the Holocaust were no longer able to speak. In the words of Boder's original study, nobody 'could interview the dead'.

At the same time the discipline of History was ill-suited to dealing with the memories of individuals. History is generally, and perhaps inevitably, suspicious of the witness – precisely because History claims to be able to see the past more wholly, more objectively, than any one witness constrained by their personal experiences. Yet such interest in the general means that individuals are unable to square their memories with the wider vision of history. As Anita Shapira has observed, the grand narratives of victim behaviour – either heroism or collaboration – were not really able to accommodate the nuances of individual recollections, which perhaps did not paint such black or white pictures.[6] Added to all of this, the social sciences in general and historians in particular lacked a vocabulary and indeed a methodology for dealing with ordinary people and their experiences. History largely remained in thrall to the politics of great men, and at the same time social historians, right up to the late 1960s and into the 1970s, remained concerned to paint in broad brush strokes, concerned with social structure rather than with individuals and certainly not individual memories.

However, testimonies of survivors *were* written and recorded. And, just as material from the ghettos almost stood in the stead of historiography, so published testimony was allowed to stand, without interpretation, as the vehicle for a history of, amongst other spaces and places, the concentration and death camps. Even before the war ended, testimony of the victims from the camps was used to try to draw attention to the sufferings of Jews, such as Rudolf Vrba and Alfred Wetzler's report from Auschwitz-Birkenau which was handed to allied governments in the spring of 1944.[7] From 1946 onwards the Wiener Library published 'survivor reports', which existed alongside historiography – offering both confirmation of the fact of the Nazi genocide and a view into the Nazi nightmare from a different vantage point.[8] In comparison with the sheer volume of survivor testimonies that exist today, either in written or oral form, then the number of survivors who told their stories publicly in this fashion was undoubtedly small. Alongside the *Yizkor* memorial books and projects like that at Wiener, seventy-five memoirs were published between 1945 and 1949.[9] Many, like Mary Berg and Marek Edelman, were former ghetto fighters – and thus were immediately cast in the pervasive heroic vocabulary.[10] Others such as Primo Levi's *If This is a Man* used an entirely different vocabulary but had little impact on the larger narratives inside which the victims' stories had been told, or perhaps were trapped.

These narratives included, as well as celebrations of heroism and condemnations of collaboration, the idea that survival was itself heroic, that it pointed somehow to the enduring triumph of the human spirit. Terence Des Pres' *The Survivor*, one of the first published studies of Holocaust survivors in the late 1970s, developed this theme, suggesting testimonies were evidence of the sheer will to survive.[11] Alexander Zapruder argues such narratives are first seen in the original reception of Anne Frank's diary as an articulation of hope rather than despair. As such while this was not necessarily created by historians or inside historiography, historians' evident failure to confront the testimonies of Holocaust survivors did little to challenge such assumptions.[12] There were other familiar discourses too into which survivor testimonies were moulded. While the Holocaust forced a reconception of both Christianity and Judaism, the former in terms of its relationship with Judaism, the latter concerned to locate God in a world that created Auschwitz-Birkenau; survivor narratives were often awarded a rather conventional religious significance. Both Olga Lengyel's and Primo Levi's first post-war testimonies were domesticated within a familiar religious vocabulary for their readers. Levi's If This is a Man was declared to be a 'literally a report from hell', Lengyel's Five Chimneys was proclaimed as a 'picture of utter Hell'.[13]

The number of survivor testimonies published, and thus survivors who bore witness to their experience, increased exponentially from the mid-1960s – although this should not be taken as a sign that anyone, especially historians, has been listening more intently to what they have to say.[14] This second wave of testimonies was the result of a complex variety of factors. Undoubtedly the trial of Adolf Eichmann was important. The prosecution determined to use surviving victims to construct a picture of Eichmann's crimes and many were therefore called as witnesses. Not only did this encourage these witnesses to tell their stories, but it convinced other survivors to do the same. With the passing of time, of course, survivors grew older. As a consequence the internal urge to bear witness grew stronger too, and many wished to articulate their stories to their own children and even grandchildren. The external pressure on individuals to bear witness also increased. Threats to the state of Israel led to a strong desire to articulate the potential consequences of anti-Judaism, for example.[15] At the same time the more witnesses there were, the idea of witnessing itself became self-fulfilling as survivors themselves began to construct the idea of the obligation to bear witness, an obligation placed on them by the very fact of their survival.[16]

According to Henry Greenspan the idea of the 'survivor' also gained a cultural currency during the 1970s in the USA – 'as much wider preoccupation with public and private disaster, destruction and victimisation' took hold.[17] And, of course, popular interest and concern with the Holocaust, as we now know it, emerged in the late 1970s in the USA, spreading throughout the West.[18]

The ongoing boom in published testimonies was also mirrored by much more active collection of survivors' oral testimonies. This practice, pioneered in the 1940s by the Wiener Library and Yad Vashem, was revived in the 1980s, especially in the USA. An archive of oral testimonies was established in 1982 at Yale, which now holds thousands of accounts. Interestingly the driving force behind that collection was Dori Laub, who was not an historian but a psychologist.[19] After the project at Yale came the collection of testimonies for the United States Holocaust Memorial Museum in Washington; then the project funded by Steven Spielberg – the Survivors of the Shoah Visual History Foundation – amongst others. Such developments are not confined to the USA. Memorial sites in Germany commonly collate testimonies, especially since reunification. Although occurring later and on a much smaller scale too, there have been similar developments in Britain: the collection of testimonies at the Imperial War Museum and at the Beth Shalom Holocaust Centre for example. Although it is impossible to tell how many, there are now many thousands of testimonies of survivors recorded throughout the world.

Yet this explosion of testimony has not encouraged historians to use this material. In part this is because, similarly to the material emanating from the ghetto discussed in the previous chapter, survivor testimony is itself an exercise in interpretation and exegesis before which the scholar stands rather inadequately. Whatever historians can theoretically claim about the ability of their practice to illuminate the past, they are understandably nervous about potentially contradicting the witnesses themselves. Many testimonies have thus been allowed to stand as wider interpretations of the victims' experience during the Holocaust.

Perhaps the most important example is provided by Primo Levi. Levi's notion of the 'grey zone' developed most fully in his last memoir The Drowned and the Saved, has become perhaps the most important conceptual device for evaluating Jewish life inside the concentration and death camps. Levi, noting the narratives of heroism that surrounded the victims, argued that while the world demanded that the camps be understood simply in terms of good and evil, the reality was much more complex. The Nazi system deliberately blurred the line between victim and perpetrator, so that in reality there was no clear 'space' between the two. Instead Levi suggested there was a 'grey zone', where 'the two camps of masters and servant both diverge and converge'. Prisoners were thus turned into instruments of domination – like the so-called *Kapos* who literally ruled over prisoner barracks, and even those like Levi who were drawn into the system of the camp itself. Jews who served the camp – from those who sorted the belongings of the dead in 'Kanada' to the *Sonderkommando* who manned the crematoria – inhabited this 'grey zone'. Part of Levi's purpose in outlining the 'grey zone' was to complicate and indeed disallow the easy moral judgement of the victims that abounded in heroism and collaboration narratives. Levi also wished to reveal the base 'perfidy' of the Nazi system, that the victims were forced to become part of the system that dominated and destroyed them. This, Levi wrote, was National Socialism's 'most demonic crime', which shifted the burden of guilt on to the victims themselves and so 'deprived them of the solace of innocence'.[20]

In refusing to sanctify the victims, Levi also characterised life in Birkenau as a ceaseless struggle *between* inmates. He depicted the prisoner population as engaged in a 'covert and continuous struggle' against one another.[21] Such arguments are, of course, profoundly challenging, and it appears that historians were rendered mute by them. Take two histories of the Holocaust with a specific focus on the victims as an example. Lucy Dawidowicz's *The War Against the Jews* was simply unable to engage with the subject of Jews' social relations inside the camps; her history of 'Jewish behaviour in crisis and extremity' seems to have ended at the ghetto wall.[22] And Leni Yahil's *The Holocaust*, which it is worth remembering was, because of the degree to which it was based on secondary material, really a reflection Israeli historiography more widely, could also only really consider the history of the camps in terms of resistance and rescue. The question of staying alive in the camp was thus avoided.[23]

Historians have, however, attempted histories of the Holocaust using the testimony of victims and survivors, although it is questionable how far such histories really articulate the victims' stories.

Martin Gilbert's monumental *The Holocaust*, published in 1987, deliberately focused on 'the Jewish tragedy' and attempted to use the testimony of victims who survived, and those who did not, to illustrate his narrative of the 'Final Solution'. As Dan Stone has argued however, Gilbert's desire to offer a single narrative of the Holocaust is problematic – because it implies a coherence to the events he describes which he really created himself. Coherence is certainly not derived from the testimony of survivors.[24] Indeed, as Tony Kushner explains, Gilbert's narrative is not really driven by the testimony of survivors at all. The chronology of the 'Final Solution', into which the testimony of survivors is interwoven, was created by the Nazis – not the men and women whose lives they engulfed.[25]

It is perhaps the end of the book that throws this into sharpest relief. Gilbert's desire for closure is such that the end of the Holocaust is declared unambiguously with the defeat of Nazi Germany on 8 May 1945. Indeed his main narrative ends with the words 'It is over'. But of course for the victims it was far from over, indeed perhaps the one over-riding lesson of survivor testimony is that it was 'never over'.[26] Many victims would die in the liberated concentration camps in their first weeks of freedom – such as those who died because of their inability to digest the food given to them by British soldiers in Bergen-Belsen.[27] Survivors then faced the task of rebuilding shattered lives, very often in foreign lands. Trude Levi's Holocaust memoir tellingly devotes over half of its pages to the period after liberation, to the struggle to find home and belonging.[28] Trude certainly experienced what Primo Levi described as a 'life to begin all over again, amid the rubble, often alone'.[29] Indeed the very act of testimony, the act of bearing witness, is itself evidence of the survivor's enduring and ongoing effort to come to terms with the past, the attempt to negotiate between two worlds that exist for them in memory, but as both present and past. As such Gilbert's declaration of an end seems problematic at best.

Gilbert also wished to find an optimistic note on which to end his history, to provide his narrative with a comforting closure:

> To die with dignity was in itself courageous. To resist the dehuman-
> ising brutalising force of evil, to refuse to be abased to the level of
> animals, to live through the torment, to outlive the tormentors, these
> too were courageous. Merely to give witness by one's own testimony

was, in the end, to contribute to moral victory. Simply to survive was a victory of the human spirit.[30]

Both Lawrence Langer and Dan Stone have critiqued this attempt to place the *entire* history of the victims within the heroic tradition. Stone regards it as an 'understandable' desire to find meaning in the Holocaust, but as 'historically inappropriate' because it is quite simply contradicted by testimony itself, not least by Levi's 'grey zone'.[31] Similarly Langer has condemned Gilbert for an attempt to impute moral meaning where there is none, for trying to build 'a monument to hope on the rubble of decay'.[32]

Predating Gilbert's book, Claude Lanzmann's film *Shoah* is the most comprehensive effort to produce a victims' history of the Holocaust and is much more challenging than Gilbert's conservatism. While of course the film is a landmark in Holocaust cinema, and indeed in documentary film-making in general, it can be rightly considered a work of History too, although Lanzmann himself argues that it almost constitutes an *anti-History* – a deliberate rejection of how the *Shoah* is approached by historians. Lanzmann's attempt at revisionism was enforced by the survivors themselves: 'there was an absolute break between the bookish knowledge I had acquired and what these people told me. I understood nothing anymore.'[33] Thus Lanzmann tried to rupture the sense of chronology provided by standard narratives of the 'Final Solution'. The idea that the Holocaust has a history without end is, for example, captured in the final sequence of the film of a train rolling which Lanzmann explains:

> When does the Holocaust really end? Did it end with the last day of the war? Did it end with the creation of the state of Israel? No it still goes on. These are events of such magnitude, of such scope, that they have never stopped developing their consequences.[34]

Lanzmann's history without end was also set in the present (as in the moment that the testimony was given) rather than the past. He used no archival footage and thus questioned the very ability of himself as a film-maker and us as historians of accessing the past.[35] All that we have is the surviving remnant to mediate the past to us. The constant presence of Lanzmann on the screen, and very often his translator too, act as a continual reminder that this testimony is made *now*, not then. At times it is clearly very difficult for the survivors to articulate their memories. In one exchange Lanzmann interviews Avraham Bomba who had been a barber in Treblinka. In the middle of his testimony Bomba breaks down, he wants to stop talking, he pleads with the film-maker 'don't make me go on'. But the relentless Lanzmann forces him to continue: 'We must go on.'[36] Thus the testimony, the past, is dragged into the present.

Lanzmann's is a devastating film, the exchange with Bomba typically forces the audience to see and even feel the survivor's pain. But in many ways the presentness of the testimony, that it is of now rather than then, re-emphasises the problems that historians have had in using such material. In many ways Lanzmann is implicitly saying that you cannot make a history from such material, just an anti-History. Robert Rosenstone has argued that films offer an alternative manner of engaging the past to the historian's medium of the written word.[37] Lanzmann is in effect arguing through his film that historians cannot use the testimony of the victims – this mediation of the past through the present – in their conventional narratives, if they continue to be in thrall to their desire for certainty and closure, because neither is on offer. The past, Lanzmann implies, is forever elusive but forever present too.

Histories of memory: making use of survivor testimony I

Can historians use the memories of individuals? Can they incorporate them into their narratives? These are obviously questions for historians in general, not just those engaged in considering the Holocaust. And during the last two decades, there has been a growing sense, albeit only on the margins, that History as a discipline *needs* to come to terms with the testimony of individuals, of 'ordinary people', survivors from any past. This is partly a consequence of political pressure to bring into view those excluded from traditional historiography – not least the experience of ethnic minorities for example; and is partly a consequence of the postmodern critique which suggests that History is just one mode of narrating the past, and as such it must take seriously other modes of narration too. Perhaps inevitably the focus of this development has been on oral history, i.e. history recorded through orally narrated memories, but it does not exclude the writing of ordinary people either. The result has been a massive upsurge in interest in oral history and 'life history' or the history of everyday life, which has provided the impetus for development in perpetrator histories too. Often the drivers of this change have come from outside academic History – witness the huge numbers of local public History projects that have sought to interview and thus document the lives of ordinary citizens[38] – and this represents the central achievement of the oral history movement too, the expansion of the subject of historical investigation to include the everyday lives of those who might previously have been 'hidden from history'.[39]

Crucially practitioners of oral and life history have not simply dismissed the easy critique that people's memories are too unreliable to constitute historical evidence. The idea that memories 'pose a challenge to the historian' is, in fact, almost the starting point for such research.[40] But instead of being disabling, such an observation represents the very opportunity of such material. As Michael Fritsch wrote in an essay first published in 1972, memory should become the 'object' of oral history and not just its method:

> What happens to experience on the way to becoming memory? What happens to experiences on the way to becoming history? As an era of intense collective experience recedes into the past what is the relationship of memory to historical generalisation?[41]

As such, one of the defining features of such historiography is the observation that the line between the past and present is blurred, and that the job of the historian is not just to make sense of the past but to understand the processes by which we make sense of it too. The historian is thus concerned not only with the past, but with the relationship between the present and the past.

To be able to investigate how individuals construct their memories, historians have been forced to look outside their own field. Psychology has had much to tell about the creation of life stories – and the tendency for individuals to narrativise their own lives in order to give their memories meaning.[42] Ironically within the study of the Holocaust this has meant historians are turning back to look at some of the original work done by psychologists with Holocaust survivors in the aftermath of war. Donald Niewyk, for example, has recently republished some of the testimonies from Boder's original study, although Niewyk betrays the traditional prejudices of the historian when arguing that these narratives are

interesting chiefly because of their proximity to the events themselves.[43]

Interest in the way the past is constructed in the present has not
been confined to the study of individuals. Since the 1970s scholars
have increasingly borrowed from sociology the observation that
remembering is a *collective* process, that it takes place within a
social context. Indeed central to debates about the nature of
History as a discipline has been the observation that History (and
historiography) represents just one manifestation of the past in the
present, just one of the ways in which society remembers.[44]
Archives, ceremonies of remembrance, heritage sites, films, festi-
vals, memorials, museums, television programmes, tourism –
represent just a handful of the other ways in which especially
modern societies construct their past, create their memories.[45]
Indeed Holocaust Studies, in a debate to which this book is a contribution, has been increasingly concerned with how societies
come to terms with genocidal pasts – how the Holocaust is, as it
were, remembered.

Yet it is not just the idea that societies have memories that has
been of interest to students of personal testimony. Practitioners of
oral history have also observed that individuals remember inside
social contexts, that there is a 'social framework' for individual
memory too.[46] That memory is constructed within a collective
sense of the past and present is not a new idea. The French sociologist Maurice Halbwachs first sought to identify the 'social
framework' for collective memory in the 1920s.[47] Ironically Halbwachs perished at the hands of the Nazis. Thus the idea that *The
Myths we Live By* are socially as well as individually constructed
has itself had a long history and is intimately involved with the history of the Holocaust. And it is an idea that has manifold
implications for the use of Holocaust testimony. Individual testimonies can often be constructed within a familiar overarching
narrative, to conform to ideals that have a much wider resonance
within the culture in which witnesses are doing the remembering
(rather than the culture being remembered). Perhaps the most
obvious example, which will be explored in more detail later in the
chapter, is that memory can be gendered – and as such women frequently remember their Holocaust pasts within the framework of
traditional gender expectations, constructing themselves and other
women as care-givers and home-makers. Men can construct their

memories according to conceptions of masculinity too, construct-ing themselves and other men as aggressive, self-centred and involved in a ceaseless struggle for survival.

Overall then, the idea that there are many routes to the past, and as such that we cannot dismiss memories as simply unreliable; and the idea that historians should be concerned with the process by which the past is made, how the past is remembered, is now vogue. The question for us is how has that been reflected in Holocaust *History*? What follows is a summary of the important debates on how to deal with survivor memory articulated inside Holocaust studies in the last twenty years. It is notable that comparatively few of the scholars discussed would necessarily define themselves as historians.

As we have seen some the most important studies of Holocaust memory have come from Lawrence Langer, who is chiefly a literary scholar rather than a historian. Langer argued that some of the concerns surrounding Holocaust testimonies were unfounded. The complications of distance and time, the idea that memory fades, are, Langer suggests, not applicable to survivors. He felt that because of the nature of the trauma experienced by the victims, Holocaust memories are an 'insomniac faculty' that remained con-stantly near the surface.[48] Geoffrey Hartman, another literary scholar who has worked on the testimony archive at Yale, agreed because 'evil is a greater force in etching details on our memory than good or ordinary life'.[49] Thus the problems of Holocaust testimony – for example where different survivors recorded contradictory stories – could not be explained away as simply the result of mis-remembering. Instead they pointed to the dizzying complexity of the Holocaust as an experience.[50]

Yet however close to the surface they were, Langer acknowl-edged that survivors had to *translate* their memories to render them understandable in the present. This was in part because the survivor's audience had not experienced their nightmares. At its most basic the language that survivors used to describe their 'hunger', their 'cold', their 'fear', could only by understood by the audience in terms of *their* 'hunger', *their* 'cold', *their* 'fear'. As such experiences from *inside* the concentration camp could only be explained using a vocabulary that only really had a meaning, for the non-survivor audience, *outside* of the concentration camps. The Holocaust was, to use the words of Giorgio Agamben, both 'absolutely unforgettable' to its survivors and absolutely 'unimaginable' to their audience.[51] Although the past lurks close by then, it is out of reach.[52]

For survivors themselves this problem of communication speaks of the unknowability of the Holocaust for those not witness to its horror. As Elie Wiesel wrote in 1970:

> To set oneself the task of bringing back to life the hallucinatory reality of a single human being, in a single camp, borders on sacrilege. The truer the tale the more fictitious it appears. The secret must remain inviolate. Once revealed it becomes myth, and can only be tarnished, diminished. In the end, words lose their innocence, their power to cast a spell. The truth will never be written.

Wiesel was articulating the problem of the gap between experience and expression, while at the same time claiming the authority of the witness, the bearer of the secret who can only 'allude to the unspeakable truths' which only they understand.[53]

But for scholars such as Langer, and then later psychologists Cathy Caruth and Henry Greenspan, the division between the witness, the survivor, and his audience is not quite so neat as it was for Wiesel. The line between those who understand through experience and those who patently do not, between those who were there and those who were not, cannot be so easily drawn. I will consider Langer first. To explore his thesis we must remember that his main concern was to overturn 'heroic' representations of Holocaust survivors as somehow testament to an enduring 'human spirit'. Instead Langer argued that the 'ambivalence' of the victims' experience meant all such moral judgements should be suspended because they subjected the specific and unique moral universe of the concentration camp to evaluation through an entirely different and alien ethical framework. While the main culprits here were those who evaluated testimony, like Martin Gilbert and Terrence Des Pres,[54] Langer also claimed that survivors themselves subjected their own stories to such moral evaluation. If testimony is, by its very nature, an effort at explanation and self-justification,[55] then such evaluation takes place *now* rather than then, producing 'narratives stained by the disapproval of the witnesses' own present moral sensibility'.[56] So for Langer although the past was close by, it was actively being made in the present, out of reach of *even* the survivors themselves. Similarly Henry Greenspan has argued that the survivor is no privileged witness, because the fact of their being there cannot 'solve the problem' of the impossibility of retelling their experiences. 'Survivors', Greenspan wrote, 'are no more able than we to retell the essence of what they endured'.[57]

While superficially there are links between the ideas of unknowability as expressed by survivors such as Wiesel and theorists such as Greenspan, Caruth and Langer, the implications are quite different. Wiesel's claims of authority demand that the survivor and their testimonies or texts be treated with reverence, as the closest approximations of the truth. As he wrote elsewhere 'any survivor has more to say than all the historians combined about what happened'.[58] But especially Henry Greenspan's words seem to demand that those same texts and testimonies require *interpretation* because they are no nearer capturing the essence of the past than any other narrative construction. Unsurprisingly the gulf between these two views is the cause of some tension between survivors and scholars of the Holocaust.

One of the uncomfortable realities that those attempting to interpret testimony have to face is what to do with the many 'inaccuracies' of memory that survivor accounts can contain. Zoë Waxmann recounts two such 'inaccuracies' in the testimony of an Auschwitz survivor: that during the *Sonderkommando* uprising four crematoria chimneys were blown up (there was only one chimney destroyed), and second that the soap victims used was made of human fat (a claim for which there is no evidence and which most Holocaust historians do not believe occurred).[59] Traditionally the view might have been taken that such infelicities of memory confirmed the unreliability of such sources which historians would do better to avoid. Yet contemporary scholars of testimony believe that this is to miss the point, because such mistakes themselves reveal something profound about the victims' experience. First the inflation of the number of chimneys destroyed is itself an indication of the profound importance of that moment in the survivor's memory – a moment which symbolically or otherwise challenged the absolute power and domination of the camp system. As such exaggerating the number of chimneys exploded might testify more eloquently to the historical significance, and thus the 'truth' of the event, than strictly accurate reporting of 'what happened' – if such a thing were possible anyway.[60] The second example is a very common 'mistake' and it allows several important observations. First, that the victims lived in a closed world in which rumour played an important role. They were not privy to the intentions of their tormentors, and thus the scale of the Nazis' depravity and what lay in store for Jews in the future was a constant topic of conversation.[61] As such what is revealed is how the events which engulfed the victims were understood.[62] Second, the regularity with which the soap legend reappears in testimony might also testify to the process by which memories are made – in that they are filtered through extant ideas and narratives. Memory is therefore mutually reinforcing. After all, one of the social contexts in which survivors remember is the survivor community itself.

Such interpretations are challenging, not least because they suggest both that the line between 'fact' and 'fiction' is blurred and intriguingly that what are effectively fictitious ideas about the Holocaust can speak to a more profound truth. As David Roskies has argued, testimonies, written or oral, are thus efforts at exegesis and interpretation, not reflections of facts at all. They then require deconstructing in the same way that any text would. Roskies did this with written testimonies which he studied as a form of literature itself – demonstrating that they were very often placed in a similar narrative pattern to other forms of witnessing within the historic Jewish tradition.[63] Much more recently Andrea Reiter has acted on Roskies' desire to subject memoirs to critical analysis, concluding that they often employ or mirror existing genres of writing such as 'the Hasidic tale or the travel novel'.[64] Narrative form is not neutral and it can therefore have an impact on the meaning of testimonies in the same way it would any other narrative.[65] Although survivors often attempt to argue that their experiences represented a radical break therefore, like Wiesel when quoted above, their efforts to report that radical break belie such a claim. Not only is the language they use not novel, neither is the form in which that language is presented.

The suggestion that Holocaust testimonies can be read like any fictional text is unsurprisingly difficult for survivors, not least because there have been notable attempts at producing forged or fictional memoirs, the most infamous being Binjamin Wilkomirski's *Fragments* published in 1996. Wilkomirski had been a child in Auschwitz and Majdanek and his remarkable memoir was received to great acclaim – both as a work of literature and as an articulation of memory.[66] *Fragments* was presented not as a coherent narrative but as a series of loosely connected portraits which captured the terrifying essence of the child survivor's burden, where memories lacked clarity and dwelt in shadows. Wilkomirski was thus especially feted by other child survivors who testified to relief that finally their story was being told.[67] But Wilkomirski was actually Bruno Grosjean, the adopted child of Swiss middle-class parents. He was not even a Jew, and had lived out the war in the relative peace of neutral Switzerland.[68]

At first glance that Wilkomirski was a fraud, that his text was fictional, simply disallows his testimony. But actually it presents a rather more complex problem. Before Wilkomirski was revealed, child survivors had thanked him for giving voice to their memories. As such Wilkomirski, fictionally or not, communicated some kind of truth about children's experiences during the Holocaust. As Elena Lappin wrote 'wasn't it enough that its prose was so moving and powerful that it made hundreds of thousands of readers think about and perhaps "feel" – if not understand – the Holocaust'.[69] Unnerving as the implications of this argument might be, is it possible that Wilkomirski articulated the 'unspeakable truths' of the Holocaust despite not actually having been there, not being a survivor? After all survivors themselves have written fictional accounts which we accept tell us something about the Holocaust, such as Elie Wiesel's *Night* and Tadeusz Borowski's *This Way for the Gas*. Is it only the fact of their authors' survival, of having been there, that awards these texts authenticity?

Certainly if it is the text itself that communicates the 'unspeakable truths' then Wilkomirski's fraud, his fiction, could be argued to be as useful as Borowski's or Wiesel's. This suggestion may be intuitively unpalatable, especially in a world which also includes Holocaust deniers. However, the logical fulfilment of an academic discourse which insists both that survivors themselves struggle to articulate the essence of their experiences, and that all testimony is a translation and mediation of the fragments of the past into the present which blurs the boundaries between fact and fiction, is that Wilkomirski's text can still be judged as an important articulation of Holocaust memory.

While this is not the place to speculate why Grosjean posed as Wilkomirski, it is clear that he gained some comfort from the memories he invented and especially their reception. Grosjean as an adopted child, had a fractured identity – and a Holocaust memory gave him both an identity and a community. In the words of Stefan Maechler, Grosjean was 'the boy who would one day write his story, because he had none'.[70] And the argument that testifying to the Holocaust, bearing witness, is on a personal level often part of a search for and articulation of identity in the present is often expressed by scholars. Even in perpetrating the fraud then, Wilkomirski revealed something about the nature of bearing witness to the Holocaust, and the reception of his memoir equally so. As one of the historians responsible for unmasking him wrote, Wilkomirski has 'written a very powerful book. [He] captures perfectly how no-one ever leaves the camps, even long after the war.'[71]

Perhaps for historians this blurring of fact and fiction simply goes too far. However what it does demonstrate is that in the dominant discourses around Holocaust testimony since the beginning of efforts to incorporate it, the past seems to remain elusive. It eludes historians and survivors alike – often lurking tantalisingly close by but forever out of reach. Perhaps in making such an observation I reveal myself as an historian, who at bottom wants testimony to tell something concrete about the past and specifically 'L'Univers Concentrationairre'. It could be argued that by making such demands I am in thrall to the Nazi chronology, and I am not doing as Henry Greenspan has instructed I must, and 'listening' to survivors. If I did then I would come to the conclusion as Greenspan, Caruth, Langer and others have that the purpose of studying the testimony of survivors is not to learn something about a concrete past at all, but to learn something about the nature of being a survivor, of living with the Holocaust and its memory, and about the attempt to articulate that memory.

According to Langer testimony is an agonising private, and ultimately fruitless struggle to articulate a 'continuous pain and suffering',[72] – witness Lanzmann and Bomba's barbershop exchange. Thus the act of bearing witness is not some noble demonstration of the enduring human spirit, it is not even really a window into a traumatic past, but simply a demonstration of the pain and difficulty of being a survivor. As such it is less evidence of the experience of the 'Final Solution' and its impact on its victims, than it is evidence of the experience of being a survivor of the 'Final Solution' and the long-term struggle to come to terms with its memory.

Greenspan argues (in a sense echoing Langer) that we do *not* study testimony to recover the past, 'to uncover what survivors really mean. Rather, it is to enter into the process by which survivors find words and meanings at all in the face of memories that undo their words and meanings.'[73] To illustrate this point Greenspan used the example of Manny, who failed to describe adequately both for himself and his interviewer the horror of his arrival at Auschwitz. Manny tried to evoke 'the tears, the separations from, from parents, from children, the agony – , the, the, the, – , sorrow', confessing that 'I don't know if there is a word. For the pain'. Ultimately this communicative struggle defeated Manny. 'He simply stopped trying' Greenspan explained.[74]

According to psychologist Cathy Caruth, these kinds of observations demonstrate the true worth of studying testimony because they reveal something about the very nature of trauma. But perversely, what is highlighted by these attempts to articulate the truth of the Holocaust is a 'crisis of truth' itself. Caruth writes 'for the attempt to understand trauma brings one repeatedly to this peculiar paradox: that in trauma the greatest confrontation with reality may also occur as an absolute numbing to it, that immediacy, paradoxically enough may take the form of belatedness'.[75]

This 'crisis of truth' has a further implication when using testimony in an history of the Holocaust. Despite the claims of survivors like Wiesel, and a minority of oral history practitioners, Holocaust testimonies cannot just speak for themselves, they cannot simply be presented without any scholarly intervention.[76] Perhaps the most successful example of the necessity of such scholarly intervention is Mark Roseman's study of the life of a single Holocaust survivor, Marianne Ellenbogen, in *The Past in Hiding*. Ellenbogen had lived through the war inside Germany, protected first by the military intelligence agency *Abwehr* and then latterly in hiding looked after by a little-known resistance group called the *Bund*. When Roseman came to write her biography towards the end, and after the end, of her life, he discovered not only that much of Marianne's past had been kept hidden from her own family, but that perhaps she had also hidden parts of her past from *herself*. In writing the biography, Roseman unearthed evidence which suggested that some of the accounts of her life that

Marianne provided had involved subtle and small, but not insignificant, changes in detail. Perhaps the most revealing was her retelling of her escape from the Gestapo in August 1943. In Marianne's account she had slipped out of the family home when Gestapo agents were searching the cellar. She had intended to take her brother with her, but he had however chosen to stay with his parents. All had subsequently been murdered. Other evidence suggested that Marianne had opportunistically escaped when Gestapo agents who were upstairs in the family home had allowed her to go downstairs to get some food.

Roseman argued that this small change was peculiarly significant, because Marianne's version of events allowed the possibility that her brother could have accompanied her, but the other suggested no such possibility and that Marianne had abandoned her family to their fate. Roseman's purpose was not to suggest that the latter judgement was correct, but that it may have been Marianne's internal judgement – she spoke often of her guilt at having survived when her family did not. Thus this apparently minor change masked a peculiar trauma for Marianne, and she adapted her memories in order to make usable what was otherwise an unbearable past. Far from great trauma etching the past indelibly in her mind, it was at moments of such great trauma where the 'crisis of truth' had occurred. Thus Roseman's work revealed in great detail that survivors' memories were at their most useful when they contained such mistakes of detail – because it was here that both the process of memory and the burdens of living as a survivor were most clearly revealed.[77]

Roseman's micro-history is an example of the 'life-history' approach to survivor testimony and stands in great contrast to that employed by Martin Gilbert discussed at the beginning of this chapter, which attempted to use testimony in the most general terms. By focusing on a single individual Roseman has both enriched our understanding of the Holocaust – by outlining a life spent in hiding during the Holocaust years and thus revealing the real problems of rescue – and enriched our understanding of the memory process. As psychologist Henry Greenspan instructed, Roseman 'listened' to Marianne as a survivor, and although he ultimately challenged the detail of some of her testimony, in doing so he heard more clearly the trauma to which she was trying to bear witness.

History and memory: making use of survivor testimony II

In a recent survey of the possibility of victim historiography, Tony
Kushner has suggested that Roseman's is a model of really the *only*
way that historians can successfully engage testimony. He does
acknowledge however that this represents a significant challenge
to the historian's instinct – which is after all to explain, to generalise, to attempt (as we have seen throughout this book) to create
smooth, closed and coherent narratives. This kind of life-history
approach explicitly disallows such generalisation, and is according
to Kushner a 'radical vision' which, to quote Donald Niewyk,
'buys texture and historicity at the expense of coherence'.[78] And
more to the point for Kushner, it is also a more realistic representation of how the Holocaust was experienced by its victims – as
confusing and disrupting.

Yet does this 'radical vision' offer simply the only way forward?
Can testimony be used as evidence of, in effect, the elusiveness of
the past and nothing else? Can the memories of eye-witnesses not
be used conventionally? Christopher Browning has recently suggested that in fact it *is* possible to use the testimony of survivors
to write a history which exploits the historian's traditional skills
of generalisation and contextualisation 'creating a coherent and
as accurate as possible narrative from an array of differing perspectives and memories'.[79] And, although few and far between,
there have been efforts to write such conventional histories. Do
they suggest a way forward for conventional history-writing in this
area?

There are certainly what might be called conventional historiographical debates using survivor testimonies – that is
interpretative struggles as to the general meaning of the past. In
many ways Lawrence Langer's writing about testimony is a contribution to a conventional historiographical debate, as well as an
argument for a revision of conventional approaches to the past. In
seeking to overturn judgemental histories of victim behaviour
which indulge in celebratory accounts of the enduring human
spirit, Langer points to the 'meaninglessness' of the Holocaust
past – and thus suggests that no general lessons can be learnt. And
yet in historiographical terms Langer has also developed the idea
that Jewish victims faced a series of 'choiceless choices' during the
Holocaust. He argues that it is not possible morally to evaluate
such choices, for example the 'choice' between death or serving in

the Auschwitz-Birkenau *Sonderkommando*. But despite this, such a concept does use testimony to paint a picture of especially communal life inside the Nazi concentration camps.

Langer's thesis is of course a challenging one. Under the impact of 'hunger's ceaseless tyranny', he paints a picture of camp life which accords with Primo Levi's war of all against all, as simply a struggle for survival. In this environment there was no heroism, little altruism, little 'sharing support' or 'self-sacrifice'. Such 'spiritual possibilit[ies]' Langer argues 'turn out to be a luxury for those not on the brink of starvation'.[80] It is true that this was a disordered world in which no two experiences were alike, but this is still a general historical interpretation based on a quantative evaluation of evidence. To use Browning's phrase, Langer has produced a thesis by doing 'what historians do'.[81] After all, Langer bases his interpretation on the fact that 'few witnesses mention them [gestures of heroism] in their testimonies'. What is more Langer is criticising extant historical narratives which promoted the idea of heroism because they implied that victims could make active moral choices – including the scholarship on resistance reviewed in the previous chapter.

Attempts to counter this picture of camp life have also employed a traditional historical approach to testimony material. Langer's principal critic Tzvetan Todorov, although a philosopher rather than an historian, produced his alternative account using testimonies 'paradigmatically' and indeed denying that individual testimonies could stand alone as accounts of either the camps or human behaviour within it.[82] Once again, this sounds like what historians do. Rejecting Langer's idea that testimonies seldom refer to the endurance of moral life or 'spiritual possibility', Todorov argues alternatively that in fact very few testimonies do not contain such references. Crucially however Todorov suggested that survivors themselves do not always recognise the significance of memories of an enduring moral life. As a consequence Todorov explicitly rejects Primo Levi's interpretation of Auschwitz-Birkenau because, although Levi argues for an atmosphere of continuous struggle, he also contrarily writes at length about his clearly sustaining friendship in the camp.[83] Todorov's is a discussion of the functioning of memory too – arguing that survivors emphasise the brutality of camp life because of an enduring existential guilt at having failed to come to the aid of others.[84] But ultimately Todorov reaches a moral historical judgement:

> even under the most adverse circumstances imaginable, when men and
> women are faint with hunger, numb with cold, exhausted, beaten and
> humiliated, they still go on performing simple acts of kindness …
> enough to reinforce even augment our faith in goodness.[85]

It is notable that Todorov frames his historical interpretation in such universal language, and attempts to utilise the Holocaust within a much wider interpretation of the human condition. Once again Holocaust history is used in a discourse about us, and about now. As Geoffrey Hartman has pointed out, and as has been argued throughout this volume, much of Holocaust historiography is similarly concerned to make a traumatic past more comforting.[86]

These efforts at historicisation are deeply problematic. The willingness to use testimony remembering different places, at different times, to produce a universal account of life in 'the camps' is to ignore and elide substantial differences in context. It is clear that even individual camps were very different places throughout their history. The women's camp at Ravensbruck for example became a much more lethal institution towards the end of its existence; the camp at Mauthausen was literally transformed in the latter half of 1944 from a punishment facility to an effective part of the 'Final Solution' when Hungarian Jews began to arrive there; and Auschwitz-Birkenau itself went through very different phases.[87] In ignoring such context they also tend both to ignore the individuality of survivors and their stories. It is not clear how either side of the debate deals, for example, with the many witnesses who contradict them. Todorov can only really account for narratives that testify to the brutalisation of the victims by suggesting they are mistaken. As such the moral purpose of writing an history driven by testimony is subverted, because there is no way of fitting discordant or dissenting narratives into the interpretation. All we are left with is the observation that ultimately all accounts are true reflections of this meaningless past.

There are other examples of such historicisation too, some more respectful of context, but which still tend to universalisation. Nicholas Stargardt's history of the experience of children at war includes reflection on the victims of the Holocaust. Stargardt quite deliberately attempts to evoke specific places and times, for example he includes an analysis of the 'family camp' in Birkenau. Yet it is unclear, in methodological terms, how one gets from the individual testimonies on which the study is based to the self-consciously broad statements made on children's experiences in general. In the 'family camp' Stargardt writes:

> if the younger children wanted to play at wielding power, older children learned to use what power they possessed. They found that they could exchange their white bread ration for larger amounts of rye bread … and older children learned to trade sex for food. Bacon remembered how a friend of his with a pretty sister became her pimp, charging a packet of cigarettes a time.[88]

By what methodology the single testimony becomes a general interpretation is not clear. Wolfgang Sofsky also incorporates victim testimony into his analysis of the 'concentration camps'. Sofsky argued that the camps witnessed a new form of domination which he labels 'absolute power'. It is notable that Sofsky also uses individual testimony as necessarily representative, and as such single, often unnamed, quotations are used to illustrate general points of interpretation. Again it is not clear, in methodological terms, how this is achieved, what route one takes from the particular to the general.[89]

Despite this, it seems that there might be further opportunities for utilising testimony historically. Christopher Browning's history of Wierzbnik Ghetto and Starachowice slave labour camp demonstrates the degree to which testimonies can be used as evidence of the behaviour of the perpetrators of the Holocaust and their approach to their task. Browning concludes, using the evidence of the testimonies, that there were three basic German 'types' in the slave labour camp: 'dangerous', 'corrupt' and 'decent'.[90] Nathan Cohen similarly used the testimony of the *Sonderkommando* to develop a picture of the perpetrators.[91] Given the extant and ongoing debates as to the nature of the perpetrators, it seems perfectly possible that survivor testimony could have a great deal to tell us about the way that Germans interacted with their victims and as such their motivations. Thus, Browning's study does suggest that survivor testimony might be used in conventional historical narratives, but hitherto this has not been widely manifested.

History and herstory: making use of survivor testimony III

Perhaps the most fruitful use of Holocaust testimony in historiography has been the investigation of women's specific Holocaust experiences. But here again, this scholarship suggests an enduringly problematic relationship between survivors, memory and History. The development of first women's and then gender History occurred at the same time as the growth in the use of oral and written testimonies. This is not surprising; in many ways the developments were interlinked. 'Life history' often focused on the private sphere and those 'hidden from history' – two categories into which women in many societies would fit.[92] The emergence of an historiography of women in the Holocaust was therefore a consequence of the development of a wider interest in women's history, and perhaps an inevitable result of the turn to the victims and to testimony – because of the assumed marginalisation of women's voices. Historians have more and more frequently posed the question 'where were the women during the Holocaust' then, because so much historiography was written by men, about men based on the evidence of men's testimony.[93]

It has, from the very outset, been a controversial field. Many felt that the very act of differentiating between the victims was a distortion – because it blurred the fact that Jews had suffered for their race, as Jews. Jewish women were persecuted as Jews and not as women, and the argument was proposed that to investigate a specific gendered experience was to reduce the Holocaust as something secondary to political feminism. Such objections seemed to have more to do with the politics of identity than they did with the Holocaust past. In this vein, Cynthia Ozick accused the organisers of a pioneering conference on women and the Holocaust in 1982 of 'lead[ing] us still further down the road of eradicating Jews from history'.[94] But, Germans *did* treat Jewish men and women differently – in the original *Einsatzgruppen* massacres men were the first to be targeted, but in the complex of labour and annihilation at Auschwitz-Birkenau it appears women were more likely to die; and Jewish women *did* play specific and gendered roles in pre-Holocaust Jewish communities, focused very often on the private sphere. At the very least this suggests that there is a possibility that Jews' misfortune would have been perceived and understood through the filter of a gendered world. And indeed the question of gender differentiation had been raised at the time by the victims themselves. *Oneg Shabbat* had sought very specifically to document the impact of German occupation on the lives of Jewish women.[95]

The study of the victims as women was also linked to the application of the category of gender to the perpetrators and German society. A significant debate emerged there as to the degree to which German women could be argued to be 'victims' of the Nazi regime, by the very fact of their gender. Fascist regimes have traditionally been understood to be at least anti-feminist, and the Nazi state has appeared similarly in historiography.[96] In terms of the perpetration of the Holocaust this was a crime committed almost exclusively by men. However, Claudia Koonz revised this view, suggesting that in retreating to the private sphere (as per the aims of the Nazi state) and thus providing shelter and comfort, German women made a significant contribution to the genocidal regime. The Nazis, Koonz claimed, relied on women to create a stable home and thus an 'ersatz sense of decency in the men who could work most closely with mass murder'. At its most fundamental level Koonz argued that by contributing children to the Nazi project, by revelling in the Nazi ideal of the family, 'women provided in a separate sphere of their own creation the image of human values that lent the healthy gloss of motherhood to the Aryan world of the chosen'.[97] This is not the place to resolve such a debate. However, it is important for our purposes because it points to the emergence, in and around Holocaust studies, of the idea that there was an interaction between Nazi racism and sexism. Racism was in that sense gendered – women were sanctified as mothers in the German community while similarly reviled as the potential carriers of a future generation amongst the Jewish victims.

Testimony has been used chiefly to consider the role that gender played in women's survival. Contrasts have been drawn between male and female survival strategies, and it is commonly argued that specifically gendered characteristics made Jewish women more resilient – especially for example in the women's camp at Auschwitz-Birkenau. Sybil Milton first proposed such an argument in 1984, suggesting that women had 'significantly different survival skills and techniques than did men' including:

> Doing housework as a kind of practical therapy and of gaining control over one's space, bonding and networks ... the use of incon-

spicuousness and possibly even sex ... women swapped recipes and ways of extending limited quantities of food.[98]

Michael Unger's study of the Łódź ghetto seems to confirm that women were 'better able than men to tolerate the ghetto conditions' because, starkly, they were less likely to die in the ghetto.[99] Certainly women's testimonies of the camps are replete with examples of women forming surrogate families as a survival strategy. Ruth Kluger remembers her mother's adoption of a girl called Susi in Auschwitz-Birkenau. This saved Susi from 'a certain degree of psychic damage: the mental self-neglect that sets in when nobody gives a hoot whether you exist or not.'[100]

Trauma could be gendered too. Women's testimonies recall with particular horror the public nakedness that invariably accompanied the initiation ritual in most camps. While it is often asserted that the incidence of rape was rare during the Holocaust, something usually explained with reference to the prevalence of German fears of so-called race defilement or *Rassenschande*, it is clear that the degradation of initiation was for women a sexual scenario, pregnant with sexual threat. Women often testify to SS men using sexuality, and their victims' fears of that sexuality, as a means of terrorising women.[101]

The issue of rape in the victimisation of Jewish women during the Holocaust is complex and begins to reveal some of the problems of this area and the extent to which the past is elusive here too. It bears repeating that it is commonly claimed that the incidence of rape was rare and it is certainly the case that stories of rape, perpetrated either by Germans, other perpetrators of the genocide, or indeed by fellow victims are 'not easy to come by'.[102] It is also true that historians display a level of discomfort in discussing this subject.[103] Yet historians are increasingly aware that rape has invariably been an off-shoot of genocidal violence and even a weapon of genocide itself. The experience of Tutsi women in Rwanda is testament to that.[104] And it is also increasingly clear that the presence of an ideology which denies the humanity of the 'other', does not protect the women of that 'other' from sexual violence. As Katherine Derderian has recently argued, rape was a central tool in the dehumanisation of women during the Armenian genocide.[105] As such it may once again be the case that this apparent silence in Holocaust testimony tells us more about memory than it does about the past itself and the contexts in which the Holocaust is remembered.

First, the idea of rape of Jewish women by German men enforces a revision of dominant images of the 'Final Solution' itself. It certainly does not fit with the idea of a clean, scientific genocidal policy directed from the centre, not substantially shaped by the homicidal intentions of its perpetrators.[106] It may also be that the absence of rape from women's memories is itself self-ful-filling, with the silence around the issue discouraging other witnesses from testifying to their experience. The level of trauma that these memories invoke may also make them even more unbearable and thus enforce their absence too, especially if rape was at the hands of one's fellow victim rather than the perpetra-tors, as such stories *necessarily* involve criticism of the victim community.[107] It has also recently been argued by Helene Sinnreich that the silence in oral testimony was often enforced by interview-ers who avoided this difficult subject – it seems that if survivors are asked *specifically* about sexual abuse they are much more likely to discuss the issue.[108] Of course women's post-war identities may themselves prevent the memory and discussion of such sexual trauma – both as women and as survivors. Rape is often perceived as a personal trauma which may seem unrelated to the wider trauma of the genocide, of which the victims are survivors, and crucially about which they have been asked to speak – again a view which is compounded by the assertion that rape was not part of the genocide itself. It is accepted that women find it difficult to dis-cuss rape in the present, that it is an experience which can evoke feelings of shame and guilt, and it may well be that this applies to the past too. Rape is and was taboo.

The issue of sexual violence reveals, once again, the complex relationship between present and past in Holocaust History, and the historiography of women and the Holocaust is somewhat undermined by that complexity too. As Joan Ringelheim, who had previously written herself on women's more successful survival strategies during the Holocaust, argued in a stinging self-critique in the mid-1980s, there is a distinct tendency to attempt to fit the image of women during the Holocaust into an existing construct of the ideal woman. As such the image of women as care-givers, nurturers, home-makers was imposed on the Holocaust in an almost celebratory fashion. In effect the practitioners of women's

Holocaust History were constructing and applying a rather stereo-typical view which had itself previously been regarded as tyrannical – the beginning of women's history had been to com-plicate the view of women in the past, rather than simply to celebrate 'feminine qualities'. This also problematically trans-formed the Holocaust into a narrative of hope and celebration, not despair. But as Ringelheim suggested, expressing similar senti-ments to Lawrence Langer, 'the Holocaust is a story of loss not gain'. Women's Holocaust historiography seemed to be suggesting that 'in spite of the rape, abuse and murder of babies … in spite of everything ugly and disgusting, women bonded, loved each other'.[109]

The source of these images is as likely to be women's own idealised image of the feminine as it is the Holocaust past. As such, perhaps some work on gendered experience of the Holocaust reveals not that the experience of women was different, but that the memory process is itself gendered and is filtered through the gendered assumptions of the survivor and their audience.[110] The same, of course, could be true for men. Famously Roman Frister's memoir *The Cap or The Price of Life* celebrated the vio-lence that he had employed in his *struggle* for survival. Frister self-consciously portrayed himself in stereotypically male terms.[111] For Ringelheim pictures of the Holocaust that paid tribute to the 'femininity' of the victims also constructed a fundamentally false image of the past, and had a negative impact on survivors whose memories did not conform to this idealised image. What of women who were excluded from relationships? What of women who fought, who struggled to stay alive in a way that seems to have been accepted within male but not female testimony? But overall this positive image of women's Holocaust experience seemed to mask one more fundamental fact – that Jewish women were more likely to die in the 'Final Solution', especially in the death camps. If they were pregnant they would be murdered if discovered, if they had young children then they faced either death or separation from their children who would die. In a world where work could keep you alive, after all the selections kept those able to work from the gas chamber, assumptions as to the ability of women to under-take work meant that women were more likely than men to be sent to their deaths.[112]

Overall the implications of the Ringelheim critique are once again troubling for efforts to use survivor memories in the writing of Holocaust History. The past remains elusive in historiography of women's Holocaust experiences too. When the past does appear more tangible, such concreteness may actually be, through the complexities of the memory process, provided by the present and not the past.

Conclusion

Whichever way we turn then, we are brought back to the position that using testimony is problematic. For conventional historical narratives it may be hopelessly so, and it remains to be seen whether survivor testimonies can be successfully integrated into the history of particular Holocaust spaces and places in the manner that Christopher Browning has suggested is possible. If the memory of survivors is to be integrated into wider Holocaust narratives it would appear however that its role must be to disrupt. At its most basic a chronology of the Holocaust that begins with an arbitrary date in the history of Nazi persecution (be that 1933, 1938, 1941) and ends with the destruction of the Nazi state and/or the liberation of the concentration camps is clearly not appropriate, or at least has no meaning for its victims. Similarly a history which sees the victims as just Jews and not as men, women and indeed children, is a history which elides the differentiation of the victim community.

However the memory of survivors appears to be disruptive on a much more fundamental level too. All scholarly use of testimony seems to point to its role in exposing the relationship between past and present, and the process by which the past is made present by individuals and thus also the degree to which the present *makes* the past. When Henry Greenspan or Lawrence Langer implore us to listen to survivors, it is because they have a great deal to tell us about the experience of living with the past and of bearing witness. Yet the idea that those memories can be controlled, and forced into the kind of stable narrative that History as a discipline has traditionally thrived upon, seems to be unwelcome and indeed even *morally* problematic. For as soon as testimony is used to create a controlled history of the Holocaust then it starts to shape a narrative which may well exclude the memories of survivors. If historians argue that moral life survived in the Holocaust then the memories of those who remember only struggle are excluded; if historians suggest that women had better survival strategies than men, then the women whose memories of survival do not include nurturing are again necessarily excluded. To return to the work of Lawrence Langer that this chapter began with, it seems that *any* conventional historiographical act which employs the testimony of the surviving victims may be to subject the Holocaust past to a moral judgement. Overall then, although there are points of conventional historiographical controversy, the lesson of attempts to deal with survivor testimony seems to be that the history of the victims can only be harnessed in a 'radical vision' of History. This is difficult for the historian as it is a vision that eschews generalisation and points only to complexity, in other words an *anti-History*.

Notes

1   Lawrence Langer, *Holocaust Testimonies: The Ruins of Memory* (New Haven: CT, 1991), pp. xi-xii.
2   David Boder, *I Did Not Interview the Dead* (Urbana: IL, 1949)
3   Donald Bloxham and Tony Kushner, *The Holocaust: Critical Historical Approaches* (Manchester, 2005), p. 32.
4   Shoshana Felman and Dori Laub, *Testimony: Crisis of Witnessing in Literature, Psychoanalysis and History* (London, 1992), p. 207.
5   Benzion Dinur, 'Problems Confronting *Yad Vashem* in its Work of Research', *Yad Vashem Studies* (Vol. 1, 1957), p. 20.
6   Anita Shapira, 'The Holocaust: Private Memories, Public Memory', *Jewish Social Studies* (Vol. 4, No. 2, 1998), pp. 40–58.
7   The text is reprinted in Rudolf Vrba, *I Escaped from Auschwitz* (London, 2006), pp. 327–64.
8   See for example Mordechai Lichtenstein, 'Eighteen Months in the Oswiecim Extermination Camp', *Jewish Survivors Report: Documents of Nazi Guilt* (No. 1, May 1945) – copies of the Survivor Reports can be accessed in the Parkes Library, University of Southampton.
9   This figure comes from Bloxham and Kushner , *The Holocaust*, p. 29. It is also in Zoë Vania Waxman, *Writing the Holocaust: Identity, Testimony and Representation* (Oxford, 2006), p. 100, who points out that these were published mainly in Yiddish, Hebrew and Polish.
10 Mary Berg, *Warsaw Ghetto: A Diary* (New York, 1945); Marek Edelman, *The Ghetto Fights* (New York, 1946); see Waxman, *Writing the Holocaust*, p. 100 on this.
11 Terence Des Pres, *The Survivor: An Anatomy of Life in the Death Camps* (Oxford, 1976).
12 Alexandra Zapruder (ed.), *Salvaged Pages: Young Writer's Diaries of the Holocaust* (New Haven: CT, 2002), p. 5.

13 Levi's If this is a Man was described in those terms in Werner J Cahnman, 'Review of If this is a Man', *American Journal of Sociology* (Vol. 65, No. 6, 1960), p. 638; Olga Lengyel, *Five Chimneys* (London, 1959), see back cover for quotation.

14 Henry Greenspan, *On Listening to Holocaust Survivors: Recounting and Life History* (Westport: CT, 1998), p. 45.

15 Waxmann, *Writing the Holocaust*, p. 117.

16 See for example Felman and Laub, *Testimony*, p. 204 which cites Elie Wiesel on the duty of witnessing.

17 Greenspan, *On Listening to Holocaust Survivors*, pp. 46–7.

18 See Alan Mintz, *Popular Culture and the Shaping of the Holocaust in America* (Washington: DC, 2001), p. 22.

19 Joanne Weiner Rudolf, 'A Yale University and New Haven Community Project: From Local to Global', published online – www.library.yale.edu/testimonies.

20 Primo Levi, *The Drowned and the Saved* (New York, 1988), pp. 42, 53.

21 *Ibid.*, p. 38.

22 Lucy Dawidowicz, *The War Against the Jews, 1933–45* (London, 1987), pp. 410–26.

23 Leni Yahil, *The Holocaust: The Fate of European Jewry* (Oxford, 1991), pp. 370–2 – these are the two pages that Yahil devotes to life in the camps.

24 Dan Stone, *Constructing the Holocaust* (London, 2003), pp. 153–7.

25 Bloxham and Kushner, *The Holocaust*, pp. 33–4.

26 Kenneth Jacobson, *Embattled Selves: An Investigation in the Nature of Identity through Oral Histories of Holocaust Survivors* (New York, 1994), p. 7.

27 See Joanne Reilly, *Belsen: The Liberation of a Concentration Camp* (London, 1997), p. 152.

28 Trude Levi, *A Cat Called Adolf* (London, 1994), pp. 57–163.

29 Levi, *The Drowned and the Saved*, p. 71.

30 Martin Gilbert, *The Holocaust: The Jewish Tragedy* (London, 1985), p. 828.

31 Stone, *Constructing the Holocaust*, p. 157.

32 Langer, *Holocaust Testimonies*, p. 165.

33 Lanzmann quoted in Geoffrey H. Hartman, *The Longest Shadow: In the Aftermath of the Holocaust* (Bloomington: IN, 1996), p. 145.

34 Claude Lanzmann quoted in Felman and Laub, *Testimony*, p. 241.

35 *Ibid.*, p. 205.

36 Claude Lanzmann, *Shoah: An Oral History of the Holocaust* (New York, 1985), p. 117.

37 See the introduction to Robert Rosenstone (ed.), *Revisioning History: Films and the Construction of a New Past* (Princeton: NJ, 1994), pp. 3–14, for a brief discussion of this idea.

38 For a British example see the Moving Here project, http://www.movinghere.org.uk/about/default.htm (accessed 05/03/2009).

39 Robert Perks and Alastair Thomson, 'Introduction', *The Oral History Reader* (London, 1998), p. 1.

40 Raphael Samuel and Paul Thomson (eds), *The Myths we Live By* (Routledge, 1990), p. 1.

41 Cited in Perks and Thomson, *The Oral History Reader*, p. 2.

42 *Ibid.*, p. 1.

43 See Donald L. Niewyk, *Fresh Wounds: Early Narratives of Holocaust Survival* (Chapel Hill: NC, 1998), p. 1.
44 Paul Connerton, *How Societies Remember* (Cambridge, 1989), especially pp. 6-40 for a discussion which touches on the role of historians in the production of 'social memory'.
45 For a discussion of the ways in which societies create memories (rather than history) see Pierre Nora, 'Between Memory and History: Les Lieux de Mémoire', *Representations* (No. 26, 1989), pp. 7–24.
46 See Susan A. Crane, 'Writing the Individual Back into Collective Memory', *The American Historical Review* (Vol. 102, No. 5, 1997), pp. 1372–85.
47 Maurice Halbwachs, *On Collective Memory* (Chicago: IL, 1992). See also Barbara Misztal, *Theories of Social Remembering* (Buckingham, 2003) for a discussion of the various theoretical perspectives in this field.
48 Langer, *Holocaust Testimonies*, p. xv.
49 Hartman, 'Learning from Survivors', p. 135.
50 Langer, *Holocaust Testimonies*, p. 21 and *Versions of Survival: The Holocaust and the Human Spirit* (New York, 1982), p. 6.
51 Giorgio Agamben, *Remnants of Auschwitz: The Witness and the Archive* (New York, 2002), p. 12.
52 Langer, *Versions of Survival*, p. 11.
53 Naomi Rosh White, 'Marking Absences: Holocaust Testimony and History', Perks and Thomson, *The Oral History Reader*, pp. 172–3.
54 Des Pres, *The Survivor*.
55 Samuel and Thomson, *The Myths we Live By*, p. 10.
56 Langer, *Holocaust Testimonies*, p. 122.
57 Greenspan, *On Listening to Holocaust Survivors*, p. 5.
58 Cited in Waxmann, *Writing the Holocaust*, p. 180.
59 *Ibid.*, pp. 167–8.
60 Felman and Laub, *Testimony*, pp. 59–60. This is cited by Waxmann, *Writing the Holocaust*, p. 167.
61 James Young, *Writing and Rewriting the Holocaust: Narrative and the Consequences of Interpretation* (Bloomington: IN, 1988), p. 33.
62 *Ibid.*, p. 3.
63 David G. Roskies, *Against the Apocalypse: Responses to Catastrophe in Modern Jewish Culture* (Cambridge: MA, 1985), p. 35.
64 Andrea Reiter, *Narrating the Holocaust* (London, 2000).
65 'Narrative is not merely a neutral discursive form ... but rather entails ontological and epistemic choices with distinct ideological and even specifically political implications', Hayden White, *The Content of the Form: Narrative and the Discourse of Historical Representation* (London, 1992), p. ix.
66 Binjamin Wilkomirski, *Fragments: Memories of a Wartime Childhood* (New York, 1996). The *New York Times Book Review* described it as an 'extraordinary memoir', See Blake Eskin, *A Life in Pieces* (London, 2002), p. 8; Anne Karpf described it in *The Guardian* as 'one of the great works about the Holocaust', cited in Carl Tighe, *Writing and Responsibility* (London, 2005), p. 90.
67 Stefan Maechler, 'Wilkomirski the Victim: Individual Remembering as Social Interaction and Public Event', *History and Memory* (Vol. 13, No. 2, 2001), p. 79.

68 For the story of Wilkomirski's unmasking as a fraud see Stefan Maechler, *The Wilkomirski Affair: A Study in Biographical Truth* (New York, 2001).
69 Elena Lappin, 'The Man with Two Heads', *Granta* (June 1999), p. 15.
70 Stefan Maechler, 'Wilkomirski the Victim', p. 60.
71 Cited in Lappin, 'The Man with Two Heads', p. 52.
72 Naomi Rosh White, 'Marking Absences: Holocaust Testimony and History', Perks and Thomson, *The Oral History Reader*, p. 178.
73 Greenspan, *On Listening to Holocaust Survivors*, p. 6.
74 *Ibid.*, p. 13.
75 Cathy Caruth (ed.), *Trauma: Explorations in Memory* (Baltimore: MD, 1995), p. 6.
76 This possibility is raised by Rhoda Lewin in *Witnesses to the Holocaust: An Oral History* (Boston: MA, 1990), pp. xv–xx.
77 Roseman, *The Past in Hiding*, pp. 460–75; See also Mark Roseman, 'Surviving Memory: Truth and Inaccuracy in Holocaust Testimony', *Journal of Holocaust Education* (Vol. 8, No. 1, 1999), pp. 1–20.
78 See Bloxham and Kushner, *The Holocaust*, pp. 46–50; Niewyk, *Fresh Wounds*, p. 1.
79 This is a quotation from Browning's review of Bloxham and Kushner, *The Holocaust*, in *Patterns of Prejudice* (Vol. 41, No. 5, 2007), p. 526. For Browning's attempts at this history see Christopher Browning, *Collected Memories: Holocaust History and Postwar Testimony* (Madison: WI, 2003).
80 Langer, *Holocaust Testimonies*, p. 26.
81 Browning, 'Review of Bloxham and Kushner, *The Holocaust*', p. 526.
82 Tzvetan Todorov, *Facing the Extreme: Moral Life in the Concentration Camps* (New York, 1996), p. 259.
83 *Ibid.*, p. 34.
84 *Ibid.*, p. 37.
85 *Ibid.*, p. 290.
86 Hartman, 'Learning from Survivors', p. 143.
87 See Irith Dublon-Knebel (ed.), *A Holocaust Crossroads: Jewish Women and Children in Ravensbruck* (London, 2009); Gordon J. Horowitz, *In the Shadow of Death: Living Outside the Gates of Mauthausen* (London, 1991), p. 22.
88 Nicholas Stargardt, *Witnesses of War: Children's Lives Under the Nazis* (London, 2005), p. 217.
89 Wolfgang Sofsky, *The Order of Terror: The Concentration Camp* (Princeton: NJ, 1997), pp. 259-67 for an example of his use of testimony concerning the *Sonderkommando* at Auschwitz.
90 See Browning, *Collected Memories*, pp. 50–4.
91 Nathan Cohen, 'Diaries of the Sonderkommandos in Auschwitz: Coping with Fate and Reality', *Yad Vashem Studies* (Vol. 20, 1990), pp. 303–6.
92 Indeed one of the first works of women's history used this title: Sheila Rowbotham, *Hidden from History: 300 Years of Women's Oppression and the Fight Against it* (London, 1973).
93 That Holocaust History is written by and about men is a point made in Roger W. Smith 'Women and Genocide: Notes on an Unwritten History', *Holocaust and Genocide Studies* (Vol. 8, no. 3, 1994), pp. 315–34.
94 Quoted in Joan Ringelheim, 'The Split Between Gender and the Holocaust',

Dalia Ofer and Leonore J. Weitzmann, *Women in the Holocaust* (New Haven: CT, 1998), pp. 348–9.

95 Samuel D. Kassow, *Who Will Write Our History? Emmanuel Ringelblum, the Warsaw Ghetto, and the Oyneg Shabes Archive* (Bloomington: IN, 2007), pp. 239–51.

96 See for example Bonnie S Anderson and Judith P Zinsser, *A History of their Own* (New York, 1988), vol. 2, pp. 213–14.

97 Claudia Koonz, *Mothers in the Fatherland: Women, the Family and Nazi Politics* (New York, 1987).

98 Sybil Milton, 'Women and the Holocaust: The Case of German and German-Jewish Women', Carol Rittner and John Roth, *Different Voices: Women and the Holocaust* (St Paul: MN, 1993), p. 227.

99 Michael Unger, 'The Status and Plight of Women in the Łódź Ghetto', Ofer and Weitzmann, *Women in the Holocaust*, p. 127.

100 Ruth Kluger, *Landscapes of Memory* (London, 2003), p. 146.

101 See for example the introduction to Vera Laska, *Women in the Resistance and in the Holocaust* (Westport: CT, 1983) – Laska was a survivor of the resistance and as such this is part monograph part memoir.

102 Joan Ringelheim, 'Women and the Holocaust: A Reconsideration of Research', Rittner and Roth, *Different Voices*, p. 377.

103 This is particularly the case with Sybil Milton's original and path-breaking essay, 'Women and the Holocaust', p. 231.

104 Rape was employed systematically as a genocidal weapon in Rwanda. See Linda Melvern, *Conspiracy to Murder: The Rwandan Genocide* (London, 2006), p. 253.

105 Katharine Derderian, 'Common Fate, Different Experience: Gender Specific Aspects of the Armenian Genocide, 1915–1917', *Holocaust and Genocide Studies* (Vol. 19, No. 1, 2005), pp. 1–25.

106 This point is made by Helene Sinnreich, '"… And it was something we didn't talk about": Rape of Jewish Women During the Holocaust', *Holocaust Studies: A Journal of Culture and History* (Vol. 14, no. 2, 2008), pp. 1–22.

107 Ringelheim, 'The Split Between Gender and the Holocaust', p. 345.

108 Sinnreich, 'And it was something we didn't talk about', p. 5.

109 Ringelheim, 'Women and the Holocaust', p. 388.

110 On the gendering of memory see Anna Reading, *The Social Inheritance of the Holocaust: Gender, Culture and Memory* (Basingstoke, 2002).

111 Roman Frister, *The Cap or the Price of Life* (London, 1999).

112 See Ringelheim, 'Women and the Holocaust', p. 400. See also Judith Tydor Baumel, *Double Jeopardy: Gender and the Holocaust* (London, 1998).

CONCLUSION

Although attempts to incorporate the voices and memories of the victims and survivors offer profound and unresolved challenges to historians, it would be wrong to end on a note of despair. The contested role of memories demonstrates Holocaust History is an ongoing discourse, with a future as well as a past. Even if the only way to incorporate memories is with new methodologies, this still points to further discussions rather than to closing them down. As such, it would seem fitting to conclude with some thoughts about where those *Debates on the Holocaust* might be heading. But, before looking to the future, I want to return to where we started by considering what this book has revealed about both Holocaust History in particular, and more generally about the nature of history-writing and the discipline of History as a whole.

Attempts to historicise the Holocaust began before the death camps had claimed their last victims. The period at and after the end of the war contained the beginnings of a search for the context in which to understand Nazi violence and destructiveness. The persecution of the Jews was often seen only in a universal light during this period – the experience of the victims telling us about universal human reactions to trauma and degradation; the policies of the perpetrators considered in their much wider contexts, such as general population movements or in the comparative contexts of totalitarianism or colonialism. Where vigorous debates were concerned only with the Jewish victims of Nazism, they were often internal discourses concerned with Jewish behaviour. The tendency toward universalisation reflected both the peculiar trauma of the Holocaust and the urgency of understanding its relationship with modern state and society in general. It is an urgency that has not departed, and that central question of where the persecution of the Jews fits into an understanding of modernity has remained at the forefront of Holocaust studies.

Holocaust historiography from the late 1950s onwards is in many ways the story of an attempt to escape those original contexts, and to assert the persecution of the Jews as a subject in and of itself. Yet even if the focus of Holocaust scholarship became more particular then the tendency towards universalisation remained. Once the destruction of the European Jews had been wrenched from some of its wider contexts, exemplified by the universal adoption of the term Holocaust, then modernist, singular, all-encompassing explanations of its development and perpetration followed. The Holocaust was often accounted for using one of two competing metanarratives. Broadly speaking those 'intentionalist' and 'functionalist' narratives were both concerned, again, to relate the Holocaust either to modernity or its discontents. The *Shoah* was identified as either the consequence of a maniacal and irrational ideology and the defeat of reason; or alternatively as the consequence of a peculiar state and society.

That debate raged for several years, exemplified by the 'dating game' Holocaust scholars played with regard to the beginning of the 'Final Solution'. Yet the search for an order for the 'Final Solution' was about discovering not just the beginning of genocide but its *origins*. If that debate has still not been resolved, more recently singular analyses and answers to the question have broken down. Regional and local contexts appear much more important than universal explanations in the postmodern Holocaust. 'Final Solutions' have replaced the 'Final Solution' as it were. The micro contexts for the perpetration of genocide have been revealed across Europe – and the idea that mass murder was driven forward as much by the lower levels of the Nazi machinery of destruction as by central authority has almost become a truism. Yet the absence of central authority which characterises many contemporary Holocaust histories should not be misunderstood as a victory for the abstractions of 'functionalism'. Indeed hatred has returned to the explanatory crucible of Holocaust studies. If the dominant images of modernist renderings of the Holocaust were the murder factories of Birkenau and Treblinka then the destruction of the European Jews has recently been more commonly embodied in the killing fields of Eastern Europe.

Throughout its development Holocaust History has been divided. The histories and historiographies of victims and perpetrators have, despite some notable exceptions, remained rather separate – even if they have developed in parallel. The historiography of the victims of the *Shoah* – despite early interest in the memories of individuals in the immediate post-war period, was at least in the 1960s and 1970s dominated by a debate as to the reality of Jewish resistance. Such an historiography was much more concerned with representative organisations than with the individual victims themselves. Just as the History of the perpetrators has turned away from the machinery of destruction, so too has attention turned to the life stories of victims and survivors as individuals. The source material provided by their memories, which although collected since the end of the war historians had traditionally sought to avoid, has forced historians to examine whether or not their discipline is capable of producing histories that are meaningful to the survivors themselves.

History's struggle with the 'ruins of memory' typifies the degree to which it has been invariably concerned with more than just the past – Holocaust History has been an ongoing discourse about, amongst many questions, our very means of accessing the past. As such Auschwitz remains, at the very least, symbolic of many discourses. A disagreement about the purpose of historical investigation, and the moral responsibilities of the historian lay at the heart of the two original and opposed metanarratives of 'intentionalism' and 'functionalism'. At the same time the historians involved seem to subscribe to different evaluations of enlightenment progress, and attempted to fit the Holocaust into those world views. Debates about the 'bystanders' to the Holocaust have always been concerned with political and moral questions too; as well as, again, disagreeing to a great extent about History as a discipline and especially what could or could not be the subject of historical investigation. Even contemporary debates about Holocaust perpetrators are grafted on top of much more fundamental disagreements regarding the nature of morality and responsibility in the modern world.

Holocaust History has also been revealed to be a function of wider social, political and cultural developments. In just the last two decades, we can relate developments in Holocaust historiography to the contemporary growth in antisemitism, discourse concerned with the ideas of individual choice, national debates on belonging and identity in the aftermath of the Cold War. Looking back much further, historiography has its roots in attempts to prosecute the perpetrators, or at least reactions to such prosecutions. As such History, politics and culture have been for-ever entwined.

Yet this is not to say that the past is unimportant in History. Documents, the fragments of the past with which historians work, are a crucial part of the story of Holocaust historiography's devel-opment too. Sometimes their presence or absence does indeed seem to have been inconsequential – it is difficult to imagine that new documents could much disrupt the ritualised scholarship on the Holocaust's bystanders for example. Some historiography has developed in a void left by 'missing' documents – not least the never-ending debate as to the 'origins' of the 'Final Solution'. However, at times it is new documents that have revolutionised perspectives on the Holocaust as much as changes in social and political context, not least the more comprehensive picture of regional occupation regimes revealed by documents brought to light after the end of the Cold War.

Holocaust History is then genuinely a conversation, a dialogue, *between* past and present. The process of rendering the past as History is a complex interaction between the social and political contexts of both the writers and readers of History and the Holo-caust that they struggle to represent and understand. History seldom offers a clear view. Even the eye-witnesses, those present in the past as it were, cannot render their experiences cleanly and unproblematically in the present, so what chance have historians? This is a past in living memory that even its survivors cannot ade-quately articulate, nor avoid attaching meanings to that are made in the present not the past. In that sense the experience of Holo-caust History makes the frailties of the discipline of History unavoidable. The idea that History can offer a window on this or any other past appears to lack any credibility at all in the light of an investigation which has emphasised time and again the sheer presentness of Holocaust historiography.

Yet my purpose here has never been, and still remains not, to pour scorn on History as a discipline. Just because the 'truth claims' of History are problematic does not mean that the disci-pline is moribund. I cannot follow Keith Jenkins' argument that we should look forward to a world without History, that History's time as it were is up. Indeed, it seems to me that the worth of His-tory has been revealed here in the degree to which it is a discipline that *is* engaged with the world, that seeks to provide the tools to navigate through and understand the complexity of the present by finding meaning in the past.

So what of the future of Holocaust History? This book has presented a picture of a divided historiography, separately concerned with the perpetrators, the victims and the bystanders. Efforts at integrated histories of the Holocaust have been notable by if not their complete absence, then their rarity.[1] Perhaps that rarity is the result of the enduring desire, even in the postmodern world, to produce histories which explain the Holocaust as a whole – the lingering modernist will to capture the quintessence of events, to render their single meaning. And the neat categories of perpetrator, bystander and victim lend themselves to such explanations. But the consequence of such neat categorisation, such straight lines is that singular explanations inevitably fail. The perpetration of the Holocaust may or may not be convincingly explained by an analysis of the functioning of German bureaucracy, but such theses certainly have little meaning for the Holocaust's victims. The question then is how to produce Histories which do integrate all categories, which have meaning for the victims as well as the perpetrators.

As the postmodern insistence on the past holding a variety of meanings is further embedded in Holocaust histories, it may well be that such integrated histories can be achieved. It is unlikely that they will occur when attempting explanations for the Holocaust as a whole however. If there is one single lesson of this book it is that no single explanation for the Holocaust will suffice. And the tendency in contemporary Holocaust studies is not towards the 'global' but the 'local'[2] – witness the emphasis on diverse regional initiatives in the transition to genocide. Such a tendency has a contemporary political context too. In a globalised world in which the interaction between local events and global meanings becomes clear, there is a growing emphasis on the need for local action to meet the challenges of global problems. Think, for example, of the importance of local solutions to the crises of climate change and food shortages in the contemporary world.

And it is in local studies of single places and spaces that there might be the greatest potential for 'integration' in Holocaust histories. But integration should not simply be concerned with putting the categories of victim, bystander and perpetrator together and asking how they interact. In fact it really requires that we challenge those categorisations altogether. It is in the 'intimate' histories of the Holocaust in the Galician countryside, or in Polish and Ukrainian towns for example, that we see how local populations could be perpetrators, victims and bystanders interchangeably.

Yet the emphasis on the local does not remove the imperative to integrate the Holocaust into 'global' history. In this sense the study of the bystanders might become less about outrage at inadequate responses to the *Shoah* and more concerned with understanding the contexts in which the Holocaust could occur. Those contexts might include the interactions of global politics, and the actions and inactions of states. But they might also include the many and various local interethnic relations and rivalries in interwar and then wartime Europe which require explanation and understanding at a micro level, like those revealed in Jan Gross's study of the destruction of the Jewish community of Jedwabne.

As I have attempted to demonstrate here, the story of Holocaust historiography is really the story in recent years of the rediscovery of its contexts. Those contexts are not always local. One of them is the history of violence and mass murder that extends far beyond the Nazi treatment of Europe's Jews. Such is the relentless recurrence of mass violence in the contemporary world, there appears an increasing moral and political imperative to integrate the Holocaust into a general understanding of the history of genocide.[3] As the growing tendency to situate the Holocaust within a history of European colonialism demonstrates, this can be part of an attempt to link the history of the Holocaust to the familiar. Alternatively, as the use of the political religions paradigm shows, it can be used to link the Holocaust to the unfamiliar or the alien. In either case the Holocaust becomes the mirror in which we examine ourselves, in which we see either 'us' or 'them'. Whatever the answer, the fundamental question seems to remain the same: Just who do we think we are?

Notes

1 The most prominent exception is Saul Friedländer, *Nazi Germany and the Jews Vol. 2: The Years of Extermination* (New York, 2007).

2 See for example Thomas Kühne and Tom Lawson (eds), *The Holocaust and Local History* (London, forthcoming).
3 See for example Ben Kiernan, *Blood and Soil: A World History of Genocide and Extermination from Sparta to Darfur* (New Haven: CT, 2007) and Mark Levene's multi-volume study *Genocide in the Age of the Nation State* (London, 2005–2008).

GUIDE TO FURTHER READING

This guide to further reading is arranged thematically - dealing with issues in the order that they arose in the rest of the book. Many more titles can be found in the notes and references of this book, and indeed the following selection represents only a tiny fragment. Inclusion here simply signifies that these texts are among the most important and accessible. What follows is, therefore, a place to start.

General Holocaust histories

Hannah Arendt, *Eichmann in Jerusalem: A Report on the Banality of Evil* (London, 2006)

Donald Bloxham, *The Final Solution: A Genocide* (Oxford, 2009)

Lucy Dawidowicz, *The War Against the Jews 1933–45* (London, 1987)

Deborah Dwork and Robert Jan van Pelt, *Holocaust: A History* (New York, 2002)

Saul Friedländer, *Nazi Germany and the Jews, Volumes 1 and 2* (New York, 1997 and 2008)

Philip Friedman, *Roads to Extinction: Essays on the Holocaust* (New York, 1980)

Raul Hilberg, *The Destruction of the European Jews* (New Haven: CT, 2002)

Helmut Krausnick and Martin Broszat (eds), *Anatomy of the SS State* (London, 1970)

Holocaust history, historiography and memory

Donald Bloxham and Tony Kushner, *The Holocaust: Critical Historical Approaches* (Manchester, 2005)

Zvi Gitelman, *Bitter Legacy: Confronting the Holocaust in the USSR* (Bloomington: IN, 1997)

Michael Marrus, *The Holocaust in History* (London, 1993)

Dan Michman, *Holocaust Historiography: A Jewish Perspective* (London, 2003)

Alan Mintz, *Popular Culture and the Shaping of Holocaust Memory in America* (Washington: DC, 2001)

Peter Novick, *The Holocaust in American Life* (New York, 2000)
Dan Stone, *Constructing the Holocaust* (London, 2003)
James Young, *Writing and Rewriting the Holocaust: Narrative and the Consequences of Interpretation* (Bloomington: IN, 1988)

The Holocaust in context

Michael Thad Allen, *The Business of Genocide: The SS, Slave Labour and the Concentration Camps* (Chapel Hill: NC, 2002)
Götz Aly, *Final Solution: Nazi Population Policy and the Murder of the European Jews* (London, 1999)
Hannah Arendt, *The Origins of Totalitarianism* (New York, 2004)
Zygmunt Bauman, *Modernity and the Holocaust* (Cambridge, 1989)
Daniel Goldhagen, *Hitler's Willing Executioners: Ordinary Germans and the Holocaust* (New York, 1996)
Robert Koehl, *RKFDV: German Resettlement and Population Policy 1939–45* (Cambridge: MA, 1957)
Hans Mommsen, *From Weimar to Auschwitz* (Princeton: NJ, 1991)
A. Dirk Moses and Dan Stone (eds), *Colonialism and Genocide* (London, 2007)
George Mosse, *Toward the Final Solution* (1977)
Robert Jan van Pelt and Deborah Dwork, *Auschwitz 1270 to the Present* (New Haven: CT, 2000)
Peter Pulzer, *The Rise of Political Anti-Semitism in Germany and Austria* (London, 1988)
Jurgen Zimmerer, 'Colonialism and the Holocaust: Towards an Archaeology of Genocide', A. Dirk Moses (ed.) *Genocide and Settler Society* (New York, 2004)

Bystanders to the Holocaust

Victoria Barnett, *Bystanders: Conscience and Complicity During the Holocaust* (Westport: CT, 1999)
Martin Gilbert, *Auschwitz and the Allies* (London, 1981)
Tony Kushner, *The Holocaust and the Liberal Imagination: A Social and Cultural History* (London, 1994)
Louise London, *Whitehall and the Jews 1933–48: British Immigration Policy and the Holocaust* (Cambridge, 2000)

Michael Phayer, *The Catholic Church and the Holocaust* (Bloomington: IN, 2001)

John K. Roth and Carol Rittner (eds), *Pope Pius XII and the Holocaust* (London, 2002)

William D. Rubenstein, *The Myth of Rescue: Why the Democracies Could not Have Saved More Jews from the Nazis* (London, 2000)

Bernard Wasserstein, *Britain and the Jews of Europe 1939–45* (Oxford, 1988)

David Wyman, *The Abandonment of the Jews: America and the Holocaust 1941–45* (New York, 2007)

The origins of the 'Final Solution'

Martin Broszat, 'Hitler and the Genesis of the Final Solution: a reply to David Irving', *Yad Vashem Studies* (Vol. 13, 1979), pp. 73–115

Christopher Browning (with Jürgen Matthäus), *The Origins of the Final Solution: The Evolution of Nazi Jewish Policy September 1939–March 1942* (Lincoln: NE, 2004)

Gerald Fleming, *Hitler and the Final Solution* (London, 1985)

Henry Friedlander, *The Origins of Nazi Genocide: From Euthanasia to the Final Solution* (Chapel Hill: NC, 1995)

Christian Gerlach, 'The Wannsee Conference, the Fate of German Jews, and Hitler's Decision in Principle to Exterminate all European Jews', *Journal of Modern History* (Vol. 70, 1998), pp. 759–812.

Ian Kershaw, 'Improvised Genocide: The Emergence of the 'Final Solution' in the Warthegau', *Transactions of the Royal Historical Society*, 6th Series, Vol. 2 (London, 1992), pp. 51–78

Peter Longerich, 'The Wannsee Conference in the Development of the Final Solution', David Cesarani (ed), *The Holocaust: Critical Concepts in Historical Studies* (London, 2004)

Jürgen Matthäus, 'Controlled Escalation: Himmler's Men in the Summer of 1941 and the Holocaust in the Occupied Soviet Territories', *Holocaust and Genocide Studies* (Vol. 21, No. 2, 2007)

Karl Schleunes, *The Twisted Road to Auschwitz: Nazi Policy Toward German Jews 1933–39* (Chicago: IL, 1970)

National Holocausts

(Covering those areas dealt with in the main text)

Yitzhak Arad, *Belzec, Sobibor, Treblinka: The Operation Reinhard Death Camps* (Bloomington: IN, 1987)

Randolph Braham, *The Politics of Genocide: The Holocaust in Hungary* (New York, 1981)

David Cesarani (ed.), *Genocide and Rescue: The Holocaust in Hungary 1944* (Oxford, 1997)

Tim Cole, *Holocaust City: The Making of a Jewish Ghetto* (London, 2003)

Martin Dean, *Collaboration in the Holocaust: Crimes of the Local Police in Belorussia and Ukraine 1941–44* (London, 2000)

Jan Thomas Gross, *Neighbors: the Destruction of the Jewish Community in Jedwabne, Poland* (Princeton: NJ, 2001)

Ulrich Herbert (ed.), *National Socialist Extermination Policies* (Oxford, 2000)

Wendy Lower, *Nazi Empire Building and the Holocaust in Ukraine* (Chapel Hill: NC, 2005)

Michael Marrus and Robert Paxton, *Vichy France and the Jews* (Stanford: CA, 1981)

Bob Moore, *Victims and Survivors: The Nazi Persecution of the Jews in the Netherlands* (London, 1997)

Jacob Presser, *Ashes in the Wind: The Destruction of Dutch Jewry* (London, 1968)

The Perpetrators of the Holocaust

Christopher Browning, *Ordinary Men: Reserve Police Battalion 101 and the Final Solution in Poland* (London, 2002)

David Cesarani, *Eichmann: His Life and Crimes* (London, 2005)

Ernst Klee, Willi Dresden and Volker Reiss (eds), *"The Good Old Days": The Holocaust as Seen by its Perpetrators and Bystanders* (New York, 1991)

Robert Jay Lifton, *The Nazi Doctors: Medical Killing and the Psychology of Genocide* (New York, 1986)

Yaacov Lozowick, *Hitler's Bureaucrats: The Nazi Security Police and the Banality of Evil* (London, 2002)

Hans Safrian, *Eichmann's Men* (Cambridge, 2010)

Gitta Sereny, *Into That Darkness: From mercy Killing to Mass Murder* (London, 1974)

German society and the Holocaust

Götz Aly, *Hitler's Beneficiaries: Plunder, Racial War and the Nazi Welfare State* (New York, 2006)

Frank Bajohr, *Aryanisation in Hamburg: The Economic Exclusion of the Jews and the Confiscation of their Property in Nazi Germany* (Oxford, 2002)

David Bankier, *The Germans and the Final Solution: Public Opinion Under Nazism* (Oxford, 1992)

David Bankier (ed.), *Probing the Depths of German Antisemitism: German Society and the Persecution of the Jews* (Jerusalem, 2000)

Robert Gellately, *Backing Hitler: Consent and Coercion in Nazi Germany* (Oxford, 2001)

Jeffrey Herf, *The Jewish Enemy: Nazi Propaganda During World War II and the Holocaust* (Cambridge: MA, 2006)

Ian Kershaw, *Popular Opinion and Political Dissent in the Third Reich: Bavaria 1933–45* (Oxford, 1983)

Jewish resistance to the Holocaust

Samuel D. Kassow, *Who Will Write Our History? Emmanuel Ringelblum, the Warsaw Ghetto, and the Oyneg Shabes Archive* (Bloomington: IN, 2007)

James M. Glass, *Jewish Resistance During the Holocaust: Moral Uses of Violence and Will* (London, 2004)

Israel Gutman, *Resistance: The Warsaw Ghetto Uprising* (Boston: MA, 1994)

Hermann Langbein, *Against All Hope: Resistance in Nazi Concentration Camps* (London, 1994)

Ber Mark, *The Scrolls of Auschwitz* (Tel Aviv, 1985)

Jacob Sloan (ed.), *The Journal of Emmanuel Ringelblum* (New York, 1958)

Ghetto society and Jewish leadership

Gustavo Corni, *Hitler's Ghettos: Voices from a Beleaguered Society 1939–44* (London, 2002)

Yisrael Gutman (ed.), *Patterns of Jewish Leadership in Nazi Europe 1933–45: Preoceedings of the Third Yad Vashem Historical Confernece* (Jerusalem, 1979)

Raul Hilberg *et al.* (eds), *The Warsaw Diary of Adam Czerni-akow: Prelude to Doom* (New York, 1994)

Samuel Gringauz, 'The Ghetto as an Experiment of Jewish Social Organisation', *Jewish Social Studies* (Vol. 11, No. 1, 1949)

Shimon Huberband, *Kiddush Hashem: Jewish Religious and Cultural Life in Poland* (New York, 1987)

Janusz Korczak, *The Ghetto Years 1939–42* (New York, 1978)

Avraham Lewin, *A Cup of Tears: A Diary of the Warsaw Ghetto* (Oxford, 1988)

Vladka Meed, *On Both Sides of the Wall* (Tel Aviv, 1973)

Calel Perechodnik, *Am I a Murderer? Testament of a Jewish Ghetto Policeman* (New York, 1996)

Isaiah Trunk, *Judenrat: The Jewish Councils in Eastern Europe Under Nazi Occupation* (New York, 1972)

Holocaust testimonies

Judith Tydor Baumel, *Double Jeopardy: Gender and the Holocaust* (London, 1998)

Cathy Caruth (ed), *Trauma: Explorations in Memory* (Baltimore: MD, 1995)

Shoshana Felman and Dori Laub, *Testimony: Crisis of Witnessing in Literature, Psychoanalysis and History* (London, 1992)

Henry Greenspan, *On Listening to Holocaust Survivors: Recounting and Life History* (Westport: CT, 1998)

Gideon Greif, *We Wept Without Tears: Testimonies of the Jewish Sonderkommando from Auschwitz* (New Haven: CT, 2005)

Geoffrey H. Hartman, *The Longest Shadow: In the Aftermath of the Holocaust* (Bloomington: IN, 1996)

Lawrence Langer, *Holocaust Testimonies: The Ruins of Memory* (New Haven: CT, 1991)

Primo Levi, *The Drowned and the Saved* (New York, 1998)

Dalia Ofer and Leonore Weitzmann, *Women and the Holocaust* (New Haven: CT, 1998)

Carol Rittner and John Roth (eds), *Different Voices: Women and the Holocaust* (St. Paul: MN, 1993)

Mark Roseman, *The Past in Hiding* (London, 2001)

Tsvetan Todorov, *Facing the Extreme: Moral Life in the Concentration Camps* (New York, 1996)

Zoë Vania Waxman, *Writing the Holocaust: Identity, Testimony, Representation* (Oxford, 2006)

INDEX

INDEX

INDEX

INDEX